The Black Manager

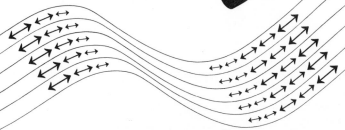

MAKING IT IN
THE CORPORATE WORLD

Revised Edition

Floyd Dickens, Jr.
Jacqueline B. Dickens

amacom
American Management Association

Library of Congress Cataloging-in-Publication Data

Dickens, Floyd.
    The Black manager : making it in the corporate world / Floyd
Dickens, Jr., Jacqueline B. Dickens.—Rev. ed.
        p.   cm.
    Includes bibliographical references and index.
    ISBN 0-8144-7770-4 (paperback)
    1. Afro-American executives—Vocational guidance. 2. Career
development—United States. I. Dickens, Jacqueline B. II. Title.
HD38.25.U6D53   1991
658.4'09'08996073—dc20   91-53055
                                                          CIP

Printing number

10   9   8   7   6   5   4   3   2   1

To our three young adults, Daphne, Floyd III, and Karen: We opened the door to success, and you entered with dignity, pride, and joy. You are on track for continued success. We are so very proud of you and wish you the best that life has to offer. Remember, never ever forget your fellow human beings.

To General Roscoe Robinson, Jr.: Our country owes you a debt that we can never fully repay. As a pioneer, you forged a new link in the chain of success for Afro-Americans. You are a beacon of success and a role model for our youth. It is an honor to know you. May life continue to reward you for your intellect, vitality, and commitment to excellence in all you do.

Contents

Foreword

Jacqueline Dickens and Floyd Dickens, Jr., have produced a very valuable work based primarily on an effective combination of diligent research and their personal experience in the corporate world. The developmental model they describe will surely draw various reactions from different readers. For young black managers starting out on their first project, it is a primer on how to cope with different situations they can expect to encounter in the work force of the 1990s—detailing issues they must be prepared to address properly if they are to succeed. The book offers a process for moving forward and hope for the future for middle managers. Those individuals who may not have climbed the corporate ladder as far or as fast as they thought their qualifications would take them may again feel the pain that accompanied an earlier disappointment. The book enables black managers who have reached the top to reflect on their own professional preparation, the obstacles they had to overcome to survive, and the dogged determination they found necessary to achieve success.

Two aspects of this book are especially worthwhile. First, although *The Black Manager* was written primarily for black managers, it is essential that both minority and majority managers have a clear understanding of the issues discussed. The ability to manage a diverse work force is taking on added importance because the composition of the work force continues to change as we approach the twenty-first century. Successful managers—minority or majority, male or female—must demonstrate that they have the interpersonal skills to ensure maximum productivity from that diverse work force.

Second, the applicability of Jackie and Floyd's book extends beyond corporate America. The principles enunciated are important in any activity in which *people* are primary targets. My own experience of almost thirty-five years in the United States Army—the last twelve as a general officer—involved the management of people at every level. Successful officers managed their personnel by applying good leadership techniques very similar to those discussed in _The Black Manager_. The traits of the military leader that I consider most important— integrity, dedication to duty, commitment, job knowledge, and sense of responsibility—are also important for the corporate manager to possess. In addition, managers, like military leaders, must realize that they are continually being scrutinized. Their performance in pressure situations, in group activities, or in routine tasks could give a clear indication of their technical competence, their professional standards, or their leadership styles.

Among the important responsibilities of the manager who has personnel resources, the ability to take care of "people concerns" ranks high, in my opinion. This means that the manager must create a healthy work environment, keep subordinates meaningfully employed and well informed, and maintain open channels of communication. The manager must learn how and when to delegate authority and use the organizational "chain of command." It is also important for those in management positions to develop their subordinates and to continue their own professional development through self-study or training programs offered by their organization. In _The Black Manager_, Floyd Dickens, Jr., and Jacqueline Dickens have properly emphasized the significance of setting goals and establishing priorities, and they have demonstrated an understanding of the relevance of various leadership techniques in the development of successful managers.

Roscoe Robinson, Jr.
General, U.S. Army (Retired)

Preface

The first edition of our book was a resounding success. We are therefore happy and thrilled to share additional learnings and information gained since this book was first published in 1982. Welcome aboard the revised edition of *The Black Manager: Making It in the Corporate World.*

Since 1982, we have been blessed with the opportunity to travel extensively throughout the United States to speak to and teach many managers, leaders, and employees of all kinds of organizations. We have also talked with students of various racial groups in high schools, colleges, universities, and trade schools. We found these individuals to be energized when we talked about the diverse work force that we now see in U.S. organizations. However, many are eager to know why minorities, especially blacks, are having difficulty rising in organizations. They know that minorities have the credentials and experience to be managers and leaders but for some reason do not seem to be in higher-level, decision-making positions.

The question, Why haven't more minorities made it up the corporate ladder? becomes even more important when you look at the February 1988 issue of *Black Enterprise* magazine, published by Earl G. Graves Publishing Company, Inc. It contains an excellent article entitled "The 25 Hottest Black Managers in Corporate America." These managers hold positions ranging from director of organizations to chairman and CEO of companies. Their total compensation packages range from $250,000 to $1.2 million. A secondary question now arises: Why did these managers make it while most others didn't? Is it because they were the chosen few or because they worked harder or smarter? Are they basically more intelligent than others, or are they better-educated? Did they get some breaks other managers didn't know about? We believe there are others in the work force who may be just as smart and just as educated as these individuals. We also believe you cannot depend on a lucky break. Then, why did they advance while others didn't? There are many answers to these questions. We believe, however that these individuals made it basically because *they learned the fundamentals of success and gained mastery* as they traversed four distinct phases leading to success.

We believe that an understanding of the four-phase model is important to those who aspire to rise in corporate America and other American institutions. The model can point out barriers that will be faced by individuals on the way to the upper levels of organizations. Although there are no guarantees of success, if you become aware of the terrain that must be traversed, then you have an opportunity to prepare for the journey. Our book is dedicated to helping you move through the phases to success without quitting or burning yourself out.

For many years, we wondered why some blacks were successful and moved up in white institutions (corporations, school systems, the armed services, and so on) while others of equal intelligence struggled, floundered, gave up, and were set aside. Our wonderment and deep curiosity took a positive turn in early 1970. We started to document our personal observations of blacks and whites as they interacted. From 1972 to 1974, we attended night school to take courses in psychology and social psychology. We subsequently participated in and led racial awareness and personal development groups consisting of both blacks and whites in community, service, and profit-making organizations. We also attended numerous seminars on personal development and management techniques. Throughout this time period, we counseled and coached both blacks and whites on how to become more effective in an integrated work environment. As a result, we discovered a behavioral process that blacks undergo while working in white institutions. We then developed this into a four-phase structured model of black development.

Jackie returned to school in 1976 and obtained a master's degree in social work from Ohio State University in 1978. She fulfilled her thesis requirements by conducting exploratory research on some key skills utilized by a group of black managers who became successful in major white corporations. These events, coupled with our burning desire to share information that might be helpful to others, caused us to feel we should publicly document our learnings; therefore, in 1978 we decided to write a book. However, we did not sit down to the task until the fall of 1980. At that point, our vision of the status of blacks in American organizations was sharp and clear.

Since racism pervades every walk of our lives, it has always presented barriers to success for the minority individual in addition to whatever his or her personal shortcomings may be. Since corporations and other American institutions represent a microcosm of our larger society, it is safe to deduce that black managers will face racism and must therefore acquire coping behaviors in addition to those acquired by managers in general. We firmly believe black managers bring cultural differences, as do other races and ethnic groups, that enhance or hamper their development and attainment of success in predominantly white organizations.

There were four primary reasons for writing the original book: (1) The foremost reason was because no book existed in the marketplace that gave practical, day-to-day how-to solutions to the management problems faced by black men and women managers. (2) There was a need for blacks to have basic information on how their blackness and culture impact their daily work interactions. (3) There was a need to collect, organize, and share data and techniques on how both blacks and whites become successful in a multicultural environment. (4) We wanted to share new, creative, and different ways of managing in the multicultural environment that resulted from the entrance of blacks and other minorities into the professional ranks of all-white institutions.

The first edition was based on research data collected from a number of black managers who shared their experiences to help Jackie realize a thesis requirement. The overwhelming response to the thesis findings by all who read them led to the expansion of the thesis data and the development of the original book.

The research study was conducted in an attempt to pinpoint some attitudes, emotions, behaviors, and job skills learned by a number of black male managers in adjusting to and becoming successful in the white corporate world. In the study, *success* was defined as earning at least one promotion in the company. The results of the study and the four-phase model have been well honed and refined by our working with numerous minority and white managers, both male and female, in training sessions throughout the country since the publication of the original book. The four-phase structured model of development for black managers in white corporations identifies and organizes the experiences both of black managers and of other minorities in white environments. It provides a way to understand the personal dynamics that occur on the job.

At this time, we feel it is important to revise our book because a third and fourth generation of blacks are joining the ranks of American institutions. It is important that these generations not forget the lessons learned by those who preceded them. For those blacks who have been around for a while and have not yet given up on advancement, this book will help them restart their stalled careers. For those blacks who have undergone or about to undergo downsizing or a corporate take-over, the lessons that can be learned from this book will help them survive and prosper. For those who have been bitten by the entrepre-neurial bug, as Floyd has, this book can help speed your departure from corporate America. Floyd left Procter & Gamble in July 1986 after nearly twenty-one years of taking advantage of excellent learning opportuni-ties. Together we now work full-time for 21st Century Management Services, Inc., which we started in 1981.

There is a more compelling reason that drives us to revise our book. A quick review of Figure P-1 shows that in the 1990s, the growth in the work force will be among minorities. The work-force growth rates for white men and white women are projected to drop, whereas increases are projected for all blacks, Asians, and Hispanics. Such increases can have potentially disruptive effects. As a result of the changes in the management ranks of corporate America, power will start to shift from whites to blacks and other minorities sometime in the next century. Power will shift because as blacks and other minorities join organizations they will move into hierarchical positions in large numbers; whites will have no options other than to share power with the minorities. For the sake of maintaining the growth of the American economy, this must be a smooth transition.

Shortly after the year 2000, as white males become a minority in the work force and the resulting shift in power and control of various organizations in this country occurs, there will be a tremendous need for information on how to effectively manage a diverse work force. This book will supply managers with some of that information, both now and in the future.

Writing a book can be quite a staggering experience, especially since the first edition was our first book. Revising it can be almost as over-whelming because there is so much we would like to say but cannot because of space and cost constraints. In preparing this revised edition, we discovered that the first half of the book required only minimal changes, whereas the second half required major changes.

Parts One and Two—"The Developmental Model" and "The Way to Success"—did not need extensive revision because, unfortunately, very little has changed since we first collected and organized our data and wrote about our findings. The issues, problems, and concerns for

Figure P-1. Work-force growth rates.

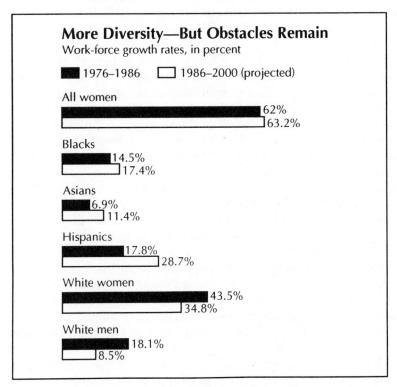

minorities working in corporate America remain essentially the same as when the first edition was published. However, we *have* revised this portion of the book to deal with additional critical issues that have arisen during the 1980s and the few gains that minorities have made in the business world.

Jack, the black manager who tells his story in Part Two, must continue to battle his way through the doors of corporate America and, once inside, he must battle his way up the ladder just as his predecessors did. Although today blacks and other minorities are no longer stymied at the entry level as they were ten years ago, they are now hitting against a "glass ceiling"—an invisible barrier encountered by minorities as they seek advancement toward corporate boardrooms and the top levels of management. It is sad to note that as we move into the 1990s, few organizations have raised that ceiling significantly higher for blacks than it was in the 1980s. Some experts would argue, in fact, that there has been a reversal in the progress made by blacks in the corporate world.

The material in Parts Three, Four, and Five—"Beyond Success," "Critical Guidelines for Success," and "Facing the Future"—is either new or extensively revised. We provide additional approaches and strategies for the black manager and have included more charts, graphs, and concise steps for problem solving. We have also simplified some of the concepts presented in the first edition and addressed some additional issues currently facing both blacks and other minorities as well as whites in today's work world.

Our new effort has been sustained by our ever-increasing conviction that we owe it to ourselves and others to share the secrets of success that have been shared with us. We feel there is a continuing need to share our experiences, as well as those of the people we interviewed and those minorities with whom we have worked over the years. We believe this is important because each year minorities will continue to enter the professional ranks of white institutions. Because minorities have now been in these institutions long enough to begin building a large body of successful operational learnings, they should no longer need to proceed solely by trial and error or based on a lack of knowledge about how to be successful.

Existing literature generally fails to provide information about the psychological and behavioral processes of minorities in white settings and the movement or devlopment that evolves as a result of struggling for success. In this book, we identify common experiences and patterns of behavior and fit them into a model of predictable behaviors and typically held attitudes and emotions. We describe some strategies used by successful black managers. We also present and discuss data relating to job mastery beyond success, which can help the corporate manager break through the glass ceiling to gain entry to top-level corporate positions.

We want to help make individuals in business environments aware of some prevalent problems minorities face in succeeding and advancing in white corporations. Bosses and subordinates will be alerted to the everyday issues and barriers blacks must overcome to succeed. Many white managers who feel a need or commitment to help minorities succeed have had few places to go to learn how to proceed; they will find many of the answers here.

We feel a personal commitment to point out the positive aspects of black success models in white corporations. Some of these aspects may have previously been seen in a negative light. Blacks are often beset by confusion and self-doubt. Clear explanations of what is happening to them may help make these reactions understandable. We would also like to assure blacks in white corporations that they are not alone in their experiences. We assure you as well that many experiences and barriers are common to all minorities who work in corporate America.

This book is for everyone who wants to be an effective leader and manager. It is critical to the white manager who works with or for minorities. For the minority manager in a white corporation, being able to recognize issues and formulate solutions may make the difference between success and failure. The structured model of development can help minority readers organize their experiences into a usable framework in preparing for success. White readers can use the model to understand the needs of minority managers and facilitate their development.

There are whites who feel a responsibility as a part of the dominant system to provide fair and equal treatment and offer opportunities to minorities. The information presented in this book tells those persons what can be expected in terms of growth and coping attitudes and behaviors of minorities in white organizations as minorities seek success. We also discuss how whites can prepare themselves to respond to the needs of minorities so that both white and minority managers can interact successfully.

The patterns of successful black managers are embodied in the model. It offers specific tools that people can use to understand what is necessary to get ahead in a predominantly white working environment. In Chapter 6, "Job Mastery Phase," we take a look at those more refined skills, attitudes, and emotions that must be acquired to position the black manager to step into the highest levels of a corporation.

Our intent was to write a book that would be theory-based and practically oriented but written in a simplified format in everyday language for a wide general audience. This book can therefore be used by individuals who are already managers, by those training to become managers, and by those starting new jobs. We not only describe what happens but also offer viable solutions that have worked effectively for others. We present good practical management strategies that emerged because of the existence of minorities in white institutions; however, these strategies can be used successfully by *all* managers.

In the past, blacks were not generally found in policy-making positions in American institutions. Because of this, learning about how blacks must operate in the white corporate setting to be successful (multicultural management) occurred at lower management levels. The basic precepts of multicultural management skills had been formed primarily at the lower to middle levels of hierarchies. Now, we also have data from many of those who have "made it."

As companies downsize, it is essential to maximize the use of all resources. People are a valuable resource regardless of whether they are male or female, white, black, Hispanic, Asiatic, or members of other ethnic or racial groups. When a company purchases a raw material for use in its products, it is with the intent of using as much of that substance as possible. It is the same with human resources. If managers are to get their "money's worth" from their employees, it is necessary to learn how to allow each one of them to move toward his or her greatest potential—to gain from using the "whole" person. Multicultural management is the process of effectively and properly using human resources. A part of multicultural management is learning how to successfully manage diverse groups of people in the workplace—how to get the additional value that different groups bring beyond their experiences or academic training.

The number of black professionals entering the work force before the 1970s was only a trickle compared to the number of white professionals. Some of the black professionals became successful, but at a great cost to their self-esteem, self-respect, and self-concept. These blacks paid a price that must no longer be extracted from them. Other minorities are paying as well. Much black talent has been lost as a result of both racism and sexism. In the 1990s, America cannot afford to lose *any* creative talent in our professional work force.

Even though black professionals are still faced with racism, a small number of blacks have made it to the boardrooms and into policy-making positions in major white institutions. We are now in a position to learn the vital information associated with blacks' moving into positions of corporate responsibility previously held exclusively by white males.

Yes, blacks have made great strides. Given their potential, however, only the surface has been scratched, and the valuable resources of this underutilized group of people have not been fully tapped. The future challenge for our country relative to black professionals is to remove those barriers that prevent blacks from fully utilizing their creativity and competencies and, in doing so, also remove the restraints that hinder the progress of other minority groups.

This revised edition, like the original, represents a consolidation of our struggles, our pain, our joy, our excitement, and our learnings. To the best of our knowledge, *The Black Manager* was the first book to discuss the management of a diverse work force. We have been honored by a robust and excited readership for the last nine years. To all those who have become successful through the sharing of this information, we thank you for allowing us to help.

As we revised and updated this book, we remembered with gratitude all those who were instrumental in the creation of the first effort. We give a very special thanks to Janice Cochran, who was our support, our editor, and the one who kept us on track for the revisions of the book; and to Dr. Jerome Jenkins, Henry Brown, and Lloyd Ward, who helped us to explore and refine many of the concepts added to this edition. As always, we also thank the many minority managers who, through their struggles to reach the top of their organizations, have shared with us what they have learned.

F. D.

J. B. D.

Introduction

This book deals with the many solutions to the most common problems minorities face in corporate America, from entry through upper-level management. As the American work force becomes more diverse, managers will need to learn additional management techniques to help them get the most from their employees. This revised edition is designed to help minorities, their bosses, and their subordinates to develop the kind of relationships that will foster the maximum output from each individual.

As we traveled across the country to work with both majority and minority managers, we noted that different racial and ethnic groups have the potential to *add value* to organizations. As a result, we developed training modules to help managers identify the added value of people, especially minorities. *Added value*, in relation to a group of people, is a term indicating those additional cultural assets (apart from formal education or generalized mainstream experiences) that the members of a group bring to an environment and apply to some task and/or to problem solving because of their cultural background and cultural socialization as well as past cultural experiences. When we speak of added value in terms of culture, we are talking about those values, attitudes, skills, techniques, paradigms, emotional mind-sets, etc., that have traditionally been handed down from generation to generation by a group of people as a result of their accumulated experiences. The "handing down" is done in many ways: through communication—either verbally or nonverbally, by watching the behavior of significant others in a person's life; through the sharing of group experiences and attitudes; and through formalized instruction.

Unlike many countries, the United States has a large population of diverse people from many cultural and racial backgrounds. Just think how economically powerful our country could be if managers only knew how to harness the added value of their diverse employees. We believe that creativity and productivity can be enhanced if the added value of various cultures can be identified and used.

We have all heard how the United States has become a melting pot because of the numerous ethnic and racial groups that have come to our shores down through the years. However, if you were to look in a melting pot, its contents would appear pretty much the same; if you were to taste the contents, you would find one predominant flavor subjugating all the other flavors. A melting pot represents a *monolithic* society, where everyone strives to be the same, where people act, think, and behave alike. We believe that America should be more like a *salad* and not a melting pot. A tossed salad is a dish where you can pick out each ingredient and taste its unique flavor or mix in other ingredients to get different tastes. In other words, each ingredient retains its unique taste, texture, color, and aroma. Salad ingredients are like people in the work force. To take full advantage of their added value, they should be allowed to bring their unique skills into the workplace to be used for the benefit of all.

Minorities—blacks, Hispanics, Asians, and others—face the same socialization process in organizations as white males, and much of the socialization is a necessary part of the joining-up process for all new members of organizations. However, when minorities are taught to behave, talk, think, and perform all business tasks just like the dominant white male culture, they lose their ability to use their added value. At that point, both the organization and the minority individual lose. Our book can help minorities withstand oversocialization, which will cause them to become "whitelike" in their behavior and lose their added value.

The Organization of This Book

This book is divided into five parts to facilitate its use as a reference.

Part One explains the developmental model and how readers can use it for personal growth and success. The model may also be used to help individuals gauge where they are in terms of their personal development.

Part Two contains basically the same four chapters as in the first edition. They help readers understand the phases that successful black managers traverse (i.e., entry, adjusting, planned growth, and success) and show how each phase of the developmental model works, step by step, as managers develop within an organization. Each of these chapters points out the critical issues that are generally involved for managers as they negotiate a particular phase of their development. The critical issues are analyzed in terms of the process used, how-to solutions are developed, and the basic concepts involved in arriving at those solutions are explored. Understanding the concepts allows readers to develop and apply solutions to whatever unique situations they encounter in each phase of their own development.

Part Three consists of an all-new chapter dealing with the issues, problems, and solutions pertaining to managers who have moved beyond the success phase toward breaking through the "glass ceiling." This chapter deals with the often complex issues facing top-level managers and the different demands made on them. Here, basic concepts and solutions are also explored.

Part Four discusses in a step-by-step fashion how to implement effective behavior to overcome difficulties. It contains four chapters, each of which deals with critical guidelines for managerial success. The first three of these chapters present strategies involving the internal, external, and environmental systems in which black and other minority managers must operate. The final chapter in this part provides additional insights into how minority managers can achieve success in a predominantly white corporate setting. One key focus of this chapter is career planning, which must start soon after a manager joins an organization, to increase the odds of realizing career objectives.

Part Five consists of two chapters that look toward the future of blacks and other minorities in the increasingly multicultural corporate and institutional world of the 1990s. The first of these chapters deals with the management of diversity—how to identify and fully utilize the added value of minorities. The second chapter outlines the challenges that corporations and institutions face in responding to changes in the composition of the work force and offers some practical suggestions for how they can respond to those challenges.

Black Professionals

In the 1960s, America found itself in the midst of racial disorders. The National Advisory Commission on Civil Disorders, appointed by President Lyndon B. Johnson in 1967, identified at least twelve grievances deeply held by the black population. The second greatest injustice felt by blacks was unemployment and underemployment; the fourth was inadequate education.

With the passage of the Civil Rights Act of 1964, educational and professional job opportunities were opened in fields previously closed to blacks. The private industrial sector established programs to encourage the hiring of blacks in more varied professional fields. For the first time in history, blacks in relatively large numbers were entering previously all-white universities.

Looking back at the 1960s, we can see that the upheaval contributed significantly to the knowledge we have gained about blacks. Racial violence is not new to America, but this time, it had two important results. The Civil Rights Act was signed into law, and the National Advisory Commission on Civil Disorders was established. This commission identified central issues that the nation was ordered to rectify; discrimination in employment and education was high on the list. If orders were not complied with, penalties were to be assessed by the government. Some of the penalties would take the form of loss of funds, loss of government contracts, and fines. Colleges, universities, and professional schools all over the country opened their doors to blacks. Then companies started to seek black professionals.

When companies first started hiring black professionals, they hired *qualifiable* people. These were blacks who supposedly were not qualified but could be trained. Many companies felt they were lowering their standards to admit blacks. Whether this was true or not, blacks managed to move into the higher levels of management in these companies. Generally speaking, industry had not found workable means of training and developing blacks for high managerial positions, but neither had existing racial barriers stopped the trickle of blacks moving upward.

In the late 1960s and early 1970s, many corporations established affirmative action programs to help identify qualified and qualifiable blacks and to continue to ensure employment opportunities. This included identifying and developing blacks with high potential, seeking to help industry learn ways of evaluating black growth and development for upward mobility, and helping to ensure that discriminatory practices were not used in hiring and firing blacks. The expressed purpose of these plans was to increase the number of black professionals in a particular corporation. Corporations had not yet begun to deal with the internal problems that arose after the black professionals were hired.

If blacks managed to slip through the doors opened by equal employment opportunity legislation and, in addition, progressed to higher levels with little help from the white industries, then what types of factors were involved in surviving and being successful in these institutions? The historical data indicate that the institutions were hostile to the survival of blacks. How is it that some blacks have managed to be successful in spite of the barriers facing them? What kinds of attitudes have they developed? How did they behave? What was their emotional mind-set? What kinds of job skills did they develop in order to survive and be successful? As blacks have moved into the upper and top levels of management, what kinds of learnings have helped them rise, what prices have been paid, and what challenges have been met?

One way we may be able to understand what has happened is to examine the attitudes, emotions, behaviors, and job skills of blacks who have been successful under adverse conditions. In the past, many of the studies of blacks were completed by white researchers who did not attempt to understand or accept racial differences as positive factors. Many of these studies focused on blacks who were unable to survive—who were unable to cope with a hostile environment. Studying those blacks does not reveal the characteristics of success or show what it takes to be successful. It is certainly time to take a look at the positive side of survival and success for blacks in a white setting.

In the late 1980s and early 1990s, a few black managers have moved beyond the middle-management ranks to the upper levels in various corporations. Blacks are now "knocking on the boardroom doors" of *Fortune* 500 companies. Some have positioned themselves to become general managers and vice-presidents of line and staff organizations. Other blacks at companies such as McDonald's, American Express, AT&T, IBM, Ford Motor Company, Xerox, Procter & Gamble, and Equitable Life have titles such as chief executive officer, senior vice-president, executive vice-president, general manager, executive director, and president of different groups and divisions.[1] These black leaders have risen from the middle-management levels of corporate America to important decision-making positions that affect bottom-line profits and results. They are the fortunate ones, who, in essence, have moved beyond the "glass ceiling." They represent what can happen when blacks traverse the four-phase developmental model discussed in Part One.

Although a fortunate number of blacks are rising in major corporations, we are now seeing a trend toward others' dropping out of the corporate scene to start their own businesses. This trend results from blacks' hitting the "glass ceiling" at the middle-management level. Black

1. *Black Enterprise* (February 1988).

managers are also leaving corporate America because they are under-utilized and their creativity is being stymied. In many cases, white managers are threatened and stressed by the level of creativity, aggressiveness, and intelligence of their black subordinates. Unless corporate America allows itself to use more of the potential of its black professional work force, the "black drain" will continue.

According to the *Statistical Abstract of the United States*, of the 115.0 million people employed in the United States in 1988, 95.2 million (82.8 percent) were white and 19.9 million (17.3 percent) were nonwhite. Of that 17.3 percent, 11.6 million (58.3 percent) were black.[2] Significant gains in equality have been made in the job market, but they are clearly not enough. Table I-1 shows the percentage of blacks among various groups of workers in 1988. As the statistics indicate, blacks are still heavily employed in blue-collar and service oriented jobs.

Multicultural Management

Multicultural management is defined as the act, art, and practice of leading and directing people of many cultures in attaining organizational and personal goals. With the increased number of minorities and women joining the work force, there is a need to manage each culture and sex

Table I-1. Percentage of blacks in various sectors of the work force.

	Total Population	Percentage Black
White-collar workers	29,190,000	6.1
Blue-collar workers	67,010,000	10.3
Service workers	15,332,000	17.6
Farm workers	3,437,000	6.6
Total workers	114,968,000	

Source: Statistical Abstract of the United States: 1990.

2. *Statistical Abstract of the United States: 1990*, 110th Annual Edition (U.S. Department of Commerce, Bureau of the Census).

differently and appropriately. Minorities and women cannot produce to their maximum potential as long as they are managed with the standard management techniques that were designed for white males. Although most of us can understand that *all* people are fundamentally the same biologically and capable of the same emotional responses to external and internal stimuli, we must also remember that each race and sex is socialized differently. Our society makes different demands on its various groups of people and specifies different roles for each group. Therefore, we need additional management teachniques that will take those different needs and motivations into account to reach women and members of minority cultures and capitalize on their potential. We cannot afford to lose these valuable resources in today's organizations. Multicultural management can provide the body of knowledge that can be used to effectively manage blacks and other minorities. The following are some key precepts of multicultural management technology:

1. *Feedback or input on minorities must be probed.* Supervisors must probe both negative and positive feedback on minority subordinates more than they do for feedback on white subordinates. Testing the feedback for validity is a way of removing racism and sexism from the input. Blacks, women, and other minorities must insist that this be done.

2. *Minorities must be included in decision-making processes.* It is essential that minorities be included very early in making decisions that will have a major impact on them. If not, the assumptions made by white male managers will generally be wrong. For example, women should have early input when an organization is setting its policy on maternity leaves. In this way, supervisors or organizations can ensure that the appropriate minority perspective is obtained and that trust barriers do not spring up as a result of the decision. Obviously, such action would not be necessary in an organization where all the people were of one race and gender. Including minorities in decision-making processes also provides them with an opportunity to buy into the decision early, and they will support it.

3. *Supervisors must behave appropriately and take into account a minority's perceptions, experiences, and assumptions about a situation.* Before sharing organizational skill information with a minority, a white male supervisor must explore the minority individual's perceptions, experiences, and assumptions about the situation. Otherwise, it is difficult for the supervisor to understand that using the skill information may have

negative consequences for the minority individual. Supervisors must realize, when telling a minority to use an organizational resource, that some of the resources may be racist and sexist. The supervisor may need to include additional information that will help the minority obtain information effectively from the resource.

4. *Supervisors must interact in an open, up-front, and to-the-point manner with minorities.* Effective interactions occur between white supervisors and minorities when supervisors behave in this way. The white American corporate style of interaction is not as open and up-front as the cultural style of many minorities, especially blacks. Because minorities continue to be victims of racist and sexist behavior, they tend to be suspicious of white managers who are not open in their interactions with minorities. This suspicion will, in turn, negatively affect the minorities' work performance.

5. *Racist behavior and black rage (anger and resentment) must be managed by both whites and blacks.* White supervisors must be aware of how racism can cause inappropriate behavior in the boss-subordinate relationship; it must be managed appropriately. This enables blacks to manage their rage, which is a reaction to the racism of others.

6. *Entry-level jobs for minorities must be programmed.* Appropriate attention must be paid to programming the proper jobs and preparing the work environment for minorities as they enter an organization. A hostile environment can program a minority for failure. It is of the utmost importance that a sensitive and skillful first boss be selected for a minority individual to help ensure success. The first job should be one in which the minority can realize early success while also being challenged. One of the boss's key tasks is to make subordinates successful.

7. *Supervisors should be aware of differential consequences.*[3] A white supervisor must be attuned to the *differential consequences* that a given behavior can have for a minority versus a white individual operating in a similar manner. This means that when a white supervisor asks a black subordinate to perform a task, the supervisor should examine the request to see whether it could produce a negative result. If so, corrective and/or supportive action must be taken. An example of differential consequences would be a manager's addressing or referring to a subordinate as "boy." If this word were spoken to or about a black subordi-

3. *Differential consequences* is a term coined by Dr. Duke Ellis while he was serving as assistant dean of student affairs, School of Professional Psychology, Wright State University, Dayton, Ohio.

nate, it would be taken quite differently than if it were spoken to or about a white subordinate.

The preceding are but a few concepts from the technology of multicultural management, a field of study that needs to be continually expanded and developed. We have only begun the task of adding to the larger body of management knowledge.

Management of Diversity

Management of diversity is the process of successfully managing people of different cultures and is a part of the total technology we call "multicultural management." The condition of being different does not mean that one is right and the other is wrong, or that one is superior and the other is inferior. Being different only adds another perspective or dimension to a situation. The ultimate objective of the management of diversity is to identify and use the added value of ethnic groups and cultures in a positive way to meet the needs and objectives of a corporation. Each cultural and ethnic group has added values that need to be identified and utilized in order to improve productivity and efficiency and reduce the interpersonal dysfunction that inevitably seems to plague people of various cultures who must work together.

Concrete Coping Behaviors

This book provides a framework for understanding what happens to minorities psychologically and the learnings they gain in order to survive and succeed in the corporate setting. We will present a road map of what minorities might expect to encounter and offer strong suggestions about which roads to travel. If properly used, these data can steer minorities on a course of *positive* coping that will enable them to grow and develop. Whites will find information here that will help them understand how they might approach minorities in order to facilitate the development process.

An important aspect of our book is that it focuses on the strengths in minorities and the output of positive, concrete coping behaviors. As stated earlier, much of the information gathered in the past about minorities, blacks in particular, has pointed up deficits or weaknesses in their struggles. Most blacks, regardless of their position or status, tend to be lumped with the poor and defeated. As blacks and women have moved into white male institutions over the past twenty-plus years, a wealth of positive coping behavior has been displayed by those individuals who have been continuously successful.

Successful blacks have developed a facility for focusing on behavior. They have learned the art and process of behavioral observation—that is, they have learned to recognize the conditions in which behavior should be closely observed. They know what to look for, especially in a conflictual situation. Successful black managers have learned how to extract key messages by observing behavior and then design and implement a plan to get what they want from an interaction.

Commonality of Experiences Shared by Minorities

For blacks and other minorities in an organization, the information in this book can be supportive in helping them realize that what they are going through is not an individual experience. Rather, it is a group experience—one that results from a minority person's entering a corporation staffed predominantly by another race whose norm is to be in a position superior to that of the minority. History tells us that difficulties will arise when these individuals must operate on a peer level or when the minority person holds the superior position.

This book moves us from the ostrich stance of "We have no problems" to a position of "We *do* have problems, so what can we do about them?" Many of the experiences, feelings, frustrations, and attitudes of minorities are shared by *all* managers seeking the few positions available at the top. Minorities, however, share the common additional experience of an environment that is hostile to their attainment of success because of their lesser status assignment in society or because the norm demands the complete socialization of the minority. Oversocialization causes minorities to attempt to be "little white people"—to so emulate white males that the important cultural learnings of the minority that would benefit the organization (i.e., the added values) are thrown away. We discuss the added value of blacks and other minorities in Chapter 11.

The Need to Share Learnings

Whites must understand the importance of sharing the dominant organizational norms and goals with minorities. Minorities must learn to appropriately share their experiences, attitudes, and perceptions, for the mutual success of both minorities and whites depends on each other.

A win-win boss-subordinate environment can be created by sharing the kinds of learnings that are discussed in this book. In such an environment, minority and white bosses with minority and white subordinates can all succeed in their pursuit of organizational and personal goals. The win-win approach will greatly reduce the time and energy wasted on behavioral reactions to racism and sexism. People tend not to misinterpret or fear things that they understand. Understanding can be fostered by sharing multicultural management knowledge and learning how to manage diversity.

Unfortunately, fear and mistrust still exist, particularly between whites and blacks. There are many causes for this. A lack of contact and an unwillingness to share information or exchange viewpoints are results of both racism and sexism. Many whites still fear violence and retribution from blacks for past injustices. Remnants of the belief that blacks are inherently incapable of measuring up to white standards can still be found among some whites. There is a belief that the old tried-and-true methods of performance (that is, white male) are best, that women should be in the home and blacks in the fields. The list can go on and on.

Some blacks, on the other hand, perpetuate the aforementioned beliefs by deliberately withholding certain information from whites. Sometimes this is because blacks feel as though they possess cultural secrets that, if they were known by whites, would give whites additional power over them. But much of the reasoning behind withholding information from whites is the firm belief of many minority individuals that whites will in some way use the shared information to the detriment of minorities. This belief is fervently held by many blacks because of its proven historical foundation.

We are at a point in this country, however, when the fears, mistrusts, and misunderstandings to which we cling may well ruin the future for everyone. Just as our society learns more about itself through the comparative study of other cultures, whites may learn more about themselves through the study of blacks and other minorities. Insights into how and why others behave the way they do often lead to insights about ourselves. Americans of different cultures can no longer afford to continue living in isolation from each other. When our economic welfare is threatened, we are all threatened, regardless of color, race, national origin, age, or gender. We are united in the common cause of keeping a competitive edge in the world marketplace. No other country in the world has such diverse talent and experience at its disposal. We must learn to use this diverse expertise and these vast resources to maintain our competitive edge. This revised edition of *The Black Manager* is dedicated to helping achieve that end.

Part One

The Developmental Model

Part One consists of Chapter 1, "The Developmental Model," which provides an in-depth discussion of the effects of racism on black managers in their everyday work life. This chapter offers readers an understanding of why some behaviors and skills that blacks learn are either different or different by degree from what whites learn. This portion of the book lays the groundwork for an understanding of the developmental model and how it can be used in daily work life. Parts Two through Five will then concentrate primarily on providing information on how black managers can effectively operate and succeed in a predominantly white setting. If properly used, this information can provide benefits for both black and white managers.

Chapter 1 will probably shock, surprise, and anger some readers because they are unaware of how institutional and personal prejudices can critically impact what appear to be insignificant behaviors and attitudes of black individuals working in largely white environments. Although equal opportunity laws have changed some aspects of our society, certain individuals remain prejudiced and are intent on acting this out in the workplace. Chapter 1 not only presents a useful working model of behaviors but also establishes a foundation that helps readers understand why certain behaviors need to be displayed by blacks, what attitudes will be shown in response to certain stimuli, and the reasons behind the behaviors and attitudes of blacks in the marketplace.

If you are white, understand that the information presented here is from a black perspective, and some of it may initially seem strange or incomprehensible to you. We ask that you try to understand rather than react. Reacting at this point will not be helpful to your understanding. As we learn about each other, we must *all* learn to look at things through someone else's eyes.

If you are black, understand that eliminating the effects of prejudice must be a *shared* task. *All of us* must be responsible for ending injustices in the workplace; one group cannot bear the responsibility alone. To become an equal participant in the corporate world, minorities must understand what motivates majority managers and learn to appropriately manage their responses.

Although we were counseled to dilute the information in Chapter 1, we decided to give it to you straight. We are sharing this material because in the past, many people have been less than candid in sharing this kind of information. If we are to truly understand ourselves, then we must at some point be honest with each other in facing certain truths about how we see our world and how we feel about each other.

1

The Developmental Model

In 1968, we became very sensitive to and interested in the behavior exhibited during interactions between blacks and whites because we were members of a new breed—black professionals entering white corporations. At that point, we were limited to observations. In 1970, we started to take notes on our behavior and personal interactions with whites and our observations of the interactions and behaviors of others. The notes included data that led us to identify helpful and dysfunctional concepts.

Night-school course work provided us with a framework in which to place the results of our observations. We now knew the "legitimate labels" that we could use to verbalize our experiences and observations.

Frustration and a strong desire to succeed motivated us to attend seminars on personal development and management. Often, we had to experiment with what we learned to adapt it to our own experiences, because for the most part, these seminars were developed for white male managers. During this period, we worked as consultants in team-building and racial awareness workshops, both inside and outside of corporations, and developed various affirmative action programs. With this experience as a background, in 1975 we placed our observations and knowledge in a tentatively structured five-phase model of black development.

The purpose of the exploratory research Jacqueline decided to conduct was to ascertain whether the data we had collected and the tentative model we had formulated would stand up under the scrutiny of research.

A structured questionnaire was given to a group of black male managers. The questions were designed to identify attitudes, emotions, behaviors, and job skills held by the managers from work entry to their present status in the company. This questionnaire was followed by a taped, private interview during which each manager could talk freely about his experiences. This provided a broad overview of what happened to the black managers from their entry into the white corporation to the present. We then compared the research data to our model and to the data we had previously collected. The research data verified our developmental model and also supplied additional refinements to it. One refinement occurred because we found that two of the phases were closely related. Therefore, we moved to a more concise four-phase developmental model.

We did not initially consider writing a book. We undertook our research because we were striving to survive and control our destiny as we sought success in a white-oriented world of big business and large corporations. Often, our major efforts were geared toward survival and circumventing painful experiences and costly mistakes.

Explanation of the Developmental Model

In compiling and analyzing the data in the research project, from the entry period through the success period, we recognized a growth pattern. From this pattern, we developed a model that can be used as a guide to the movements of blacks in large white corporate settings. These movements represent the learning process exhibited by black managers as they pass through the four phases of development: (1) Entry Phase, (2) Adjusting Phase, (3) Planned Growth Phase, and (4) Success Phase (see Figure 1-1). This is a close-looped model because it repeats itself. After an individual reaches the Success Phase, a new cycle will begin with a major job change or reassignment to another organization. Each time a cycle is completed, it will take a shorter period of time to traverse the cycle in subsequent job changes.

At the beginning of any new job, the employee starts at the Entry Phase of the developmental model. This phase is characterized by:

- No movement in terms of job growth
- Little or no direction from the boss
- Little or no direction in terms of personal goals
- A feeling of "I've got it made" (because of having secured the desirable job position)

Figure 1-1. The four-phase developmental model.

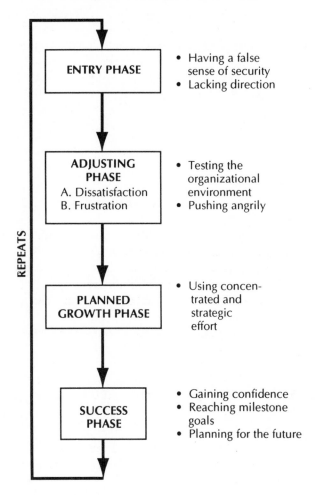

- Contained anger; interpersonal and job discomfort is ignored or not dealt with
- Reserved behavior, or "Don't make waves"

In time, the individual moves into the Adjusting Phase of the model. This phase is divided into two parts, a dissatisfaction stage and a frustration stage.

Dissatisfaction Stage

- A negative reaction to whites (regarding interactions with whites and a desire to mete out punishment)
- Rage that slips out periodically; minorities begin to display anger
- Low self-confidence
- Beginning to see inequalities but still holding anger inside most of the time; may complain a lot
- Negative reaction at seeing white peers get better jobs and more responsibility and the company taking more chances on white potential

Frustration Stage

- Rage that cannot be contained or managed (may be seen by whites as a "bad attitude")
- A lot of verbal, interpersonal fights with whites (may be seen by whites as "militant" or "noncooperative")
- No movement in terms of personal growth or job growth and production (the degree of anger inhibits growth)
- No increase in job results (dysfunctional behavior can help produce job stagnation)
- Becoming more vocal, tending to speak out about feelings, usually inappropriately

At some point, managers will come to a crossroad in their development. It may be precipitated by a number of things. They may become weary and see their behavior become debilitating in the area of job growth. They may become fearful of losing their jobs or may realize they are getting less job responsibility and being shoved aside. Whatever the reason, successful black managers move into a phase of planned growth. This is a time when managers make a conscious and concentrated effort to grow in their jobs and in terms of personal development. The Planned Growth Phase is characterized by:

- Management of rage; controls indiscriminate outbursts; chooses things at which to become angry
- Style changes; behavior becomes smoother; tends to initiate fights with whites less and less often
- Start moving toward goals; career plan is established
- Establishment of firm goals; begins to see what to reach for

- Rough periods; may slip back to the frustration and dissatisfaction stages

As the Success Phase is reached:

- Basic goals are met; progress can be seen.
- New and harder goals are set.
- Style is developed. (There is no longer a need to fight with or punish whites in interactions.)
- High confidence is developed (as a result of successes).
- High-quality results are produced; managers become aware of how the system works and acqure skill in using it.
- Strokes become less important. (Managers no longer depend on verbal OKs and praise from others, particularly from whites.)
- Results become more important. (Jobs well done speak for themselves.)
- A success affect is developed; self-confidence and importance are displayed.

Our research has shown that these phases are never skipped, nor do they occur out of sequence. The time spent in each phase varies, however, because of individual differences. Different levels of awareness of self and the environment can reduce the time spent in each phase. A person may also become stuck in one phase or even regress to an earlier phase. This regression can take place even from the Success Phase, since nothing remains static. Getting comfortable, dropping one's guard, and getting tired of the output of energy can be causes for regression. Failing to realize that growth must continue may be another cause.

The thesis research clearly showed that black managers felt they must develop a higher degree of job skills, especially in management, than their white peers. They felt that in order to survive and be successful in a major white corporation, there were some skills blacks had to learn that were different from the skills learned by whites. Two of these, which will be discussed later in this chapter, are the management of racism and the management of conflict.

To sum up, the two major issues of concern in our model are survival and success. The two main phases associated with survival are Entry and Adjusting; Planned Growth and Success are the main phases associated with success. Each phase is characterized by different attitudes, emotions, behaviors, and job skills. In separating these factors, we will look first at what they mean in terms of the black manager's survival—how they operate and why they exist. Then we will look at them in terms of attaining success.

Entry Phase

Attitudes

Most minority readers of this book can personally connect with the early feeling of doubt about making it in the white corporate world. Several factors can cause this doubt. As with all people, personal feelings about oneself can cause a black person to have doubts about making it. Blacks, however, are affected by additional doubts caused by other factors that do not plague whites. Racism in this country and the way our society perceives the competence of blacks can cause blacks to feel unsure of themselves. Blacks are affected by these perceptions even if they are not actively aware of this situation. Although all blacks do not believe "all" the negative perceptions that society has about them and their competence, these negative perceptions are usually internalized to some degree by all blacks.

Another factor contributing to the doubts of blacks is the realization that they are sometimes hired "because" they are black. Many blacks still must face the fact that they are being hired for reasons other than being the best person available for the job. Since this possibility always exists for the black individual, this doubt can get translated into, "I wonder whether I'm as prepared for my job as my white peers." This perception can be further compounded if the black manager has graduated from a black university. Even though this does not make the training inferior or the black person less qualified than white peers, prejudicial perceptions about the quality of education at black schools can cause additional doubts.

We are all reminded today in various books and journals that education does not prepare new hires for the realities of the everyday work environment. For blacks, this can be a particularly crushing blow. Naïveté often causes blacks to assume that racial attitudes within the company will be more positive than those of society at large. Blacks expect to be treated fairly and to be rewarded for their hard work. They may not expect to have to work in very close conjunction with whites as a team. In other words, blacks often expect the company and its members to disregard their blackness and judge them in the same manner as their white peers are judged.

The word *career* seldom holds the same meaning for blacks as it does for whites. Gratitude for having acquired a "good job" with a "high salary" can cloud the black manager's vision beyond basic day-to-day responsibilities and task accomplishment. Also, the stereotypical white boss–black subordinate role status continues to make it difficult for many blacks to see themselves in the upper-level positions normally held by whites or to understand the power dynamics of this role reversal.

Emotions

At the entry level, most blacks experience a moderate to high degree of stress. Many managers may see this stress as typical of any person in a new situation. However, the degree of stress depends on how black managers interpret their preparedness to work in a white corporation. Among the concerns that produce stress among blacks are (1) how they will fit into the normal corporate picture; (2) how they will fit in socially; (3) whether they will get the quality of help needed to do the job; and (4) whether their education will compare favorably to that of their white peers.

Shortly after joining the company and beginning the job, some blacks become angry and hostile without knowing why. Blacks are aware of racism in the larger community but are often not aware of the subtle ways in which it gets translated into behavior by whites in the corporation. Blacks may feel certain levels of visceral discomfort in some of their job interactions with whites, but often, they cannot pinpoint where and how that discomfort originated. A common emotion that blacks experience in their job interactions with whites is "feeling crazy."[1]

Behaviors

Two primary behaviors displayed by blacks are "fit-in" and "avoidance" behavior. These two extremes are indicative of the black manager's need either to "overcome" blackness and belong or to avoid the "unpleasant" task of any interaction with whites beyond getting the job done. Both extremes can be dysfunctional for the black individual.

1. Edward W. Jones, Jr., "What It's Like to Be a Black Manager," *Harvard Business Review* (July–August 1973), pp. 108–116.

Job Skills

Most blacks, like their white peers, feel technically competent to do the job for which they were hired. A major difference, however, appears to be in the area of awareness of the need for managerial skills. There are still too few black role models and black coaches in upper-middle and top corporate positions to help train, advise, and support young blacks. For this reason, many blacks at the entry level do not truly see themselves becoming top-level managers of whites. It takes some time for blacks to recognize the need for managerial skills, even though they are often held accountable for not displaying these skills.

During the Entry Phase, companies often neglect to offer training or encourage black employees to seek it and develop managerial skills. Since blacks are not a normal part of the corporate "club," the informal opportunities for encouragement to which whites are privy are, for the most part, denied to blacks. The corporate club that exists in most companies refers to the after-work socializing done by members of the various organizations who have common interests and enjoy activities together—e.g., playing cards, golfing, and fishing. Minorities tend to be excluded from these activities.

We would like to remind the reader that the time spent in each phase of the model varies from person to person and depends on differences in the environmental situation. In reality, there is considerable blending or overlapping as the person moves from one phase to another. The speed at which the person develops is determined by individual learning rates. Keeping this in mind, we are now ready to move into the next phase of survival, Adjusting.

Adjusting Phase

Attitudes

Gradually, the doubts experienced by black managers dissipate as they become more acclimated to the white corporate setting. Usually, the gradual gain in confidence results from experiencing successes on the job. Blacks who do not experience these successes, however, will become increasingly less confident and will continue to operate with entry-level attitudes for a long time. The more successes black managers have, the more confidence they gain. The obvious conclusion is that since blacks who enter white corporations experience an initial drop in confidence, they need to be positioned in the kinds of jobs where they can see early successes and quick results.

Black managers usually change their attitudes about a company after they start work. One important attitude change is dropping the general belief that hard work alone will net a reward. Blacks tend to come into companies believing in the Protestant work ethic—work hard, keep your nose clean, and you will be rewarded accordingly. Highly successful people, however, are successful because they do *more* than adhere to the work ethic. Because positions at the top are limited, other considerations come into play in competing for those places. For blacks, the barrier of racism prevents them from receiving their appropriate reward. Black managers cannot *just* practice the work ethic and automatically get fair treatment from a company or realize a lot of positive results from their efforts. Black managers must use strategy to make others see what they have produced and push an organization in some way to obtain an appropriate reward. The large number of black managers who believe the work ethic applies to them is surprising. They do not realize corporations are large entities with very few managerial slots relative to the number of employees. Therefore, opportunities for a reward in the form of a promotion are limited.

The naïveté of black managers about the norms and values of the white corporation creates a painful adjustment period for most blacks. Since the Protestant work ethic alone does not determine who gets ahead, then the question becomes, What does? Corporations have developed a method by which certain people are moved ahead: People higher up in the hierarchy sponsor other people for managerial slots. The sponsor, or mentor, may coach and guide the individual who is being sponsored. The sponsor may also push the organization to gain a promotion for that person. Many blacks are still not aware of this, and many whites do not know how to sponsor blacks. Whites' sponsorship of whites is a normal corporate process for pushing bright young whites up the corporate ladder. This process breaks down with blacks because companies do not initially possess the criteria for selecting blacks with potential, nor do blacks know how to give whites this information. Blacks tend not to know how to develop or affect a relationship with a potential white sponsor. The reverse also tends to be true: Whites do not know how to develop or affect a relationship with a potential black sponsoree.

A factor that inhibits blacks from getting sponsors is the black manager's need to feel emotionally attached to the sponsor. Whites tend not to have this need. Anger and hostility felt by black managers as a result of the racism directed toward them can also inhibit them from seeking a sponsor. Many blacks stubbornly refuse to affect any kind of relationship with whites in the hierarchy and instead focus on their anger. Many blacks ask themselves, "Why do *I* have to take the initiative? I didn't create this situation; why do I have to be responsible for changing it?" This can prolong the period of adjustment.

Understanding the company's norms and values is an important factor for black managers in adjusting their attitudes to the corporate milieu. Most companies, regardless of the product they produce, have established a norm that states, "Technical competence is more valued then managerial competence."

When black professionals enter white corporations, they tend not to possess the managerial experience to manage the black-white inter-actions necessary to do their job. This happens because they have not had preparation or work experience in the area of multicultural manage-ment. This is true of most white managers also. In most instances, however, whites are not required to use good black-white management skills. But a black manager's survival depends on it. On entering the company, blacks appropriately sense that technical competence is more important to the company than managerial competence. However, they have to deal with racial barriers and issues using managerial skills and interventions. White managers are only required to manage with the same managerial skills they have always used.

Black managers have to accomplish their job by using managerial competence, which is less highly valued than technical competence by their company. However, white managers will tend to judge the techni-cal competence of blacks by the way they display managerial compe-tence.

The final point with respect to Adjusting Phase attitudes is that black managers experience a gradual realization that racism directly affects them. In the entry period, most black managers can identify an uncomfortable feeling in their interactions with whites. In the adjusting period, they come to understand that race is a real issue and that it does affect their work output. They also realize that racial issues have to be dealt with and cannot be avoided. It is in this phase that blacks begin to be aware of some specific kinds of barriers that affect their progress.

Emotions

In the Adjusting Phase, black managers experience a very important psychological event. As we said earlier, blacks come into corporations with some degree of stress, as all new employees do. Blacks, however, are hit head-on with institutional racism and neoracism[2] in terms of their work-task accomplishments. *Neoracism* refers to the more sophisticated, subtle, and indirect forms of racism that are evidenced by individual white attitudes and behaviors.

Today, neoracism is the danger in the integrated community, and its assault is most commonly aimed at undermining the black's self-confidence, self-esteem, and self-worth.

At this point, most blacks will be stunned and will consequently experience a lack of technical and managerial growth. However, all is not lost; most blacks will start to grow again when they discover what is occurring. Two things that will allow them to grow and develop are the acquisition of cultural paranoia[3] and the use of protective hesitation.[4] *Cultural paranoia*, as used in the context of this book, is a sociological and anthropological concept referring to a person's expectations of mistreatment. It is a cultural phenomenon that has evolved as a group coping mechanism to deal with the real consequences of racism. It does *not* refer to the psychological concept that implies an individual mental disorder. *Protective hesitation* is the behavior associated with cultural paranoia in which a black individual hesitates in order to protect himself or herself from possible psychological assault before interacting or preparing to interact with a white individual. Cultural paranoia and protective hesitation are healthy coping reactions of blacks to the very real dangers of racism.

Another emotional reaction of blacks in the Adjusting Phase is the very strong negative feelings that result from prejudicial interactions with whites in the corporation. Blacks are culturally sensitive enough to pick up prejudicial behavior in whites, and this, in turn, affects the blacks' work output.

In the past, as a result of their sensitivity to whites' negative behavior, black managers tended to seek closer contact with other blacks in a company. This was done for psychic support and to determine whether other blacks were having similar experiences. The need of

2. The term *neoracism* was suggested by Robert Blaunder and discussed in John P. Fernandez, *Black Managers in White Corporations* (New York: John Wiley & Sons, 1975), pp. 196–197.
3. William H. Grier and Price M. Cobbs, *Black Rage* (New York: Basic Books, 1968), p. 149.
4. *Protective hesitation* is a phrase coined by Dr. Duke Ellis while he was serving as assistant dean of student affairs, School of Professional Psychology, Wright State University, Dayton, Ohio.

blacks to seek close contact with other blacks points out why companies should, when possible, hire blacks and other minorities in groups rather than one at a time when they initially hire minorities into a previously all-white environment. Increasingly, however, in the past five to eight years, we have seen more and more young blacks enter corporations and become fearful of seeking each other out for support. Lack of psychic support from other blacks in the organization makes adjustment more difficult. The message to black managers from white male managers is, "Be white like me, and you will have a better chance to succeed." For many blacks, this seems to be true—at least, to a point. When the organization calls upon black managers to use their added value, they no longer know what it is. The downside for black managers is a lengthened stay in the Entry Phase or a very painful adjusting phase.

Behaviors

In the Adjusting Phase, the behavior exhibited by black managers usually results from trial and error in interactions, using resources, and linking with the informal communications network. An informal communications network exists in most companies, but blacks are normally excluded from it. To become a part of the network, blacks have to be friendly with whites. They do this by either seeking an authentic friendship or, as a minimum, affecting a relationship with whites in order to get them to share company information. Blacks must behave in what appears to be a friendly manner with whites in order to be able to function more effectively in the corporation.

There are some other prominent behaviors that black managers exhibit in the Adjusting Phase. Confrontive behavior is more important to the survival and success of black managers than it is to their white peers. White managers can afford the luxury of avoiding confrontation as much as possible, but for blacks, confrontation is seen as necessary in many situations to avoid constantly running the risk of having their input dismissed. Unfortunately, in this period of development, confrontation can often be dysfunctional for blacks. It is in a later period that the black manager learns to become smooth in handling confrontational interactions with whites.

Blacks tend to take greater risks in the Adjusting Phase than in the Entry Phase. They are literally forced to do this because of a high level of frustration. The frustration results from an inability to effectively manager various black-white interactions. Whereas in the Entry Phase, behavior is restrained because of the perception that punishment may result from aggressive actions or because of a high need to fit in and be accepted, the Adjusting Phase is a time to cast off restraints and aggressively pursue one's goals at all costs. Generally speaking, the higher the level of risk taken, the higher the potential rewards granted.

In the Adjusting Phase, blacks exhibit a great deal of sensitivity to people. Since blacks have historically been disadvantaged, it is fairly easy for them to understand the needs and desires of others. One reason this occurs is probably because blacks have always had to be sensitive to some degree to survive from the days of slavery to the present. Even in the cotton fields, blacks had to be sensitive to the overseers to survive from day to day under the tremendous demands placed on them. Therefore, we see this sensitivity as a cultural trait handed down from generation to generation.

Another important behavior that can be observed in blacks at this point is resistance to organizational power. Blacks in this phase are able to resist power more than they could in the Entry Phase. This resistance is important because, when blacks enter previously all-white institutions, some whites may position blacks to fulfill their negative and prejudicial stereotypes. To prevent this, blacks begin to learn how to resist that power.

An overall conclusion we reached is that blacks enter a corporation armed with their own cultural behavioral patterns, which they soon find cannot be *fully* used in the corporation to accomplish results. It becomes obvious during the Adjusting Phase that blacks have to develop additional behavioral styles and skills. This does not mean that blacks should discard their cultural style. It does mean, however, that blacks should acquire an additional behavioral repertoire to accomplish results.

Job Skills

The Adjusting Phase is the beginning of a more active period of learning for blacks. It is when they learn the more subtle aspects of getting the job done. The desire to learn behaviors and skills that will help them advance in the organization is in contrast to the *self-induced* satisfaction that many blacks feel in the entry phase. We say this because we think some of the difficulty experienced by blacks is self-induced for various legitimate reasons, as discussed in the "Entry Phase" subsection.

In the Adjusting Phase, black managers start to test the environment in ways unlike those used in the Entry Phase. A new struggle is begun, employing trial-and-error behavior. To ascertain what can and cannot be done, a person often acts inappropriately and may get into difficulty with the organization in some way. At other times, he or she will do things correctly and get appropriately rewarded. The person will make a conscious or unconscious note of the specific behavior and the reward that resulted from it. Therefore, the job skills that the manager starts to acquire result from testing and probing the environment.

Since black managers have not yet gained the self-confidence they will hopefully gain later and do not have a lot of positive experiences at this point, they do not have a good feel for what they are doing. They seldom exhibit behavior in a planned manner. Instead, they act upon and react to various stimuli—the people, the values of the organization, and the norms—without understanding them. Blacks do not have a clear understanding of the organizational norms because they are just starting to learn how to tap into and use resources.

Blacks can be seen adjusting their behavior in the areas of managing rage and other emotions, managing interfaces with other people in the organization, managing conflict, and reading corporate cues. Let us look more closely at one of these areas.

White managers of blacks often complain that blacks are too emotional. Blacks and women in general tend to display and use emotions very openly. This behavior in a corporation can cause problems for them. White male managers tend not to behave as emotionally as blacks and women do. Therefore, most corporate norms include a rule that states, "Keep emotions down to the bare minimum to get the job done." Blacks will restrain themselves emotionally in the Entry Phase. In the Adjusting Phase, however, they cast aside restraint and vigorously display rage and other emotions. Blacks respond emotionally at this point because of a high level of frustration. They become frustrated because they have high job interest and energy but cannot seem to produce the correct job outputs. Emotions tend to be close to the surface; rage cannot be constrained or managed.

Extreme emotions can cause a person to become almost irrational. We are not suggesting, however, that the display of emotions is wrong or bad. There are many occasions when the display of strong emotions is both right and very functional if it is used as part of a person's strategy.

Another Adjusting Phase struggle for black managers is connected to the corporate messages they receive. As noted earlier, most organizations emphasize the technical aspects of the job more than the managerial aspects. Rewards seem to be given for results produced and not for how well the people doing the job were organized, directed, and developed. Therefore, during this phase, black managers seldom get rewarded for displaying managerial competence; however, they do get punished for displaying a lack of it. The ambiguity of the situation adds to the frustration of black managers in the Adjusting Phase. They must work to find some balance in their job performance between what is seen by the organization as technical competence and what is seen as managerial ability. Black managers in this phase struggle to be considered technically competent while attempting to handle personal and group interfaces in a functional manner.

In essence, in the Adjusting Phase, black managers are dissatisfied and frustrated. The resultant behavior is often volatile and emotionally charged. Such behavior can be frightening for whites and dysfunctional for blacks.

Planned Growth Phase

Attitudes

The Planned Growth Phase is a period of consciously structured activity for black managers. The attitudes of planned growth center around personal improvements that facilitate growth and development. Since the organization may not become less racist, black managers begin to accept the responsibility for changing their own style and methods of operating.

Black managers will work hard to improve their personal style of interacting with whites in an effort to be more productive and get needs met. They will consciously look for successes and for strokes from others to help build self-confidence. Black managers will start not only to recognize others' prejudicial attitudes toward them but to learn how to keep those attitudes from being obstacles to their progress. This action causes some whites to become less prejudiced.

Black managers in the Planned Growth Phase will work to make better use of resources. Many black managers discover the importance of sponsors and will actively seek out one or more and cultivate relationships with them. In this phase of development, black managers give up much of their reactiveness to the environment and learn how to become proactive on the job. They become involved in success issues rather than survival issues. In this manner, barriers are overcome, prejudice is managed, and rewards are obtained.

This period represents a major milestone for black managers because it is a turning point in their development. Bitterness and anger in the extreme inhibit growth when an individual decides the system owns all the problems. Managers moving toward success will separate the system's problems from their own. In this development phase, black managers make a conscious effort to change those attitudes and behaviors that prevent them from being effective.

Emotions

In the Planned Growth Phase, black managers begin to control their angry outbursts and understand how anger can work *for* them if it is used strategically. As confidence grows, presentation of personal style becomes smoother. The need to fight with whites diminishes because now black managers can channel their frustrations into consciously planned goal-seeking activities directed at their own personal growth.

Behaviors

Overcoming mistrust of input from whites is a lingering issue for most black managers. Trust may be established in a one-to-one relationship between a black and white manager, but it is seldom a generalized attitude held by blacks. However, in the Planned Growth Phase, black managers will elect to keep their misgivings to themselves, choosing instead to behave in a manner of trust. Sponsors must be identified, sought out, and accessed. Resources must be used, racist or not. A commitment to succeed becomes paramount.

By now, black managers know that waiting to be adopted by a white sponsor in the hierarchy is chancy. Instead, they must take the initiative to access potential individuals in the hierarchy and select a sponsor. Then it becomes a matter of establishing a relationship and contacting the sponsor when certain needs arise. Black managers must make sure their sponsors have an understanding of their value and potential in the company. A reciprocal relationship may be encouraged by the black manager so the white sponsor can learn more about blacks and thereby put the black person in a giving and sharing position.

In most corporations, people have to interact to accomplish work tasks. Because many technologies and work processes are very complex, it is difficult to do most jobs without seeking the expertise of others. In the Planned Growth Phase, black managers will more readily use white resources than in earlier phases. However, they may still be hesitant to do so and may distinguish between the kinds of information sought from whites and from blacks. Black managers will more readily seek whites as resources for technical job issues but may hesitate on questions of strategy, particularly pertaining to interpersonal relations. Blacks continue to seek out other blacks for help in interpersonal strategic planning. There are reasons other than trust for this; these include common experiences, the perception by blacks of more honest feedback from each other, and the tendency to be straightforward with each other.

Black managers in the Planned Growth Phase often find that their organization has allowed them to fall behind their white peers in job growth and development. Their first concern then becomes having to expend extra energy to catch up to where they should have been all along. Other black managers fortunate enough to have stayed abreast of their white peers will begin to use resources to help them chart career paths—that is, to plan their advancement in some structured manner. Many blacks will in various ways exert pressure on their organization in order to advance. For instance, a black manager may be able to point out the company's inequities toward its black managers or may confront the organization directly about his or her current status in relation to white peers. Whatever the initial activity, black managers in the planned growth phase begin to take conscious charge of their destiny.

Job Skills

Two of the most important job skills acquired by black managers in the Planned Growth Phase are what we call conflict management and the management of racism. These skills are seen as necessary if blacks are to continue to advance in white corporations. Many behaviors and strategies make up these management skills. Blacks see conflict management as a skill that must be more highly developed by blacks than by whites. The management of racism is a management skill unique to blacks. In recent years, however, we have begun to teach whites how to manage racism in themselves, in other whites, and in their institutions.

Conflict management is just what it sounds like—that is, managing conflicts between people, groups, and situations. Most blacks have learned that whites have options to confronting conflicts. Whites may deal with conflicts or, as is usually done in organizations, avoid them. Black managers must learn how to deal with conflicts productively, or they are apt to be scapegoated as a cause of the conflicts. Culturally, confronting conflicts has been a simpler process for blacks than it has been for whites. As we stated previously, blacks tend as a group to be more open and straightforward in their interactions than whites. (In recent years, we have seen some white managers learn from black managers how to confront conflict directly and gain rapid results in terms of problem solving—a heady experience for white managers in conflict-avoiding companies.)

A big difference in the way blacks and whites handle conflict involves their approach. When faced with a conflictual situation, a black manager will more likely confront the person immediately. If that is inappropriate, a black manager will do it later in private. A white manager, on the other hand, will tend to discuss the conflictual situation with the person's boss. The white manager may also talk about the situation indirectly with the person or with peers, usually to get the unpleasant feelings off his or her chest, or the white manager may opt to do nothing. The success of a black manager often depends on how well conflict is handled on the job because, as we said earlier, invariably some part of the conflict will be attributed to the black individual.

Management of racism involves a group of behaviors uniquely developed by blacks to counteract and neutralize demeaning, prejudicial behavior directed toward them by persons of another race or ethnic group. The management of racism is connected with both the survival and the success of the black manager. A large amount of energy goes into the development of this unique black management skill. Whites do not need to develop this as a job skill because they are not targets of racial discrimination. However, many whites today want to learn how to manage racism because they have seen how productivity is increased and loss of time due to dysfunctional behavior is reduced when the correct management skills are used. Black managers need the skill of managing racism above all others in the Planned Growth Phase. Black managers can survive without managing conflict, although it may limit their success, but they will not survive for long without managing the racism of others.

Some management of racism is learned by all blacks by virtue of their survival in the society at large. It is like being a member of a big family and having the skill passed down from parent to child. How much the black manager learns in the corporate setting and how difficult it is to acquire additional skills in this area often depend on accessibility to other "family members." Blacks provide each other with coaching, guidance, feedback, and so forth, just as whites provide other whites with an understanding of corporate norms and expectations. Fortunately, a few training events that successfully teach the management of racism are now available. Usually, black managers learn this skill from other blacks through shared experiences and shared knowledge on a one-to-one or a group basis.

From a shared perspective, black managers learn how to manage racism through planning and implementing strategy. They learn by controlling the behavior of others and by self-control. Racism is managed by using the company's norms, values, and communications network effectively. The individual behaviors used in the acquisition of these skills are discussed in later chapters.

Success Phase

Attitudes

In the Success Phase, black managers combine all they have learned and felt and understood as they struggled to reach this phase. The degree of success is directly linked to their degree of sensitivity to themselves as well as to the environment. Black managers are successful when they have learned the appropriate skills that apply to their unique position in the white corporation.

One of the key learnings in the Success Phase is that making mistakes or failing is not an option for black managers. When a white person fails, the failure reflects on that person. When a black person fails, that person fails for the group. Every black failure reinforces the expectations of the white system.[5]

Black managers who have become successful have accepted protective hesitation as a way of life in the corporation. They are very careful about identifying and using resources, remaining cautious in their interactions with whites. (Complete openness is a luxury afforded to whites by whites.) Preplanning becomes a necessary part of the protective hesitation process. Careful thought is taken before a move is made.

Black managers in the Success Phase are aware of their blackness at all times and how this impacts the white corporation. Blacks must keep in mind that if they want to be successful, they must constantly remember who they are and how they are seen. Black managers must understand how their blackness affects the people they work with and how it affects relationships with others in the corporation.

Black managers have learned to be aware of the racism around them. To forget the impact of racism is tantamount to losing or giving

5. This message is clearly communicated by John H. Johnson in "Failure Is a Word I Don't Accept," *Harvard Business Review* (March–April 1976).

up one's survival instincts. They have learned how to be unusually perceptive in interactions with others. They must listen with "two sets of ears" and see with "three eyes." In other words, black managers must be sensitive to the many cues, especially the racist cues, around them—not in order to respond to them all but in order to be able to respond to those that threaten them or that offer them opportunities.

In charting the attitudes of black managers from entry to success, we found that many come to the corporation with a positive, but naive, attitude. They encounter personal as well as corporate racism and become angry, hostile, and culturally paranoid. Hopefully, they will make the decision to adjust and plan their growth rather than allow anger and resentment to stifle it. As black managers plan their growth, hard work must be applied to earlier attitudes to make them positive again. Once this is done, negative attitudes cease to be a barrier to learning. Therefore, successful black managers will retain a positive attitude even in the midst of racist behaviors.

Emotions

In the Success Phase, black managers know they must sublimate emotions. They learn to use anger and rage as a part of their strategy to enhance job productivity. Through trial and error, they have taken the rage and channeled it into something that could produce better results. They no longer allow emotions to be a barrier to progress. Experience shows that whites will not tolerate uncontrolled emotions from blacks. Whites will negatively evaluate the black manager who displays uncontrolled emotions and will make sure that manager does not succeed.

Behaviors

Black managers in the Success Phase behave in a manner that conveys confidence, knowledge, and the appearance of being in charge. They now better understand how to negotiate the system. They have high control of self and others.

Successful black managers possess the unique ability to turn racism around and make it work *for* them, not against them. They know whites will allow other whites, but not blacks, to be dysfunctional. Therefore, successful black managers no longer allow the system to trap them into dysfunctional behavior.

A smoother interpersonal style emerges for the successful black manager, who develops a high ability to influence others. Black managers have to use more influential behavior than white peers do and charismatic power rather than real position power in order to get whites to work for them.

Black managers can now use resources that are obviously discriminatory. They learn they must confront whites in a way that leaves whites their dignity. If not, racism will dominate the whites' behavior and cause them to become illogical. This prevents the reaching of closure on any issue. As previously stated, being sensitive to the environment is more important to blacks than to whites because blacks have had to protect themselves from hostile surroundings to survive.

Under certain circumstances, black managers have to resist the power of whites in order to prevent a master-slave relationship from developing. Blacks perceive they must use more physical and psychic energy to get tasks done than whites do. In addition, successful black managers discover ways to tap into informal communications networks to seek out the norms, values, and other information that is otherwise a normal part of their white peers' job system.

By the time black managers reach the Success Phase, they have forged a track record. They have produced outstanding results and gained respect from others. However, this merely means they have won the opportunity to work to maintain that record, the opportunity to prove competence to the company again and again. This is a failure on the part of the system. The noticeable difference for white managers is that they normally move through the organization on the basis of perceived potential. Black managers can continue to cement their own confidence in their competence relative to white peers. They can look outward at the events they experience and place blame appropriately instead of always turning inward and perceiving failure in themselves. At this point, black managers can make the system own more of the failures, and they can own fewer.

Job Skills

One thing that stands out in performing the job is the need for black managers to use strategy more than their white peers do. This is particularly true for the management of conflict and the management of racism. It is necessary because external forces work on blacks to reduce their impact on the system. It is difficult for minorities in general to get their input heard. Black managers must develop a strategy against racist resistance in order to impact the system. Preplanning is needed in order to affect the outcome of any given situation. Everything becomes important—dress, style, and timing.

To implement the strategy, successful black managers develop high levels of interpersonal-behavioral skills. Blacks in the Success Phase understand that their interpersonal style is quickly evaluated in an all-white organization. Black managers also learn that getting the title and position at the next level is often anticlimactic. This occurs because, in reality, a black manager has usually been carrying the responsibility and doing the job at the next level for some time prior to the actual promotion. One plausible explanation for this phenomenon is that it eliminates the fear among white managers of setting back affirmative action goals by promoting a black who then fails. The system continues to test the black manager to make sure he or she can handle the job. Successful black managers must continue to reestablish their credibility with each new job, as if their track record will not hold up.

Job Mastery

Job mastery is the name we give to the group of advanced skills, attitudes, and emotions possessed by black managers who have moved beyond the middle-management levels of organizations—beyond the "glass ceiling." Job mastery goes beyond the Success Phase of the four-phase model. The state of job mastery places an individual outside and beyond the four-phase model. The individual who has gone beyond the Success Phase has developed a mind-set that places capability, competence, action, and other leadership issues in his or her hands and not in those of the organization. This individual no longer relies on the organization to totally set his or her course. Instead, the individual feels empowered to develop ideas and enroll others to implement them to meet organizational goals.

Every upper-level black manager we spoke with has a personal list of "key principles" that he or she has used to become successful in the job. These lists have been developed and honed from personal experience—hands-on losses and wins—throughout their careers. Although information was learned from books or courses, much was passed along by sponsors or mentors—by the skillful use of resources and consultants—and some was gained from trial and error.

Attitudes

We have found one common key attitudinal principle among black upper-level managers using job mastery techniques. These managers regard seemingly negative situations as "opportunities." They seem to know how to look at a situation in a positive light instead of a negative light (as lower-level managers tend to do). It does not seem to matter whether the situation involves a personnel problem or a technical problem; these managers have the ability to get others to see the problem in a positive way as an opportunity. It is much easier to get a group of people to work on an "opportunity" than it is to get them to work on a "problem." Job mastery separates those who will make it through the "glass ceiling" from those who will not.

Emotions

Job mastery exacts a different kind of stress. "Excitement" and "commitment" seem to best describe it. In the job mastery state, self-confidence is now a part of the manager's natural self. However, this is not to say that the responsibility of top management does not bring periods of anxiety. The manager knows that responsibility and account-ability stops at his or her door, but this is normally seen as a challenge rather than a burden. Occasionally, there are moments of fear and disbelief. The fear is of failing or not "measuring up." There is self-imposed pressure to do the best possible job—as measured against one's own capabilities, not against one's peers. Disbelief occurs when the black manager experiences the environment into which he or she has traveled. Few blacks are prepared for the relative opulence and power that top-level managers command.

Behaviors

Top-level black managers have learned to operate in a smooth interpersonal manner. They have mastered a behavioral style of interact-ing with people (especially whites) that puts them at ease and encour-ages confidence. Black managers at the top of their organization know they are walking a tightrope. We have seen this manifested in two distinct ways.

One type of black manager seems to have ridden the crest of the various affirmative action programs through the years. He or she ap-pears to have been in the right places at the right times. We do not suggest by this that the person was incompetent or lax in the job. We do say that the individual got there by "playing" to the white hierarchy and by supporting the status quo. This person made it by distancing himself or herself from the other blacks in the organization. This is discussed in more detail in Chapter 7, in the section entitled " The Neoconservative Black."

The second type of black manager to push himself or herself up the ladder to the top made it by dealing effectively with the organization's hot issues. This manager is able to keep his or her finger on the organization's pulse and respond to the difficult challenge of resolving "sticky" problems, especially those involving people issues. This manager relates well to all levels of the hierarchy and is usually seen as "one of us" in the ranks. He or she is aware of the additional dynamics and responsibilities of being a black manager in a top position and will use added value to enhance his or her corporate value.

Job Skills

A major job skill acquired at this level is understanding the ability to play corporate politics well. At the top levels, black managers no longer see this as threatening or as a moral issue, but rather as how business is conducted among competing resources. They also understand how business is conducted in their organization and how to use the organization's resources to get products or services to the marketplace. They acquire the skill of taking a conceptual panoramic view of how the organization functions and providing the necessary resources for effective output by others.

How the Model Can Be Used

By Black Managers

In general, black managers can use the developmental model to explain what happens, why it happens, and how individuals can change to become successful or more successful. Specifically, the model relates the individual black experience in the white corporation to the experience of other blacks in the same circumstances. It helps explain, in part, what happens to blacks psychologically as they face the difficulties of prejudice and discrimination. The model can be used to help black managers ascertain where they are in terms of their organizational growth. It can also help black individuals ascertain where they are in their organizational skills.

The model can give black managers personal insight into themselves and the reasons for certain behaviors. It can help them become more aware of how racism impacts their daily life so that they may gain more control over themselves and their responses to the environment.

The essence of the model for black managers is that it offers an explanation of what is real, insight into how to go about changing things, and a personal hope for their future.

By White Managers

White managers will find that the model offers an explanation of what happens to blacks in predominantly white corporations. White managers can be very anxious about a situation involving blacks if they do not have a clear picture of what is occurring. Knowledge of the model can help white managers speed up the joining-up process for blacks. White managers will have a clearer picture of what to expect from blacks in the Entry Phase. Proactive steps can be formulated by white managers to help accelerate the development process for blacks. The model suggests that whites can help eliminate institutional racism. Since white managers will know what behaviors to expect as well as the reasons why blacks behave the way they do, whites will have a responsibility to remove the institutional barriers that cause dysfunctional behavior. The model will make both blacks and whites aware of some of those barriers.

It is of the utmost importance for white managers to understand that much of the behavior they see in a black subordinate is a minority-group experience as opposed to an individual experience. Taken as a whole, the model gives white managers hope that the interface between a white manager and a black subordinate can be made more effective.

Transferability of the Model and Data to Other Minorities

Because of the response to our developmental model by members of other minority groups, we know that the model and data are transferable to other minorities. Historically, Hispanics and blacks have been, and still are, members of an oppressed class of people; to some extent, this is also true of Asians and white women. Hispanics and blacks are not an equally accepted part of American society. Asians are seen as apart from society. This is more true in some parts of the country than in others. Discrimination separates nonwhites and women from the mainstream of life. Oppression creates issues within and between groups of people.

Minority psychology is a field of study that applies to all minority groups. Some commonalities among minorities are:

- Oppression
- Exclusion from the mainstream activities of society
- Feelings of being different (in a negative way) from those in a dominant position
- Low self-concept, self-esteem, and self-confidence
- Being positioned in a one-down status
- Being barred from, and not encouraged to seek, a better position and status in society—or in life
- Lack of equal opportunities

The subordinate position of various minority groups to a dominant group makes the model transferable because minorities tend to display similar attitudes and behaviors in response to being in their subordinate position.

Part Two

The Way to Success

The everyday functioning of black individuals in the workplace is shaped by America's racial attitudes. Blacks who are not aware of this try hard to fit into organizations by not associating with anything involving black activities. Some white managers encourage this behavior by saying, "I don't see any difference in you," or, "I don't see your color when I look at you." In some organizations, if two or more blacks are seen together, white managers wonder what they are conspiring to do to the organization.

Organizations sometimes rob themselves of the talents of their black managers because the blacks are busy using up their energies to fit into the organization. We equate the capacity of people to that of computers. If a computer is built to store only four megabytes of data, it will store no more than four megabytes. Likewise, people have a finite operating capacity; if some of that capacity is used to produce fit-in behavior, then they will operate at a diminished capacity. The more blacks are forced to fit in, the more their operating capacity will be diminished.

In defense of their status, however, blacks have developed a unique way of operating in an interracial setting and, as a result, have learned a group of interpersonal skills that can be helpful for *all* interactions by *all* minorities. Part Two of this book is dedicated to freeing blacks and other minorities from having to inappropriately try to fit into their organizations.

Part Two illustrates the dynamic functioning of the four-phase developmental model as it intimately affects black managers. Each chapter begins with a list of the critical issues that black managers deal with on the job during a particular phase. An in-depth discussion of these issues follows.

In Part Two, you also meet Jack, a black manager who talks to you about his development as he moves through each phase of the model. Jack is a composite of the experiences, feelings, perceptions, and realities of most minorities who work in a white setting. He could just as easily be Evelyn, Ruby, Maria, Huiling, or Carlos. The ethnic background may vary, but the experiences remain essentially the same. His story offers white readers an opportunity to look into and feel the world of a black individual. It offers minority readers insight into the confusion they may now be experiencing and the questions they may have.

Following the story of Jack in each chapter is an analysis of the critical issues involved in that particular phase. How-to solutions for dealing effectively with these issues are then presented, together with the basic concepts used in these solutions.

2

Entry Phase

Critical Issues

Attitudes

- Lack of self-confidence (especially in a racial context)
- Pseudoconfidence
- Attributing the job situation to luck or, at the opposite extreme, to personal brilliance
- Inadequate preparation for the realities of what is involved in the work world (especially interpersonal interactions)
- Naïveté (particularly about racial attitudes in the workplace)
- Belief in the Protestant work ethic
- Being overly satisfied with the job
- Belief in autonomy (not needing anyone's help)
- Lack of clear job goals and/or understanding of career objectives and advancement opportunities
- Unawareness of racial issues in day-to-day operations or interfaces

Emotions

- High stress level (particularly in interactions with whites)
- Confusion in interactions; willingness to accept responsibility for poor interactions with others
- Inability to identify sources of visceral discomfort in interactions with whites
- Feeling crazy
- Feeling grateful
- Arrogance; feeling self-important

Behaviors

- High need to fit in with whites or, at the opposite extreme, avoidance of whites
- Being "nice" no matter what the situation: smiling, agreeing, laughing at jokes, etc.
- Seeking support for psychic well-being
- Avoiding black support and allowing isolation to occur
- Problematic behavioral style
- Permitting interpersonal style to overshadow work or job competence
- Primary concern for job tasks; little concern for managerial interactions
- Working alone, with a need to avoid "making waves"

Job Skills

- Unaware of how to become appropriately socialized
- Lack of managerial skills or appropriate managerial skills
- Lack of understanding of how organizations function; concern only for tasks
- Lack of opportunity to obtain training and development in the job
- Inability to translate white-oriented training material for effective use by blacks
- Unrealistic (or nonexistent) expectations of the job and people
- Not future-oriented in the job and people
- Inability to effectively use (or understand how to effectively use) the communications network

Overview of the Critical Issues

Attitudes

That first significant job as an adult is important to most of us—whites and blacks alike. All of us have critical issues to deal with on any new job, and these include promotions into new positions as well as new assignments. Minorities must face and resolve these issues as well as the additional issues that are a product of living as the victims of racism and sexism.

Many of today's young people have been taught to be more confident than their parents were, although a lack of confidence is still pervasive among black professionals. The lack of self-confidence can admittedly be a product of personal background and upbringing. For the black person, however, society is also responsible to a certain degree for this feeling. Individual and family experiences with discrimination determine how a black person will feel about himself or herself in relation to functioning in the larger society:

> *"I felt I was capable of doing a good job, but I feared asking questions of whites. They would think I was dumb. I felt whites had better training and experience than I."*
>
> *"I felt college had prepared me to do the job, but I never had whites as peers before and I felt they had to test me first."*
>
> *"I felt whites had a lot of negative ideas about blacks. I felt evaluated when I asked questions. Asking questions became painful for me."*
>
> *"I didn't go to whites because I felt they would think I was dumb, I should already know it all. So I tried to know it all alone as fast as I could so I wouldn't be seen as dumb."*
>
> *"I thought I'd do well, but my performance review made me wonder how I was being seen by whites."*
>
> *"I felt like the dumbest nigger in town, and whites treated me like I should have automatically known everything even though they had shared nothing about the job with me."*

These comments are but a small sample of the feelings and experiences expressed by blacks about their self-confidence in a predominantly white setting. Many also attributed the acquisition of their job not to hard work and tenacity but to luck, government pressure, or "they just needed another black."

A number of young professionals, particularly those from Ivy League and top ten white universities, enter corporate America cocky and overconfident. They believe they had had the best education and preparation for the job. What they have dismissed as nonexistent is the impact of personal and institutional racism on the day-to-day execution of the job tasks. These young blacks believe they were hired only because they were the best:

> *"I've associated very well with whites all my life. I never believed I would ever have a problem making friends in my new job or fitting in with my colleagues. But everyone here acts like I don't exist outside of my job."*
>
> *"I've been here about six months, and at first, everyone was so nice and seemed enthusiastic about my joining their team. Now, relationships seem strained, and I don't understand what has happened."*

> "I attended one of the best schools in the country, and I'm thought of as very creative and very smart. I had one of my company's highest test scores, and the recruiter confided to me that I had impressed him very highly. So I don't know what happened. Every time I try to share an idea in a meeting, I either get talked over or dismissed."

> "I graduated summa cum laude in my school's toughest program. So why do my bosses treat me like an idiot? I have to justify everything I do."

One of the biggest complaints about education today is that it does not prepare people to deal with the day-to-day realities of the work environment. Often, young white employees are jolted into the realities of the work world that they are not academically prepared to handle. For blacks, this experience is doubly or triply jolting, as evidenced by some of these comments:

> "I expected to do my job with minimal help from whites."

> "I expected to come in, do the job laid out for me, do nothing extra. I wasn't thinking of moving ahead, and that's how the company treated me."

> "I expected hard work to get me recognition and reward. But it didn't, not by itself. There was no support for blacks, and I got evaluated on white standards and norms."

> "I expected to struggle day by day to make the grade. I worked hard to be accepted by whites, but I got little information or help."

> "I thought I just needed technical things and that I wasn't sure of myself. I expected to get help but instead got protected, sheltered, and killed with kindness."

Naïveté in the Entry Phase, particularly about racial attitudes in the work force, is a common characteristic of the black manager. No matter how well versed blacks are about society's discriminatory practices, there seems to be a belief that such practices are not a factor on the job. Blacks have generally bought into the Protestant work ethic, and somehow racism has no place in this concept:

> "I was not prepared for interactions with whites. I didn't understand racism behaviorally."

> "I had no concept of what an organization was. I was just doing a job without having to interact much with whites."

> "I wasn't aware of racist issues or other goings-on. I thought people in a corporation would be more professional."

> *"I was very naive about subtle racism. I wanted to trust whites and believe in goodness, fairness—to do the job and get rewarded, not have to worry about interactions."*
>
> *"I expected the company to give me what I wanted without forcing it. I wasn't prepared for resistance. I had a basic lack of understanding."*
>
> *"I was naive, expecting to be seen and treated the same as whites."*
>
> *"I was arrogant and thought I would be rewarded because I was so competent in my job."*

In addition, some blacks feel they can do their jobs alone. They do not need sponsors—no coaching, especially from the other black employees who have been around awhile. They adopt the attitude that their competence alone will get them ahead in the organization; the other blacks don't understand; racism is no longer an issue in corporate America, and a person is advanced on merit regardless of who he or she is:

> *"I expected people to leave me alone and let me do my job. That's what I thought I was doing. When my upper-level boss told me people were having a problem with me, I was shocked! My immediate boss never said anything to me other than I was doing fine."*

These statements and informal discussions between blacks often reveal how unaware they are of racial issues, except when these issues result in negative evaluations and prevent their advancement in the workplace. Whites and blacks often assume most blacks know all there is to know about discrimination and its effects, but much discrimination, especially today, is subtle. For this reason, blacks often miss much of the discriminatory behavior until it results in some harmful overt action.

Many black families, with the endorsement of the general dominant society, inadvertently teach their children that they must be grateful for the chances they get in life to better their status. This means being grateful to whites for that "good" job. Another prevalent theme today is, "Get in there and show them [whites] what you can do." The idea is that if you are supercompetent and a hard worker, you will be noticed and rewarded. Your job and career are set. Job security is a major issue. If whites are concerned about job security, you can safely assume it is a paramount concern to blacks. With this in mind, is it any wonder that many black managers may be, or may appear to be, perfectly satisfied with their jobs? Although, in reality, black managers are often dissatisfied, they tend to inhibit their own feelings of dissatisfaction. Many are unable to see themselves in progressively higher positions of responsibility or are too fearful to push their organization with regard to increased responsibilities and opportunities. With few role models and little or no support and encouragement from the whites in the organization, many blacks feel fortunate "just to have a good job":

> "I figured if I did an outstanding job and didn't make waves in my organization, I would be rewarded."
>
> "I wasn't looking ahead to reward, just doing a job and getting paid."
>
> "I wasn't looking for reward. I was just lucky to have a job with a great company."
>
> "I thought I'd cause trouble for myself if I complained to my boss that I wanted more responsibility."
>
> "I had no goals for myself other than learning, alone, how to be good in my job."
>
> "I wasn't thinking ahead to being rewarded for superior competence. I was too busy surviving day to day."

Emotions

The emotions experienced by blacks in the dominant white setting at the entry level can be confusing, debilitating, and often dysfunctional for black managers. The dysfunctional aspect of the Entry Phase emotions is the willingness of blacks to accept responsibility for poor interactions with whites. In this phase, black managers are unable to divorce themselves from the process of the interaction to ascertain what part they own, what the other person owns, and what the situation is contributing to the interaction. Often, there is only visceral discomfort to cue the person that something is amiss. Black managers frequently experience a high level of stress because they cannot identify the source of the discomfort. Those black managers who do realize that something is wrong spend a lot of psychic energy in denial. They talk themselves out of believing what just happened or rationalize the incident away. All this confusion of emotion, self-debasement, denial, and conflicting desire to acknowledge their own competence leaves many black managers with the feeling of "going crazy":

> "I had not thought about how racism would affect me. I was not prepared for corporate life. I soon became bitter, and my self-confidence dropped."
>
> "I wasn't prepared to work with whites and was soon caught up in proving myself."

"Sometimes I would go home after being in meetings half the day and ask myself if I was losing my mind."

"I didn't know what was going on, but I began to be upset and became full of stress as I realized I was being stereotyped. I had been satisfied with wooing whites to be accepted and not be mistreated."

"I was not prepared to deal with whites or know how to get what I wanted; I was generally satisfied; I believed the propaganda; I had some fear and a feeling of helplessness."

"I was in no way prepared for anything I got on my job and was in and out of emotional upsets most of the time."

The most amazing finding among black managers in the Entry Phase is a lack of anger and hostility. This is probably due to an inability to identify the sources of their discomfort and a desire to see their organization as fair and paternal:

"I had no anger or hostility. Intellectually, I knew racism existed, could recognize it in the outside world, but I did not see the subtleties in the company. I just wanted to get along in the work setting."

"I wasn't angry or hostile. I was unaware of how racism got played out. I wanted to fit in but couldn't seem to."

"There was no anger or hostility in me. I ignored racism and acted white."

"I felt no anger or hostility. I ignored racism. I wanted to fit in in the worst way, to be accepted. I wanted to be liked by whites, be on the bandwagon."

"I didn't feel any anger or hostility. I isolated myself. I was not involved with the racial issues around me. I didn't respond much to it."

Behaviors

One of the most obvious behaviors observed in blacks in the Entry Phase is the striving to belong to the group—to feel a part of the organization as they perceive whites would. Feeling accepted and being comfortable are of paramount importance. However, avoidance behavior can also easily be seen. It is almost as common as seeking to belong. These behavioral extremes are indicative of the alienation blacks feel from the mainstream of society. It boils down to trying too hard or not trying at all. Being "nice" and not making waves become critical to day-to-day well-being and to just being able to get the job done. Like it or not, everyone's behavior affects the cooperation of others, which is needed to do a job. This is especially true when blacks need the cooperation of whites; a black person's behavior affects how cooperative others will be:

> "I didn't seek out my boss very often, nor did I speak up."
>
> "I was quiet, didn't speak out. I didn't interact with anyone much."
>
> "I didn't clique with the other workers. I had a fear of being seen as lazy, so I didn't do much socializing."
>
> "I smiled a lot and made friends with whites. I ignored racial digs to be accepted."
>
> "I laughed at the whites' jokes, even when they weren't funny. I wanted to make them think I was their friend. I worked to make them feel comfortable around me."
>
> "I didn't interact much with whites. I am quiet, but whites saw that as a weakness in my style. I was told I'm too low-key."

Intellectually, everyone can accept that there are individual differences in *all* people's personalities. However, for blacks, these differences often get exaggerated and usually are evaluated negatively by whites. For these reasons, interpersonal style becomes problematic for the black manager. More often than anyone imagines, interpersonal style overshadows work or job competence.

> "I knew I was technically sound, so I thought I could run. But I got poor performance appraisals and suffered a lack of confidence for a long time. Now, I realize how much of that appraisal focused on personality differences and conflicts."
>
> "I was told I was doing a good job, and I felt very arrogant about it. But I was not rewarded for it because of my interpersonal style, I was told."
>
> "I expected to be evaluated on what I could do, nothing else. I stayed to myself. I thought I was doing well from the results. Later, when I was evaluated, I realized more went into the job than completing the tasks."

In the Entry Phase, blacks focus on the tasks. Whites enter corporations with careers on their minds. Until recently, blacks felt fortunate merely to have been allowed to hold jobs once reserved exclusively for white males. Today, most blacks still have a limited vision of their chances to rise to the very top of large corporations. Given the statistics on how many blacks hold such positions, these black managers are rather realistic about their expectations for advancement in most corporations.

Whether the black manager tries to belong or to avoid social interaction with whites, the need for psychic support often overrides these considerations. Many black managers seek someone in the organization to talk to, gripe with, or glean information from. When no other blacks are available, then often a sympathetic white is sought. However, many other blacks seek support outside the company from mates, family, or friends:

> *"I got support from blacks. I turned the place upside down to find other blacks."*
> *"There were no other blacks around. I traveled a lot, so all my support had to come from my superior."*
> *"I was isolated my first year, so I got most of my support from a black friend."*
> *"I sought support and sharing with a black friend from another company."*
> *"I really suffered. I had to listen to my boss, who told me what to do. The only other black around wasn't at all supportive."*

Job Skills

The most damaging shortcoming for black managers is the lack of managerial skills. This becomes a critical issue for blacks, because organizations evaluate blacks, but not their white peers, negatively if they do not very early display an ability to manage others. This translates into showing such behaviors as being able to (1) run meetings smoothly and handle the conflict that arises; (2) use and manage resources; (3) manage one's frustrations and angers; and (4) manage the racism of others.

In the Entry Phase, newly hired black managers are destined to failure in these areas for all the reasons discussed so far in this chapter. In addition, most black managers do not initially have a good working understanding of how organizations function. Where would blacks as a group acquire this information? There has been little or no historical basis or cultural opportunity for blacks to learn. Given the limited number of years since blacks were first allowed into the corporate world and the relatively small number of black corporate managers who can serve as role models, blacks have still had little exposure to corporations. Most black parents who have worked in corporate America left their troubles at the office, so most young entrants have heard little of what corporations are about, except for what is offered in academia. Furthermore, few companies provide black managers with specific opportunities to obtain the necessary training and development in the areas of managerial and organizational skills.

Such training is not always necessary for white managers, because they can acquire most of the needed managerial and organizational skills by generalizing their own cultural experience to the organization. That is, the primary style of interacting within an organization is a reflection of the behavioral styles of white America. Therefore, white managers are normally accustomed to a style of interaction that allows them to use resources and obtain new skills in this environment. The style of white managers is generally consistent with the style of those who are evaluating them. In this sense, whites can be said to inherit skills that are directly related to their survival within the organization.

On the other hand, most blacks have a different cultural experience and, consequently, a different style from that of whites. This is a handicap in the white organization, and blacks are consequently penalized for not having had the experiences of the dominant group. In this phase of development, black managers are further handicapped by having to translate much of the training material and data into a minority framework. Often, black managers cannot use the training material as it is presented because they would meet resistance or receive a negative evaluation:

> "I couldn't use the managerial training I got. It was all slanted to whites' needs. I didn't know how to translate it for my use."
>
> "My company didn't deal with issues blacks would face. All the managerial stuff was white-middle-class."
>
> "The managerial training was geared to white boys. I didn't get anything out of it."
>
> "I was never encouraged to get any kind of training."
>
> "I found out from a friend about management seminars. I went outside my company on my own to improve my interpersonal skills. My black friends helped me to strategize to go."
>
> "My managerial training didn't give me an appreciation for what I was running into. When I used the training, it didn't work."

An additional handicap for most blacks in the Entry Phase is that they do not understand how they can effectively use the existing communications network. Whites can readily identify effective behavior and relate to successful managers through the formal and informal systems of sharing information. In this way, they use the energy, skills, and knowledge of others who share a common cultural experience.

Therefore, whites have a built-in support system. Circumstances allow white managers to have a forward-looking orientation. That is, whites generally have an image of the future that includes the clear possibility of growth within the organization. In contrast, black managers have trouble maintaining such a positive image of the future because of the absence of sufficient role models to support that belief. Black managers expend more energy in the Entry Phase on activities designed to ensure survival:

> *"I knew I wanted to do the best job they'd seen. That was all I was concerned about—not about becoming a manager or being successful."*
>
> *"I was excited about my job—growing, developing, and taking on more responsibility. I had a vision of how I was going to move up in the company. But now I've become angry and bitter. It takes all I can do just to struggle to survive in this place."*

Black managers in the Entry Phase tend to be unrealistic in their expectations about the quality of their jobs and about the people who share their work world. Their expectations are a product of wishful thinking. Continuous doses of the reality of their unique situation will sooner or later propel black managers either out the door or into the next stage of development.

Jack: A Story of Blunders

My name is Jack, and I'm thirty-seven years old. I've been asked to talk openly and frankly about the Entry Phase in my first job in a predominantly white organization. I don't profess to speak for all blacks, only about my experience and what I know and have seen. We all have different backgrounds, personalities, and have been in a myriad of different situations. Even I can't go into them all here. But one thing I do know—blacks in white institutions have faced the same problems, the same emotional responses, and the same personal trials. I've found, though, that not all of us reach the same level of consciousness about it, nor are we willing to face the brutal truth about ourselves or the discriminatory systems we work in. Still fewer of us are ready to speak out to others and tell it like it is.

Perhaps you'd like to know something about my personal background. OK, that might help you understand why I'm the kind of person I am. Let me get it straight with you, now. Just because I haven't reacted to my environment the same way you did or the way you've seen others do, don't think the same feelings weren't there. It was just a difference in training, friend.

I was born and reared in the South during the time before black was beautiful. It was an average-size town. It was just big enough for all the blacks *not* to know each other.

I was an above-average student in my desegregated high school. When I graduated, I decided to go into the army. My older brother, Fred, had not gone to college but had decided instead, two years before my graduation, to go into the small construction business our father owned.

My parents, like nearly all the black parents I knew, were working people. Both my parents had only a high-school education. Now, my brother also had stopped there. Fred and my father were pretty close. Fred hung around Dad all the time, helping in the business, so no one was surprised when Fred starting working full-time with Dad after high school. I never saw much of my father. He was always gone working on a job, sometimes until late at night. For blacks at that time, he made a good living for us.

My sister, who was a year behind me, wanted desperately to go to a teacher's college in another state. We had talked a lot about it, knew it was going to cost a lot of money, so I made things easy by joining the service. I'd thought about college for myself, but it didn't seem as important as having my sister go.

Not too long after going into the army, I was sent to Germany. I worked as a personnel specialist, responsible for keeping track of people, making assignment changes, and keeping personnel records. Since I'd been a pretty good student in high school, I decided to fill some of my time by going to night school.

Now, you should understand where I was coming from, so you'll understand the why of some of the choices I made. Growing up in the South (I've since learned this happens all over the U.S. of A.), I was inadvertently taught that blacks are not as smart as whites.

Man! Now, there I was in night school with white guys from all over the country. So what do I do? I start taking courses—not college courses, but more high-school courses. My first course was a ninth-grade English course. Of course, that was no challenge, so I took a twelfth-grade English course next, then a twelfth-grade algebra course. Those weren't any challenge either.

But what surprised the hell out of me was the whites in the classes wanted to know how much college I had taken. I was impressed. I started to feel so good that I thought I'd move on and take some University of Maryland courses. So I took two years of college courses. I was able to do this because the university conducted extension courses on the army base.

I had planned to make the army my career, but a white sergeant encouraged me to leave and go to college. I left the service and enrolled in a black southern college, worked hard, and again was a very good student.

A large, nationally known company hired me off my campus immediately after graduation. I was one of the first black people in my field of study to be hired at my school by this firm.

By then, I had married and had an infant child. We moved North. Neither of us had lived in this area of the country before. The company provided us with no help in getting settled. Theoretically, we could live anywhere (especially up North, we thought) but practically, we had trouble finding housing. Many empty apartments were mysteriously filled when we showed up.

I started my job in an office with all whites around me. I had replaced a black manager, James Peoples, who had been moved to another office. At first, everybody was really nice, you know—the people I talked to on my interview, the recruiting people. And, man, everybody was calling me "Mr."! I really felt like I had it made.

But everything got off on the wrong foot for me right away—the first day! My immediate boss was away from the office for two weeks. He left notes on my desk telling what he expected me to have done when he returned.

I looked through the papers; my anxiety shot straight up. How was I going to do this stuff? I didn't even understand it. There was nobody around to explain it to me. He'd just left me out there—on my own.

I thought about it for a while. Frankly, there was reluctance on my part to go ask the whites around, so I went and found James and asked him about the work. I felt more comfortable doing that.

See, I felt I'd had an inferior education. That's what I had been taught, what I grew up with: that blacks who go to black southern schools have an inferior education.

You want to know why I felt that way? OK! I knew white companies had almost never recruited on black southern campuses before the civil rights laws. You learn this from other places, too. For instance, at school, our black teachers would say, "You've got to study and work hard because you know those whites are over there, too." The white teachers just sort of ignored you, assuming that if you learned anything, that was good.

Another thing, you look around, and there are few black role models for us anywhere except in music and sports. At one time, teachin' and preachin' were high-status jobs in the black community. Even today, what few of us are out there making our mark seem to be invisible. Our black kids still don't see they can be somebody important.

Man, oh man! I'm getting on my soapbox! Where was I? So! I was reluctant to ask whites questions because I didn't want them to think I was dumb and didn't understand what I was doing.

I felt uncomfortable; I could look around and see there weren't any other blacks in my field except James. That told me something.

Two weeks later, my boss returned. I hadn't finished the work because I didn't understand it. I had started and had tried to gather some material on it.

At this point, I didn't know what my job was—didn't know how to go about accomplishing my job—and hadn't met very many people.

During this time, I felt lost. I had no direction. There was one white individual down the hall, a quiet, sympathetic-looking guy. I did go ask him questions. I depended on him a lot for help, and he gave me what he could.

Yeah! There was something else, too, that first year. I could sense the other people around me—as though they were smirking. It was like . . . a lack of respect. It's a strange feeling and difficult to explain. For instance, I had been on the job about two weeks when one of the whites in the office with a two-year degree . . . well, uh, I had asked him earlier in the day what I thought was a legitimate, intelligent question. In less than an hour, he had gone down the hall and told everybody how dumb I was because I had asked him a question. After finding that out, I was really afraid to ask whites any questions.

Of course, years later, I realized that was the wrong thing to do because it hurt me in terms of my development and learning process.

If I couldn't find a black person to ask a question of, I wouldn't ask questions. Oh, and there was another one! A young white peer of mine from the office across from me—a smart ass. He would come ask me basic kinds of questions. If I gave what he thought was the wrong answer, he'd look at me, smile, and then proceed to explain the correct answer to me. So I figured he was trying to find out if I really knew anything. I knew he had never interacted with blacks before because he would come in and try to get very intellectual with me.

Oh yeah! We had a white supervisor, too. He would come around and tell what amounted to "colored folks jokes." At first I used to laugh because . . . well, I guess, uhm . . . like a victim or a slave—if I didn't laugh and be nice, I'd be in some kind of trouble. Or maybe people wouldn't be nice back to me.

You know, I stayed to myself. I interacted with whites as little as possible, only when necessary. Now I know I hurt myself with this behavior. I'm sure I was negatively evaluated for this. I didn't socialize with whites; I didn't want to be around them after work; I didn't want to go to their parties—although I'd force myself to go in some instances.

Let me tell you what bugged and confused the hell out of me. I noticed white managers coming into the company the same time I did and after me, getting bigger jobs, larger projects to work on than I did. I know because I ate lunch with them every day.

I was damned uncomfortable most of the time. I really wanted to go eat with some black folks. I had met some other blacks, but they worked in other areas of the company. I didn't eat with the blacks, though, because I felt pressure to eat with my group. Because the whole group always ate together.

Occasionally, James and I would go out to eat—just to get away from everybody else. We wouldn't talk about the job. Instead, we talked about baseball, our families . . . to relax, laugh, talk, and enjoy each other's company.

Like with most companies, I had training and orientation sessions to attend during that first year. Needless to say, I was the only black manager at these sessions. We had to stand, give our name, and tell something about our background, including our school. When I mentioned my school, everybody wanted to know where that was—never heard of it before. The other people were mentioning Harvard, Yale, Princeton, Columbia, Stanford, schools like that. That was very intimidating to me. I dreaded having to go to these sessions. But somehow, I hung in there.

Once, a vice-president came to visit our sessions. At the time, the company was pushing equal opportunity, and they sent a photographer to take a picture of James and me to put in a brochure the company was putting together. A couple of the newer whites wanted to know why they weren't included, why only our pictures were being taken. The VP looked at me, and again I felt embarrassed, uncomfortable, and put on the spot. Somebody had to go explain to the whites what was going on.

But you know, meetings in general were a hassle until I learned how to handle myself. I wouldn't speak up. And when I did, I'd always sense something wasn't right. It's like people would talk right over me. They wouldn't listen to me. For instance, in one of my meetings, we were dealing with a problem that was definitely in my area of expertise. My boss was in the meeting, too. So instead of asking me questions directly, whites asked questions of me through my boss by directing their questions to him. After about the third time this happened, I asked myself, "Didn't I make myself clear, or don't they know I speak English?" My white peers were there with their bosses. This didn't happen to them. They were talked to directly.

Oh, and another thing! Speaking of bosses, I didn't have regularly scheduled meetings with my boss. He told me I could come in if I had a problem. Now, think about that. The implication was, "Don't bother me unless you have a problem!"

Now you *know* I certainly wasn't going to admit I had a problem I couldn't handle. Sooo, I had little interaction with my boss. Again, this hurt me.

You know what? During that first year especially, I really experienced periods of high stress. There were plenty of blacks around, but not in my area. I saw whites get better jobs than I had, and I didn't like that. James was from a northern city, and he didn't understand some of the things about southern blacks or what differences we had in some of our attitudes. He was just insensitive to what I might be going through.

James didn't understand, for instance, why I wasn't as aggressive as he was. Hell, I was from the South. I know I was pretty damn unaggressive. I always knew what the situation was. I've always been a fast learner.

I knew about racism, but I never thought it would exist in a large corporation like this. I thought they were in business to make money and wouldn't tolerate crap like that. Of course, that was an inappropriate assumption for me to make, because companies are just people from the larger society. I guess I just didn't think.

Being in a new city, having to make new friends added to my stress. I was used to a black society—now it was integrated.

Stress came from old learnings from my growing up in an environment—all of society—telling me, "Whites are smart; blacks are dumb and lazy." I guess, like a lot of blacks, I had unknowingly bought into a little piece of that.

Yeah! Sure it made me angry when I thought about it. I felt *if* whites were smarter, it was because they had better opportunities. And besides, they made all the rules determining what was and was not considered smart.

Looking back, I see now that in order to escape some of the pressure, I allowed myself to be maneuvered into becoming "the expert" in my work area. I've found out since, that's death for a minority. You get steered and directed so that you end up specializing in one piece of something because whites can feel that they know you can do that piece well. You're also comfortable being an "expert." But you don't get the broad-based training and development you need when that happens.

See, let me tell you. I had this one little piece that was mine. Later on, when they tried to broaden me, I fought it. They had channeled me into a narrow path to make sure I didn't fail. I knew this because I was only given this kind of work to do. They didn't introduce me to anyone else, either, to help me get my work done so I could move on to something else. So when they tried to broaden my area of responsibility, it was too late; I resisted. I had gotten their message. They wanted me to work in this narrow channel, and that was nice and safe. When they finally offered me others to help me on the project, I didn't want it! I didn't trust those other people. I felt they'd screw up what was mine.

I guess you know, I was really confused now. I said, "Wait a minute! You wanted me to stay in this area, now you want me to get out." I couldn't read the messages. I didn't understand. And *nobody* took the time to explain it to me.

You better believe I felt anger from time to time—but I didn't express it at work. I knew if I did, I'd be looked down on and ostracized.

One day at work, my boss came in and asked me, "Why is it taking you so long to do this job?" I exploded! I told him I was upset—he was pressing me—I needed more time! I was new with the company! I hadn't been there ten years and didn't automatically know how to do that stuff. "I've got to learn how to do it like everybody else," I told him.

He thought I was taking too long. Looking back, I probably did take too long.

But what he didn't understand was, being black and not having access to resources the way whites do, I would take damn near twice as long to make damn sure that everything was in order; I checked and rechecked and checked again.

The same thing in meetings—you have to get up in front of a bunch of white people and explain things. You're under a lot of stress when that happens. You're fearful that if you make a mistake, that'll just confirm what you know whites are thinking in the first place.

At the time, I didn't know there were people someplace around there whose job it was to do some of the tasks on my projects. Hell, how was I supposed to know? I didn't even understand the organization or how things worked. No one ever explained it to me.

Sometimes, my boss would stand over me and watch me work on my project and make comments about it. We argued all day one day over a simple decision I had made.

Now I'm feeling crazy! Why would a person do that? You know, if you asked me right now to explain it to you, I'd have to say I didn't think about trying to explain it to myself. I couldn't explain it! I just didn't think about it. I guess I didn't think about any of it much. I wasn't angry . . . and if anger threatened to surface over some incident, I'd usually swallow it. Sounds strange, doesn't it?

Thinking back, I guess I was thankful I had this job. In fact, when I joined this company, I figured I might not last the year. Somewhere inside me, I felt that I might leave or they would fire me because they would discover some deficiency in me. I know that's not logical—but then neither is racism logical nor the effects it has on all of us.

I ran into a lot of things that worked to undermine my confidence. I saw younger whites come into the organization and other whites take them aside and tell them things, share information. I saw the new whites interacting with other people I didn't even know. That wasn't done with me or for me.

Now I'm feeling real strange.

At first—not for a long time, really—I didn't attribute my weird feelings to racism, though. I thought it was *me!* I thought *I* was doing something wrong.

James didn't even realize I was feeling this way. He'd been there longer and, being from the North, seemed to get along better than I did. James and I didn't discuss discrimination or many of the incidents at work or our real feelings about things.

Of course, there did come a time when everybody had just about had enough! Whew! Did we talk to each other then. Like when James got put on a really big project and ran headlong into several people who wouldn't work with him. But that's another story.

In retrospect, it took too long for me to get angry. I'm surprised I don't have an ulcer. I guess it had to come to the point where the damn job was less important than my dignity and self-respect.

There were even problems when I had to go out of town to one of the branch offices. Surprise showed on people's faces whey they discovered that the trouble-shooter sent out to them was black.

Once—get this—it got so bad that every time I made a suggestion, this one big, red guy would stand up and ask insane questions, pick at my answers, and just agitate. It got so obvious, this guy's boss told him to get a cup of coffee. "Just leave!" he shouted.

At this point, I guess, it finally hit me—"This is happening because I'm black." No whites had complained about stuff like this. And the thoughtless racial remarks— but I was still "nice." Like Jackie Robinson—you can't fight back.

Another time, returning to the northern city where I'd been transplanted, I had trouble getting a cab home, which was in the black part of town. I complained and learned other blacks had this problem, too.

Change came gradually. I found myself talking more to other blacks about survival issues. We were no longer merely seeking each other out for relaxation. Now we were also sharing experiences, asking questions of each other, and working strategies.

We discovered that we were all trying to survive . . . having the same kinds of problems and dealing with the same kinds of issues.

I know, I've often wondered myself why it took so long. I guess we all felt this couldn't possibly be happening to anyone else, so why even discuss it? Perhaps, too, in a way, we were covering up something we probably took more ownership of than we should have.

What precipitated my opening up? Yeah, I remember what happened. I had made friends with a black manager who had joined the company after I did. This was a few years later; I had gotten pretty fed up with a lot of things, and I told my friend, Harold, I was going to look for another job. I was going to leave the company.

Hal got alarmed and asked me why. I told him I didn't think I was getting anyplace here. That's when Hal looked at me and said, "I'd like to do the same thing."

Glory! Man, I felt . . . *good!* I was relieved. It wasn't just me! Yeah. That's when we started to level with each other. In fact, all the black managers started leveling with each other after that.

Do you know what? I told my boss the same thing—that I was fed up and going to leave. I found out later that turkey didn't tell anyone about our conversation. That's also when I realized that if I was going to get out of the survival state, I'd have to preplan my every move—to outwit and outfox some of those racist SOBs! Obviously, my boss didn't care if I quit or not.

At parties, over lunch, whenever we black managers were together, we talked more about what was happening to us. I could see the sad looks in my friends' faces as we talked about the crazy things we were putting up with.

Some of us were being checked up on to see if we were going where we said we were. Can you believe that?

Frank Smith told us he'd always ignored racism. It didn't touch his life much growing up sheltered in an all-black community. "I didn't perceive any problems," he said. "I thought things would be like they always were. But I got poor performance appraisals, even though no one offered to help me. I'd always succeeded before when I tried something. I asked myself, 'What's happening to me?' I've gotten bitter. They assigned me to a boss who's a company reject. I'd been thinking there was something wrong with me. My self-confidence has dropped to zero." Now where had I heard that before?

John Neil spoke up: "I was really impressed with this company coming in. But like a lot of you, I've gotten small jobs, small projects. I didn't think anything of it at first, but I've noticed the new whites coming in getting big jobs and projects right off the bat."

We got the message—the company was going to test the blacks first to see what they could do before risking more.

John continued: "My jobs have been too easy. But I've been satisfied. Sure I've been mad, but I wouldn't dream of being aggressive. I know if I go to meetings and get aggressive, the whites would accuse me of being pushy."

You know, I'm glad there's a lot of us that don't care about those kinds of tags. Oh, no. Don't for a minute think that alone will get you over. You just get a different set of the same kind of problems. *Militant* is a tag that will get all kinds of doors shut for you. Knowingly or unknowingly, the black who's aggressive will get himself punished. The punishment most likely will come in the form of the type of jobs he'll get. He'll be passed over for promotion. His white peers will say he's "got a chip on his shoulder." He'll get cut out of what information flow whites might share—and so on.

The message to all of us is: Don't upset anyone. And for the love of God, don't act emotionally! One of the first things I noticed was that whites tended to be very unemotional. Show a white manager you're upset, or show you're angry, and watch his face and behavior. What'll happen? Chances are he'll try to shut you down by cutting you off—he'll just interrupt, that's what. He'll imply you don't know what you're talking about—say that you cause problems.

Evaluations were a revelation to all of us. I'd been on the job for nearly a year when I was called into my boss's office—my boss two levels up—and told that my immediate boss had given me the best performance evaluation he had ever seen. And that's essentially all he said. *Ten years later,* I got to see the performance evaluation, and it was damn near perfect.

But hell! I didn't need to see it ten years later. I needed to see it then—when I was feeling a gross lack of confidence. When I'd go to branch offices, people would write my bosses and tell them what a good job I'd done—but it was ten years later when I saw that information, too. So they really withheld positive information from me.

Look, I'm going to tell you one more war story, and then I'm going to take a break. The more I talk, the more I remember, the madder I get! Man, this stuff is painful for me. I had to go out to one of the branch offices to help straighten out some foul-up in the books. We worked overtime until we got it all straightened out. Then I went back to the motel. Next morning, the books didn't check out. The branch supervisor got on me—asked, "What the hell is going on?"

What had happened was that one of the white clerks had tampered with the books—and he did it because he and some friends wanted to play a trick on the "nigger." That's what I heard later.

But you know what's interesting? I was walking around there, and it's like I wasn't really angry. I guess—out of frustration—I said, "What the hell! Why even get angry when somebody would do a stupid thing like that?"

OK, now I let you see a little piece of my world and get a feel of my gut. You said it would make a difference if I were honest about it. Sure, white America has run a number on me, but I let it happen. Hell, I'm no victim. Once I realized that, I started to do something about all this stuff. Yeah, yeah, whites helped, too, once I stopped hiding everything. Let me rest now; I'll tell you more later!

Analysis of the Critical Issues

Jack's story is one of blunders—Jack's, his coworkers', and the company's. They are all casualties of ignorance and a racial system that discriminates against people like Jack. At this point, let us take a look at Jack's blunders and why the preceding statement is true.

When Jack came on board at his company, his boss was absent, and Jack did not understand what his job was or how the work he was given was to be accomplished. Jack made no attempt to seek out anyone who could provide him with the information he needed. Nor did he complain to his hierarchy about having to begin his job without proper assistance. Also, Jack's boss was not astute enough to understand that because his new employee was black, he had to do something different to help Jack join up. If the boss assumed that others in the organization would look after Jack, then the boss was indeed insensitive in failing to recognize Jack as black and therefore different. By dismissing Jack's differentness, a subtle racist message gets passed. When whites try to see blacks as the same as whites or make blacks somehow colorless, the message is that blackness is a negative to be avoided. Jack could pick this up unconsciously and be uncomfortable, stressed, or angry and not know why.

Jack refused to ask questions about his work, even to relieve his own stress. He laughed at jokes that were offensive to him without telling his coworkers he thought they were insensitive. By laughing at the jokes, Jack encouraged his coworkers' thoughtless and sometimes cruel behavior toward him.

In meetings, Jack allowed people to talk to his boss instead of to him about things for which Jack was held responsible. He never confronted that issue. This is another example of the subtle form discrimination can take. Often, blacks find their presence ignored. This lack of respect toward them is usually *felt* in the Entry Phase of development instead of *consciously acknowledged*. The person feels uncomfortable without being able to pinpoint the source of the discomfort. Jack, typical of most minorities at this phase, disowned his negative feelings.

When Jack did make contact with another black in the company, James, he further hampered his progress by remaining closed to sharing his problems and seeking information from his black coworker. If he had, he could have gleaned valuable information, since James had been in the organization longer and had a perspective and outlook similar to his own. In other words, at first, Jack did not know how to effectively use his psychic support system.

Another blunder Jack made was not speaking up when it became obvious to him that his white peers were getting bigger jobs than he was. Again, Jack in his naïveté did not realize this was subtle discrimination against him. The company was sending Jack a message about its faith in his competence. Unconsciously, Jack picked this up. Since this message was not in conflict with all the other messages blacks get from society as a whole, Jack accepted it and continued to doubt his own competence.

To relieve the resulting tension Jack felt between the messages he received from his environment about his lack of competence and his own desire to recognize and realize his competence, Jack allowed his company to position him as a specialist. This further prevented his growth and development. Jack's major blunder here was making *comfort* his prime objective.

Carl Sandburg said, "First, there must be a dream." Some years before, Jack had a dream that he worked to fulfill. He had left the army, which held no real future for him, finished college, and went into a field that few blacks had dared to enter because there were so few jobs for them. Jack had gotten that job; his blunder was to stop his dream there. Without a dream, we become complacent, we do not push forward to obtain better things for ourselves. The first big barrier becomes a permanent block. Jack needed to set higher goals and career objectives for himself shortly after entering his job—or at the very least, he needed to develop survival objectives.

Jack was too trusting of a system he knew, if only intellectually, was discriminatory against blacks. He blundered when he did not insist on *seeing* his boss's evaluation of him as opposed to just being told it was good. Jack inappropriately assumed everyone had his best interest at heart. His friends also made similar blunders when they did not insist on having their evaluations explained to them.

Jack should have demanded regular meetings with his boss for reasons other than discussing problems. Instead, he sat back and waited for people to come to him. Jack should have insisted that someone introduce him to all the people he would be working with in his area of responsibility. In addition, Jack should have let his boss know the kind of treatment, good or bad, that he was receiving at the branch offices.

In light of the information we have discussed, Jack's lack of self-confidence is understandable. Jack grew up in America and was taught as a child, in various ways, that whites are smarter than blacks and that whites are better-educated. He also came to understand that whites have the power and control. Therefore, any lack of self-confidence got compounded for Jack because of the reinforcing messages he received from the society at large.

Whites in America are also programmed to believe that blacks are mentally and educationally inferior to whites, and many whites do believe this. Their beliefs are often sustained because they have no real interaction with blacks. Many whites still know very little about blacks except what they see and hear in the media. Even in integrated situations, whites seldom get to really "know" the blacks with whom they interact. Racial prejudice breeds mistrust, and neither blacks nor whites are open to each other. Because of these prejudices, blacks are constantly put in the position of having to prove themselves over and over. Jack's inexperience with subtle racism prevented him from realizing this. Since Jack did not understand, he was trapped. He had to work twice as hard to get the same evaluation as his white peers.

Many blacks get angry about this situation. Often, a black individual will be angry and not realize it. This explains, in part, the feeling of "going crazy." This anger can affect a person's performance and output. It can manifest itself in a lack of confidence and cause withdrawal. In this case, the person will not seek external information that would be helpful to growth and development or in acomplishing the job tasks. Therefore, energy output, of necessity, will be twice as much as that of white peers.

The anger in the Entry Phase is different from the anger shown in the Adjusting Phase, when blacks seem to be angry at the whole world. In that phase, the anger and self-doubt are expressed by lashing out at everything and everybody and/or becoming bitter. People who react in this way are usually seen as having a chip on their shoulder. It is also understandable that their interactions with whites will be minimized.

Although Jack only once specifically pointed out his feelings of gratitude or good fortune at having gotten his job, those feelings are implicit throughout the narrative. Jack stated that he felt he had it made and never mentioned any other black who had attained a position similar to his. This strongly implies that Jack thought he had attained great heights not open to other blacks. He showed his gratitude to the company by not speaking up and not making waves. Jack was careful not to cause problems. For example, he would not ask questions or complain about the lack of help in doing his job, even though he hurt himself by not doing so.

Because Jack felt lucky to have the job, he thought he must be careful or he might lose it or at least be proved incompetent somehow. Jack, during this phase, could not see that he had worked hard for his position in the company and that he had earned it. In the conversations Jack reported having with his friends, again the implication is one of gratitude, because they were for the most part satisfied with their jobs—and this was in the face of seeing their white peers get better jobs and more responsibility. A white manager can easily interpret this attitude as complacency and a lack of inner motivation, or the attitude can feed into a stereotype that says blacks do not want much out of life anyway. Neither of these conclusions could be further from the truth.

To sum up the situation in very general and rather simplified terms, blacks are subjected to the racial inferiority propaganda to which all Americans are subjected. If blacks believe any part of that propaganda, then they are automatically grateful when given a job. A person's attitude might sound something like this: "Even though whites don't think I'm worthy, at least they thought enough of me to give me this job, so I'm going to behave in a way that will show them I'm grateful. I won't make waves, and I won't cause problems." Or the attitude may sound more like this: "I'm very smart, and I worked hard to win this position. I'm going to prove my competence by being the best, and I'm not going to play into any stereotypes. I won't cause any problems by making waves."

Jack was not prepared for the realities of his job. He was not prepared to be thrown out on the job to sink or swim. He lacked information about how his organization worked. For reasons already discussed, he was not about to ask. He expected to be given some tasks, laid out for him in very clear terms by someone, and then be left alone to do his job. He did not anticipate needing a lot of help. Jack certainly was not prepared for interactions with all kinds of people. As with most blacks, nothing in his background prepared him to be able to deal with corporate functioning, power, and politics. We would venture to say that most blacks have adjustment problems in these areas, because these are the areas in which blacks have historically been the most powerless.

A lot of Americans, both black and white, believe in the Protestant work ethic. Very successful whites learn early on that it takes more than that belief to get what they want. For blacks, it becomes a painful lesson to learn that the system will not reward them in proportion to the results they produce. One reason they are not sufficiently rewarded may be that some people are honestly not aware that blacks face greater obstacles in producing results than whites do. On the other hand, some people are aware, but they do not intend to give the extra credit deserved. In Jack's case, the Protestant work ethic also worked against him because he did not realize he was putting forth extra effort to get the same results as whites. Nor did he understand that working effectively depends in large part on successful interactions with others.

Many people may find the degree of racial naïveté among blacks difficult to believe. Obviously discriminatory behavior is easy to see, but few blacks are aware and sensitive enough to see all the subtle ways in which they are excluded from mainstream participation. Jack and his friends are very typical in this respect.

Jack had enlisted in the army, where he interacted in an interracial environment, yet he still made the basic assumption that a white profit-motivated corporation would not allow racial matters to become a hindrance to making a profit. These kinds of assumptions are common among blacks. Therefore, blacks are seldom prepared to deal with racial resistance. They tend not to be consciously sensitive to the subtleties of corporate interracial interfaces. Although most black adults today have had extensive interactions with whites, blacks remain inexperienced in understanding the subtle cues of racial prejudice and the barriers they present.

It would seem that people in general are not aware of the effects that racial prejudices can have on a profit-making operation. That tells us a lot about the nature of racism. It can affect bottom-line results. For an example, Jack could have produced more results per unit of time from the beginning of his new job. In other words, Jack was paid for working thirty days, and he was unable to do what his boss had asked him to do. If Jack and the corporation had known what Jack was going to face, they both could have been positioned to work through some of the problems early. Then Jack could have finished his work and made a much smoother transition into the corporate milieu. So racial naïveté on the part of both blacks and whites can certainly affect bottom-line results.

Because of his inappropriate assumptions that race was not an issue in the corporation, Jack lowered the sensitivity he had acquired from previous experiences in interacting with whites, such as in the service. Jack, like most people without help, generally lacked sufficient insight into his own feelings and motivations. Without this, he could not see much of what was happening to him.

A missing factor for Jack, as for many blacks, was the clear concept of career. Whites, on the other hand, are often brought up and educated with the idea of building a career in life. Blacks are generally brought up differently because, in the past, this country did not offer blacks opportunities to build careers. Jack did not go into the company thinking in terms of a career. He went in thinking in terms of a job. He was struggling with such basic issues as keeping the job and doing well. He had not expanded his mind to the point of assuming he could have a viable career. Also, there were few black role models—no blacks he could look up to and say to himself that there is a possibility of having a real career here. As Jack pointed out in his narrative, not much hope is offered young blacks in terms of what they can expect for themselves in the job world. They can verify the validity of that pessimistic outlook when they look around and try to count how many blacks are on corporate boards.

At school, no one taught Jack that you must set career goals when you go into an organization and that these should be well-planned and laid out. This idea was alien to Jack. However, this is a responsibility Jack's boss should have assumed upon his return to the office. He should have helped Jack develop some goals. Companies need to let minorities know what they can ultimately offer them in terms of career opportunities. It is unfortunate that many companies are unclear themselves about their policies concerning career advancement for minorities.

For this reason, there is usually a lack of appropriate training opportunities for both minorities and whites to learn the kinds of managerial skills needed to effectively work together. Any kind of managerial training to which the minority individual is exposed is geared for the most part to meeting the needs of white male management. Black managers must translate the training material into something that they can use, because of their unique relationship to the dominant culture. Initially, few blacks are able to do the necessary translating; therefore, much of the training material is lost to them.

As we can now readily see, Jack's career opportunities were realistic from his viewpoint. He saw a lack of commitment from white institutions toward his equal participation and advancement, and there were few black role models to assure him that the opportunities were there. He was constantly reminded that his interpersonal style was problematic to whites, and he saw that his style often overshadowed others' evaluations of his job competence. Paradoxically, this usually drives black managers to become even more concerned about their work tasks rather than the interpersonal interactions that are in reality the crux of the issue.

In face of seemingly overwhelming odds, Jack, like many black managers, was able to overcome the various barriers and succeed. Now that we have some insight into many of the problems confronting the black manager, we will discuss how these problems may be solved.

How-To Solutions and Basic Concepts

Many critical issues and situations leap out from the story about Jack's Entry Phase—too many to deal with adequately in this volume. Therefore, we will present, in general terms, what we consider to be some of the key problems that hinder the progress of many blacks in the Entry Phase. After each problem, we present one or more solutions, followed by one or more basic concepts that were applied to solve that problem. Please keep two things in mind: (1) These are certainly not the only possible solutions, but it is hoped that they will trigger additional thoughts and approaches. (2) Many of these concepts can be applied to more than one problem, even though, to avoid repetition, we have explained each concept only once—following the first problem to which it applies.

Problem I

How to overcome reluctance and hesitancy in asking work-related questions of whites.

Solutions

Solution 1. The first solution deals with yourself. Have a conversation with yourself and ask, "What is the worst thing that can happen to me if I ask questions of one or more white people?" The worst possible thing that can happen is you will get fired. That becomes the highest possible risk you have to be concerned about. Asking a question about your job is certainly not grounds for dismissal. Therefore, being fired is highly unlikely, and the risk becomes negligible.

Now ask yourself, "What is the best thing that can happen?" The answer to that is, "I will get an answer to my questions that will allow me to produce results."

Your next question may be, "But what if they think I'm dumb?" Then you will have to face your feelings about what is more important at this moment—the other person's perceptions of you or the fact that you now have information that will help produce results. In this case, the results are the important factor. This is a solution for individuals who are less concerned about the perceptions of others.

Solution 2. For individuals who are more concerned about their image with whites, the "power model" is useful. The power model is used in this fashion. When preparing to ask a question, preface the question with a statement like this: "Mr. [or "Ms."] Jones, my boss told me that you would be a good resource for me on this kind of question and that if you can't help me, I should come back and let him [or "her"] know." Then ask the question.

What that does is position the resistant individual to give you an answer to prevent your going back and reporting to the boss. It also implies you have the support of the boss. This can be done because you will already have had meetings with your boss. (See problems II and III.)

Solution 3. A third way to approach this problem is to pre-position the white individual to receive your question. You can say, for example, "I want to ask you a question. Now, the question may seem elementary to you, but I'm not really concerned about how you view it." Then ask your question.

This positions the person to focus on the question instead of evaluating the person who asked it. People don't like to be told beforehand how they are going to react to something, so they will work hard to do the opposite of what you suggested. It is simple reverse psychology.

Concepts

Concept 1: Talking to the champ. This concept is based on the old adage that says, "When I want to talk to someone nice, I talk to myself." Talking to yourself is not the silly exercise we tease each other about. It can be used for a variety of helpful and often healing purposes. It can be calming in stressful situations. When other people are not present to say the appropriate things you need to hear when you need to hear them, you can do it for yourself. You can provide the factual, logical information you need in order to see a situation as it is. You may discuss things with yourself in private that you would be hesitant to discuss openly with another person.

Talking to yourself can give you the opportunity to dig out, crystallize, and verbalize thoughts and feelings that lie just below your conscious awareness. You can look at, experiment with, and examine your thoughts and feelings from various perspectives without having to worry about how you are being perceived by another person. You can give yourself that pep talk you may so badly need at the moment you need it.

Concept 2: Checking out both sides of the street. This concept involves risk analysis and assessment. It is a good practice, especially for minorities, to assess the risks involved in any managerial problem. You need to assess the risks to you as a black individual so that you will be able to relax with the decisions you make. The usual result of risk assessment is that you find you have overestimated the risks to yourself. This is particularly true for black managers in the Entry Phase.

The important method to remember in risk analysis is to ask yourself the question, "In this particular situation, what is the *worst/best* thing that can happen to me?" Now you can weigh the worst-case/best-case answers relative to each other and get a picture of what are most likely to be the *real* risks to you. In other words, check out both sides of the street. This method of risk assessment takes you out of the areas of the unknown and of uncertainty.

Concept 3: Using the power of the boss. When you find yourself in a situation in which you have little organizational or personal power—which is typical in the Entry Phase—there will be many instances when you will be empowered by the organization, through your boss, to do certain things. It is appropriate to use that power. In solving problem I, the power was used by telling a resource your boss told you to contact him or her and asked to be advised if the resource was unable to help. It is correct to use the power of the boss in this case because, if you must interact with someone who displays racist or sexist behavior, it will put pressure on that person to behave appropriately. This is a good concept to use whenever you are in a relatively powerless position and must manage or influence a resistant individual.

Concept 4: Pre-positioning. This is a useful concept for reducing dysfunctional interactions. People can be positioned by giving them information or messages about what you want or how you expect them to behave. The average person will then work hard not to behave in a dysfunctional manner.

Concept 5: Reverse psychology. This concept is by no means new. It is most familiar in the context of child-parent relationships. However, knowing adults respond to this also, we suggest it can be used effectively in managing people in an organizational setting as well. Tell a person that you expect him or her to feel or react in a certain way, and the person will probably respond in the opposite manner. People do not like to have their feelings and behavior predicted, especially face to face. Of course, reverse psychology does not work on everyone. Therefore you must use your own insight about human behavior to pick the personality types on which it will work well. Stubborn and resistant people tend to be good candidates for reverse psychology.

Problem II

How to define your job role.

Solution

Ask your boss for a roles write-up or a job description for your position. If that is not available, or if you are not satisfied with what exists and you need more detail, then write your own. This is permitted; people are seldom told this, but it is quite acceptable to write your own job description as long as you review and work it with your boss. Start by interviewing your boss and one or two people with whom you must interact in your job role; ask the following questions:

- What are my major job tasks?
- What are my major roles in terms of how this organization operates? In other words, how do I fit in the organization? What is my role relative to my boss and others in the organization?
- Who are the clients who will receive the output from my job?
- What is my output?
- What are your major expectations of me, expressed in terms of "I expect you to _____"?
- Who are the resources or experts for the tasks associated with my job position?
- With which people or organizations will I interface in performing my job function?
- What are the priorities associated with my particular job function? Which things are important? In what order?

Sit down and think about the answers to these questions. Then summarize the answers and appropriately place them under the following categories:

- Job role
- Job tasks
- Job expectations
- Major outputs
- Available resources
- Job priorities
- Major interfaces (names of people, organizations, clients)

A minority individual cannot afford the luxury of not knowing what his or her job is. Once the information is pulled together under the appropriate categories, have it typed and give it to your boss and others you interviewed with a note that says, "This is how I view my job role at this time. Please review this and comment." If there are corrections to be made, then discuss the misunderstandings with the boss and get them resolved; reach a mutual agreement on what your job is. Remember to factor in the feedback from the others you interviewed. The boss owns the yardstick by which you will be measured. You need to know what that yardstick is as early as possible.

This procedure should be completed in your first few weeks on the job.

Concepts

Refer to the "Concepts" subsection for problem III, which discusses the concepts that apply to both problems II and III.

Problem III

How to set a positive direction in your job.

Solution

After you have worked at your job about a month, and after your job has been documented, make a list of the things you would like to learn in the next year. Make the list as specific as possible. List those things that you like to do, that you are interested in, and that will make you produce at your optimum level. Try daydreaming about what you will be doing a year from now and what tasks you will be executing when you are feeling good about your job. Write down the ideas suggested by your daydreams. Summarize them in a presentable form.

Bounce your list off a friend, mentor, sponsor, your mate, or a trusted peer for comment. Then use their input to revise the list. Bounce the revised list off your boss for his or her comment. Now turn your list into quantified objectives, using the following format:

> **To:** (action verb) (task) **by** (date).
> **Example:** To learn my organization's basic marketing strategy
> by September 19__[1]

1. This is the most simplified form of an objective and will suffice for the entry phase. However, if you are interested in more information on how to write better goals, see Robert F. Mager, *Goal Analysis* (Belmont, California: Fearon Publishers, 1972).

Next, set up regularly scheduled meetings with your boss to take advantage of his or her expertise as well as resolve any problems you may have with your job. You may also use this time to obtain any additional information or training that you need. Remember, *all* bosses have some area of expertise, no matter how incompetent they may appear to be.

Concepts

Concept 1: Publicizing the yardstick. In a white corporate system, there are built-in organizational cultural norms that get transmitted among the various members of the organization in an informal manner. Whites tend to conform to these easily, as has previously been stated, because these norms are merely extensions of their cultural learnings. When blacks, with their different cultural norms, are introduced into the system, the informal communications network does not function as well for them. White male bosses will tend not to be as comfortable or as informal with blacks as with other white males. Therefore, blacks must seek means of finding out what the yardstick is that will be used to measure them.

White bosses may also make some inappropriate assumptions about a black manager's ability to get this information. They may think that the information is as readily available to blacks as it is to white males. They do not usually perceive that blacks are often excluded from the activities where information is informally passed. So black managers are put in a position where it becomes important to set up their own measurement device with the sanction of the boss. It must then be legitimized in the organization by making it public.

Concept 2: Collaboration. We suggest black managers use this concept often, particularly with their bosses. This may be difficult in some instances where an adversary relationship exists between the boss and the black subordinate. However, regardless of what the relationship is, the white institution will expect black managers to be able to collaborate with certain people on various issues. This means that in some instances, you will have to learn to collaborate with the boss.

Collaboration can also protect the black manager and the boss. In our how-to solutions to problems II and III, boss and subordinate collaborated on job definition and goal setting. Collaboration protects the subordinate and the boss because the decisions they make are a shared responsibility. The white male boss has the organizational power to legitimize the work done by the black manager, and the black manager does not have to face the consequences of acting alone.

Concept 3: Navigation of your life. Take a moment and think of your life as a ship and the corporation as the ocean in which you are sailing, with you as the navigator—it is your responsibility to plot the course. You cannot assume that the corporation will know in which direction to set the course of your life any more than you would assume that the ocean would know how to set the course of a ship. How would the water and winds know where you wish to go? So do not sit back and expect the boss or the corporation to set your career course. Granted, it is a joint venture and responsibility, but *you* should initiate it. This is especially true for blacks. Black managers are so new and few to the corporation that the system is just learning how to help these managers set the direction of their careers.

Concept 4: Fantasy and autosuggestion.[2] The basic premise is that in order to reach a goal, you must fantasize that you have already reached it. You must use autosuggestion to actually see, feel, touch, and taste what you want; doing this facilitates your setting and obtaining the goals you wish to reach.

Concept 5: Using resources. This concept can be found throughout most of these problem solutions. Essentially, there are two ways to use resources: (1) to provide additional information on what you already know how to do well or (2) to provide information on what you do not know how to do well. (More will be said about this in Part Four.) The important thing about using resources is to use the *right* resources. This is where your boss, peers, and friends can be helpful in terms of identifying resources for you. First, identify your needs, and then identify the resources to tap for information.

Problem IV

How to be successful with interpersonally insensitive people.

Solutions

Solution 1. Spend more time asking than giving information. This works because as long as you are asking questions, the other person will be concentrating on giving answers instead of getting information

2. *Autosuggestion* is a term taken from Napoleon Hill, *Think and Grow Rich* (New York: Fawcett Books, 1960), pp. 67–73, 89–100.

from you to use to evaluate you. This works well with people who in the past have displayed prejudiced attitudes. Often, this works further in your favor because people tend not to waste time answering questions from people they do not value. Since they are responding to you, their opinion of you will tend to improve.

Solution 2. Confront the insensitive person directly. Say, "After looking at our situation, I'm somewhat confused. Maybe you can help me. You seem to be upset about something." Or, "Can you help me. You seem to be upset about something." Or, "Can you help me understand what is upsetting you? I need to understand in order for us to meet the objectives that we have in mind. We *are* working toward the same end, aren't we?" The person will then have to deal with your "confusion" by looking at his or her behavior and interactions with you.

Solution 3. Sharing your feelings with the person is often appropriate. Say, "When you say or do that, I *feel* this way. I wish you wouldn't say or do that." Insensitive people are then made to realize that you will not hesitate to make them face your feelings. They are also put in the position of having to alter their behavior or be subjected to your evaluation. This approach should be used between peers—not between you and higher-ups.

To put this solution in less personal terms, which is the best course of action when dealing with a person in a position higher than yours, try this approach: "When you say or do that, it causes me to have a problem with it." Then follow up the response.

Solution 4. There are some people who seem oblivious to others' feelings or who simply do not care. In this circumstance, your sole recourse may be to interact with them only when absolutely necessary. When you do, interact rapidly and cordially. Work out the issue or task involved as quickly as possible and move on. Perhaps it would be even better if you asked someone else to obtain the information you need. Select someone who has a rapport with the other person.

Concepts

Concept 1: Questioning-diversion technique. This concept, which is used to deal more effectively in some interpersonal interactions, is helpful in avoiding situations where blacks find themselves giving too much information or talking too much about themselves. By "too much," we mean providing information that may inappropriately show another person that you are overly stressed. Running off at the mouth at this point is not helpful. All too often, this is used against you to meet the other person's needs.

Many times, blacks may find themselves unwittingly feeding into a white manager's negative racial sterotypes of blacks by offering unnecessary and inappropriate information. Black managers should ask questions of white managers about the issues being discussed to elicit their opinions, feelings, ideas, and so forth. In this way, the interaction can be focused on the issues under discussion or on the white person and will leave little time for the black manager to allow himself or herself to be placed in a positon to be evaluated.

Concept 2: Confrontation. This concept is very familiar to most of us. There are some instances when nothing we try seems to work. The chemistry between people is just not right. There may be too great a personality difference between the parties involved. In these cases, you will have to confront the issue. Remember, we said confront the *issue,* not the person. It is very important for entry-level black managers to confront the issue and not the person because this is linked to their survival in the organization.

Appropriate and successful confrontation is not only a concept but also a skill blacks will learn to develop as they grow and mature in the organization. Successful confrontation will be addressed as a separate topic in Part Four, because it is a very important job skill needed by black managers.

Concept 3: Sharing your feelings. This concept is similar in some respects to confrontation but differs principally in that it lacks a menacing affect. That is, your feelings may or may not be presented boldly to the person on the receiving end of the interaction. The sharing of feelings is important to minorities because there will be some instances when you are so frustrated you cannot think of anything else to do. When you get to that point, the simplest thing to do is share with others how you feel about an issue. That positions people to deal with the issue. It also points out to others that you do have feelings and are being affected by their dysfunctional behavior. In addition, this action demands that other people respect and respond to your feelings.

Concept 4: Avoidance behavior.[3] This concept should be used *only* as a last resort. If all else fails, avoid the person or the situation for the moment. When everything breaks down, leave the scene of the action. Here, the old proverb "Discretion is the better part of valor" applies. At

3. This concept is also suggested in Charles C. Vance, *Manager Today, Executive Tomorrow* (New York: McGraw-Hill, 1974), pp. 1–28.

times, avoidance behavior is quite appropriate. Remind yourself that nothing is solved by unnecessarily subjecting yourself and others to fights and punishments that neither lead to good problem solving nor prove anything. Return when there is a viable plan to solve the problem.

Problem V

How to become more comfortable in social interactions with whites.

Solution

As we previously explained, many blacks feel stressed when interacting with whites. Such stress may be attributable to lack of experience, lowered confidence, or both. When feelings of stress or awkwardness appear, the black individual tends to do most of the talking. This only causes more stress.

Instead, strike up a conversion and become the listener. Ask questions and listen. Look at and listen to the other person to determine what subjects or areas he or she gets excited about. Try to find topics of mutual interest, like hobbies and sports. Get involved in the other person's interest in those topics. Stay away from topics that may raise your anxiety or call attention to how different you may be from the people with whom you are conversing. Do not position yourself to be left out of the conversation or to be made to feel alienated.

Initially, allow the other person to do most of the talking while you summarize or restate what has been said to make sure you understand. The whole process of restating will help you become more comfortable in talking to the person. It also takes unwanted attention from you and puts the focus on the other person.

To give individuals the impression that you are interested in them and what they are saying, ask them questions about themselves. It is always safe and interesting to talk about where a person grew up and attended school. Ask how he or she has seen things change over the years in the company, city, or community. Talk more as you feel more comfortable with the person and the topic. Be sure to look the person in the eye. Avoid looking down at the floor or up at the ceiling, which could give the other person negative messages about your interest or self-confidence.

Watch the other person's facial expressions when you talk. If you do not, you may miss 50 percent of the interaction. Avoid talking with your arms folded or hands hidden in pockets. Such actions may reveal your discomfort.

Concept

Interest transference. This concept is used to help you deal with stressful or awkward situations. It involves transfering your awareness from your own discomfort to an active interaction with another person. This merely means that you can deemphasize your stress or awkwardness by using your mental energies to get involved in an interaction with another person and his or her interests. If you truly involve yourself with what the other person is saying, you will discover that you have little energy left to be wrapped up in how you are feeling at that moment and that your feelings of discomfort have vanished. The other person will be flattered by your interest and will usually return the favor by a warm response to you. This concept is important for black managers because they frequently find themselves in conversational situations where they feel like outsiders.

Problem VI

How to be comfortable and successful when you are the only black participant (or one of two) in a meeting.

Solutions

Solution 1. Before the meeting, tell yourself that you are an integral part of the meeting. It is important to remind yourself of this because whites may tend to dismiss you or not acknowledge you. A solution that works well is to allow the other participants to talk first. Then, when you do speak up, ask a question for clarification. This can also help you become more comfortable in the meeting. Asking questions causes others to acknowledge your presence. It forces the group, even if momentarily, to deal with you by responding to your question.

If the meeting is for decision making, it is usually best to wait until the group is near closure on the decision. Then ask questions that will cause the group to be clearer about the decision-making process. A black manager can handle himself or herself well in a meeting by assuming a consultant's role. That means taking a look at what was said, by whom, why, and how it relates to the main business of the meeting. Your questions should point up some facts that the others may have missed.

If the meeting is leaderless and you are black, it is advisable that you not be the person to take that leadership role initially, because the group will fight you. Since the leadership role shifts during such meetings, it is nearly always best that you assume that role later when the group is in need of your special talents. Instead, let the other participants organize their thoughts and start talking. Do not forget to ask questions periodically to get clarification and people's attention.

As the group gets bogged down in issues, ask questions to help clarify the group's position as a consultant might. The group will then seek clarity as a result of your questions and pay more attention to your input. This will give you an opportunity to lead the group or at least be heard. At any rate, the group will listen to you more. It is at *that* point that you should switch from asking questions to giving information. This is an effective strategy for black individuals to use in meetings.

Solution 2. Another option open to blacks in meetings is to just speak up and demand to be heard. If you are a very open, strong, and verbal person, you may prefer this method. You must be very careful as to *when* you speak up; timing is important. Since you are black, the odds are that your comments will be dismissed if you attempt to speak up first. If you wait to voice your input until after the third or fourth person has spoken, your chances of being heard are better.

The solutions in the Entry Phase presuppose that you as a minority are not the designated leader. If you are, you must deal with some different dynamics. The black individual as the manager or leader of an all-white or predominantly white group is discussed in Chapter 8 in the section entitled "Successfully Managing Subordinates."

Concept

Proper timing. This means sensing when it is appropriate to carry out some activity or behavior. In many instances, as in the solutions to problem VI, timing can be crucial. You must learn to sense the best time to act on an issue. Proper timing is like a sixth sense; some people seem to have it naturally, whereas others must acquire it. It appears to be learned through trial and error. It is essential that black managers acknowledge the importance of this skill and seek to develop it because it is often the critical ingredient that can ensure success. We know of no sure way to teach this skill, but we suggest that finding a role model who displays this ability and copying that person's behavior may help.

Watch your role model and ask questions concerning his or her sense of timing. Study what is done and under what circumstances decisions are made. This may give you some insight into what is involved in proper timing.

Problem VII

How to ensure that you are heard in meetings.

Solutions

Solution 1. In meetings where the boss is present, it is very common for white participants to talk to black participants through the boss instead of talking directly to them. After this has happened to you once, sit back in your chair, relax, and cross your legs. Wait for the behavior to be repeated. Now place your hand on your boss's arm or hand or shoulder, if he or she is close enough, and say, "I would like to answer that." If you are not close enough, lean forward, put your elbows on the table, and say to your boss, "Bill [or whatever], I would like to answer that if it is OK with you." It is almost as if you were asking permission. Or say, "May I answer that?" Then answer the question.

If, after this, someone in the meeting still insists upon not talking directly to you, lean forward, put your elbows on the table, touch your boss if you can, and say, "Bill, since this is my area of responsibility, I'm more than willing to [now turn to the meeting leader or the person who asked the question] answer the questions in this area." That should do it; the odds are that people will begin talking directly to you. If not, continue to use the aforementioned methods.

This solution is based on the assumption that there are no high-level managers (vice-presidents or above) at the meeting. If they are the ones talking to you through your boss, you had better allow them to go ahead without interference. In this case, it is better to try to correct the situation using the indirect method suggested in solution 2. After the meeting, discuss the issue with your boss to reach an agreement on how to handle such a situation in the future. If the participants in the meeting are at your boss's level or one or two levels up, however, solution 1 works well.

Solution 2. As a variation to solution 1, you may, depending on what suits you better, choose to be less direct or more direct in handling this situation. Perhaps you would rather let the situation continue without interrupting the meeting. When you leave the meeting, you might say to your boss, "Bill, was there a particular reason for your not telling those people to direct their questions to me? I suggest the next time that happens you tell them to ask me. There are negative implications associated with their not talking directly to me." Then explain further if it becomes necessary.

Solution 3. If you are more comfortable in meetings and tend to be the aggressive type, and if solutions 1 and 2 did not work, you may prefer this method. Put your elbows on the table, lean forward, and say to the person who keeps talking to you through your boss, "Perhaps you didn't hear what I said earlier. That is my area of responsibility, and I'm more than willing to answer any questions you may have in that area. If I can't, then between my boss and me, we will certainly be able to answer your questions."

Solution 4. Here is a situation somewhat different from the one above. You are in a meeting—it does not matter whether your boss is there or not—and you say something. The people in the group disregard your input or act as if they do not hear you. Let this go for about five minutes. After this, interrupt someone and say, "That really is a good point and certainly a good piece of input to this issue." Then lean forward and say emphatically, *"As I said a few minutes ago . . ."* and repeat what you had said.

Or you may choose to escalate the situation in the following way and make the group deal with their behavior toward you: Get a quizzical, dumfounded look on your face and say, "I'm confused. I made a statement a few minutes ago, and perhaps it wasn't heard because no one responded to it. I would like to have a response to my comment. Let me repeat it." Then go ahead and repeat your earlier statement.

Concepts

Concept 1: Taking the critter by the neck. This means using your sense of timing to determine when it is appropriate to speak up in an aggressive manner to take momentary control over a situation. In the case of problem VII, the black person senses that he or she is being dismissed in the meeting, does not like it, and becomes angry. This individual does not feel a part of what is occurring in the meeting. The input from the person may be important but nevertheless gets overlooked. It is not only appropriate but essential that blacks aggressively cause their presence and input to be acknowledged by the group.

Concept 2: The SSS (sudden seizure of stupidity) syndrome. This means that at some appropriate time, you choose to affect confusion, misunderstanding, lack of knowledge, or just plain ignorance in an interaction with someone. You may shrug your shoulders or even say, "I don't understand. You've lost me," or something like that. Often, it helps to frown as though you are really struggling with what is being said.

You may want to use this concept to buy thinking time in a difficult interaction by positioning the other person to give you additional information. Or you may use this concept to place responsibility for another person's attitude, behavior, or emotional outburst back where it belongs. This technique frequently calms the person who is accusing you of something that you did not do and forces that person to reexamine his or her data. It puts responsibility back on the originator to explain his or her behavior.

Problem VIII

How to keep your work experience broad enough to help position you for advancement or increased responsibility.

Solutions

Solution 1. Keep your energies focused on your responsibilities, and produce good results in your job. When you have mastered your present responsibilities, ask your boss and your peers questions about other responsibilities that relate to what you are currently doing. It is advisable that the peers you approach be people you trust. This helps eliminate the possibility that they will make unwarranted assumptions about your motivations and gives you some sympathetic support in gathering this information.

Learn more about and get interested in the other areas. Tell yourself, "If I am to grow and develop in my career or job, I need to expand to avoid becoming stagnant." Select new job responsibilities that fit within your general area. Ask your boss whether there are additional things you may do—such as helping the boss produce a report or doing some other job in which the boss is involved. If your boss is competitive or hostile in the relationship with you, then it is not a good idea to ask for any part of the work your boss may be doing. In this case, you must find other means to increase your responsibilities. You can do this through your peers or the bosses of your peers who have good relationships with them by simply inquiring and then asking for the work.

Keep adding to your responsibilities as you become proficient with the new ones. At some point, you can ask to be moved to another job area. You may have reached that point when both your old and new responsibilities become too simple. *Never* become comfortable with one area and refuse to move. This is a no-no, a *trap* for blacks. Understand that it is all right to ask for more responsibility and to be moved to another area in your company or organization.

Solution 2. After you have been on the job for a while, ask you boss about what other jobs relate to your job area. Then ask whether you will have an opportunity to work in the other area(s) at a later date.

After getting this information from your boss, turn it into growth objectives and document them. This documentation can be used as a yardstick for both you and your boss to keep track of how well you are setting and meeting your job objectives. It will also indicate to your boss when you should be given more responsibility.

Solution 3. Ask your boss early in the job, "How do I keep from becoming too specialized in a particular area so that I can continue to obtain broad experience?" Then, with the help of your boss, plan and document a course of action for the future. Make sure your plan provides some means to prevent your becoming too highly specialized.

On the other hand, if you already have a job that is highly specialized, if that is what is required of you in your job description and you do not want this, then it is best to consider terminating that job position. Your career movement under these circumstances will be highly restricted. If you see yourself working to climb to upper corporate levels, you will need varied experiences.

Concept

Data sorting. This concept involves the judicious use of resources. Data sorting is the idea that you should sift through the mound of information you have collected from your resources and pick out *only* the data that are relevant to your particular case and to what you are trying to do. In other words, keep in mind the objective you are aiming for and select only the information that helps you reach that particular objective.

Problem IX

How to let your hierarchy know that you are ready for more responsibility.

Solution 1. Set up learning and performance objectives, as stated in the solution to problem III. During your regular meetings with your boss, test yourself against the objectives. For instance, you should have an objective that states that by such and such a date, you will be able to perform at a certain level. Test this with your boss by asking whether you are performing at that particular level. If the answer is yes, mark off the objective and move on to another one; if not, correct the situation so that you meet the objective.

As you accomplish each objective, set new ones, as suggested in the solutions to problem VIII. Have your boss participate in the setting of the new objectives. If you follow this process, you will automatically get increased responsibility with the sanction of your boss.

Solution 2. Another option is to ask your boss, after you have been on the job for two or three months, what his or her criteria are for determining when you are ready for increased responsibility. Document this and give your boss a copy. When you think you have fulfilled the criteria, take out the paper and discuss it with your boss. Then you can legitimately ask for more responsibility. Your boss will be more responsive to your request because the criteria are the boss's.

Concept

Taking the initiative. This relates to some of the other concepts, in that the black individual does not sit back and wait for someone else to decide what his or her next move should be. Blacks must learn quickly in the Entry Phase to be concerned and thoughtful enough to initiate some moves to ensure that their needs are met and their concerns resolved. If you encounter procrastination on the part of your hierarchy, then be persistent and appropriately demanding. *Appropriately demanding* here means do not be dysfunctional in your demands and get pushed aside by the system. Be sensitive to when to pull back.

Problem X

How to translate material from training and development sessions for use by black managers.

Solution

After attending a training or development session, you will have notes and other material from which you can compile a list. The list should consist of the important techniques and action steps you feel may be useful in performing your job. It is seldom helpful to include more than nine good techniques or action steps, because trying to handle too many can cause you to spread your energies too thin.

Now examine each item from your list one at a time using the following process:

- Look at each of the techniques and action steps through the eyes of a white manager, using your knowledge of the perceptions and assumptions of whites about blacks. The white manager represents the system in which you work.
- Imagine the reaction of a white manager upon receiving data about or viewing another white manager performing an activity related to the important technique or action step you are translating.
- Now imagine the reaction of a white manager upon receiving data about or viewing a black manager performing the same activity.
- Compare the reactions—how a white manager would perceive the same action done by a black and a white manager—and examine the differences.
- If the white manager's reaction is neutral or positive when the activity is performed by the black manager, then use the behavior suggested in the training session.
- If the reaction is negative, then identify some alternatives to the action suggested in the training session. The alternative behavior or action steps should accomplish the same purpose or desired results, but with neutral or positive consequences.

To help clarify this solution, let us look at an example—the "shotgun memo."[4] A shotgun memo is written as though you were talking to someone. It is short, to the point, and hard-hitting. It states in very direct terms what you expect from people. Now be a white manager for a moment looking at a shotgun memo written by a white male manager. The assumption is likely to be, "Wow, this guy is really on top of his job. He knows what he wants. He's hard-hitting and to the point. He tells his people exactly what he wants, and he's very aggressive."

If you are a white manager looking at a shotgun memo written by a black manager, however, the perception is more likely to be, "Hmm, this fellow has a communication problem. He doesn't write well. He's too pushy and not being supportive of the people." Now you can see

4. American Management Association's course "Executive Productivity Training," March 19–21, 1979, course notebook, p. 40.

that for a black manager, the consequences of writing and sending a shotgun memo are negative. So this means black managers must develop some alternatives to the original training material they received. If you still like the concept of the hard-hitting memo, you may decide to alter it in this manner.

You might start with an introductory paragraph stating the problem and the objective you or the company are trying to reach, then follow with the hard-hitting memo. When white managers see this memo written by a black manager, they will tend to view it in a more positive light. Their response is more likely to be, "Hmm, this person really lays his stuff out, knows what he wants, is directing his people well. Although some people may react negatively, at least the objectives are in line with those that I want the people to have."

Concept

Behold! The other side of the coin. This concept means that in order to make good decisions or understand another's viewpoint, you will have to look at the situation through the eyes of the other person, using what you perceive to be his or her assumptions, perceptions, and cultural background. This arms you with additional data so you can understand why people do certain things or behave in certain ways in given circumstances, and it also helps you understand your own behavior, attitudes, and motivations in the same circumstances. For many people, this can lead to new discoveries and make them more sensitive to people who have differing cultural perspectives.

Problem XI

How to develop and effectively use a psychic support system.

Solutions

Solution 1. You can develop and use a psychic support system through social interactions at work. Take your coffee breaks with a black friend or any friend whom you trust, respect, and can garner support from to enable you to deal with the stress and strain of your everyday work environment. It is helpful to talk about your feelings and reactions to things. Catharsis—that is, the relieving or cleansing of one's emotional self—is very good for your psychological well-being.

Periodically, eat lunch away from the job, if permitted, with a black friend or other associates. At times, have lunch on the premises away from your work group (if you are in the habit of eating as a group) with a black friend to talk privately. Seek out new blacks as they come into your job area and offer to help in any way in order to be supportive to them. Check in with them periodically. Go on breaks or eat lunch with them occasionally. At these times, make a point of discussing job situations with them. Talk about how you feel about your job and your reactions to it. Seek advice or ask the friend to just listen.

Solution 2. You may be interested in developing and using a support system after work through sports and social interaction. Such a support system has always been a part of the white corporate culture. The golf course is often used for this purpose. White managers tend to play golf with each other, and blacks have tended to be excluded from this. Unfortunately, in many places, that exclusion is still operative.

Playing or watching sports with a black friend can be an integral part of a good support system. This is true for both men and women. It gives you the opportunity to enjoy and relax around a common interest. It also provides that important opportunity to talk about the stresses and tensions of the job in a relaxed environment that is conducive to thoughtful and helpful suggestions. Tennis, racquetball, golf, swimming, fishing, as well as a myriad of other active and sedentary pastimes, can all be used to stimulate the supportive relationship.

What happens if you are a black in an all-white work environment? Odds are you will have to develop a two-part psychic support system—one part white and the other black. The black support system will be developed after work, and the supporting individual(s) will most likely not be directly involved in your work environment. Sometimes, this can work to your advantage, in that you may be offered a broader perspective on many of your job situations. The white system will be developed at work. Whether or not this is extended beyond the work environment will depend on the people involved and the nature of the relationship.

The dynamics of the relationship between the black manager and the black support system will differ from the dynamics of the relationship between the black manager and the white support system. In the first case, the individuals involved will share a common cultural background that will help in the understanding of problem issues. In the second case, there will be some difficulty in understanding because of differences in cultural perspective. However, astute black managers can use these differences to increase their understanding of the perceptions of the dominant culture.

One thing that is apparent throughout all the solutions in this section is that the black manager is going to have to *speak up*. This is very important. There is nothing that can be said or done to get people to speak up. They have to do this themselves.

Concepts

Concept 1: Seeking help and support. This is similar to the concept of using resources; both embody the informational process of giving and receiving data. However, seeking help and support has the added dimension of emotional encouragement and support.

Concept 2: Socializing. This is a concept with which most people are familiar. It is very important for black managers to learn and understand its significance as applied to the corporate culture. Blacks tend to have a different attitude toward socializing than whites do. Blacks tend to want to have some emotional involvement with the people with whom they socialize; that is, they want to like the people they are with. Whites, on the other hand, tend to be able to comfortably socialize without necessarily feeling any emotional involvement. They have learned to use socializing for reasons other than being with friends.

It is a normal part of white corporate culture to use socializing to informally gather information, seek favors, make contacts that may lead to opportunities, and so forth. Black managers need to be aware of these differences in social attitude in order to take advantage of opportunities to be a part of the informal corporate culture. Be aware that *no one* is demanding that you relinquish any part of your black identity. There is no need to do that. Socializing is an accepted, legitimate tool that can be used to obtain the opportunities to do the things that need to be done in order to move from a state of survival to success.

3

Adjusting Phase

Critical Issues

Attitudes

- Reality testing
- Low self-confidence (may run into a lot of criticism)
- Readjustment of expectations about the company to fit new perceptions
- Allowing self to see how racial prejudice affects progress (identifies barriers)
- Periodic concern over whether organization will be capricious, vindictive, or unfair relative to money, position, and responsibility
- Thinking that whites are not as competent as they would like everyone to believe
- Thinking whites are insensitive because they either don't want to understand or are incapable of understanding the situation blacks are in
- Wanting to punish whites because of their apparent or perceived lack of caring and/or understanding
- Separating self from other blacks in order to be thought of as just another manager

Emotions

- Change in stress level (disappointment in work ethic and disillusionment over company/organization's taking care of employees)
- Frustration
- Anger or rage

- Fear of retribution from the organization
- Clinging to hope (expectations of the possibility of "making it" because of the few scattered role models seen in organizations)

Behaviors

- Struggling to identify and learn appropriate corporate behavior
- Linking with informal communications network
- Learning to identify the skills one brings to the company
- Negative reaction to whites (may have a lot of arguments with whites)
- Becoming more vocal, often inappropriately
- Acting as whitelike as necessary to be rewarded in the organization
- Rejecting and being critical of data that focus on racial/ethnic differences
- Refraining from networking with blacks on the job (becoming isolated because of lack of acceptance in the white network)

Job Skills

- More positive perception of one's own competence
- Struggling to acquire managerial skills
- Continuing to see white peers get better jobs, more responsibility (the issue of potential versus proven competence)
- Perceiving little job movement and few results
- Learning the criteria by which blacks are evaluated on competence
- More leadership skills (more experience)

Overview of the Critical Issues

The Adjusting Phase is probably the most turbulent period of development for black managers. In the Entry Phase, black managers are less aware of the issues they face because of inexperience with the workings of the white corporate culture. Blacks believe in integration and tend to think that racism will not be tolerated when it interferes with bottom-line profits. They also tend to deny negative activities they begin to see in order to get along well on the job. As they move into the Adjusting Phase, black managers become increasingly aware of all types of issues involved in getting along on the job. The act of denial now becomes harder to sustain as inexperience gives way to growing experience and greater understanding of how the white corporate culture operates. They begin to see how subtle prejudice gets in the way of producing results on the job.

Reality testing is one aspect of adjusting in the corporation. The Entry Phase attitude of acceptance changes to suspicion of the motivations and activities of the corporation regarding the survival and success needs of the black manager.

In the Adjusting Phase, many black managers may still retain an attitude of lower self-confidence about their competence than they will experience in future phases. This is particularly true where blacks experience a lot of criticism of their job performance and are not told when they are excelling. However, blacks will *see* the good results they produce on the job and will compare these results against the results produced by white peers. As black managers experience more and more the discrepancies between how the organization treats them and how it treats their white peers, they will begin to push back on the organization and test it. This testing not only helps build self-confidence but also helps provide a more realistic picture of how the black manager must operate in order to grow and be successful in the organization:

> "I started to overcome my competence problem by showing myself and others what I could do. I could see myself becoming more aggressive."
>
> "When I compared my skills with those of my peers and even some of my bosses, my skills were better, especially my managerial skills."
>
> "I kept looking around for my competition, and I didn't see any. I started hesitating every time I did something because I was so used to getting interference, people bothering me. Whites had been telling me that what I was doing or saying was wrong."
>
> "I was concerned that white people like me. It has become less important. I don't care now. I do care that they behave in a way to let me get my job done."
>
> "I don't use all my energy any more to counteract the feelings I get from whites, that blacks are 'less than.' I now know better than that."
>
> "I got respect even though I can't say people liked me very much. I got results; what could they say?"
>
> "I got a few accomplishments under my belt. That gave me confidence and freed me up some."
>
> "When I realized I had some power and authority over what happened to me, I became more assertive and verbal."

In the Adjusting Phase, black managers realize that the organization is not a benevolent institution and that the same barriers that exist in society at large exist there as well. The system will not allow industrious activity alone to determine who succeeds. The growing realization of what an organization is all about is coupled with the increasing ability to identify real barriers to a black manager's progress—barriers with which white peers do not have to deal:

> *"When I looked around at what everybody else was doing, I felt qualified to move up; but I knew that unless I did something about it, no matter how well I did my technical job, it would never happen."*
>
> *"I began to realize that I was going to have to strategize to get anyplace in this outfit. I'd have to be clever, tenacious, to absorb the punishment and outthink the whites."*
>
> *"I now know that 'The harder I work, the further I'll go' is not true. There are limitations and obstacles. I began to wonder how far I wanted to go; it may not be worth it, that is, with what I have to go through."*
>
> *"You have to strategize to just get things done in your job. You have to become a superstar—no less than that."*
>
> *"Learning the elements of politics goes more for blacks than whites."*
>
> *"You have to put pressure on the organization . . . 'cause nobody's going to give you anything, no matter how good you are. I'm being more proactive."*

In the Adjusting Phase, younger blacks, those who grew up in the late 1970s and 1980s, find their organizations to be places of great hostility. Older blacks, the first and second wave of managers, believed that white corporate America was naive and unschooled about blacks, that education and association would make a difference. Today's black managers tend to see whites as deliberately holding the managerial reins for themselves and for those few blacks who can manage to behaviorally "pass" as whites. The popular belief today among black managers is that whites do not care to understand the different pressures black managers are under, and blacks are not about to tell them because they fear retribution. Many black managers punish their hierarchies by being closed (the prevalent excuse is that of being an introvert or having a shy personality). These blacks withhold information and are subtly uncooperative:

> *"When I get in meetings with whites, I don't say much because whites own the organization and they will do what they want to do regardless of what I say or do."*
>
> *"Our organization is always working affirmative action stuff. All they*

want to do is ease their guilt and keep the black managers quiet. Here we go again with another training event that gets nothing changed. Why should I learn anything different when I know that the hierarchy is only going to let a few blacks be promoted? They will only promote those who can act the whitest."

"We don't take our problems to the whites because they'll think we're causing trouble."

"I just do an outstanding job on all my projects and let that speak for itself. That's the only way whites will see your competence. Nothing I say will make any difference."

Emotions

As the black manager gradually moves from the Entry Phase into the Adjusting Phase, there is also a gradual change in the kind of stress experienced. On much more than the previous superficial and intellectual level, black managers begin to realize that a lot of people in their organization are running to get to the top. Stress results from now knowing that they are also running, but with a handicap that presents barriers to their upward movement. At this point, black managers are not sure who is responsible for what barriers, and there is great frustration because they do not quite know what to do about the barriers.

More frustration is felt because of the trial-and-error activity required to learn the appropriate corporate behavior and discover what does or does not work for a black manager. Feelings vacillate from mild irritation to anger and sometimes rage. Expressed emotions range from anger directed at the organization in general to verbal attacks on specific persons. Black managers often feel anger and resentment over the extra and sometimes excessive energy they must pour forth in order to get simple tasks done when interacting with whites. The anger gets intensified when blacks stop to think about how whites operate with each other in relation to how they operate with blacks:

"People will blatantly lie to you and use you in detrimental ways. The company won't look out for you. You look out for yourself. The best person won't always get the job."

"Blacks have to prove competence. Whites can be assumed to have it. Blacks don't fit the white picture of a manager, so the company tests blacks. And whites expect blacks to be messiahs around people problems."

"I don't have much faith in the organization because most people around

> *here are insensitive. They just don't know what it takes for me, a black person, to do the job. There is no problem seeing what whites do, but I have to reinterpret everything so the organization can see what I do. My values are higher than their expectations."*
>
> *"A lot of your energy is used just surviving racist pressures. I have to use energy on whites playing games with me. Blacks can come to the brink of failure because of racism.*
>
> *"I put everything I did under a microscpe and kept all mistakes to myself. I was careful no one else saw them. I have been anxious and frustrated over what it takes to get across to whites that I'm competent."*

Because of mergers, downsizing, cutbacks, and corporate take-overs, all Americans are nervous about job security. Now, in addition to the black manager's normal concerns, there arises the specter of "last hired, first fired." Many black managers will wonder, "Is my organization just looking for legitimate reasons to get rid of me?" With this as a backdrop, it then comes as no surprise that blacks are reluctant to challenge or push their organization relative to appropriate treatment and opportunities for minorities. "Making waves" is seen as a danger-ous activity in today's marketplace.

An additional factor for today's black managers is the hope of success that has been fostered by the increased visibility of successful black role models. Such noteworthy magazines as *Black Enterprise* and *Ebony*, to name only two, showcase successful blacks in the marketplace. This says to blacks, "It can be done." *How* some blacks make it to the top of their organization is the question that concerns many blacks.

> *"I had some really creative ideas about how my job should be done. I believed very strongly in this. So . . . I went to the mat with my organization, and now I've got fewer people working for me and less responsibility. You can't convince me that my organization did not punish me for speaking up."*
>
> *"I don't want to get involved with 'black manager' kinds of things because I don't know whether I'm going to stay with this company."*
>
> *"I don't have any problems as a black manager. All you have to do is be poised and don't create problems."*
>
> *"From what I see, the minorities that make it up the ladder in their companies are the ones who can most emulate whites."*

Behaviors

As mentioned earlier in this section, black managers make con-certed efforts in this phase to learn appropriate corporate behavior. In addition, more attention is paid to trying to link with the existing informal communications network. If possible, black managers will begin to expand more energy in finding each other within the organization and forming their own grapevine for information sharing. This grapevine often leads to support systems for the managers, providing such help as feedback that is more easily trusted and coaching. The coaching from other blacks is very important in identifying one's own skills, building confidence, and providing the kinds of assistance whites get informally from each other but are not able or willing to share with blacks. Many black managers who have become more vocal in the organization and who are behaving negatively toward whites can learn how to use their anger and behavior in more acceptable ways.

The grapevine is so important in helping blacks adjust to the organizational culture that we suggest that if a person is totally isolated, he or she should seek help outside the company. This means making contact and estabishing relationships with other blacks who are in similar circumstances and can help in information sharing and coaching:

> "I learned appropriate corporate behavior through trial and error. I used resources both inside and outside my company. I developed a push-and-retreat technique to use on whites. Their reactions taught me a lot."

> "I sought out other blacks to find out how things got done in an acceptable manner."

> "I'd check out a lot of things with other blacks to see how they sounded before doing something like giving a presentation. We would work out strategies together, so I would come across well and my input would not get dismissed."

> "I did a lot of eyeballing both whites and blacks and doing things through trial and error."

> "At first, I patterned myself after whites but later turned to blacks for help because I wasn't getting what I wanted."

> "I listen in on white peers' conversations to get information. For instance, at lunch, the topics you are interested in are things they may not want to talk about, so you are there as sort of an invisible person. So I take advantage of being a good listener and learn what kinds of things are happening in the organization."

> "I got asked to a lot of parties, and I felt there were consequences for not going, so I'd go and put it on a business basis for myself. I would try to get something out of it and use it as a chance to talk to some people I didn't get a chance to at work."

> "I have found a few sympathetic whites who would sit down and share information and one or two who would look out for me."

"I draw a lot of energy from being around blacks, talking with them, etc. It helps me understand myself better."

"Sometimes, I have this overpowering need to get with blacks because I get sick of dealing with white racism. With other blacks, I can get new ideas, put my guard down, and relax."

"There's enough of us at my company now to share a variety of experiences, compare notes, look for trends and flaws."

"You have to have a balance. I stay close enough to blacks and some distance from whites to keep from being socialized too much."

"I never got angry in general, but I sure blew up over some incidents and at certain people."

"At first, I felt frustration, then anger. Finally, I was in a rage as I became more aware of the inequities of the system. I was ready to take on anybody that tried to screw me."

"I'm frustrated and angry. I find myself in a lot of arguments because nobody believes we can come up with our ideas so fast and do as well in our jobs as we do despite the barriers."

Some of the Adjusting Phase behaviors that have helped black managers get beyond the entry level and rise to middle management are not accepted by the younger black managers now entering the business world. "This is a new day for the black manager," say the young black turks from the top ten white academic institutions and the Ivy League schools. What American institutions fail to teach and what young black managers are not aware of is the impact of differential consequences on minorities as they do business in corporate America:

"We have learned the corporate norms and rules. We understand the culture and how business gets done, and we know what behavior gets rewarded. We are brave and competent and will succeed on our own merit without help from other blacks."

In the Adjusting Phase, too many young black managers learn to become oversocialized—i.e., they give up the additional nonacademic skills they have acquired from being black in America (see Chapter 11, "The Management of Diversity"). Yet this is precisely the creative energy that American corporations seek in order to keep their competitive edge. A part of the "glass ceiling" that exists for blacks today is forged from the inability of top-level black managers to use the additional cultural strengths needed by the organization to increase productivity. When there is no difference between top-level white managers and top-level black managers, the only reason for black managers to be there, then, is in response to affirmative action concerns:

> "I try to talk to young blacks coming in, but they don't want to listen to anything I have to say. They tell me I don't understand, that things have changed. So I just shut up and let them get burned. You know, it's sad."
>
> "I thought I had to act just like the whites here to get ahead. But I'm not getting any further than the other blacks in the company."
>
> "We have one black upper-level manager here, and I thought everybody respected him. We sort of accepted that he didn't associate with any blacks. I thought that was how it was. But man, oh man! I accidentally overheard these two white top managers talking about him, and one said, 'Yeah, I told him, _____ was our resident Uncle Tom.' Man, I didn't sleep that night thinking about that."

Job Skills

Competence issues remain a concern until black managers realize a sense of success on an intellectual as well as an emotional level. Then, in spite of what else happens, they still feel OK about themselves. Blacks tend to recognize soon after entering an organization that the acquisition of good managerial skills is critical to their success. Whites, on the other hand, often succeed without acquiring these skills. In part, the reason managerial skills are so important to blacks is because the system places so much responsibility for good black-white interactions on the black manager. When communication breaks down, it is usually the black manager who must bear the blame, in people's minds if not publicly.

No matter how hard blacks work at their tasks, they tend to be rewarded and recognized less than their white peers who do the same tasks. The message is, "Prove yourself again and again." In order to prove yourself, you must know what the rules are and by what criteria you are being judged. Many black managers in the Adjusting Phase begin to see that their competence in doing their job tasks is evaluated in direct proportion to how well they are able to manage others. Unfortunately, this is a slow and usually painful realization that nobody warned them about and for which their recognition of racism did not prepare them. The following comments provide a disturbing picture of how quite a few black managers see the technical aspect of their job compared with the managerial demands and how their organization perceives and evaluates them:

"I'm pretty average at my task performance, but I've lost interest in doing the ordinary task work. I'm seeing that I'm one of the best managers in the company. Few can hold a candle to me, but the company will not take risks on blacks. You have to do the job to get the job. Every time you get moved, you get tested again. They are more stringent on blacks than whites. The average black manager will have a difficult time making it. The company thinks I'm good at my job because I can conceptualize. When whites evaluate blacks, they tend to talk about the blacks' managerial abilities; when they talk about whites, they tend to talk about their technical abilities. Even when the black is technically solid, whites reserve their technical strokes for whites. I'm so public, so visible, that whites have no recourse from my results but to praise my work. When whites can't do the job, it's the fault of the system; when blacks can't, the fault is theirs."

"I know I have survived by doing my tasks exceptionally well. I really didn't want to get involved in interpersonal things. Blacks don't fit into any images whites have of managers. I was already doing this job before I got the title and moved up. Whites get promoted on potential; they don't have to first prove they can do the job. Even though I've been tested over and over, I still get the job done. I have to manage interpersonal interactions; all whites do not. The company has recognized my persistence as well as my ability to get people to do things, but I am not adequately rewarded for what is involved in being a black manager. I can't get honest feedback from whites. I have to do extra things in my job to offset racism that whites don't."

"I don't question my technical competence anymore, and I don't allow anyone else to either. I've shown superior interpersonal skills. My ability to deal with interpersonal issues; direct, guide, and steer people; deal with conflict in a positive manner have all helped me. There is no in-between for blacks; you have to be good in every area. Whites expect excellence from blacks before they can make it. Whites can make it on being average. Blacks will get penalized for making mistakes. The organization can put questions in the system about you to undermine you instead of openly saying something negative about you. Blacks have to manage all kinds of interactions and others' racism. With all the pieces I have handled successfully—a white wouldn't have to do all that and then get underrewarded as I have. A company has no perspective around how much it takes for a black to do the job. I have to face the stereotypes the organization plays out on me. The company will quickly get their negative report if I make a mistake."

"I got a bad performance evaluation, and when I asked for the details on

where I was missing the mark, I could see I was not meeting my boss's
stereotypes of blacks. Blacks have to amplify managerial skills so much to
survive that the task component seems unimportant. Many job tasks get
misinterpreted as managerial tasks and then turned into a negative."
"My performance appraisals have always been subject to interpretation by
my supervisors. Everything I do is relative to my being black."

In the corporate world, younger blacks have more opportunity to exercise leadership during the Adjusting Phase. Black managers in the first wave were more frustrated in taking leadership during this period because of low trust and expectations by their organization. Those expectations and trust levels have been raised because of the successful groundwork laid by the earlier managers; but even so, they remain too low.

The Adjusting Phase is the most active phase in terms of struggle. However, with all of its surface negativism, it is the most positive phase relative to the great learnings acquired by the black manager. Both the Adjusting Phase and the Planned Growth Phase are periods of rapid growth and learning. The two phases differ in the nature of the learning and the methods used. The Adjusting Phase can be compared with the period when a young child learns to become aware of his or her environment and manipulate it. Much of the behavior displayed is trial and error, and the attitudes are those of reality testing. This development stage lays the foundation for the next great learning period, the Planned Growth Phase, which is more structured and goal-directed. The manager in the Planned Growth Phase can be compared with the student who studies in a structured, goal-directed manner in preparation for acquiring a job in society.

In the Adjusting Phase, black managers correct misconceptions and inappropriate assumptions about how the corporation operates. Values are reexamined, and managers begin to crystallize goals and seek a direction in their jobs. They make way for the more structured learnings to come in the next phase. The next great task ahead is to be able to use these learnings by organizing experience and laying out a plan to achieve success. When managers are able to do this, they move into the Planned Growth Phase of development.

A word of caution: Black managers will experience many Adjusting Phases throughout their careers. It is necessary to propel a person out of a stagnant period into one of growth. The danger lies in remaining in the Adjusting Phase and thrashing around until you burn out. Remember, the key to moving on is to organize your experience and learn from it.

Now let us return to Jack's story.

"Everything Not as Great as I Thought"

Man, oh man! Just stretching and walking around did me a world of good. My muscles had gotten pretty tight just sitting here. Guess I was really into remembering things and got tight.

Yeah, I'm OK. Let's see, where were we? Oh yeah. I was talking about my entry period at my company.

Now you want to know what happened next, what changed me, and how I got into the next period of development. OK. Let's go back to the day I told you about, when I went and told my boss I was going to look for another job, because I didn't feel as though I was growing and developing.

Now the real reason I told him that was because I got angry! I looked around . . . I'd been angry all along, but now I allowed the anger to just seep up, to engulf me, to . . . to just permeate my every little fiber. That's how strong I felt about it.

So I went to him and told him I was going to quit—and the real reason was because I looked around and I saw some whites who had come in along with me; they had much better jobs than I did. Much, much more responsibility.

I figured, damn! I can't be *that* dumb! So dumb that they're not going to give me some better jobs and more responsibility. It's like they gave me little bitty jobs— to see if I could do them. Then if I could do them, I'd get another little bitty job. And then, maybe, the third time it would be a little bit more responsibility. And it ticked me off!

And also, when I was working with my boss during our weekly meetings, he'd give me, like, some little side job with some little minor problem where I'd have to go and dig up stuff, something that had nothing to do with what I was really doing.

And that ticked me off! Well, it was like I had a private training session. Like I was so dumb that I *needed* a private training session. And it really made me angry. I was just fed up with it because I didn't see myself going anyplace.

Now, my boss . . . just about two weeks passed, and nothing happened. So, I . . . I figured out how to get a message to my boss's boss's boss. And I did it through a white guy I knew who worked in the office around the corner from me. He was in personnel.

The way I did it was to tell him I wanted to help him in personnel, to help in his office with some of the minority problems. Then the personnel guy, Mike, went to the upper-level boss and asked, "Can Jack help me in personnel?" And the boss said, "No!"

I knew the boss would come looking for me, and he did. We went in one of the empty offices and stayed about two to three hours.

He asked me what was wrong, and I told him that I didn't feel as though I was growing and developing, and uhh . . . I felt that I had talents that I wasn't using. And he agreed.

Then he shocked me! 'Cause he looked at me, and he said, "I'm so glad you feel this way." I almost fell out of my chair! He said, "Well, it finally sounds like you're ready to make some movement." Which implied that that's what they were waiting for. But damn it!! Why didn't they tell me that!

What? What were they waiting for? For me to . . . to, uhhh, get angry. Exercise some initiative. Say, "I want this and I want that." And . . . and just make some movement. Just get off the dime! In other words, stop accepting peanuts and ask for more. I guess, that's what they—

No. No, I don't think the whites were asking for more. I think they just did their jobs, and then the next time, they got more responsibility automatically.

Why did I have to make noise before I got better jobs? Why didn't I get automatic increases like my white peers? Now that's a good question! One which I can't answer—other than they were testing me because they didn't think I could do the job in the first place.

Even when I did the damn job, I didn't automatically get as much responsibility as the whites got. Maybe they were asking, but I doubt it. I just don't have any explanation for it.

Anyway, there we were in this room. I was explaining to my upper-level boss that I was upset. And he was shocked when I told him that I had told my boss I was going to quit, 'cause nobody had told him. He didn't know about it.

I was so angry at this point that I looked at him and said, "I don't need *you* or this *damn company!*" I said, "People are afraid of you, but you're a damn man like I am. You put your pants on exactly like I do, and I'm not afraid of you!"

I know he was surprised, but anyway he said, "I'm glad to hear you say that."

Anyway, the result of that meeting was his admitting they weren't using my skills. He asked me not to quit, and I got the biggest pay raise I'd ever had. That was designed to keep me there. In the meantime, I'd asked to transfer to personnel, so he made arrangements for me to do that.

Now, my second-level boss got into the act. He worked for the boss I had the big conference with. This second-level boss called me up and asked me if I wanted the personnel job and called me "boy" in the ensuing conversation, which further ticked me off. That was adding insult to injury!

I then moved to the personnel office. Now I know that this was when I had moved completely into an adjusting period. Realizing how angry I was and wanting to quit my job and telling my bosses is probably what pushed *me* over.

Yes . . . yes, I know it was because I was just so damn angry. I got even angrier when I got to the personnel office and saw the kind of things they were doing— because they were saying, "We can't find any blacks." Well, hell, they were only looking in white schools!

They were also saying, "We have trouble orienting blacks. They don't respond to the training." I couldn't believe this. There were no black recruiters or black input in the orientation program planning.

So the first thing they did—you're supposed to be in middle management to go out and recruit—they let me recruit without the promotions. I went out and found so many blacks in each of the job areas they wanted that they had to force me to stop.

Nobody in that office understood any racial stuff, so they didn't do a good job. The staff wasn't organized. People didn't know what their jobs were! So I organized the office. I got people to write up their job responsibilities, drew up a chart showing the process involved in the operation of the personnel office and its various responsibilities.

From that, I convinced them to put in a computer management system. But I had to bug the—

Now, see! Here's the difference. If I'd been white, they'd have paid attention to me. But it got . . . I had to literally *bug* the *hell* out of them! It got so bad that every time I met with my boss, I'd mention it again. He got ticked off—talked to his boss, and he got ticked off.

So finally—just to shut me up, I guess—they allotted some money to study the thing. And the study showed the computer system really would pay off. In the meantime, I had taken some college graduate courses in a nearby city a couple of years before that. I guess it was to test myself—to see how I stacked up against supposedly sharp whites. My army service didn't really count, I felt, because there are a *lot* of people in there who would have trouble making it on the outside. Now I went back to this school to take courses that related to the computer system I wanted in the office. Finally, they put it in.

Man, I had my hands full. The next step was to upgrade the orientation program, so I got interested in organizational development. I was concerned about what happened to black folks once they got through the doors.

No way! No! My anger hadn't gone away now that I was handling more stuff. My anger was building and building—reaching its zenith. I guess that zenith was when I was so damn frustrated at what I saw happening to blacks coming into the company. I saw the games people were playing—saw racism in action.

Man, it was like—my hands—I was just one person. My hands were tied. I couldn't change the whole thing. So I went outside the company and got some help. I got these people to put on some racial awareness sessions in my organization so they could see for themselves what was happening.

Some of the top-level managers heard about it and wanted to attend. So we started giving some sessions that included managers on every level. Now everybody could see what was going on. The upper-level managers decided to do something about the situation, so they allotted me a sizable budget and some latitude to do some things that needed to be done.

Now wait! Before you decide everything is OK, remember this is the period when I was so angry and frustrated that I fought every white manager I came in contact with. Just exploded all over them! And I did some inappropriate things with upper-level managers in big meetings. It got so bad that people were saying that I didn't know when to fight or how to fight or, in essence, I didn't know how to act in the corporation—that's what they were saying.

This was happening to other people too—not just to me. For instance, John. You know, I mentioned him earlier. Well, he told me about the time—we can laugh about it now; it wasn't so funny then—he blew up in a meeting in front of a lot of white managers.

We were talking about some of the things we'd learned, and swapping war stories and insights—oh yeah, you can see a lot of things later—twenty-twenty hindsight. But it helps to talk to someone who's going through the same thing.

Anyway, John said he was in this meeting with a couple of his bosses and some peers, and something he had asked to be done for his project wasn't done. He said he started getting all kinds of excuses about why it wasn't done. He was already mad because he had not been able to get cooperation all along. His input was dismissed; his peers wouldn't do what he had asked, and his bosses weren't supportive worth a darn.

John had had it at this point—so he blew his stack! He stood up, and took the papers he had in front of him, and threw them down on the floor. "I don't want this to ever happen again!" And he kept on yelling, letting off some steam.

Well, John said the papers hit the floor, scattered all over, and he had to go pick them all up while everybody sat there looking at him. He said he felt like an idiot, an angry idiot who would have liked to smash some noses. He felt set up at the time, and he just got angrier . . . and was angry at himself for letting them make him lose control. He said he got his point across in that one incident, but it didn't do the kinds of things he wanted for his image.

Of course, we've talked about those days and realize now that maybe we needed to go through some of this to learn. We know anger is appropriate, but as a tool—not a relief valve.

What was I doing with my anger and frustration? Oh. Oh yeah! One thing I did inappropriately was to get into meetings with upper-level managers, and instead of bringing up an issue and then discussing it, I would sit and watch things happen until my anger just made me explode, and I just kind of erupted. I would just, kind of, uhh—rage! Yeah! That's it! I'd use my black rage.

Yeah, man! It wasn't really aggressiveness—it was black rage! I'd just jump all over people! People who were two and three levels higher than me, because I didn't give a damn anymore. I saw I wasn't going anyplace. I wasn't learning anything, so I said, "Just to hell with it." And I pulled out all the stops. OK?

Now what else? Oh! Sometimes I would, uhh . . . yeah, I would see something in writing that I would react to because it would be racist, a racist reaction to something that happened on the job. Like, when they were figuring out minority numbers, they would count black women twice, OK? They'd count them as blacks and as women. To me, this didn't make sense.

I went to one upper-level boss's office to ask about it, and instead of being strategic, I jumped all over him—and he never forgot it. Years later, he still remembers that I did that. And *I* thought I was being cool and calm.

See, the corporation does not allow for a lot of display of emotion among its members. But blacks are more emotion-based than whites. And that's something that usually gets us blacks into trouble.

But man, see . . . whew! I'd got frustrated! I could see what needed to be done, but I couldn't do it because people were too busy trying to *test* me to see if I knew what the hell I was doing.

There were a lot of fights. And they weren't just with white managers above me; they were with white peers also. I just . . . it was just a display of anger! I was trying to make reason out of a maze of confusion.

What things did I see that didn't make sense? Well, uhh . . . Oh! One thing I could very clearly see was that sharp whites could propose something, and people would listen, ask a few helpful questions, and make plans to try out the idea. If a black manager did that, they would quiz the hell out of the person and then proceed to tell him or her why it wouldn't work.

Also, they'd move blacks from one area of the country to another and assume everything was going to be all right. They'd move black people down South, for instance, and never once give thought to where they would live, how they would get a phone, where they would go to the doctor, where they would get their hair cut—stuff like that.

When we tried to explain that to the whites, they looked like—duhhh! When we tried to tell them to assign a black to a new black person coming into the area, they said, "Why?" Just insensitive—totally insensitive!

Oh! Wait! Another thing! When I got the money to make changes in the personnel department, they put in these silly little controls—like, I had all this money and couldn't sign a request to use it! So to hire somebody to come in to consult—well, I could pick the consultants, but I couldn't pay them. That really gave others veto power over a lot of things.

Now in all this, I still had a white boss who wanted to always take a look at how I was going to solve a problem, even if it was a black problem. And he wanted to override authority . . . until one day I'd had enough of it.

So you know what I did? I taped him a message and left it on his desk because I was just *sooo* angry. I just—I knew if I put it in writing I'd lose it, and I knew I couldn't sit in front of him and say it because I'd probably jump in his chest! OK?

And in essence, what I was saying was, "How the hell can you as a white man evaluate what I'm gonna do? You couldn't solve the problem: that's why you got me involved."

That's the kind of crazy things that would happen. Whites would question me to death every time I made a proposal. They didn't do that with other whites.

Whites would use the informal communications network to learn things, but I wasn't privy to that. Why not? Well, it's because they were uncomfortable with blacks; even our bosses were uncomfortable with us.

How do I know? Very simply. They talked to each other differently, spent more time with each other, told each other different things—offered more help.

Even when I ate lunch with them, they'd share information with each other, but they wouldn't give me any. I'd have to ask, and when I did, I'd get short, to-the-point answers—but no conversation. They'd look disgusted with me. Their faces and voices changed.

When I led meetings and sessions, if a white was doing the session with me, the people in the room would look toward the white individual for leadership . . . including any blacks in the room. Everyone seemed to have trouble accepting black leadership, even the blacks.

I was feeling extremely bitter—crazy at times trying to explain to myself some of the very same things I've been telling you about today. I was looking for an explanation, and—damn it! I couldn't come up with one; I had no explanation. How could all this happen? How could you get a budget like this and then not be allowed to sign for anything? That's crazy! Then, when I was told to make a major decision, my boss told me I didn't know enough to make the decision.

I had a lot of stress—paranoid-type. At times, I had a feeling that, after I confronted whites about looking over my shoulder with everything, they'd do the reverse. They let me go out and do stuff without any checkpoints, and if something happened, they'd come back and jump on me.

But I must have been doing something right. Because once every two weeks, I had to meet with four upper-level managers, and it was their job to keep me in check.

And that was crazy, too. Now, why would you put one black person in a room with four upper-level white managers? It was intimidation. So what they were trying to do was slow me down by intimidating me.

Man, did I ever need a lot of psychic support, and I got that from other blacks. We'd meet after work. Then we were at a point where everyone needed that support, so we'd meet at work.

At one point, if more than three blacks got together during working hours, the phones in the white bosses' offices would ring, and they'd want to know, "Well, what are the blacks doing?" And you'd go in the dining room, and if you ate with each other, you ended up at a table with all blacks, and people would start whispering and talking and asking, "Well, why do you blacks eat together?"

It's very interesting, but none of them ever came over to sit with us. So the same applies to them, "Why do all you whites eat together?"

Hell, yes! A lot of what I learned was from trial and error, and I got into a lot of trouble. I remember one meeting with all upper-level white managers one time, and we were discussing some plans I had laid out for the personnel program. One manager made a comment which to me was stupid, so I turned and jumped all over him—and I got about six messages from six different top managers saying, "Don't do that again."

Now, everybody was telling me what *not* to do, but nobody was telling me what *to* do. So there I was, more frustrated—and left out in the cold. That's why I had to learn by trial and error.

We blacks who had gotten together formed a grapevine to keep track of what was going on and to pass information and ways of surviving in the company.

I was frustrated over not having the correct interpersonal skills. Now, in this big meeting I was telling you about, obviously, I didn't have the correct interpersonal managerial skills. Right? But I didn't know what was correct. I had nobody to tell me, and . . . and sometimes I couldn't sleep at night. I felt crazy trying to figure out, well, how the hell should I act? I wasn't about to act white.

See, black managers are caught in a chasm. Over here, you've got what is so-called black cultural behavior. And over there, is white cultural behavior. Now, the black cultural behavior is not corporate-based. Obviously, I wasn't, uh . . . Some blacks like to try and act white—but I wasn't going to. Then that meant there was a third thing I had to develop. Well, what did it look like?

How do you behave? I had no way of knowing that! So I had to learn how to survive and test the system relative to what things I could or could not do.

Obviously, the company could not read black potential and take a risk with blacks, because with me, and other blacks, we . . . we had to display competence and show results, or else we didn't get an opportunity to do more things that required more responsibility. It's like we had to do the job at the next level before we could get more responsibility.

My managerial abilities were questioned. They questioned both my technical competence and my managerial abilities. And this is the way the white managers can manage blacks. All they do is create doubt.

See, the trick they play on us is not to say directly that they don't think we can do the job. The say stuff like, "We question whether Jack has the right experience." See, that's what they hit you with.

Yeah, they talk about, "Well, I don't know whether you have the right background or the right experience for that job." Behind closed doors, they decide your future with "haven't had the right kind of experience." Whereas whites don't have to have the "right kind of experience." They'll promote them on, well, based on potential and then provide the experience.

Like I said, during this time, I became a helluva lot more verbal. I told people what I thought, what I felt—'cause I didn't give a damn anymore. I didn't have a damn thing to lose. I didn't have anything, so there was nothing to lose.

I became a helluva lot more aggressive, and I was pushed on by the rage—the black rage that I had within me. I had gotten to the point where I said, "This is crazy! I won't tolerate it! I won't stand for it! I'm gonna leave!"

And then . . . I really was going to leave, but then I decided not to because I got angry at that, too. I said, "Why the hell should I run away from this? If I run away, then the next black comes along, and they'll do the same thing. I'm going to stay here! I'm gonna dig in my heels, and I'm going to change this organization."

Racism motivated the hell out of me! Now, if whites could understand how to use motivation—boy, could you improve the effectiveness of black individuals!

But they don't know how to use all that anger and energy—they're afraid of it, and what they try to do is shut it off! Whites in an organization tend not to attack problems directly. Listen, I know. 'Cause that was one thing that I had trouble with. I'd attack a problem head on—I'd jump dead on it—and whites tended to beat around the bush about what the problem is, who's to blame, what we are going to do about it . . . and "We don't want to upset the organization and change things too fast." And I'd jump dead on it and say, "Let's change things right now." Boom!

White organizations lose opportunities to really use us blacks effectively. How? Because given our cultural style, we tend automatically to deal up front with difficult problems—that is, hot issues.

Why? Because that's the nature of our growing up. We've been doing it since the cotton fields: being creative. OK? For example, overseers in the fields didn't want us "lollygagging" and talking to each other, so we developed a system of communication through song. So we've learned to be creative in difficult situations.

I also think it has to do with our emotions. They tend to be closer to our level of consciousness than whites'. We have not been taught to suppress our emotions as much.

Man, one of the biggest issues I dealt with relative to my survival was the managerial piece. You have to get people to listen to your ideas. You have to convince . . . you have to sell yourself and your ideas. And that's not technical competence; that's a managerial competence issue.

During this time, I probably threw away the work ethic, because it sure didn't work worth a darn for me. At least, I paid a heavy price for what I was given in terms of rewards by the company.

There was a lot of dysfunctional behavior going on, mine and other people's. All this just drives you further into anger and keeps you frustrated. I know why I didn't get that ulcer early on; I was saving it for now.

I noticed a lot of crazy stuff. I noticed a couple of things happened when blacks and whites interacted. One was the verbal, spoken piece, and the other was the nonverbal. And I was missing a lot. I had to learn to notice both.

A lot of managers use intimidation to control people, but it has a different effect on blacks. I'd have to try and sort out the racist piece in the manager's actions, and whites wouldn't. I'd have to try to find out if there was a difference in the way intimidation was used on me versus the whites. The reason it's important to know this is because it would probably have a bearing on how I would respond to the person using intimidation.

Also, another thing I noticed. Uhh, whites can get benevolent sometimes when you take problems to them. They can get into a parent-child mode and try to protect you. They'll say things like, "Well, I'll go and speak to that manager," instead of telling you how —or helping you—to take care of the problem yourself. That would be an adult-to-adult teaching mode. That's what a manager is supposed to do. But you get a lot of that crap. And that further frustrates you because you don't learn anything that way!

You know! That makes you angry because it feels like a put-down, like being treated like a child. I'm not a child. I'm an adult and want to be treated like an adult. Don't take care of something for me—help me understand, so I can do it myself. That's slave-master stuff, 'cause I'm black.

Now, this—this is something! I want to tell you about evaluations before I take another break. I've even seen this happen with my kid at school. The teachers have to tell us about his conduct before they talk grades.

OK! Listen! One day, I challenged a high-level manager because, given the job I had, I saw a lot of the performance evaluations on blacks and I noticed something. I noticed that when whites evaluated blacks, the first thing they evaluated, independently of their job performance, was style. With whites, it was technical competence. So that if a white had high technical competence, they would overlook some of the negative interpersonal and behavioral things needing changes.

With the black, they did the reverse. I felt like this was done from a base of prejudice. They expected blacks to misbehave. Therefore, the first thing looked at was, does the black behave properly?

Nobody was teaching us how to behave. So we all got zonked, automatically, with negative input around our style.

I'd say this happens all over. I'll be that general, that it still goes on. Because we checked it out with a very large number of evaluations, my boss had to give in and say, "You're right." So I say that happens in most institutions, corporate or otherwise. The first thing evaluated is the black's style.

Yeah, that happened to me, too. One of my first evaluations started off with, "You've got a communications problem," not with the results I got doing my job. What that meant was, "When people interact with you, they don't feel good." OK!

The funny thing was that this boss had me talk to people he was afraid of. Why would he do that if I had a communications problem? What he was really trying to evaluate was my aggressive style—which may have been rough—and I'll concede that point. But what they tend to do is evaluate you on style and lump it under headings like "communications problems" or "personality problems," and you can't do a damned thing about that.

What I was trying to find out was, what do I change if I've got a communications problem? I dug into it, and what it boiled down to was I had a problem because I didn't do everything my boss told me to.

It was also based on his idea of how blacks are supposed to behave in the company, which he wasn't clear about. What he was trying to do was to say, "When I'm told to do something, I shut up and do it. Why don't you shut up and do it?" If that's what he was evaluating, he should have said it that way.

What? Do I see any difference in how these new black managers act? Doggoned straight I do! They take a lot less, get mad, and quit! They're not as afraid of moving on to something else as I was.

Yeah. I *am* a little tired. I'm going to take a little stretch in a minute. Let me finish up by making a connection here, I mean, uh, put it in some kind of perspective.

When you finally get tired of just sitting there doing your little bitty work tasks, when you get *sooo* angry you want to explode on everything—*then* you'll quit and move on, or you'll start learning how to adjust to your environment.

In your period of adjusting, you tend to deal primarily at an emotional level. You pull out the emotional stops. You don't try to suppress or try to manage your rage and anger and aggressiveness or initiative. You just let it all hang out, so to speak. OK?

But then what will happen is that you'll discover—damn, I'm not getting anyplace this way either! It's getting worse! So obviously, I gotta do something differently. Let me look around and take in data about what other people . . . how whites make it in the organization.

Plus! Let me translate that into black terms so that I don't become white, and let me get some additional black input from other people I respect and admire.

So you get to a point where you calm yourself down. You . . . you learn to manage your rage and anger. It's at that point that you begin to plan your own growth and development. You begin to take a look at, OK, what areas do I need improvement in, and how can I get it? What are the how-tos, and how can I go about practicing the things I've learned that will work?

You start learning about taking risks. You start being aware of needing and using strategy, using the management skills you've picked up, and increasing your technical competence—all at the same time.

But that whole transition area really has to do with . . . with the black individual realizing that pulling out all the emotional stops is not going to work. So it's the realization that something must be different that swings you over into planning your growth.

Oh sure! I can tell you what did it for me. There was an incident. I had an upper-level boss, and every time I met with him, I felt put down! OK?

So one day I went to a white manager. Now, this is amazing! I went to a white manager, and I asked him, "How do you deal with this upper-level manager?" And what the guy said to me was, "Well, what I do is . . . the guy's whole style is that he appears to know everything and he asks a whole lot of questions of people. He intimidates them. And people shut down."

So right there the white manager was telling me, "Jack, the first thing you've got to do is—you've got to have a behavioral, psychological profile on the person." OK? Then you've got to strategize.

And then he said what he does is to allow the manager to go ahead and roll out his strategy, use his behavioral pattern. And then after about three or four questions, he looks at the guy and says, "Look, you asked me three questions, and the three questions seem to be unrelated. What is it you are really trying to get at?" Or, "What is it you really want to know?" And see! What you really do is get on the offensive and not on the defensive.

Now, I learned that from a white individual, but I also learned more of the same from black individuals.

I calmed down after that. And that's when I moved into a period of planning my growth, because I tried it and it worked. It was painless! It was quick! It was to the point! And I didn't turn the guy off. I didn't strip the guy of his dignity. I was strategic, and I got what I wanted! What's just as important is, I've been getting what I wanted without having to become just like another white male in the organization. I get to keep my identity. I've come to appreciate my being black because I can add a creativity to my organization that white males can't.

Look, you think about what I said. And speaking of getting what I want—I'm going for a sandwich. Can I get you anything?

Analysis of the Critical Issues

Jack's basic attitude changed drastically in the Adjusting Phase. His confidence was low, but he had fewer doubts about his ability to do his job well. Rather, he began to see and feel that he had little chance of growing, developing, and moving up in the company. Jack began to see certain things regarding his job, such as a lack of increased responsibility, that he seemed powerless to change. So Jack experienced frustration and dissatisfaction, and he became increasingly angry. This anger propelled Jack from his Entry Phase attitudes into Adjusting Phase attitudes.

Jack became so frustrated and angry over what he perceived to be so few avenues to get ahead that he no longer cared whether he had the job or not. He decided to quit and look for a job elsewhere. At this point, Jack had certainly readjusted his expectations of his company. He came into the organization figuring he would be given a job to do and be left alone to do it without having to interact very much with whites. What he found was that he could not do the job alone and did have to interact with others. He became frustrated because he did not understand the dynamics of what was occurring to him. Jack felt that no matter how dumb he was in relation to whites, he had been with his company long enough to have made a little progress. There had to be some other explanation. So Jack allowed himself to see racial prejudice in action, and he began to see how it was affecting his progress. There were a lot of things happening to him that were not happening to his white peers, and he could not explain it to himself. Therefore, it had to have something to do with race.

Jack tells us in his narrative exactly what led him to angrily confront his upper-level boss about what was happening to him on the job and how he felt about it. Jack was very surprised to find that his boss had no idea of what was going on. This is a common experience among blacks. When blacks are brought face to face with the realization of how much racial prejudice touches them personally, how hurtful and vicious it can be, their first reaction is to feel as though the perpetrator of the racist behavior must be acting consciously and deliberately against them. This is, of course, true in some, but not most, cases. Whites tend to be unaware of and insensitive to how racial prejudice affects blacks.

Jack reacted to his environment in a typical manner once he realized what was interfering with his development. In the Adjusting Phase, his need was to attack the system rather than inform it because he was now too frustrated and angry to do otherwise. Everything he had tried prior to this did not work; that is, it did not bring him what he needed or wanted.

Now that Jack was more aware of racially based practices acting against him in the company, he began to push back and test the realities of that environment. Jack asked questions about his job environment for which he had no answers. He wanted to know, for instance, why he had to make a lot of noise before he was heard by his organization. How could the organization see what his white peers were doing and not see his contribution, since he was obviously more visible, because of his difference, than the white managers? How did he become invisible? The only answer he could deduce was that the organization did not *want* to see him. Minorities in the professional work force upset the status quo.

In the Adjusting Phase, Jack's emotional state was one of great agitation because he was in direct contact with his black rage. This is the furious anger born out of an individual's blackness and all that it means in our society. Jack's reorganization of the personnel office is a good example to help us understand the genesis of his black rage. There were times when Jack could clearly see a problem and other people did not seem to see it. He even had some solutions that he could not implement because he could not convince anyone that there was a problem. It was as though Jack were standing in front of a brick wall and trying to get through. All he could do was beat his head against the wall and blow off emotionally. He would pull out all the stops and let go. Jack might have screamed at the white manager or pounded on his desk or just walked out of the room—blown his stack as his friend John did.

Jack's movement in this phase was motivated by the rage that had been suppressed, possibly for years. Now these emotions had surfaced, and Jack often had trouble containing them, but they also acted to motivate him to boldly explore his environment.

In addition, Jack was now experiencing a different type of stress than he had in the Entry Phase. It no longer came from the fear of losing his job because his organization might think he was incompetent;

instead, it came from disappointment and disillusionment over the values he previously held about the work ethic and people's inherent goodness. In the Adjusting Phase, blacks redirect their stress from inward to outward. In the Entry Phase, blacks tend to look within themselves for answers to explain what is happening to them. They also put a lid on their emotions. They suppress them for all the wrong reasons by focusing on self and whatever deficiencies they perceive within themselves. In the Adjusting Phase, emotions take a diametrically opposite turn, and now everything is focused outward toward the organization and the people who cause the frustration.

Jack had reached an intolerable degree of frustration and now doubted everything he valued and believed in connection with his job. He felt none of these values and beliefs were working for him. This is the point at which the white manager of a black should sense that something is wrong. The display of this attitude signifies that the black manager is well into the Adjusting Phase. It also means, if the company or the supervisors do not make some changes to reduce the stress, the black manager will become dysfunctional or leave the organization.

Let us point out here that we said "dysfunctional," not "irrational." Rage is a *rational* reaction to the intolerable situation in which the organization places blacks. In Jack's case, he started to leave the company but changed his mind. His momentary ventilation of anger at his boss, combined with his continuing anger, made him decide to adopt a stubborn attitude and fight it out. He decided not to run away but to stay and somehow force the organization to respond to his needs and those of other blacks. This is the type of positive perseverance that had made it possible for blacks to break down barriers and open previously closed doors. In order to place everything in perspective, let us remember that Jack was not solely responsible for this situation, because the trigger for all of this was Jack's frustration over his inability to manage and deal with the racist behavior that existed within the environment. In the Adjusting Phase, then, situations are jointly caused by the black individual and the corporation.

To recap, Jack came into the organization free of frustration and stated, "I've got it made." He went through the Entry Phase, discovered something, and had to say, "Wait a minute! I *don't* have it made; something is wrong here!" He then became stressed. As the stress built, he tried to deal with it by rationalizing and justifying what was happening to him as being his fault; that did not work. Then he tried to figure it out logically; that did not work, either. So his frustration continued to build to a point at which he just blew up emotionally.

With some blacks, this does not happen. All blacks will go through Jack's experience but will not necessarily behave as Jack did. How they behave will vary even though the frustration is there. Racism affects some individuals worse than others. The sharper, more open blacks will sooner or later publicly display their frustration. Others may not. Unfortunately, many blacks will become bitter and give up. Perhaps they were taught early that there is no point in fighting the system. They may struggle at first and then accept what is happening to them. These individuals spend their job careers in the Entry Phase or on the edge of the Adjusting Phase. Eventually, because of their long service, the organization will reward them but never in the way that their more aggressive brothers and sisters will be rewarded.

Viewing the Adjusting Phase from this vantage point, we can see that although Jack was filled with negative thoughts and feelings, he had embarked on what could be considered on of the most positive stages of his development. This development phase should not be feared, because it is the doorway to reaching success. Jack was now highly motivated. Whites who can see and capitalize on that motivation can help the black manager shorten the adjusting period and move more rapidly to the Planned Growth Phase. This is where structured learning takes place at a rapid pace and higher results are seen, with a greater payout for the organization.

As Jack continued to test his environment and use his trial-and-error behavior, he began to realize that he was not powerless to change his organization. Through outside contacts and consultants, he learned of things that were being done by other blacks to manage racism and effectively get their job accomplished. Jack had the initiative to use these resources to acquire some of the skills he needed to do this job; many of these skills related to identifying and learning appropriate corporate behavior. This was an area of difficulty for Jack, as it is for most blacks.

The angry feelings at this stage often push the black manager into snap reactions but at the same time also force reactions from the environment. This is not the best way to learn, but it is *a* way, and it may be the *only* way when the environment is totally unresponsive. Jack tells us about his friend John and John's reaction to the uncooperative staff. Jack also tells us about how he told off an upper-level manager in a meeting and was instructed through notes from his boss's peers never to do that again.

There were valuable learnings about corporate behavior associated with these experiences for both men. True, this was learning from negative responses, but it *was* learning! The men began to realize that losing their temper and putting themselves in embarrassing situations was not the answer either. They must search elsewhere. These types of experiences often form the basis for sharing information and exploring options among blacks. This process becomes necessary because the white organization tends to feel little or no responsibility to inform blacks of·what is appropriate but merely criticizes what is not appropriate.

Jack was still struggling to become a part of the company's informal communications network, where relevant corporate behavior can be learned. Because blacks rarely fit into this system, it is extremely difficult for them to sort out the mixed messages they receive from the organization. Jack and his friends were caught between the proverbial "rock and a hard place." The company chastised them for their misbehavior but presented few avenues to learn how to behave. The grapevine continues to be the system through which black managers can piece together corrective measures.

The grapevine helped Jack identify the skills that he brought to the organization. It is often used, in addition, as a pressure-relief valve for the type of frustration Jack encountered as he attempted to use his creative skills. Jack moved to the personnel office and accomplished some things no one else could. No one in his hierarchy acknowledged his creativity, but supervisors often criticized him or tried to talk him out of his ideas.

In the Adjusting Phase, it is extremely important for white supervisors to give strokes or verbal rewards to blacks. Jack identified his skills, put them to use, and did not get any strokes for them. It is important for blacks to get strokes because they have been positioned, both by the organization and by the racist behavior of others, to struggle with issues of competence and to question their own skills. When they develop some skills they can use on the job, they expect some external reinforcement and verification of their competence; they expect someone to say, "Hey, that was great!" Whites can inadvertently manage blacks negatively by *not* stroking them, by withholding positive information. This will create further stress, confusion, and doubt. As the black manager moves to the Success Phase, stroking comes more from within. In the Success Phase, blacks are able to provide internal reinforcement. Their successes are more obvious to them and to the public.

Jack saw he possessed skills that would be valuable in the personnel office. He put in a computer system, developed an organization chart showing task responsibilities, and had the staff define their jobs; but even then, he felt insecure. So Jack went back to school to ensure his success with his projects. He did not want to look bad or fail.

In the Adjusting Phase, blacks tend to underrate what they do and the results they obtain. This is a consistent theme seen in their behavior and attitudes. To Jack, what he did was simple. He saw a problem and took the initiative to correct it head-on. This, too, is typical of minorities in the Adjusting Phase. They will take the initiative in one area, and if they are humiliated or receive negative feedback, they will not do that any more. They will then initiate action in another area, and if they obtain success there, they will do more of that. If a person is consistently humiliated over a long time period, he or she may stop taking the initiative altogether. Remember that anger is a motivating force and constant humiliation can act as a weeding-out process. Out of fear or stress, blacks may decide that they will no longer take risks and will stay where they are. This is a major decision that affects black managers as well as the corporation. These managers are now stuck in the Adjusting Phase—angry, hostile, and dysfunctional.

Throughout Jack's narrative, he lets you feel the negative reaction he had toward whites and tells you about the arguments he and his friends had. He became more vocal in expressing his needs and feelings and especially his anger. He wanted others to know somehow that he was in pain, and since whites were perceived to be the source of that pain, they were the recipients of that anger. Jack was now having less of a problem with his feelings of incompetence. He was moving toward a positive attitude about his job skills because he was able to handle difficult problems better than his white peers and in a creative manner. Part of this ability resulted from Jack's lack of socialization in the white culture. This gave him a freedom to think of and try ideas that whites might not try because they know much more about the rules and corporate norms. In this way, Jack's lack of knowledge often worked to his benefit. But in the Adjusting Phase, Jack was neither aware of this nor able to take advantage of it in a strategic manner, as he would be able to do in the Planned Growth Phase.

Jack was struggling to acquire managerial skills in an unplanned, unorganized, catch-as-catch-can manner. He picked up some skills by discussing his trial-and-error activities with his friends, some from consultants, or wherever he could. Most of them came from other blacks, but Jack tells us that at least one piece of management data came from a white manager, and it was instrumental in pushing him into the next stage of development. It became a turning point because he was forced to recognize that both he and the organization had a responsibility for his attainment of success.

At some time in the Adjusting Phase, black managers learn the organization is not going to take any chances on them. Better jobs and more responsibility will not come until they have proved their competence in the job. This is not true for white peers. They will be given jobs and responsibility on perceived potential. Jack tells us proving your competence once is not enough for blacks. Your track record will not hold, so you must prove yourself over and over with each new responsibility.

Again, this is a very common experience for blacks. Today, they still have to disprove the "inferior black" concept of the dominant culture. This is a reality for blacks, whether it upsets people to hear it or not. Black professionals need to be aware of and understand this reality and plan for its occurrence because this, too, is a source of great frustration and anger. When blacks enter a white organization that operates under the rules and norms of the white culture, the majority of the whites will automatically assume that the blacks are not competent. Therefore, whites will overquestion, overtest, and withhold needed strokes from blacks.

Blacks are further frustrated, as Jack was, at finding in the Adjusting Phase that they are evaluated first on style, where as their white peers are evaluated first on task performance. Again, this relates to the assumptions of the dominant culture, one of which is that blacks do not know how to act. The trap for blacks in the Adjusting Phase is that they usually display behavior that confirms what the whites thought in the first place. Although this is a danger for blacks, they must go through it to reach success because the Adjusting Phase cannot be circumvented.

Jack also spoke of the younger blacks who get trapped into believing that a successful black is one who can become "just a manager"—that is, a *colorless* manager. The trap here for blacks is that a manager is one who directs people—*all* people—to attain organizational goals. An organization has fewer expectations of its white managers with regard to their knowing how to manage diverse groups and is to some extent both insensitive to and forgiving of its white managers' mismanagement of minorities. In contrast, the organization does expect its black managers to be more senstivie to and more able to manage diverse groups, even without training them to do so. Unfairly, black managers are eventually punished for their lack of understanding of how to manage their diverse work force.

When black managers seek to become one of a colorless group, they also render themselves invisible in the organization. Behind the closed doors of upper management, invisible and colorless black managers get overlooked and their abilities questioned by the decision makers when they discuss managers for promotion and increased responsibility. Attention is paid to those white managers who distinguish themselves from the pack, and colorless black managers fade into the background.

Occasionally, whitelike black managers will be mentored by upper-level white managers—with or without the knowledge of the black managers—and will achieve some degree of success. This encourages the notion that "colorless" blacks—i.e., those who act white in the organization—are what is sought, valued, and rewarded. The bitter truth is that at higher levels in organizations, expectations regarding performance change, and blacks are expected to share their ethnic creative energy with the organization. Unfortunately, many black managers lose their creative energy in the effort to give the organization what they think it wants from them.

As we have said repeatedly, the Adjusting Phase is a time for testing the environment to determine the limitations on personal behavior. After this has been done, the black manager is prepared to accept the planned, structured behavior required in the Planned Growth Phase.

How-To Solutions and Basic Concepts

The following solutions cannot help you skip your adjusting period but certainly can help you alleviate some of the sting or prevent some of your trial-and-error mistakes and embarrassment. If you are a fast learner, perhaps the how-to solutions can help shorten your period of adjusting. Again, we are faced with the dilemma of having more problems to deal with than space to write about them. Therefore, we have chosen the ones we feel are key to the interest of most minorities in surviving the adjusting phase.

Problem I

How to successfully bring various problems to your boss for improved organizational success.

Solution 1. A key to this solution is to hook your boss's interest around organizational issues. Go to your boss and lay out the organizational issue, *not* the problem. Now connect the issue to the high-priority work items or the organization's goals. For example, John had to get some people to do a job for him, and they would not do it. Let us say that John's people had to get him information to help develop a means to reduce operating costs. John could have gone to the boss and stated, "As you know, one high-priority organizational item we have is reducing operating costs." Then the boss would have said, "Yes, that's right." John could then have replied, "Well, I have a problem that relates to that," and stopped talking. The boss would have said, "Well, what's the problem?" At this point, the boss would have been hooked!

The second key to this solution is to stop talking and let the white boss ask you questions about the problem instead of doing all the talking yourself. It is a simple, three-step process:

1. State that the problem you are having is connected to an important or high-priority organizational issue or goal such as the organization's bottom-line profits or service. This establishes the importance of your problem and reduces the risk of your continuing to talk without getting your desired response.
2. Now stop talking and wait for your boss to ask you to state the problem.
3. As you state the problem, present it in terms of an opportunity for improvement in the work results from your organization.

Solution 2. This is a variation of solution 1. If your organization has not set clear goals and priorities for the major work tasks, you may have to do it for yourself. Make a list of about five to seven items. Sit down with your boss and tell him or her, "I have developed a list of our high-priority organizational work items as I see them. Please take a look to see if we agree on the list." After you both agree, use this list to bring up work issues by explaining problems to your boss relative to the agreed-upon list. Then proceed as in solution 1.

As an example, let us look at John again. John's people did not follow through on getting the cost-reduction information he needed. If John had had his high-priority work list, he could have gone to his boss and stated, "I'm in charge of these people and the project. It is important that we complete this project on time and at cost or under." The boss would have agreed. Then John could have responded with, "I'm having some difficulty, and I need your assistance." Then he could have stopped talking, and the boss would have *asked*, "What's wrong?" John could have stated the group's reluctance to do their tasks—you *need not discuss race*—and then John could have stopped talking again. The boss would have *asked*, "What happened?" Now John could have presented what had occurred. It would have been appropriate to look at solutions after this, not before. John could have asked his boss to meet with the group or to produce a letter; or he could have gone back and told the group he had met with the boss and discussed their problems.

Solution 3. What if your problem is not associated with a high-priority issue? Use the same general method.

Go to your boss and say, "I need your help on a problem." Stop talking and wait for your boss's question. When you are asked about the problem, lay it out. If the boss attempts to convince you that your problem is *not* a problem, then begin to express your anger, which is near the surface in the Adjusting Phase. Say, "It is a problem for *me!*" Now slowly escalate the emotion. At some point, the boss will have to concede it is a problem for *you*. Do not be afraid of using your anger occasionally in the Adjusting Phase. It is a part of the learning and developing process.

Concepts

Concept 1: Hooking Interest. Before you bring a problem to your white boss, first plan to hook his or her interest. You can do this by relating your problem to an important organizational issue or objective or a personal objective of the boss. This approach is important and works because the boss is there to solve hot organizational issues or to meet organizational goals. Also, the boss needs to know immediately that the problem you are raising is important.

Concept 2: State and wait. One way for a black manager to ensure a successful interaction with a white boss, regardless of whether that boss exhibits racist behavior or not, is to make a statement and then stop talking. The statement should be designed to elicit a question from the boss. This approach works especially well if the statement relates to an issue of concern to the boss.

This technique works because whites tend to listen to blacks better when the whites are asking questions than when the blacks are giving a lot of information. When blacks give a lot of information, sometimes whites discount it. This is particularly true if the information is something they do not want to deal with or hear. They can tune out the black who is giving all the data unless they are asking questions and are actively involved in the interaction or feel a personal stake in it.

Problem II

How to get the most from meetings with your boss.

Solution

You should have regularly scheduled meetings with your boss. If you are in the Adjusting Phase, we suggest that these meetings occur weekly and last one and one-half hours. Bear in mind, even if these meetings are in your boss's office, they are still—in part—your meetings. Meetings with your boss provide you with an opportunity to update him or her on your current projects. You may discuss any problems you are having and also use some of the time for growth and development purposes. It can be a planning and organizing session to allow you to make use of your boss's expertise. Remember, no matter how incompetent your boss may appear to be, he or she does have some expertise that you should use.

One way to successfully manage the meetings so you get what you want and still leave room for your boss to get what he or she wants is to go in with an agenda. We propose that you use the format shown in Figure 3-1.[1]

In Figure 3-1, notice that there are three categories. This forces you and your boss to use structured behavior. Everything you discuss should fall under these categories. List the topics you want to discuss under each of the categories in outline form. You may include additional detailed information, such as drawings, an expansion of your outline, or references.

Item I on the agenda, "Information Exchange," should include the topics about which you have information to give to your boss. Your boss needs only to ask questions about the subject for clarification or understanding. All you want at this point is to share information, not solve a problem.

Under item II, "Consultant and Resource," list topics about which you want your boss to share information and experience. This will indicate to your boss that you want information that will help in solving a problem or accomplishing a task. In other words, you are using your boss as a consultant and a resource. Therefore, your boss will be positioned to give you advice.

1. This agenda format was shared with Floyd by Eugene Weinshenker, an engineering manager at Procter & Gamble Company in Cincinnati, Ohio.

Figure 3-1. Suggested basic agenda format.

Agenda

Date _____

Meeting Time _____

I.   Information Exchange

II. Consultant and Resource

III. Decision and Agreement

Under item III, "Decision and Agreement," write down topics on which you need to make a decision or get closure. Also write down topics on which you need your boss's agreement. This will place your boss in a position to make a decision, help you make a decision, or agree with a plan you have outlined.

For the more "hearty" or higher-risk-taking manager, we suggest that you use the advanced agenda format shown in Figure 3-2. It is important each time you meet with your boss to take the opportunity to discuss what you are doing, what the results are, and what you hope they will be. Use your boss as a resource. Get any decisions made, if needed, and come away with action steps! Make sure these are *action*-oriented meetings as opposed to *reporting* meetings. Listing your present major activities gives your boss an opportunity to make sure your priorities are correct from the boss's perspective. This also gives the boss an opportunity to review your workload to see whether your projects are realistically staffed. You need to talk about problems, issues, and concerns you are encountering because if you do not bring these up, then your peers and the people with whom you work will. Your boss will want to know why you did not share the problems. It will then seem as if you are not on top of things. Many of the problems and concerns will be those over which you have no direct control, so do not be concerned about being viewed as incapable of handling things. Many problems will be attributable to what someone else did or did not do.

Make sure your boss is aware of what you are planning to do next. You may need his or her support. Update your boss on various projects. This needs to be handled as a separate agenda item so your boss will know he or she is merely to listen and ask questions only for understanding.

Under the "Consultant and Resource" agenda item, your boss will know you are asking him or her to share experience and knowledge and to problem-solve with you. In addition, your "Decision and Agreement" agenda items will clearly show that you want some closure on your projects and agreement on what is to be done. This leaves you with concrete action steps to take in completing work tasks.

Concept

Structuring. This is the use of an agenda to improve the odds of your having a successful outcome when interacting with your white boss. This process does just what its name implies. It structures the interaction so that it follows a predetermined course, thereby improving

Figure 3-2. Suggested advanced agenda format.

Discussion Items

Date:_____

Meeting Time:_____

I. Present Major Work Activities

II. Problems/Concerns/Issues Encountered

III. Work Items I Am Planning

IV. Information Exchange

V. Consultant and Resource

VI. Decision and Agreement

VII. Action Steps

effectiveness and efficiency. You will know you are talking about the right things and spending the appropriate amount of time discussing them. For blacks, this concept eliminates the dysfunctional pieces of the interaction that can occur between blacks and whites. When a black must meet with an upper-level manager, structuring is essential because there is an even greater need to get in, take care of business, and get out. Upper-level managers are very busy and must conserve their time.

Problem III

How to successfully interact with whites when you are angry.

Solution

The first thing you *must* do is ask yourself, "Why did I choose to get angry?" Or, "Why did I allow myself to get angry?" You must be able to answer that question before you can successfully interact with whites when you are angry; otherwise, the interaction will not be functional. No one can make us angry against our wishes.

Make a quick mental list of the things that caused you to get angry. If you are away from the interaction at the time, make a list on paper. This will help you easily visualize the issues and also give you an opportunity to dissipate some of the anger onto the paper. Push the list aside, and think about or write down what you want to get out of the interaction you are about to have.

Base whatever you do in the interaction on a need—yours, the other person's, or one you have jointly. Open the interaction by telling the white individual what you want and asking what he or she wants; that is, what is the business need? Each party must be able to state a need in acceptable organizational terms.

As much as possible, deal only with *facts* related to the issue, not with the emotions involved. Wrap the facts around the need you are trying to fulfill. This will minimize emotional outbursts. Be willing to ask questions and give explanations. Avoid blaming each other in the interaction and personalizing the issues and needs. If the interaction escalates emotionally despite your efforts, feel free to disengage. Say, "Perhaps this isn't a good time to work on this issue. Let's drop it for now and continue later."

Concept

Dealing with the need. This means when you are angry and emotionally upset and you know you are going to have difficulty interacting with a white person, you will need to approach the situation from a factual standpoint. Dealing only with the facts will help eliminate emotionality from the interaction. You can place the interaction on a logical, intellectual level, which means you must be clear about the business need involved. Stick to that business need as much as possible by dealing with facts.

Problem IV

How to sell ideas to your boss.

Solution

Blacks will encounter varying degrees of prejudiced attitudes against them, so this process is important in general. It can eliminate the need to ascertain how open your boss is to your input. Whatever the boss's attitudes, you are more likely to sell your ideas using this method.

As soon as you get an idea and are comfortable with suggesting it to your boss, you need to solicit input from others. They can help you fill in any gaps you may have overlooked. Here are the important steps for doing this:

1. Write down your idea and add major proposed actions with reasonable dates for their accomplishment. Writing your idea down makes it concrete instead of illusive or subject to inappropriate modification and forgetfulness on your part. When writing your idea or goal, use *action words* and give a reason for its implementation. For instance: "I want *to meet once a week* with all my project people so we may *better coordinate* our collective efforts in completing our various tasks. In this way, *each person will better understand* how his or her piece contributes to the whole."

2. Connect your idea to the organization's bottom-line results or goals. Remember, organizations are places where you can accomplish your personal career goals as long as they fall under the umbrella of the organization's goals. This is legitimate business and is how leaders operate. If your goal is connected to your organization's bottom-line results, it will have a better chance of being implemented. If your organization's goals are not written or are not clear, talk to your boss or your boss's boss to learn the major goals. Then connect your idea or

plan to them. Remember, keep your plan or idea within reasonable organizational economic guidelines.

3. Identify your adversaries, supporters, and resources. Be clear about whom you can trust. Use your resources to help refine your idea. They may not publicly support you but will share technical skills or knowledge and/or experience. You need to think about what objections your influential adversaries will have. You can then plan ways to nullify their objections and concerns. Consider getting your adversaries to provide input for your idea. This can turn an adversary into a supporter. If you are not clear about whom your adversaries or supporters are, offer ways in which your ideas may be enhanced by others and watch how individuals respond. Count on your supporters to share experiences and suggestions. Getting input from your supporters allows them to "buy into" your idea, thereby adding more vigor to their support of you.

4. Bounce your idea off peer resources and supporters with different specialties or backgrounds. Avoid the "groupthink" situation. Allow your idea to be examined by others with different perspectives and experiences. Go a step further and test your idea or plan by sharing it with someone you know will be critical. He or she will find the flaws and provide you with the opportunity to "plug up the holes." These resources and supporters may provide additions that can improve your plan or idea or point out whatever negative consequences may be inherent in parts of it. Do not become defensive. Subjecting your idea or plan to review by these resources can only improve it.

5. Develop a rough plan of action to implement your idea. Refine and modify your original plan of major proposed actions based on input from others. Fight the urge to retain sole ownership of the idea. Always leave room for input from your boss and be willing to share ownership with him or her. In this instance, perfection can invite criticism. Your plan needs to be specific enough to indicate the major blocks of effort to be expended. Do not detail your idea to such a degree that your boss becomes bogged down in how you are going to execute it. In your rough plan, do include approximate dollar figures and human resources requirements.

6. Share your idea and plan of action with a senior-management supporter or sponsor. This will arm him or her with sufficient information to publicly support you. Remember, upper-level managers talk among themselves. If your idea is a good one, word will get around, and it will be easier to implement it.

Try to view the situation through your boss's eyes. Guess at how he or she may react to your idea based on the kind of relationship you have with the boss. (You may want to review the solution to problem X in Chapter 2, "Entry Phase," for the exercise on imagining being the other person.) Select a time when your boss is at ease and not agitated or under pressure. Hook the boss's interest by connecting your idea to high-priority organizational issues or work tasks. (See the solutions to problem I in this chapter.)

Tell your boss you have bounced the idea off others and have solicited their input. If your boss tends to exhibit racist behavior, this approach is particularly effective because it will minimize the consequences of your boss's negative attitude toward you and your idea. Your boss will be able to say, "Oh, it's not *all* your idea; others had input." Do not worry, you will get credit for it, because your boss will have to admit you developed the idea.

Expose the facts and share your thinking about the idea. Focus the conversation on the idea and not on yourself by minimizing any personal references, such as "I," "my," or "me." If your boss tends to exhibit racist behavior, such references will have a negative impact and can easily be interpreted as bragging, and you will be negatively evaluated.

Assume your boss will accept your idea. Then analyze the risk. Is it high or low? (See problem I, solution 1, in Chapter 2, "Entry Phase.")

There may be things you did not think about. Relax and be prepared to compromise when necessary—the idea is still yours. Compromising is often a problem for blacks in the Adjusting Phase. They tend to think that an idea should be all theirs without change. When a compromise is made, they fear that the idea will be credited to someone else.

Be confident that your idea will work and be patient, but not too patient. If your plan is innovative to your organization, understand that more than the normal selling job will be required. If may be difficult to bring some people on board because something different from standard operating procedures is required. Many individuals are extremely reluctant to change what they find most comfortable. However, how can you tell when you are being too patient? You have reached that point when things start to "bog down" and you stop moving ahead toward the realization of your idea. Now you need to "stoke the fires" by pushing harder.

Be careful of being dysfunctional, though. You must not operate too far outside the normal behavioral parameters in your organization. It is occasionally appropriate to step outside those parameters, but not on a regular basis. If this occurs frequently, your people will view you as being dysfunctional and will shut you out of important events. Sometimes, they will do this even if your idea will save money.

Develop a success-oriented, can-do attitude by being persistent. If you are convinced your plan should be implemented, be aggressive, and do not let anyone stop you or turn you away from your course of action. You may have to take time to *convince* people of the importance of a new and innovative idea.

It may be helpful to assemble an "informal team" to help develop your plan or idea, especially when you need comprehensive knowledge and skills that you personally do not possess. It is still your idea; you still have ownership of it, and you are "tapping" resources to help you further develop or sell the plan. We say "informal team" because organizations will allow you to use people from other departments on an informal basis to help you develop your ideas. You do not have to pay for their time and services as long as you do not require an abundance of their time. Many blacks are never told that this is an organizational norm. Keep this thought with you always: *The smartest person is not the one who has all the information. The smartest person is the one who knows where to get the information when it is needed.*

Use a shared-risk approach; do not take all the risks alone. Get people who are interested in your project or idea to join you. Have them assume some of the risks. If there are some aspects of your project that are not adequately defined, then allow other people to refine those aspects. Sometimes, it is helpful to let others help reduce risks. For instance, if you take five people who have worked on different aspects of your project into a presentation meeting with your boss, then you have a greater chance of getting your project through the system. Plus, you have shared the project risk as well as reduced your personal risk.

Now that you have sold your idea, plan, or project, continue to refine it. Line up your resources to help implement your plan and make appropriate corrections as necessary.

Concept

Compromising. This concept is extremely important to blacks. If your boss is the kind of person who is threatened, intimidated, or made uneasy by blacks or exhibits racist behavior toward them, you may leave yourself open for automatic rejection of an idea. If you attempt to sell an idea to your boss and the boss senses that it is solely your idea, he or she may try to pick holes in it or evaluate it negatively. White bosses of blacks are more likely to accept an idea if they can add to it. You need to become comfortable with and accept this, because the idea will still be credited to you. Once you can accept the boss's addition, the boss will accept your idea. Some people, for whatever reasons, feel they must contribute to any idea formulated by a subordinate, and this is especially true in the case of a black subordinate. Do not make an issue of it. It is usually not worth it.

Problem V

How to get cooperation from others.

Solution

The first thing to consider in getting people to cooperate with you is to connect their cooperation and the task to a business need. Sometimes, you may be able to connect the cooperation of others to their self-interest. Plan their cooperation by scheduling the various tasks associated with whatever you are trying to do. Your schedule should show what is to be done, by whom, and when. The *how* is best left up to the individual worker. Document the schedule and send copies to the people involved and their bosses. You should set up milestones and check back with people to see whether they are on schedule in accomplishing their tasks. It is also very important to show who will get the results of the task. This will allow you to delegate responsibilities to others even though they do not work directly for you. Figure 3-3 shows a simple way of making your schedule.

It is important to document the tasks so everyone will have the same information regarding who is responsible for what and by when. This documentation makes everything public and legitimizes agreements. It considerably increases the odds that the tasks will be accomplished on time, because no one wants to be seen as the one who dropped the ball. It gives you a way of going back and checking with people before the deadline to make sure they are on track in completing their tasks. If they are not, you then have the opportunity to help work out any problems they may have. If they become hostile with you, the documentation legitimizes your going to their boss. This method increases your span of managerial control over people who will attempt to resist cooperating with you.

Figure 3-3. Form for scheduling tasks.

Task (what)	Date (when)	Responsibility (who)	Give Information (to whom)
1. Prepare May forecast	4/13	Doug Fisher	Ron Schaeffer
2.			
3.			
4.			
5.			
6.			
7.			
8.			
9.			

Concept

Responsibility charting. This concept is important because it involves documenting task agreements between people. It shows what, when, and who on a document that becomes public. As a black manager, you can use responsibility charting to protect yourself and improve your effectiveness. Unfortunately, there are many instances when it becomes necessary to cover yourself because, as we stated earlier, blacks tend to be easy targets for blame when something goes amiss.

Problem VI

How to tap into the informal communications network.

Solution

Accessing the informal communications network is a touchy problem for blacks in the Adjusting Phase. They tend to exhibit hostile behavior toward whites at the smallest provocation and to be least inclined to socialize with whites during this period. However, when the need for information far outweighs the need to avoid social interaction with whites, this solution will work. The solution is broken into two broad areas: the social-related area and the work-related area.

Under the social-related area, there are several types of activities in which blacks might choose to engage to tap into the informal communications network. One is sports; you may join some existing company team—bowling, baseball, basketball—or you may engage in a one-on-one sport, such as tennis or racquetball, with coworkers. Some women reading this problem solution will think that we are sexist because women may not be allowed to join "male" company sports teams. If you cannot do so, then ask men or other women to join you in other sports or activities. Racquetball, bowling, tennis, etc., are all examples. While you are having fun, you will, at some point, talk about work-related topics and therefore have an opportunity to get information otherwise not available to you. A second type of activity may be hobbies you share—model railroading, building, woodworking, hooking rugs, and so forth. You may arrange to get together to work jointly on a hobby. Or you might accept some invitations to attend parties or take advantage of an informal get-together, something as simple as helping someone with a home-repair job like painting or repairing a driveway. A great deal of business information is "dropped" at parties.

Under the work-related area, one activity would be to go on a five- or ten-minute coffee break with your white peers. Go to lunch, either on or off the premises, and have an informal conversation about work issues. Have an after-work rap session on the work premises. Go to someone's office after work, sit down, and ask how things are going. Steer the conversation to the areas you want to discuss. Perhaps *occasionally* drop by a white coworker's office during working hours for a brief chat. Be careful with this last tactic because, since you are black, people will tend to think you are wasting time socializing and not doing productive work. As a black, you will have to weigh the need to avoid whites against the need for information.

Concept

Socializing. See Chapter 2, problem XI, concept 2, for a discussion of socializing.

Problem VII

How to manage your stress (making use of cultural paranoia).

Solution

There are three main keys to dealing simply with the problem of managing your stress. The first is to discuss your stress with someone you trust and respect. Relief by ventilating can have a cleansing or unloading effect for you. Second, talk to yourself about your stress. This is very helpful. Third, understand that the phase you are in is only temporary and you will pass through it. Stress is an eliminator for minorities. If you do not learn to manage stress, you will avoid those situations that are stressful, and some of those situations may have benefits for you. You will then essentially eliminate yourself from a fast track for growth and development as well as from the mainstream movement that leads to success. Understand that you cannot eliminate all stress; you must endure some of it. The trick is to manage it. Some stress is helpful in heightening awareness, which can enable you to solve problems in a creative manner. Here is a process for managing your stress:

1. List those things that cause you stress. For example, you have to give a presentation and are anxious about it.

2. List reasons for having stress around the particular situation, such as the presentation.
3. List what you think would remove the stress. After looking at your list, you will probably discover you are being unrealistic about the situation—it's not all that bad.
4. Look carefully at the list of things you could do to remove the stress and pick several to work on. For example:

   • You have a presentation that you feel stressed about.
   • One reason for the stress is lack of stage presence or smooth delivery.
   • One way to remove some of the stress would be to look as though you have done this all your life.
   • So practice your speech before a mirror and then in front of a couple of good friends who will offer corrective feedback until you are more comfortable with it.

5. Discuss your list with one or more people you trust, whose input you value. They may have some helpful suggestions. Use them as resources.
6. Talk to yourself throughout your stressful situation. Remind yourself that cultural paranoia can be a healthy and helpful response to your environment that prepares you to handle situations creatively. Tell yourself stress heightens your awareness, which helps you prepare yourself enough to ensure success. Also, remind yourself you are probably overreacting to the situation and that all this will pass.

Concept

Listing. This is the only concept used in this solution not previously reviewed. It involves writing down those issues that are important to you so you may stand back and look at them. This process is important because it helps give you a clear understanding of what is occurring. Once you are able to get the information out of your head and onto paper, where you can look at the data in black and white, you will often find things do not look as bad as they did when you were thinking about them. Your mind tends to expand problems, whereas writing them down tends to narrow their focus. Listing is a good habit to form in problem solving. It helps to clarify things, put them in proper perspective, and record them in a form that facilitates your taking action or sharing with others to solicit their input.

Problem VIII

How to use anger as a motivator for success.

Solution

The Adjusting Phase, as we have stated repeatedly, is a period of high stress, frustration, and anger. You can learn to use a period of high stress, frustration, and anger. You can learn to use the energy associated with these emotions to your benefit instead of your detriment. Use the energy by remaining angry. It is virtually impossible not to be angry in this phase if you are black. Try practicing feeling, almost touching, the anger. *Feel* what it is doing to you; then *understand* what it is doing to you.

Now mentally brush the anger aside and focus on the energy that remains. Say to yourself, "I will use the energy that my anger has produced to change or remove the source of my anger." For example, you became angry because a peer did not do what should have been done to allow you to perform some task, and it made you look bad. Feel the anger and savor it; now push it aside. Focus your remaining energy on determining how you will *not* let that situation occur again. In essence, you will be using the energy from your anger to replace the anger with a stubborn determination to change events so that the situation will not recur.

As we have stated, blacks tend to be closer to their emotions than whites are. This also explains why blacks are apt to jump onto a problem and attack it head-on. Anger tends to drive blacks to remove the source of anger. Being aware of and appreciating this tendency can help you direct the energy specifically to the area to be changed. Awareness keeps you from inappropriately dispersing the energy in directions that are not important or where no change can be made; it also keeps you from feeling guilty about being angry. The white corporation will tend to tell you that you should not get angry. Historically, the white middle-class cultural norm has been not to get emotional or angry. Therefore, at times, we as blacks will deny our anger, which means we deny a source of our energy that can help us strike at a problem directly.

The use of anger is an *overlooked cultural skill* that blacks bring to the white organization. The skill is to be able to get angry quickly, then channel the energy from the anger into creative problem solving or into attacking the problem and forcing swift resolution. That is how you can make anger work for you.

Concepts

Concept 1: Sensing. This is a concept used to get in touch with feelings from within. In sensing, you focus intently within yourself and force the anger and other feelings to the surface of your consciousness so you are totally aware of them on a physical level. It is similar to a process used by actors before a performance. This concept is useful in preventing denial and in converting the vast amount of energy produced by recognizing and drawing upon intense feelings.

Concept 2: Converting energy. This concept is closely linked to sensing. It is particularly useful in the adjusting phase because, if you are black, you will find you are angry quite often. The energy produced by that anger can be converted into something helpful, as described in the solution to problem VIII. Converting energy can be used for any strong emotion that generates energy, not just anger, and where it may be inappropriate to openly express the emotion. The energy from excitement, for instance, may be converted into a drive to rapidly accomplish something rather than be displayed in a more direct form.

Problem IX

How to resist intimidation from whites.

Solution

Blacks and other minorities tend to be more sensitive to the moods of people in various situations; that is, they can easily read where people are and what is happening with them. When blacks are interacting with whites who are attempting to intimidate them, blacks get a visceral feeling from the interaction. Not only do blacks recognize the power of others, they can feel it. When this happens to you, say to yourself, "I am *feeling* the intimidation the other person is emitting." If you think of it in terms of a radio, the black individual is the receiver and the white individual is the transmitter. Your receiver is picking up what the other person is transmitting, and that transmission is intimidation. Now you can say, "What I feel is being picked up from the other person; it is not being generated from within me. Therefore, I am not and will not be intimidated."

It is important to be aware that the feeling is not yours. As a result, you will be less likely to accept the feeling and subsequently feel fear. Our experience has shown us that on most occasions when whites feel a need to intimidate blacks, they are motivated by feeling threatened or feeling a lack of power. The white person may feel that you are smarter, quicker, or have the ability to outthink him or her to make things happen faster. In essence, we are saying that the white person is responding to you out of a feeling of perceived, or real, lack of power relative to you in certain areas. Therefore, you can now sit back, relax, and think about an appropriate response to the intimidation without the accompanying barrier of fear, because you are really in a power position. One type of response can be a question. Use the questioning technique we discussed in Chapter 2, problem IV, solution 1, or try a thought-provoking response designed to grab the other person's attention so that he or she will stop transmitting intimidation.

It takes practice to negate intimidation. Historically, blacks have been managed through intimidation and are particularly sensitive to it. But remember *no one* can intimidate you unless you allow that person to do it. Here is a P.S.: You can *always* leave the scene of the action if real physical intimidation is involved! Then communicates with the person in writing instead of verbally.

Concept

Reading. *Reading* will be familiar to many of you. This concept is a black term given to a process we like to call "high-speed calculation of interpersonal data." It is the ability of one person to perceive information from another person by observing the nonverbal behavioral cues the other gives about himself or herself in an interaction. This process usually takes place below the level of awareness of the observer. To put it more simply, all of us tell others about our personalities and about the kinds of people we are by the way we speak and move our bodies. People who can "read" others will translate this into responsive feelings about the person they are observing. Many of us grew up hearing about how well our grandmothers, other relatives, or neighbors could read people. If you wanted to know about some stranger you met, "Go ask yo' gran'ma; she's good at readin' folks." This merely meant grand-mother was skilled in observing nonverbal behavioral cues.

Problem X

How to help reduce time spent in the Adjusting Phase.

Solution

The first thing you need to do is acknowledge that you cannot circumvent this phase. You need to say to yourself, "I will stay in this phase until I have fulfilled my need to publicly express myself emotionally and have acquired the learning I need to move into a more structured phase." Although you cannot skip this phase, there are a few ways to help shorten it.

Take a really big piece of paper—say, the size used in flip charts—and write, "I want . . ." at the top of it; then list as many things as you can think of that you want from your job, such as:

1. A promotion or increased responsibility
2. Learning opportunities
3. Etc.

Now post this on your wall at home.

At the top of another large piece of paper, write, "I can move into the Planned Growth Phase when I . . ." Below that heading, make another list. For example:

1. Become more aware of how racism is acted out
2. Learn how to manage my emotions
3. Learn more about corporate norms
4. Etc.

Each day, look at these sheets of paper and use them as reminders. If you keep a work diary of your learnings, you may prefer to enter these lists there and periodically to go over them as checklists to see where you are in terms of your growth and development.

White managers need to understand that blacks go through an adjusting period in the white organization that differs from that of their white peers. White managers can offer assistance to blacks in the Adjusting Phase by taking the time to discuss needs relative to information gathering and by assisting with difficulties. A white manager can open doors for blacks by introducing them into the informal communications network. The manager can see to it that blacks are included in work activities where corporate information is discussed.

A very important point for the white manager to remember is: Do *not* take the black manager's behavior personally and overreact to it. Instead, try to understand why black managers behave the way they do. White managers may be able to provide an additional perspective by sharing their interpretations of the behavior. By understanding the dynamics of the Adjusting Phase for blacks, white managers can take their cues from this and be creative in helping the black manager through the period.

Problem XI

How to manage the process used to evaluate you.

Solution

There are five key precepts involved in this solution:

1. Involve people other than your boss in the evaluation process.
2. Test against criteria previously established by you and your boss. These criteria are to be used by everyone who gives feedback or input.
3. Use written, not verbal, responses for input.
4. Always set up an evaluation system that gives you ongoing feedback rather than a once-a-year shocker.
5. Use "step-level counseling" with your boss's boss. That is, take the opportunity to talk to your boss's boss and take advantage of his or her experience. This is not an opportunity to tell on your boss but rather an opportunity to discuss your career development and to tap into and use the experience of your boss's boss. For example, you might ask, "What kinds of things were you concerned about when you were at my level?" And, "What did you do about them?"

Here are the how-to's connected with these precepts:

1. Very early in your job, develop criteria for evaluation. Do this with your boss and then document the criteria.
2. At evaluation time, you and your boss should select the people from whom you want to obtain feedback. These people can be

peers, subordinates, and superiors. This protects you, because you get a balanced perspective.

3. Use a standard format and ask selected individuals for written feedback.
4. The boss will collect the feedback and share the written information with you.
5. You and your boss *together* can develop a mutually agreed-upon summary signed by the two of you. This is your opportunity to discuss directly with the boss what people have said about you.
6. The signed summary will be passed along to the boss's boss for review and for a face-to-face meeting with you. This session can be used for step-level counseling.

Concepts

Concept 1: Step-level counseling. This first new concept is used by a subordinate to talk to bosses above the level of the subordinate's immediate boss in the same hierarchical chain to get the benefit of their counseling, experience, expertise, and perspective. This is extremely helpful to blacks. It also provides blacks with much-needed exposure to important others in the hierarchical chain. For those all-white organizations that are concerned about the growth and development of blacks within the company, this concept could be a valuable addition to any program that may be instituted.

Concept 2: Checks and balances. This second new concept is very helpful to blacks because more than one person is included in such processes as evaluations, feedback sessions, or whatever information sharing is done with a black by members of an organization. This concept can also be used in conjunction with other concepts, such as responsibility charting. When a black manager makes copies of a task schedule and sends them to the person responsible for the task and that person's boss, that is an example of using checks and balances in connection with responsibility charting.

Problem XII

How to set up a network for black managers.

Solutions

Solution 1. White managers in many of the organizations with which we have worked truly believe that if more than two black people meet (in offices, a conference room, or the cafeteria), they are plotting something against the organization. Blacks sense this belief or know it to be a fact, and therefore, they refrain from meeting to seek psychic support and to use resources to help resolve organizational issues.

The first step in setting up a network is to develop the "appropriate attitude." Think of the network as a vehicle to help all its members learn how to operate more effectively and increase their productivity. Wouldn't the organization value this very highly? Networking provides an opportunity to learn to increase the organization's bottom-line output through its members.

The second step is to have *one* black take the responsibility of scheduling a meeting with other blacks after work or on the weekend. Discuss why you called the meeting and what you hope to gain: exchange information, provide learning opportunities, be resources to each other, etc. Schedule one more outside meeting before you start meeting on company or organizational time and premises. When you meet during working hours and are asked by whites to explain the reason for your meeting, tell them that the purpose is to learn from each other what it takes to produce higher-quality work output at a lower cost for the organization. Who can argue with that explanation? As you continue to meet, you may want to get official organizational sanction to form a group that can bring in speakers and sponsor training sessions for black managers. This is how employee groups were formed at some large *Fortune* 500 companies.

Solution 2. Instead of initially meeting outside of the work environment, start out by meeting on company time. This can easily be done by asking others to bring their lunch and meet in your office or in a conference room. This approach speeds up the establishment of the network. If some of the black managers have attended a training event recently, you can form a network for the purpose of following up on the training event. You can expand the role of the group to meet other needs the black managers may have.

Concept

Seizing an opportunity. Every organization that we know about today is concerned with the cost of doing business. Therefore, those simple, legitimate things that can be done to improve productivity and reduce cost will be welcomed. In essence, we are suggesting that you kill two birds with one stone: Use your need to network during working time as an opportunity to save dollars for your organization.

4

Planned Growth Phase

Critical Issues

Attitudes

- The need to be a superstar becomes apparent (being prepared to expend more energy than white peers)
- Taking a serious look at personal style (removing barriers to style)
- Understanding the need to get more black input
- Willingness to use whites as resources
- Realignment of expectations and attitudes about whites

Emotions

- Acquiring a sense of determination
- Building a feeling of pride
- Using anger as a strategy instead of a pressure-release valve
- Less stress around abilities and competences

Behaviors

- Consciously acting to remove barriers under one's own control
- Using strategy more to position people and company to meet one's needs
- Seeking sponsors/mentors
- Learning to effectively use white resources
- Using protective hesitation
- Learning to make proper demands on the corporation (plotting career)
- Setting and meeting goals
- Working to develop a smoother style (experimenting)

Job Skills

- Learning and using multicultural management skills
- Making strategic use of communications network
- Seeking development opportunities
- Learning how to manage

Overview of the Critical Issues

Attitudes

By the time the black manager is well into the Planned Growth Phase of development, the need to be a superstar is very apparent. Given the same job tasks, black managers see themselves having to expend much more energy than their white peers to obtain the same results. Whether black managers will admit it openly or not, the truth of the matter is that with every job task carried out by a black individual in an interaction or transaction with a white person, there is a racial component that must be dealt with effectively if job performance is to be maximized. As black managers move into the Planned Growth Phase, they are more likely to accept this fact, stop fighting against it, plan for it, and move to manage it. The extra expenditure of energy becomes the price one pays to succeed if one is black working in a white setting:

> *"I have to spend energy doing black-white activities that whites don't have to do, but I don't get any extra reward for it."*
> *"I spend a lot of extra time fighting the effects of racism. Whites in the development mode can make mistakes, but I can't. Whites tend to believe what other whites say about blacks, so you have to work with a racist listening to a racist."*
> *"The thing that tires me out is having to overexplain why I want to do certain tasks in certain ways. I have to exert greater influence than whites around issues."*
> *"I'm always trying to find an appropriate balance between which are the important racist behavioral issues to fight and which to let go."*
> *"Sometimes, you get into situations on the job where it becomes important to expend some extra energy in identifying white peers and supervisors in terms of where their racism will hurt you or help you."*

Although black managers are no longer willing to bear the whole burden of their inability to behave in the correct corporate manner, they are willing to systematically make appropriate changes under their control. Personal operating style tends to be one of the most problematic interpersonal issues for the black manager. Successful managers will understand that they are not locked into any one kind of behavior and will seek whatever personal style best facilitates the most effective and profitable interactions with others:

> *"Overcoming my own low-key interpersonal style was a problem for me. I'm a quiet person. But I knew I'd continue to get run over if I didn't learn to speak up and be more proactive. You can say I've become quietly assertive."*
>
> *"I didn't look or act competent, and that's the way people treated me, like I was incompetent. I had to relearn how to dress and walk and carry myself."*
>
> *"I learned how to be more intellectually aggressive and less emotionally angry."*

In the Planned Growth Phase, black managers know the value of their black resources and do not hesitate to use them. They have identified the learnings reaped from other blacks' expertise and draw on them for help in a variety of areas, such as (1) developing interpersonal and behavioral strategies; (2) personal feedback; (3) understanding the effects of racism and how to use strategy to get around those types of barriers; and (4) gaining insight and developing reflective observation:

> *"I often go out of my way to find blacks who will help me with management problems. I don't do that with the technical problems because there are always plenty of whites who will help with that."*
>
> *"I was a slow learner, but I have finally turned to other blacks to get the quality help I need in coaching, strategizing, and support."*
>
> *"If you want to get the real scoop on promotional information, a black has to ask another black who has access to the data."*

Whites, in the Adjusting Phase, were to some degree, seen as "the enemy" or representatives of "the enemy." Black managers in the planned growth phase begin to replace their resentments with a more realistic acceptance of whites as generally unknowing about how blacks must deal with racism in the organization. Black managers will separate the few bigots from the rest of the whites and act accordingly. This frees black managers to use whites as resources for more than technical matters. They will learn how to manage the various interfaces more appropriately:

> "My boss and I did not have much of a relationship other than he gave me the work and I did it. I didn't have a lot of respect for him, and . . . I don't know; maybe he knew it. His peers sort of talked down to him, and he seemed not to care. Anyway, his boss was a real a _ _ h _ _ _, but you know, my boss could handle him. I just noticed that one day in a meeting. Out of the whole bunch, he was the only one who could control the guy. You know, I started asking my boss about how he did that, and he just brightened up . . . and I'm learning a lot from him."
>
> "Now that I have had some black development training, I have taken time to keep my boss informed about my work progress. As a result, I'm in a state of shock! My boss has warmed up to me, and he's taken to stopping by my office just to talk a minute and maybe joke a little. He's never done that with anybody before. He shares a lot of data with me that I'd probably never get anywhere else."

Emotions

The Planned Growth Phase is characterized by determination. It is as though blacks, facing and passing through a wall of flame, are not going to let the sight of a flaming forest stop them now. With each barrier overcome and accomplishment made, there is a growing sense of pride. Confidence in one's competence and abilities is built from practicing the newly learned behaviors and skills. Old dysfunctional behavior is discarded, and a growing repertoire of strategies is built. The anger that was so prevalent in the Adjusting Phase is now more controlled and is usually employed as a last-ditch effort when all else fails. Even then, the use of anger is generally well thought out beforehand and its consequences anticipated.

Behaviors

Now black managers consciously seek to identify the various barriers to progress and remove those within their control rather than ignoring them as in the Entry Phase or angrily complaining about them as in the Adjusting Phase:

> "I suffered too long from a lack of self-confidence. I decided it was time to stop buying into racist beliefs and recognize the effect it had on me. I sat

down and laid out some changes I would make. Things looked a lot clearer written down. After that, I wrote out a whole self-improvement plan."

"My own arrogance and denial of being black in a white environment slowed me down. I refused to see how racism blocked my progress, and I made no use of my black peers and any role models to learn about how to succeed. When I saw my black peers getting bigger jobs and more responsibility than I, I had to face myself and my denials."

"One day it hit me. I had too much emotional involvement and energy in fighting racism on my job. I had to pull myself together. I started allowing business relationships with whites to help me."

"I wasn't proactive enough. So I adopted this rule for myself: 'If you don't make things happen for yourself, you'll be a long time succeeding, if ever.' "

The realization of the need for strategy in order to both survive and succeed in the corporation is very apparent in many of the statements made by black managers throughout the different phases of development. We consider strategy of such monumental importance for blacks in attaining success that it is handled as a separate topic in Part Four.

Seeking sponsors/mentors is a big step forward for blacks in the Planned Growth Phase. Sponsorship for whites in the organization is a very accepted and usually known procedure to give bright, up-and-coming young managers that extra boost they need to beat the competition in advancing. Older, more experienced managers will pick younger managers who they perceive have potential and will coach, guide, and act as advocates for their protégés. Often, a social relationship develops between them, and the young managers get special grooming for their career paths.

Rarely do black managers get picked for sponsorship; if they do, it is almost never in conjunction with a social relationship and special grooming. If a black manager has a sponsor, it is usually because that person has sought out and adopted one. The black manager must then establish a relationship with the adopted sponsor and work to, at best, develop a real alliance or, at the least, affect one.

One very big problem for blacks getting sponsored is that white managers are still often not able to recognize minority potential. Blacks tend to bear little resemblance to how the white organization thinks its managers should look and behave. Establishing a social relationship is difficult because the pressures of differing cultures, differing expectations of each other, and personal and institutional prejudices are always there to interfere. It is not impossible, but it is often difficult:

"I identified some key people in the hierarchy who are powerful and got on their good sides. I received some help—coaching—and used that to move on."

"Blacks have to get real close to a white to find out things, one who is committed to moving them on."

"I got adopted by a white manager in the hierarchy early in my job. I tried to be white and emulate the white managers, so it was easy for someone to relate to me and help me in the organization."

"I thought you'd need someone who feels he can give you a helping hand, who would reach down and pick you up. That was my first type of sponsor and that was a 'one-down' type of relationship. Since I've closed the gap between us, I've been dropped. Now I'm looking to find a sponsor type who will help me because he respects my competence and abilities."

"You have to identify someone for yourself, get established with him or her; someone who is viewed as a valuable contributor and who will go to bat for you."

Using white resources is a perplexing issue for most black managers. They are ambivalent about seeking information from whites. Black managers want to use whites as resources but are concerned about how that will be viewed. Initially, what black managers lack is an effective how-to approach to get information from whites. There tends to be a lack of trust on the part of the black individual toward the white resource and an inability to sense and properly react to racism. In the Entry Phase, some blacks are cautious about the use of whites as resources because these blacks are dealing with issues of negative self-concept. Other blacks are overly confident and use whites as resources inappropriately or not at all. In the Adjusting Phase, blacks often have too much anger to effectively use or listen to whites as resources. When a black manager does use white resources, it tends to be for technical assistance—i.e., questions about job tasks. This kind of assistance requires less trust. In the planned growth phase, blacks have learned the value of strategy and will use it to make more effective and frequent use of whites as resources for a wide variety of purposes—both technical and nontechnical.

At this juncture, we would like to reintroduce two of the concepts we defined in Part One, Chapter 1—*cultural paranoia* and *protective hesitation*. We must treat them together because they are interrelated. We think it is appropriate to redefine these concepts here because one of them is highly refined and used strategically by black managers in the Planned Growth Phase.

Cultural paranoia is a sociological and anthropological concept that refers to a protective hesitation or suspicion, a group coping mechanism that has evolved to deal with the consequences of racism. It does *not* refer to the psychological concept that implies an individual mental disorder.

Protective hesitation is the behavior associated with cultural paranoia in which blacks hesitate in order to protect themselves from possible psychological assault before interacting or preparing to interact with whites. This behavior is also used in an attempt to avoid reinforcing any negative stereotypes that whites may have about blacks.

Blacks were once taught early in life to be suspicious of whites in general. This continues to be taught in many black homes today. Historically, this was necessary for the preservation of life for blacks. Physical harm or death could come swiftly for the black person who stepped too far out of the bounds set by the dominant white society. This attitude was passed wholesale from one generation to the next until recent times. Since integration followed desegregation, many black parents do not equip their children with cultural paranoia. But cultural paranoia still exists within the general black culture because blacks, as a group, continue to be subjected to psychological and, occasionally, physical assault by the general white culture.

On an individual basis, most blacks in America sooner or later develop this attitude of cultural paranoia. For the black managers who, for various reasons, enter corporate America without this attitude, it is usually developed in the Planned Growth Phase. This hesitation blacks use when interacting with whites is an important strategy for growth. This attitude is acted out by prethinking or preplanning an idea before approaching and interacting with a white individual:

> *"Every time you use a resource, it's a risk. . . . You run the risk of being evaluated negatively. Before I use a white as a resource, I think over carefully what I'm going to say and how I'm going to say it."*
>
> *"Whites hear part of what they expect to be said and part of what is actually said by blacks; so I preplan my interaction before I speak so I can be sure to state things clearly enough to be understood correctly."*
>
> *"Before I take an idea into a meeting, I write it down and think about all the negatives—especially how people are going to react. If it's very important to me, I'll call a black friend who'll talk me through it."*

A great deal of activity in the Planned Growth Phase is directed toward career planning and setting and meeting goals. In this way, black managers are able to appropriately notify their organizations that they are ready for more responsibility and that they have career goals. Both the organization and the black manager can be clearer about their expectations of each other. (Personal and corporate planning discussed in detail in Chapters 10 and 12.)

> "I attended a seminar on career planning that my company paid for me to attend. I was very excited about it. When I returned to the job, I spent some time planning a career path for myself. I committed it to writing and had it publicized within my hierarchy."

> "I do more planning now, more discussing my career with my boss regarding the types of jobs I get."

> "First, I get the idea of what it takes to make a person promotable, then I take the information and write up a plan. I take it to my supervisor and say, 'I want these things.' We form a training program. I get input from other people about the key points of my program and how to accomplish them."

> "I've had to play catch-up. I got tired of being the underdog."

> "I've learned how to make my boss accountable for my training."

> "I see my job as a career, and I try to influence some of what happens to me."

> "I was disappointed about losing a possible position; so with the help of a black resource, I strategized, planned, and even retrained in another technology to get another management position. I now am more demanding of white supervisors, making sure they give me the right data, lay out formal criteria for getting ahead in the organization."

> "I try to be more visible in my organization. I continue to try to understand what an organization is all about. I try to find out what I'm in store for beforehand."

An important barrier black managers are forced to take a look at in the Planned Growth Phase is personal style. Blacks begin to realize that personal style impacts how whites see their job performance. Often, competence and good job results take a back seat to how blacks manage and interact in their job interfaces:

> "My arrogance held me back. My bosses wouldn't help me because I made them feel bad. I always acted like the smartest person in the room."

> "I beat up on my bosses so badly they didn't want to talk to me at all. I've had to work hard to get rid of the reputation that I'm hard to get along with."

"I've had better results in my job than my peers, but my hierarchy doesn't seem to notice. I've become an invisible man."

"Basically, I'm a quiet person. I like to do my job with as little fuss as possible, but I'm seeing that my progress is so slow because I don't speak up and fight for what I want."

Job Skills

The Adjusting Phase was a time of exploration for the black manager. The black manager learned, out of necessity to survive, many management skills somewhat different from those learned by the white manager. More correctly, we might say that some of those management skills are the same, but in practice, they contain an additional component—the skill used to neutralize the racism or sexism of others. This skill, which falls within the area of multicultural management, must be mastered by blacks in the practice of effective management. In the Planned Growth Phase, the black manager learns to become an effective multicultural manager:

"I have to use energy figuring out how to—or planning how to—communicate with my boss when I feel there is something racial in the interaction that is affecting me."

"In many cases, whites will ask for input, then go check with a white to check your data. They claim they didn't understand. You have to anticipate such behavior and put data in writing. They will pay attention and can't forget it then."

"Whites avoid telling you where they see you, so what I do is try to find out where I am by just talking instead of having regular performance reviews. I focus on positioning myself on the placement scale and giving data to help the supervisor see me."

"In meetings with whites, you are either on the offensive or the defensive. I stay on the offensive."

"In dealing with whites, you have to be always two steps ahead of their thought processes to make up for the extra stuff you have to deal with, never be thinking on the same level."

"Blacks must be friendly to whites. Whites are easily turned off by hostility or unfriendliness by blacks. Blacks have to operate more smoothly than whites in interactions."

"Whites are allowed to be dysfunctional in a behavioral sense with each other, but blacks are not allowed to be dysfunctional with whites."

"Blacks must confront a situation in a way that the white does not lose his

dignity. Whites can do that and get away with it, but a black will receive
very negative feedback."

"To keep my input from being dismissed on important issues, I preplan. I
sit down and plan out everything myself, then check it with another
black, and more if necessary, and make sure all the bases are covered.
Then I try to anticipate what all the comebacks will be from the people
I'm presenting to."

The challenge to make effective use of the communications network
continues for the black manager in the Planned Growth Phase. Blacks
must become more strategic in this area. The opportunities to network—
get data, pass information, give and receive coaching, get corporate
gossip—are less natural for blacks than for whites. Blacks have not
traditionally been part of the white communications network; therefore,
black managers must learn how to access that network for their benefit:

"Whites take care of whites; they don't worry about it. Blacks have to piece
things together, or they may have a sponsor who will share information
with them. I got a lot of information from my white supervisor, who got
it from other whites. I've been fortunate."

"Blacks are not privy to whites' mainstream informal network, which is
social, so they do not get information as fast as whites do. That always
keeps blacks in a one-down position."

"Whites don't discuss many organizational norms, criteria, etc., with
blacks. I got a lot of my data from a black who was promoted above my
level and who had access to more information. Part of his day was spent
tutoring, counseling, and developing blacks who weren't even reporting
to him."

In the Planned Growth Phase, black managers seek opportunities
for development. They are now consciously aware of how important it
is to learn how to manage effectively. The system will not reward them
without it. Even in companies where management skills are not openly
acknowledged as valuable and promotions are seen as rewards for
technical competence, blacks will be held back or punished if they do
not display effective management skills:

"When I realized how my organization viewed me as a manager, I was
mad. They said I wasn't developing my people. Hell, I was doing what
everybody else was doing. Lately, I've been doing a lot of reading, and I
think I'm going to take some management courses at night."

> *"My company is real good at providing in-house management training.*
> *But I haven't been very smart about taking advantage of it. That's going*
> *to change."*
>
> *"There's a lot of change going on in my company. My organization is*
> *cleaning up its act. We have contracted with consultants to help us*
> *become more effective managers. I'm excited about what I'm learning,*
> *and I can now see a real future for myself here."*

Now, let us continue with Jack's story.

"It Will Be a Cold Day in Hell Before They Defeat Me"

Ahhhh, that was good! OK, we'll get started again. Let me put my feet up and stretch out. Yeah, that's good! I've got to get my mind back on what I was saying.

Now, going into this next period of development was *really* exciting. It was exciting because I had an opportunity to get out of my old mode of operating. The way I had been doing things . . . uh, I guess the last period where I was trying to adjust to things was highly active, but it was also very depressing because that's when I really discovered . . . well, when I *allowed* myself to see racial reality.

It was depressing. I felt down a lot. I felt as though I was going "off," as though I was crazy. I felt nothing I did was right. I got negative input from all directions, all quarters, even though I *knew* I was making progress.

So at some point, I had to go back and recall that I had decided to stay with the company and make it, so I had to get rejuvenated. And the thing that rejuvenated me was the discovery that the harder I fought with whites, the slower I was going to progress. So I knew there must be another answer. My job now was to start out and seek and find the answer. OK?

The way I did that was to take a look at what was going on with me and set some goals and objectives. What was going on with me was that I was being asked to slay a giant with a switch or a pea shooter. That was a pretty big giant, too!

Man, what I was doing was running all over the place, being a fire fighter—consulting with groups here and there—making people feel good . . . but I wasn't accomplishing a hell of a lot in terms of moving the company ahead in the area of recruiting and good affirmative action.

This kind of thing went on until I ran into a friend of mine who had been doing some consulting on the side. He took me aside one day when I was groaning and complaining and said, "Why're you running around like a chicken with his neck wrung off when you ought to stay in your office to plan and organize your work? You'll get a heck of a lot more done." That brought me up short, and so that's exactly what I did.

So what I'm saying to you is this new phase of my development was a period in which I, uh, stopped momentarily long enough to see what was happening to me—both in terms of within myself and outside. Internally, I had very high energy because I was starting to learn how to use strategy and how to manage my emotions. I really was just wrapped up in my job, because I really wanted to make it go well.

So I was running around like a chicken with its neck wrung off, and when this black friend said this to me—it kinda hit me between the eyes, and I really *did* slow down. I slowed down and thought about what the devil I wanted. And there were about three or four major goals that I wanted. One was to develop a smoother style of interacting; two was to plan and organize my work; and three was to change the organization. So that's what I set out to do!

And to do that, I decided that probably what I needed to do was to get the heck away from the work environment and go to some management training function—to really try and see how I fit. How did I fit in relative to other people?

Where did I stand relative to people from other companies? Was I being crazy because I was only looking at my company? I was looking at myself only in the context of my company.

The first session I attended was in another state and was an eye-opener. Most of the people there were high-level whites. No blacks other than me were there—and one woman, a white female. We had two work groups. Both minorities were in the same group, and from the first day I arrived there, I intuitively knew what had happened.

See, before I went to the session, on one hand I felt like, "Crap! I'm really making progress!" On the other hand, I'm getting steadily beat up by whites. So I went to this session, and after the first day, I said to myself, "Damn! I'm a whole lot further along than I thought I was." And what was happening is the whites at work had started to see me make movement, got threatened, and gave me even more negative feedback.

Then I went with these strangers, who had never even seen me before; they just heaped strokes on me like, "Damn! Where did you learn to do that?" So what I discovered was—Shoot! I've got some sharp skills here that I, uh, I didn't even know I had. That was very helpful to me; so that was helping me take care of my first objective, which was to develop a smoother operating style.

And I worked hard in those workshops. Just testing and trying new behaviors, which I could easily do because I was away from my work environment. I think it's damn important for minorities—women, blacks, and so forth—to go to sessions like that away from the company environment because you'll get more accurate feedback. It will be more realistic.

So each time I'd come back from one of those training sessions, I'd be in good shape. 'Cause I'd just . . . I felt stronger; I felt enthusiastic. I would be really ready to attack my job . . . and just . . . I was *determined* to have a smoother style!

Each time I got back, people would see an increasingly obvious air of confidence about me. But after about a week, the same crap would start again—in other words, giving me negative feedback! But now, it didn't take. I got to the point where I'd question the feedback. I got sick and tired of people telling me I wasn't any good, when I knew I was taking care of business!

So when I'd get a negative piece of feedback, either from—well—anybody, I'd quiz them about it. When I got some from my boss, I'd quiz him about it, too. He'd get mad about that! So what I would say is, "Look, when you get feedback on blacks, you've got to probe it to weed out the racist pieces."

So even though I was in a relatively calmer phase, my boss expected me to fight with him like I did before—but I wouldn't do it!

I fought differently now!

I now fought strategically instead of being totally emotional and open all the time.

So one thing I told my boss I was going to do—because the workshops had helped me wrap my mind around the fact that I did need to get organized—so I told him, "Look, I'm going to stop fighting fires. I'm going to plan and organize my work. I'm going to become a fire marshal and prevent fires instead of being a fire fighter."

I pulled together a budget for my office and a plan for my personnel responsibilities.

The budget was fairly easy to sell because of some outstanding results we'd been getting, but it was harder to sell the new plan, which included some different management programs. But I did sell it to my hierarchy after some heated discussions.

We kicked the training programs off. I brought in some outside people to work with us. And with the first session . . . all hell broke loose!

And really! I had cleaned my desk out, because I was ready to go! I *knew* I was going to get fired!

Because about three of the upper-level white managers in that session complained bitterly, and what happened was . . . uh, was there . . . we had tapped into their racial attitudes in the session. And they, uh . . . they angrily reacted to it.

What we had to do was meet with them separately and calm them down. I did it—and here I was, at the lowest level in a room with three upper-level managers—but I was *dealing hard*, because I was *determined* that I'd just be damned if they were going to shut down this good thing we'd started.

We finally got permission to go ahead and do another session. Now, the second one came out better because the . . . I got together first with my outside people, and we strategized this one better, did some new things like changed the . . . the sequence of events slightly so we'd take responsibility off us and put it onto the participants, where it really belonged. We made the highest-ranking manager responsible for the goals and objectives for each session—and it worked beautifully. Now, that was being appropriately strategic! OK?

Throughout this time period, I began to feel better and better about myself, took pride in what I was doing . . . and I started to get respect from people, especially from whites.

And that happened because I was less harsh with whites. I still confronted them and pushed them, but I did it in a way they could handle. I stopped stripping them of their dignity, the way I used to do.

I was really excited these days and felt better about a lot of things. I could see myself making movement, smoothing and ironing out things—planning and organizing and filling in gaps. I felt like I had faced the giant and tied his hands . . . tied them by strategy, planning, and organizing.

The next step was to trip the giant and get him off his feet. The way I did that was to publish a report of the activities, findings, and results of the personnel office relative to our recruiting efforts, training procedures, and the new management programs I had instituted. I gave background information, analysis of where we were and what we needed to do, and then a broad conceptual plan.

When I presented this to my boss, he thought it was great—but he was a new boss and hadn't read the organizational norms and cues yet. But his boss just blew up!

He said, "What do you mean doing this? We didn't tell you to do this!" In other words, one norm I had violated was that I wouldn't shut up and draw—or . . . I didn't—I didn't only do what I was told to do. I was learning how to be a manager, and this really threatened some people. I was taking more initiative and being creative. Yes, I was making some decisions on my own because of outside feedback. It was more realistic than the inside feedback.

Well, the report was approved, and I got what I wanted. Oh no! I didn't get everything, but I did get a lot more responsibility—a new position and a subordinate—and a whole new ball game.

Man, oh man! Now the giant's hands were tied; we tripped him, and we were on the verge of getting him under control. OK?

What I continued to do was to refine my personal style so I could be even smoother, learn how to be an even better manager, learn how to delegate things . . . uh, how to keep people informed, and uh . . . just how to generally operate more smoothly. I looked around and identified a new concept.

It was the concept of how to deal with hot issues. I mean, find things that were important to the company and that people were having trouble doing—and jump dead on them. I handled a couple of these. I found out *that* was important for me as a black to do. It made me visible and positioned the company to take more notice of my skills.

Exactly how did I operate differently? OK. For instance, if I were in a meeting with a white individual and I said something that elicited an arrogant, nasty, or inappropriate response from the white person—well, instead of jumping back at the white individual like I used to, instead I would calm down, sit back, and cross my legs . . . relax and look at the person and say, "I really don't understand your comment. Can you help me understand it?"

In other words, instead of jumping on people and deluging them by preaching, I would take their logic and use their data and dissect it, bit by bit, so they could see what they had said to me. Half the time they'd end up saying, "Oh, I didn't realize I had said that."

People will accept that kind of interaction much more than they will accept a black manager jumping on them if they're white.

OK, another thing I discovered was that some white managers were uncomfortable around black managers—especially if the black manager could speak up and talk back and, uh, show signs of really being able to outthink some of the whites. So I found that before I went into a meeting with a white and started working business things I had to put the white individual at ease.

I'd talk about baseball, mowing the lawn, or uh . . . I'd spend five minutes or so just shooting the bull. OK? Then I'd wrap the conversation . . . or initiate the conversation by wrapping it around a business need. I had learned that when you do that you can neutralize an interaction by sticking strictly to, uh, the business needs.

See, whites tended to operate with blacks by personalizing things—by giving personal feedback or feedback about their personal behavioral style. If I got to a point where a white would start to do that, I would really take the white's information. I didn't get *defensive*, I'd get *offensive*!

For example, my boss once said to me, uh . . . he said that he'd gotten feedback from a manager that said, uh . . . how did he put it? He said I was difficult to . . . uh, interact with. Oh yeah, that's it.

I asked my boss if he had explored the information and what the feedback meant. He said no. So I said, "Well, don't you think you need to go back and find out exactly what was meant? Otherwise, it's possible that you have become a messenger—carrying inappropriate racist messages."

What? Oh, yeah, he understood what I was saying. So then he went back and talked to the individual. He discovered that the white manager had given him negative information about me becasue the white individual had discovered that, uh . . . on a particular issue, I had the ability to outthink him—probe, find out, and uncover flaws in his thinking.

Again, even on one to one, I tried to use the other person's information and put that in front of him instead of using a "give-the-black-the mike" technique—which is talk a whole lot in the hope that along the way, you'll convince a white individual of something. What that tends to do is further alienate the white, and it gives him more information to use to beat up on you.

Let's see. Oh! We're rolling along. I was given this new position—subordinates, learned how to manage them. Uhh . . . I immediately became aware that a lot of managers did the daily work tasks, performed maintenance functions, but didn't do any development of their people. So! I developed my people, in a creative manner, and I—Oh! Wait a minute! I forgot to tell you about this. It's an important piece to my development.

Before I got my new position in the personnel department—now realize, I didn't really know what I was doing at the time—but I went out and acquired three white sponsors. I figured I needed that many to institute my plans, and I inadvertently did it by asking three people if I could—upper-level managers—if I could meet with them and learn some management techniques, things like budgets, how to delegate, managing various situations. And as a result of doing that, I ended up with three sponsors. And they came in handy for me.

How did I do that? Aha! First of all, they were identified as resources in one of the training sessions for the new hires. They had expressed interest in the newly proposed affirmative action plans and wanted to help blacks. So I took advantage of that. I seized an opportunity!

I remembered what they said, and looking at my goals and objectives, I made a list of the things I needed and wanted to do better. Then I looked around at the upper-level white managers, and I said, "Who does this well?" and I put some names beside my list.

Then I picked up the phone and called those people and said, "Look, you said you wanted to help blacks; I need some help in this area, and I really think you're an excellent resource in that area."

And they were just flabbergasted! They just . . . awwww man, they just jumped at the opportunity, even though they were three or four levels above me. Other blacks didn't try that—if they had, then I guess they would have gotten the same response.

Man, it got to the point where I had set up a situation whereby, if an upper-level manager wasn't talking directly to a black, he went out and found a black to talk to because he figured that was the thing to do! It was also rewarding and fulfilling. So I inadvertently started a trend, but at the same time, I learned a *tremendous* amount of information . . . and it really paid off in terms of helping me do a better job.

Another thing I learned going to those training and management sessions was that you can unlearn negative behavior—or replace it very quickly with positive behavior—if you use behavioral change. All that means is be aware of and understand what the negative behavior is, the effect it has on people, and what you should replace it with. OK?

Now! What I did was, I looked around and found some white managers with . . . with a very smooth style in an area that I wanted to develop, such as delegating, for example, or such as, uh . . . managing subordinates—and I learned to pattern myself after them in terms of their behavior in managing.

And you know? This is a critical issue with blacks, because you have to separate that from becoming white. I did not use their specific speech patterns. I did not throw away my blackness. What I *did* do was duplicate the process they used to manage certain things. And being around upper-level managers, I was able to identify their positive behavior and duplicate it. Now, that's one way a black can change very quickly.

The other issue I had to face was how do you separate . . . how do you interact with racists—understand and realize they are racist, but separate some of the good skills and techniques they use? Now I was able to learn how to do that in this part of my development.

For example, this one individual, well, displayed obvious negatively prejudiced behavior toward blacks. He took pride in trying to outmaneuver blacks. But I was able to spot some positive skills in that person and duplicate them, even though this individual kept trying to keep me in a slave-master context—like trying to position me to have to humbly ask for everything I received from him. Oh yes! I always managed to maneuver around him instead.

A lot of people were amazed at how fast I was learning, including me. It was as though I had discovered some keys to learning. I've read a lot of behavioral stuff, so let me see if I can articulate what it was.

Let's see, it was like . . . like the keys were behavior modification—uh, behavior duplication—and getting information from outside the existing organization. And the remarks I received were that I was on an upward vector and people couldn't understand how I could change so fast and so much.

I'll tell you something else I did, too. As a result of my inappropriate behavior and a remark to an upper-level manager in a meeting and the subsequent negative feedback—then followed by a training session with some of those same managers— well, I tell you . . . I got all kinds of input about some things I should do. And, uh, it came so fast, I . . . I decided after that high-level meeting and the training session to sit down and write up what I remembered from the comments and put a date on it.

When I did that, I discovered, "Wait a minute! If I do this from now on, I'll have a wealth of knowledge in my own handwriting, dated, and I can tell who I got the information from." So I started a personal development file, which has been *invaluable* because I can periodically go back and read through it and it'll refresh my memory on certain things.

Now! Man, I'm really growing fast and just getting into it—and just lovin' it because I'm feeling, uh . . . I've got a sense of pride—uh, now using my anger as a strategy. People can see I'm making progress—but!

There was a negative side! And the negative side was, for those whites who used to have you under their wing, some of them retracted the wing! For now, I—

and they—found I was able to do some things they couldn't do. And this is very threatening to some people, especially being in levels above me.

Sure—you're darned right! I was doing a lot of things differently. When I had an idea, I would document it and go in and discuss it with my boss. I'd take it in early, before I had put details around it, and that way my white boss could feel a part of making the idea come to fruition—but I'd still get credit for the idea. I would help make both of us feel more like we were working as a team and not as competitors.

Here's another important piece for a black to learn. When you're in an interaction—especially with a white individual—there're two things going on: the content of what you're discussing and then the process of the discussion. That is, who says what to whom—body movements, reactions, and things like that.

So for a black, the process of an interaction is just as important as the content—and in some cases, maybe more important because it allows us to utilize our skill to read situations; with some of us, I think it's an inherent cultural skill.

But there're also a lot of good books out on the subject of watching the physical dynamics in interactions. Most of them are written only with whites in mind—but with a little translating and a little adding to, you can learn a lot.

In this phase of development, I used my readin' cues skills to their maximum. In essence, as they say, I'd learned how to snatch victory from the jaws of defeat. Now, you want to know what that means. For example, if I received some negative input from a white on an interaction—in one case I was told I was formal—and after digging into it, I discovered that I was very organized, not formal. I went in with an agenda, had my plan clearly laid out, and uh . . . when I discussed it with the person, he said, "Well, that's . . . well, that's not . . . I see what you mean. That's not formal; that's organized. But it's too structured." Then I asked the person, "Did I ever come in here with an agenda that you had a problem with? Did I ever refuse to listen to you or change the agenda?"

"Well, no you didn't, because you were flexible." That's the purpose of an agenda: to reflect what one person wants, and if that's not what the other person wants, then collaborate, compromise, modify, and change the damn thing. Anyway, that person had to withdraw his complaint.

Another big problem I had during this period was the standoffish reaction I got from whites because I was learning so fast. I had become smoother in conducting meetings; the way I did it was threatening to some people.

When I got negative feedback, I now had the ability to dig into it, dissect it, and make people own some of their own stuff. And I'm not saying all of the feedback was wrong! Some of it was right on and very helpful. I don't want to give you the wrong impression—I wasn't doing everything right!

When blacks take charge of meetings with whites, you always run the risk that someone is going to try to take leadership from you. So what blacks—and I—will usually do at first is to hold on to the leadership . . . overcontrol the participants. But when you get smoother, you can relax, allow people to take control and, when it's appropriate, take it back—but smoothly. You can do it by being the person who writes on the board, or who runs the agenda.

What did all this do to me? I'll tell you. I moved so fast, gained so much managerial skill and knowledge, that at times I'd go into a situation and be overstressed. My self-concept, or what I thought I could take care of or handle, had not caught up with my skill attainment. I was capable of doing more than I thought or believed I could do.

So sometimes when I'd go into a meeting, my stress would show—the white individuals would pick up that stress from me without knowing it, and we'd end up fighting when there was no need to fight. I had to learn to relax and trust my black intellect.

Aha! That's what it is! That's what has been pulling at the back of my mind— *black intellect!* This is the period when a . . . a black individual will start to develop a high level of trust in black intellect.

Now what is that? Black intellect means that, uh . . . as a result of slavery, the words *black* and *intellect* are antithetical in this country. Man, I mean for blacks and whites! For some people, black intellect doesn't even exist as a concept!

Man, I'm smiling because of the feelings involved here. When you discover that you *do* have intellect—that you can strategize, that you can adroitly handle a situation, that you can be extremely logical—conceptualize in every sense of the word that you *thought* all whites could—

Oh man, I don't mean just in your head. You might have been saying that for years. But did you believe it—with every fiber of your being? Or were you quick to say, "Look at that black person showing off. Who does he think he is? He's no better than the rest of us."

In this phase of development, blacks can learn to truly believe in and trust black intellect, your own as well as others'. You begin to lose the need to see all blacks as the same—to . . . to accept our common experience, but . . . but respect our differing intellects. Yeah, man! That's it! You know? This feels good!

It was during this period that I made closer contacts at work, talked more deeply about what happened to us, shared information, talked strategy, developed our own black heroes and black role models, and . . . and we . . . we just helped each other. We helped each other, not only to survive, but to . . . to grow and develop.

We not only learned to trust our black intellect but the intellect of other blacks, and that's why I feel so strongly that it's important for a company hiring blacks that they don't go out and hire just one or two. They need to hire blacks in larger numbers—what is called a *critical mass*—which will vary from company to company depending on company size and . . . and, well! I know a lot of companies are cutting back and all that, but for the blacks already in a company . . .

There are some things that only blacks can help other blacks learn. [Jack fell silent for a few moments; a look of concern crossed his face.]

It was during this phase that I discovered I needed a way to resist power, and I guess that's one thing I didn't master until much later.

No. No man, I guess the broadest concept to crystallize in my mind and that hit me between the eyes was the concept of *black development*. There are some areas black managers need to develop that white managers don't have knowledge or skill to help them with. These are the kinds of things that only other blacks can transmit, as I said before.

See, it's like being in a big family . . . and, like having a father hand down certain information to the sons, or the mother to the daughters. You know, like that.

What kinds of information am I talking about? Well, uh, like how to resist power is one. Another is how do you keep a positive psychological attitude about yourself as a black, uh, and . . . how do you sharpen and refine your skills to read a situation with racial components and be OK with using your skills? Oh, and how do you interact with whites over controversial issues without losing your dignity or taking theirs?

See, because we blacks bring skills to the white corporation from the streets, so to speak, we tend to throw 'em away as being out of place or not important or not useful. So what we have to do is learn to reach back and pull those skills out from our experience and history and use them appropriately in today's atmosphere. OK?

The other piece of black development that's different from whites' is how to manage the racist behavior or attitudes of others. What does that mean? It means that given that racism in corporate America is still operative at this time, and . . . and yet I still have to interact with all kinds of people and be successful, I have to continue to learn how to manage some people's negatively prejudiced behavior toward me.

The first thing I had to do about that was not be reactive to it. There was no sense reacting to it because the person was not going to change instantaneously or overnight—or even next week. But yet, I had a responsibility to be successful. So what that means is that a black is going to have to carry an extra burden, whether he or she likes it or not.

So you have to identify the behavior, learn how to control or neutralize it, and be successful in spite of it. *That's* what you can learn in black development from other blacks.

There is also the management of conflict, because now there is a different kind of conflict than in the previous phase. This is the kind of conflict where whites want to take me on around my black intellect. They want to know what skills I've developed, and they'll question them. Oh yeah! What they'll question is whether or not they are *legitimate* skills.

I had to learn how to manage that. If it's a peer, you might be able to verbally kick 'im in the behind; if it's an upper-level boss in a meeting, you'd better not or you're in trouble.

We often cause a lot of problems during this period. For instance, a lot of blacks on occasion buy into the slave-master concept. The way we do it is by positioning whites to *protect us!* And when we give them that message, that's exactly how they behave: in a way to protect us. Then at some point, we get angry about it, but we have to take responsibility for that.

You know, thinking back . . . I generally felt so good about myself during this period. I didn't wait for people to give me feedback—I went out and sought it!

How? I sent out a one-page questionnaire asking people about my area—about how they evaluated the service they received and whether or not they had any additional suggestions.

I really calmed down from that last phase. I thought a lot—planned, organized, systematically proceeded to carry out my plans. I really learned how to effectively run a meeting—not Uncle Tomming or shuffling or screaming and jumping on people; neither fighting the system full-time nor being totally socialized.

I learned how important it was to have sponsors to keep some whites from withholding helpful information from me when I started moving fast. I had to watch out for that.

What else can I say about this phase of my development? I did a much better job of separating those barriers to my success that I owned from those that the corporation owned. That was a major difference, too, between this phase and the last one. I feel competent and confident enough to own . . . to feel OK in owning the negative things I've done.

The concept of protective hesitation took on a new meaning for me. I would now take more of what you would call a calculated risk. I would expose more information about me, but I'd be careful as to who I would expose it to and what I exposed. Before, I felt I'd go into a meeting not knowing the outcome, not knowing if I'd still own my shirt afterward. But during this time, I felt I could go into any meeting and come out with my shirt intact as well as my dignity.

I used protective hesitation, not to hide myself or shut down, but to anticipate what would happen—plan my behavior—organize my thoughts and respond in an appropriate manner so that I got what I wanted, Yeah.

OK, what other questions do you have? That's about it, unless you want to hear some more war stories about this period. I haven't even mentioned some of the similar stuff my friends went through. But really, I'd just as soon move on to the next period.

Oh! Wait! There's the phone. Will you excuse me for a minute?

Analysis of the Critical Issues

The Planned Growth Phase, representing the critical turning point for blacks, is the beginning of an exciting uphill climb. Jack became aware that he could no longer continue in the same vein as in the previous phase because it required too much energy for too little results and was too depressing. He was tired of feeling crazy and having negative thoughts about himself.

Jack identified his next phase as calming and one in which he could focus his energies on something concrete that he could both understand and do something about. He started taking a serious look at his personal style, which prevented him from getting what he wanted, and took serious strides to change it. In the Planned Growth Phase, blacks put a lot of emphasis and energy into modifying personal style and identifying and removing barriers in addition to handling the normal work tasks. Jack also put more energy into using black input, and he told us why it was important. He leaned heavily on his resources, both black and white. However, he realized that those racially sensitive skills—managing conflict and managing the racial attitudes of others—must be learned from other blacks.

Jack does not say he is a superstar, but it is apparent throughout his narrative that this is the position in which he sees himself. He brings to our attention that he is aware of the extra burdens and responsibilities he as a black is willing to bear in order to become successful. When you join an organization in the Entry Phase feeling like "I've got it made" and then discover you don't, you become angry. For example, you see you are not moving as fast as your white peers, and then you will make a decision. In the Adjusting Phase, you will try to change things so you can grow and develop—or you will slip back into the Entry Phase. One thing is for sure: You will not stay in the Adjusting Phase and remain with your present employer for very long. The pressure will be too great, and your company will not tolerate your dysfunctional behavior forever. You will either go forward, or slip backward and out.

Jack chose to go forward, not backward and give up. Therefore, he knew that in order to overcome some of the difficulties he was having, he had to be a superstar. He had to be prepared and be able to expend much more energy than his white peers to accomplish the same tasks because he had to fight against a system that is inherently against his being there. Of course, we all hope someday this will change.

When whites opened the doors of industries and other institutions to blacks, many whites wanted to show that blacks could make it. As a result, whites ferreted out the superstars, not the average blacks. Blacks in the first wave, unlike the one or two—here and there—of the 1940s and 1950s, entered the newly opened institutions and were rapidly weeded out. The first group that rose into the hierarchies of industries really were superstars; they had to be in order just to survive. When Jack took on the challenge of moving ahead, he became a superstar. He had to be able to take on the demands and pressures that are unique to blacks in white organizations. He also had to accomplish outstanding job results that would make him competitive with his white peers.

This continues to be the plight of all minorities in corporate America. In order to be successful, those whom we treat as minorities—regardless of whether they are white females, blacks, Hispanics, Asians, etc.—are required to manage the job plus the dysfunctional sexist and racist interfaces of individuals and to overcome the inherent barriers that the organization erects against minorities. To do this, they must be superstars. However, the cost to many minority managers is great. To some, the attainment of success means having to totally socialize into the dominant white male culture and thereby minimize differences. This works until the dominant culture has need of the minority's creative differences and the minority cannot respond. Even when this occurs, the minority has had to be a superstar before the price is paid.

As we have seen, Jack is a superstar because he chose to go forward, but what of the blacks who chose to give up and slipped backward into the Entry Phase? What can be done in their cases? Let us take a friend of Jack's, Ansel, and see what happened to him. Ansel came into the company a few years after Jack. He was in another area of the company but saw Jack regularly because they often had to collaborate on job tasks. They had also socialized outside the company on a number of occasions.

Ansel had two degrees and, to most people, was obviously sharp, but he had been beaten down so much that he moved into the Adjusting Phase furious and highly resentful. He became dysfunctional with everyone and rejected a lot of the information sharing from other blacks. "They didn't understand," he told himself. Ansel became increasingly difficult to work with. This increased his organization's negative reaction toward him so much that it scared Ansel half to death and he went running back to his Entry Phase level and gave up.

At some point, Jack realized what had happened to Ansel and started to work with him, pulling and prodding him back to his Adjusting Phase level. Jack had to go to Ansel's managers and try to calm them down by telling them that by helping Ansel through this period, they would learn something and so would Ansel. Jack's hope was to get Ansel past his anger and disappointment and move him into the Planned Growth Phase, where Ansel could then deal with himself and the system.

Now, what if Jack had failed to help get Ansel back on track? Perhaps Ansel would be locked in because the system beat him down or frightened him too much. There may now be information in his evaluation file that marks him as a "troublemaker" or "uppity" or "militant." In this case, the company would have lost a valuable employee. Ansel would have met the negative expectations. The best that Jack could do is make a new opportunity for Ansel, not hold his hand. If Jack could succeed, he would also fulfill his need to give back to someone else the opportunity he had received—but it was up to Ansel to accept it.

Jack acquired a sense of determination in the Planned Growth Phase. He changed his mind about leaving the company; they were not going to chase him away, and he was determined to make a success of his job. Again, this speaks to Jack's superstar status—a status without which Ansel would be unable to make it. Jack's determination was often at the root of his creativity, and he often stumbled into it rather than reached it by design. For example, Jack went to his first management seminar, not because he knew it was going to provide him with such valuable learning opportunities, but because it was a chance to get away and find out what was happening outside his company. However, Jack discovered the advantages of these seminars and used them to facilitate his rapid growth.

Jack's determination and subsequent creativity brought him a sense of pride. He could see for himself the quality of his results. This pride and self-evaluation based on results and improved interpersonal style ultimately make it possible for blacks to slowly become less dependent on external praise or strokes. The pride Jack took in his results showed him that he need not expend his energy fighting inappropriately with whites, that it cost him nothing to allow others to keep their dignity, and that he could still perform his job and achieve his goals. His anger was managed; it was used only as a strategy when absolutely necessary. The energy from the anger was consciously turned into creative output.

In the Planned Growth Phase, white managers will see a big difference in the behavior of black managers. Whites are apt to be confused and sometimes upset because they have come to expect one type of interaction and will see another. Black managers struggle to smooth their style and to be more effective. Hopefully, white managers will sense this and feel free to openly discuss this subject with black managers because white managers can be a tremendous help at this time.

This can also be a great learning opportunity for white managers as well. Since blacks must struggle with becoming oversocialized into the white corporate culture, whites can expand their managerial repertoire by having blacks share some of this struggle with them. Research in the behavioral fields, for instance, has shown that blacks and women bring a more humanistic form of management to organizations. We believe one reason for this is that blacks and women have a more highly developed level of sensitivity toward people resulting from the role status they have been historically assigned. Here, then, is an opportunity for white male managers to take advantage of a different management style and to use it to everyone's benefit. The key to doing this is for white managers to first admit to themselves that something *can* be learned from black managers. Second, they must decide *what* is to be learned, and third, they must be *open* to learning.

This is an important time in the professional life of a black manager, and as we said, white managers can help. However, if a black is the subordinate of a white manager who is highly threatened, then this is going to be a rough period for that white manager because the black manager will be learning a lot of positive new behaviors and skills at a rapid pace. Instead of allowing the black manager to share and use those skills, the white manager will tend to react negatively to the changes. The white boss will inadvertently or even deliberately try to slow down the black manager. This reaction, if strong and persistent, can frustrate black managers enough to push them back into the Adjusting Phase.

In the Planned Growth Phase, the black manager develops a thick skin. Jack, for instance, could not listen to both negative and positive input and was strong and astute enough to deal with it by ensuring that it was proper and accurate feedback. He asked questions about it and accepted it when he thought it was correct. If he thought the feedback was not correct, he weeded out the inappropriate pieces and kept the helpful ones. Because he had learned about the corporate culture during the Adjusting Phase, Jack was now able to identify and separate various information and place the pieces where they properly belonged.

To sum up, blacks develop in the Planned Growth Phase the refined skill to weed out negative racial and sexual data and to determine whether a barrier is organizational or personal. Not only will blacks welcome and listen to feedback, but they will tend to go out and seek it from any appropriate person, white or black. Jack was even willing to expose himself and his shortcomings in training and management seminars so he could get the right kind of information to move ahead. This action showed how much he valued the input, because public exposure is risky for most individuals, especially for blacks. What Jack and other blacks try to do in this phase is refine those things that turn them on, juice them up, and cause them to do a good job.

Jack did not go into any detail about his discoveries regarding interactional processes, but we know from his narrative that he worked very hard to improve the manner in which he approached people to give and get information. Jack noticed, both at work and away, that there are some differences in the dynamics of the interactional processes between different groups of people. The impact of this was important because it had implications for how Jack would approach different people and what he could expect the nonverbal and often hidden issues to be. Figure 4-1 diagrams and explains three of the most outstanding issues—power, control, and trust—in the interactional process between three different racial dyads. Of course, there are other dynamics and hidden issues involved in these interactions, but those shown are basic in the corporate culture.

Because of his understanding of interactional processes, Jack could see the value of the warm-up conversation before getting into the business at hand. He knew when and why it was important, what purpose it should serve, and how to use it strategically to position people to listen and seriously consider his needs. Jack could now easily put both blacks and whites at ease and anticipate their needs and

Figure 4-1. Three dynamic issues involved in the interactional process of three different racial dyads.

Interaction: (White Person) ←——→ (White Person)

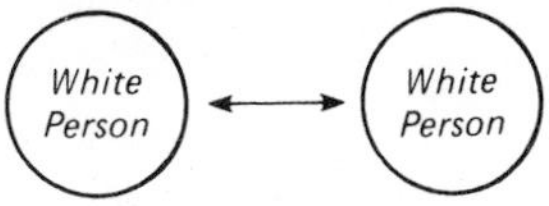

Power

- Characterized by persons seeking to identify job positions for mutual beneficial contact and/or to establish one's place in the pecking order.

Control

- Persons display intelligence or seek level of intelligence of each other.
- Persons show and discuss material goods and comforts, clubs joined, neighborhood lived in, trips, etc.

Trust

- Initially little display of trust.
- Lack of personal or emotional display in conversation.
- Trust established after positions in the pecking order are identified.

Interaction: (Black Person) ←——→ (White Person)

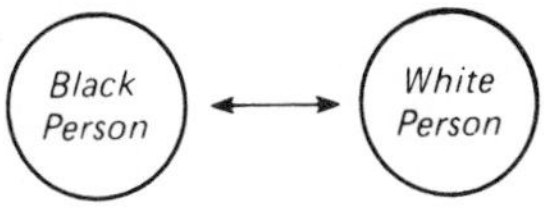

Power

- Centers around and is held by the white person, who is a member of the dominant culture.

Control

- Some fear by the white person of loss of control.

Trust

- Little trust, because there is no common base of cultural experience and may be little common base of personal experience.

Interaction: (Black Person) ←——→ (Black Person)

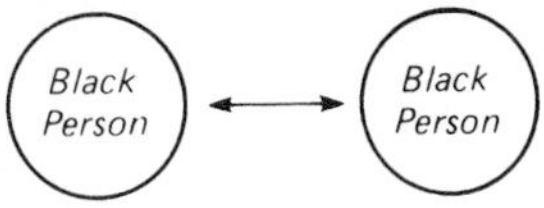

Power

- Persons tend to establish respect independent of job position.
- Characterized by a display of mental prowess and/or street sense, education, and sometimes material goods.

Control

- There tends to be an absence of control issues.

Trust

- Trust is established very quickly and often assumed because of common cultural experiences.
- Personal or emotional affect is displayed in conversation.

concerns in order to move to meet or reject them. During the Planned Growth Phase, blacks tend to focus very quickly on the differences in the dynamics that occur when individuals from different cultures interact.

Jack took advantage of an opportunity to develop and use sponsors. He chose people in the hierarchy who not only would act as advocates for him but were willing to be used as coaches and resources. That action helped Jack move faster because he could learn through the experiences of others. Also, Jack came to learn, although he did not specifically mention it, that it becomes critical for the white sponsors of black managers to know the black managers and their skills and abilities well enough to speak up for them with confidence when whites go behind closed doors to discuss promotion. Anyone who expects to move up the hierarchy needs the extra help of sponsors or mentors. As we have already stated, competition is keen, and the pyramid narrows rapidly as it reaches its apex. Blacks cannot afford to wait until someone on his or her own sees their potential to advance; that may never happen. Minorities must be aggressive enough to make their desires and abilities known to someone who is willing and in a position to help. We cannot repeat this too often or state it too strongly to the minority manager.

Jack also lets us know how important it is to set goals. The setting of goals is a main indication of when a black has moved into the Planned Growth Phase. These goals provide a road map to success in terms of attaining some of the things that the black manager wants. However, this is also the phase in which the acquisition of skills and new knowledge and the setting and meeting of goals occur so rapidly that the black manager's self-concept always lags behind the level of managerial skill that can be used to handle complex situations. This is illustrated in Figure 4-2.

At this point, you may be asking, "What are the implications of this gap for blacks?" Let us look at an example that will point out the implications. Take the case of a black manager who has to attend a meeting that will involve the discussion and resolution of hot organizational issues such as staffing, budgets, or quality control. The black manager knows that meeting participants will debate various points. A manager in the Planned Growth Phase will tend to go into the meeting with a great deal of stress, anxiety, and concern. Usually, shortly after the meeting starts, the black manager will discover that he or she is handling himself or herself very adroitly in the ensuing debate and may

Figure 4-2. Managerial skills acquired and improvement of self-concept over time for black managers.

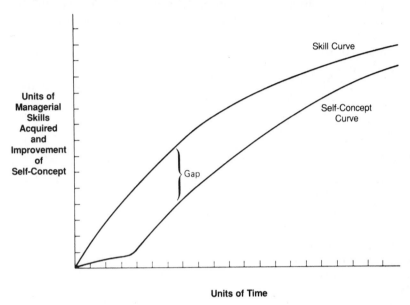

Units of Time

even wonder afterward why there was so much stress and worry before the meeting. Unfortunately, this scenario will be repeated often.

A gap will always exist, as shown in Figure 4-2. As a black manager moves toward the Success Phase, the gap will decrease significantly. For some individuals, the gap reduces fairly quickly; for others, it may take years. This depends on how rapidly the individuals can change their self-concepts in a positive direction.

In summary, blacks usually develop managerial skills at a much more rapid rate than they develop positive self-concepts. Although all of us sometimes have doubts about our ability to get the results we want, the primary difference is that whites are concerned over whether success will be achieved, whereas blacks tend to be concerned about whether failure can be avoided.

How-To Solutions and Basic Concepts

The how-to solutions tend to be more complicated in the Planned Growth Phase. They are, as we have said, more structured and more strategic than those in the two previous phases. Some of the solutions are very involved, and we choose not to go into them at this time. Therefore, we will give rather simplistic solutions to some of the problems here and refer you to another part of this book for the more involved explanations and problem solutions in that specific area.

Many of the concepts used in the how-to solutions of the Planned Growth Phase and the Success Phase are concepts previously discussed in the Entry Phase and Adjusting Phase. In the Planned Growth and Success Phases, blacks learn to use these concepts in conjunction with others to broaden their ability to solve problems. For this reason, fewer new concepts are needed to formulate solutions. For example, in problem I of the Planned Growth Phase—how to successfully manage conflict—the concepts used were confrontation and sharing your feelings from the Entry Phase in addition to dealing with the need and a broader application of compromising from the Adjusting Phase.

The concepts discussed in the Planned Growth and Success Phases will be new concepts not previously discussed. As you read the solutions in the how-to sections, you will be aware of the varied uses of the concepts. At some later time, you may find it helpful to go back to these how-to sections and see how many concepts you can find in each solution.

Problem I

How to successfully manage conflict.

Solution

This solution can apply to conflicts between black peers and white peers and between white bosses and black subordinates. (Successful confrontation is discussed in greater depth in Part Four, Chapter 8.) The solution has seven steps and is especially useful with people who tend not to be open and candid in interactions. It also works well with people who tend not to confront others. Figure 4-3 illustrates the confrontation process:

1. Spend three to five minutes discussing subjects designed to help relax and reduce stress in both you and the other person involved in the conflict. The subjects could be sports, hobbies, the latest home project, or some funny event.
2. Bring up the subject of the conflict by placing it in terms of

Figure 4-3. Steps involved in successful confrontation.

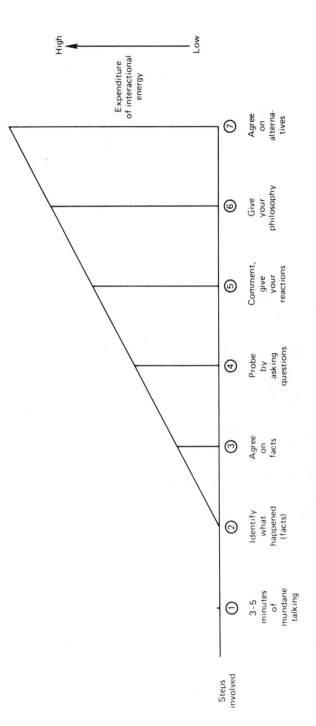

factual data. Describe the problem relative to what happened. It may be difficult to manage your emotions, but it can be done. You must do it at this point.

3. Agree on the facts—nothing but what actually took place—because a confrontation cannot be resolved if the two parties cannot start from a common base. However, if there is disagreement about the critical facts, agree on a method to get the data. Reconnect when you have the data and repeat steps one and two. Then resume the process.

4. Probe each other by asking questions. Asking how the other person felt about the incident. Find out what the person actually had a problem with in the situation or why it gave the person a problem. You need to understand the other person's thought processes. One reason conflicts arise is because people use different thought processes, and you need to find a common way of viewing the situation in question.

5. At this point, it is OK to talk about your feelings and be emotional. After you have asked sufficient questions and are comfortable with the information you have received, comment on the information. Then, give your reaction, such as, "When you do things like that, I react in this way," or, "When you say something like that, I tend to get angry." Explain, "When I get angry, I may get dysfunctional," or, "I get angry and find it difficult to cooperate with you."

6. Give your philosophy about the incident. For instance, "My general thoughts are," or, "My general feelings on that are," or, "My philosophy about that kind of issue is this."

7. The last step is to agree on some alternatives to resolving the conflict. Pick one and use it to resolve the issues between you and the other person.

Problem II

How to develop a smoother style of interacting.

Solution

We are presenting one solution to this problem. For further discussion of effective styles, see Part Four, Chapter 7.

Be aware of your need to develop a smoother style; this is half your battle. Your level of awareness and ability to accept the responsibility for changing your style will determine how much energy you will give to the task and how successful you will be in accomplishing it. If your interactions with people tend to make them react negatively rather than respond positively to you, then that is a clear signal that you need to develop a smoother style. Allow your need for success to drive you to change.

Define the specific areas you feel you need or want to change. For example, perhaps you have been given feedback that you tend to be aloof with people and, as a result, they will not share information readily with you. You may see that you are awkward in conducting meetings and people get impatient with you. You may see another manager handle conflict in an effective manner you wish you could duplicate. Be clear about what you desire to change or improve.

Pick a role model who exhibits smoothness in the areas you are concerned about. You may choose several different people as role models for various changes you wish to make; their ethnic group or sex does not matter. A good argument for picking several role models is that it is harder to generalize from one case. Seeing several people who are skillful in one area helps you ignore individual mannerisms and concentrate on the key processes involved in the skill area. Use the listing concept to identify and describe the *processes* the people use that produce the smoothness of behavior in their interactions with others. For instance, you may see that one manager has a great deal of charisma with people, and as a result, people eagerly share information with that person. You may see that another manager is quite skilled at running meetings, and people leave full of energy and ready to do their tasks. Still another manager may have the ability to confront conflict and resolve it leaving all parties satisfied. You need to describe what you see and understand how it is done—that is, pull out the process.

Duplicate the process used by the role model. Again, we want you to understand that if your role model is white, you are not attempting to become "whitelike." Your delivery and mannerisms will be your own and within the personal character that is comfortable to you.

Role-play the interaction to be changed or improved in your mind or with a friend or with your mate. Practice the behavior you want to use, such as being more personable, leading a meeting, or confronting conflict. Picture yourself in the situation, integrating your words and mannerisms into the process of your role model.

Practice the new behavior in actual situations. Greet people using a more personal affect; lead your next meeting using the role model's process; or deal with conflict by operating in a smoother manner. You probably will not get the new process and behavior 100 percent correct the first few times, but that is OK. You should realize that you are learning, and change does not happen overnight.

Make corrections and refine your behavior and the new process if you make a mistake. Keep doing this until you are satisfied with your behavior in that particular area. Do not get discouraged if people do not immediately react differently to you. They will have "old tapes" on you that they will need to erase.

Concepts

Concept 1: Role modeling. This is the idea of selecting a *specific* behavioral skill, characteristic, or quality that you admire in a person and want to acquire. You may find many different people, regardless of race or gender, with some one quality or skill you would like to possess. It is extremely rare that one person will embody all the traits and skills you are looking for. This concept is very important to blacks. Use of role modeling can free you from the fear, intimidation, anxiety, and stress that occur when you want to do something but prevent yourself from doing it. If you can handle the situation the way you have seen another person do it, then it frees you from your inhibitions.

Concept 2: Role playing. This provides you with the important step of practicing the behavior you hope to acquire. You can practice in private or in front of someone you trust. Role playing is based on the same principle you used as a child when you played mama, papa, teacher, or cowboy to practice the grown-up behavior of the adults around you. It was preliminary then for your taking a place in the adult world; role playing can be preliminary now for more effective performance as a manager.

Problem III

How to effectively probe negative feedback.

Solution

First, let us take a broad overview of the entire process. Position your psyche, or put more simply, set a positive mental attitude. Make sure you understand the negative feedback. Look at the preceptions of others as well as your own. Now look at ownership and then develop corrective steps. From this overview, let us discuss each specific step involved.

To position your psyche, you must talk to yourself. Use the concept of talking to the champ. Being black and getting feedback from a white person can be stressful. You become tense because you face these questions about the feedback: "Is it racist, or isn't it?" "Is it sexist, or isn't it?" Another question blacks commonly ask themselves is, "Is this person trying to be helpful by sharing feedback, or is he or she trying to degrade me?" Try not to react too quickly to the feedback. Try not to get defensive, even though it is natural to do so. Say to yourself, "I should not react negatively or be defensive yet because there may be some constructive pieces in the feedback. If so, I need to listen and find them. I can use them for my benefit."

Some of the feedback may not be valid or may not apply to you. It may apply to the person who supplied the feedback; that is, the person may be attributing his or her own faults or feelings to you. Therefore, you must prepare yourself psychologically to receive the information.

Make sure you understand the feedback. Ask questions for understanding, such as: "When does the bahavior occur?" "How does it occur?" "What does it do to people?" "What are the implications for me?" Also ask questions to find out the implications of your behavior for others. "Why is my behavior seen as negative by you or others?" "Why do you think I behave as I do in this situation?"

Look at ownership. Is the feedback valid as it pertains to you, or is it someone's projection onto you? Is someone reacting to you because of something that the other person owns or that is an attribute of the other person? People's perceptions of you can be influenced by your affect as well as your verbal communication. People may react negatively to your mannerisms as well as to what you say. Test this by asking yourself, "What portion of this feedback actually resulted from my behavior?" "Do I behave in this manner?" "What portion of the feedback applies to the other person as well as to me?" "Am I reacting to the person or to the situation and its becoming a reciprocal interaction?" "Does this feedback really apply to the giver because this is his or her behavioral style?"

Now analyze the information you have about ownership and other people's perceptions of you and discuss it. Sift through it. This is where you will throw away the irrelevant data and keep the constructive data. Probe to see whether others misinterpreted your bahavior; remember to be honest with yourself. Also, check to see whether you were unaware of how your actions impacted people.

You are ready to develop some specific corrective action steps at this point. The feedback may not apply to you, however, and if it is a case of inappropriate data, then correction is unnecessary.

Concept

Probing. This concept directs you to explore and thoroughly examine information for clarity and understanding and to extract additional information.

Problem IV

How to recognize hot organizational issues.

Solution

People tend to be successful and contribute more to organizations when they focus on and resolve hot organizational issues. A hot organizational issue is an existing condition that poses a barrier to effective operation and that an organization is willing to expend monetary and human resources to eliminate. The speed with which you gain success is directly proportional to your ability to recognize and resolve hot issues. All organizations have hot issues. These issues are dynamic and may change often. Some examples are: how to increase production, how to increase efficiency, how to reduce operating cost, and how to reduce employee turnover.

List those issues discussed at the highest levels in your organization. Do this by tapping into the informal communications network—for instance, by listening to the bosses at lunch and on breaks and listening carefully to company speeches. List issues by reviewing organizational goals and pulling out the high-priority ones. Ask your boss whether you may see the organizational goals for the next year. Extract key messages or issues from various pieces of correspondence. Read memos and letters written by bosses at the highest levels in the organization.

After you list the issues and extract the key messages from the correspondence, you can discuss them with your boss to get his or her input. Also, bounce them off your peers, other supervisors, and your sponsors. Do this to ascertain whether you have chosen the correct issues. Once you feel comfortable with what you think are the hot organizational issues, the next step is to work to resolve them in addition to attending to your normal work tasks. Remember to use resources to help resolve them.

Concept

Assessing the organization. This new concept means that you need to look at the organization and pull out the most important problems and issues that the company is wrestling with at the time. As a black, you need to be aware of the importance of doing something in the organization that will place you in a position to make a unique contribution. The easiest to do this is to deal with a hot issue. Resolving problematic issues for the organization will definitely set you apart from your peers and create the exposure you need to get ahead.

Problem V

How to take initiatiave in your job.

Solution

Start by clearly identifying a hot issue or a problem that your boss needs to solve. Subordinates become very valuable to their bosses when they can focus on and solve or help the boss solve some of his or her problems. First, make sure the problem is clearly stated. Develop a very rough plan to resolve the issue or problem. A problem basically is an opportunity to showcase your skills and abilities. Do this by trying to sense what upper-level managers want in terms of a resolution. Use resources by seeking their advice and thoughts on the issue or problem and the rough plan you have developed. Allow your ideas and your plan to be shaped by input from others.

Identify the barriers involved in executing your rough plan. Identify the personal risk involved for you. There may not be any risk, or there may be a very low level of risk. Identify any other risks to resolving the issue or problems. Then decide whether you are willing to take the risks.

Develop a "battle plan." This is an action plan that you will use to resolve the issue or solve the problem. Plan and organize in order to make a unique contribution to the business. Your plan should specify milestones or key events, together with a date for accomplishing them. Then execute your battle plan. Make in-flight corrections, and continue to move toward success.

Concept

Battle planning. The concept used in this solution conjures up images of generals poring over maps and plotting strategies. This is an action-oriented concept, in that it is used to solve hot organizational issues and implies that you will have to battle with some existing norms and perhaps some people in the organization. Strategy is used in close conjunction with battle planning.

Problem VI

How to acquire a sponsor or mentor.

Solution

Sponsors or mentors in an organization act as teachers, coaches, and advocates for others who are at lower hierarchical levels in the company. Sponsors or mentors give inside information relative to important company norms, share experiences, and tell what to watch out for as well as share information about appropriate and useful organizational behavior. They can also empower you to do certain things, such as asking your boss questions you might otherwise not feel free to ask. Sponsors and mentors can be used as both technical and managerial resources. They may, in addition, have an opportunity to speak up for you, recommend you for something, or defend you for some reason.

Basically, there are two ways you can acquire sponsors or mentors. One way is to seek them out; the other is to allow them to seek you out. First, let us look at how you can seek sponsors and mentors. Most blacks acquire sponsors and mentors by seeking them because it is not as easy for whites to identify black potential and interest as it is for whites to spot other sharp whites. Look around in your organization and identify those upper-level managers who are movers and shakers and get things done. Since you need sponsors and mentors to fulfill different roles, you should have more than one. For example, one sponsor may be politically well-connected in your organization and may have numerous contacts that may be helpful to you; another sponsor may know how to cut through red tape to get things done quickly; while yet another sponsor may be good at selling new ideas. They should be one to three levels above your level in the hierarchy. Select individuals who are regarded by a large number of people in the organization as sharp and powerful.

The next step is to make contact with the sponsor or mentor you have identified. Contact can occur as a result of being in a meeting with the person, hearing a speech by the person, or being in a social setting where you have had an opportunity to talk with the person. You can call the potential mentor or sponsor's office and ask to meet to further discuss some item of mutual interest. You may have an idea or a rough plan worked out that you can share and ask for input from the prospective sponsor or mentor. Use the first meeting to assess the potential relationship and begin to develop it. Do this by asking some general questions, such as, "What principles are important to success in the organization?" You can also ask questions about the event at which you made initial contact with the person.

Do not use the first meeting to ask the person how you can get to the next level, because that may be too forward and presumptuous on your part at such an early stage. First, you must develop the person as a sponsor or mentor before he or she will give you inside information—such as how to get to the next level. Ask whether the person would be willing to meet with you again. If so, mention what you would like to discuss. For example, you might say, "In the future, I would like to discuss with you the principles for successful task execution." Or, "How do you properly delegate?" You might also ask, "How do you lead a meeting smoothly?"

At the second meeting, you want to further test the person's willingness to be a sponsor or mentor. At the end of this meeting, ask whether you can have a monthly meeting to discuss various subjects; have a prepared list you can pull out and show. Throughout the sessions, be sure that you document your learnings, but do not write down confidential information or inside information of a sensitive nature. You may even find it useful to summarize your learnings and send a copy to your sponsor or mentor. Be sure to mark it "Confidential." Use your discretion about this, because there may be data your sponsor or mentor does not want passed around. However, do take notes on such topics as the principles of successful task execution.

Continue to meet as long as the meetings are profitable. As you meet, your relationship will grow and the sponsor or mentor will begin to take you into his or her confidence and provide you with the assistance you need. Be patient; allow your sponsor or mentor to get to know you because this relationship will also be a test for you. However, relax and show self-confidence. The sponsor or mentor will test your competence, listen for the logic of your thinking, and test you to see whether you can handle confidential information in a professional manner. The sponsor or mentor must have enough information about you as an employee and an individual to act as an advocate for you if the need ever arises.

The second way to acquire a sponsor or mentor is to be sought out by a person in the hierarchy. This happens less frequently, but it does happen, usually as a result of a presentation or an impressive contribution you made at a meeting, or as a result of a conversation with someone at a social event. If for any reason you are approached by an upper-level manager who strikes up a conversation with you, you need to listen very carefully for the organizational cues or indirect hints and suggestions that indicate the person is willing to work with and develop you. Listen for such things as a suggestion that you drop by sometime or that the two of you continue the discussion at a later date; perhaps you will be asked to play tennis, golf, or racquetball. *Follow up on this.* Call the person's office to set up a meeting and say you would like to follow up on a prior conversation. Allow the potential sponsor or mentor to direct the first meeting. Let the sponsor or mentor start talking first. Be prepared, however, with a couple of key questions, such as: "What are the principles for successful task execution?" "What are the important goals of the organization?"

After the first meeting, review the results. If you are satisfied, then ask for a second meeting. In fact, if you feel satisfied during the course of the first meeting, then ask for a second meeting before you leave. Use the second meeting, as we said before, to further test the willingness of the person to be your sponsor or mentor. Make sure you stroke the person and thank him or her for taking time out of a busy schedule to talk to you.

Make sure you understand what sponsorship and mentorship means. It does *not* mean that your sponsors or mentors will bypass your hierarchy and completely dismiss your bosses. Nor should you use your sponsors or mentors for that purpose. Sponsorship and mentorship *can* help maximize your potential and offer you a means of public exposure.

Concepts

Concept 1: Seizing an opportunity. Despite this concept's simple name, using it is not necessarily simple. You will have to take what may appear to be a casually made comment and recognize in it an opportunity to acquire something you need or want—in this particular case, a sponsor and mentor. Blacks need to be especially aware of casually dropped suggestions, hints, or other information. When you feel there is something you can use to your benefit, then follow through on it. It may lead to an opportunity for both you and the organization.

Concept 2: Testing. This is used often by blacks in a variety of situations and can be found in many of the solutions throughout all four phases. Testing is used in any situation in which there is a lack of clarity about where people are on issues or needs. It is a way to ascertain whether the assumptions you are making are correct. In the case of acquiring sponsors and mentors, you need to test for sincerity by the second meeting. Making and acting on assumptions can be detrimental to the survival and success of blacks in an organization. Therefore, testing becomes a critical action step for blacks.

Problem VII

How to document and continue to use your personal learnings.

Solution

Document your personal learnings by creating a personal development file. Your personal learnings relate to both the technical and managerial aspects of your job. Documentation is important for the continued use of your learnings.

There are a couple of ways you can conveniently start your file. Purchase an expandable file folder, which should be kept at home, not in the office, because these are personal learnings. Jot down the things you learn and be consistent; use 8½" × 11" pieces of paper instead of a lot of scraps. (If you happen to be a paper-napkin artist or writer, transfer your notes later to something more readable.) Work out your own filing system, so information is readily available when you need it. We can attest to the extreme annoyance that occurs when you cannot find that important note to yourself right when you need it most.

Another option is to purchase a half-inch three-ring binder and keep sheets of information there. You may want to get sophisticated and index the notebook to separate technical learnings from managerial learnings. You may choose to break those categories down to suit your own needs.

Across the top of each sheet, write the subject of the learning, the date you acquired the information, and the source, which will usually be the name of a person. This is important because when you refer to the learning in the future, if it is not clear, you can always go back to the source for clarification. Jot down as much information as you need to ensure clarity of understanding for future use. You may wish to include how the learning can be used. Read through the material every two to three months to refresh your memory. You will be surprised at how much useful data you forget when there is a large volume of learnings.

Concept

Jotting it down. This is one of the best habits you can acquire and one of the most widely and consistently used concepts. Very simply it refers to the old cliché "A short pencil is better than a long memory." When you jot things down, you capture the essence of your learning for future use, and it is always at your disposal.

Problem VIII

How to use constructive feedback.

Solution

This problem differs from problem II in that that problem dealt specifically with style development. This solution is geared more to general feedback, because feedback also covers such issues as task execution and decision making.

First, always be clear about the feedback. Ask questions for understanding and try not to be defensive or reactive. Remember to test the feedback for racist and sexist content and to use your resources, peers, friends, and spouse to help you. Sometimes, we are too close to the information to see it clearly. Ask yourself and others what would happen to a white manager in similar circumstances: Would the feedback and the data be the same? Are there extenuating circumstances surrounding the data?

After exploring the feedback, develop a rough plan to make changes in your behavior if the feedback is legitimate and genuine. Again, use a resource to test and refine your plan. The most important thing to do in using your corrective plan is to employ a behavioral-change model; that is, alter your behavior while working on your attitude. To facilitate this whole process, say to yourself, "I did this thing the way I did because this is a new situation for me, and I have not had the opportunity to learn how to act appropriately or correctly." This is a *positive* learning model. Do this instead of saying, "I did not know how to proceed because there is a hole in my educational background." This is a *negative* learning model, which is used too oftern by blacks. Sometimes, white managers will inadvertently cause blacks to use this negative model. When that happens, it merely raises the black manager's stress level and anxiety unnecessarily. As a result, the black manager becomes less open to receiving and using constructive feedback.

In short, using constructive feedback ceases to be a problem when you are able to listen without reacting, probe the data, check its validity with resources, develop a plan of correction if needed, change the bahavior, adopt a positive learning attitude, and finally, practice in private or in front of your mate or trusted peers.

Concept

Positive is better than negative. This straightforwardly named concept means what it says, that when you are in a situation in which you must evaluate yourself, it is much better to *choose* a positive viewpoint than a negative one. All situations can have a negative aspect and a positive aspect; we have control over which we choose to focus on. When we choose to indulge ourselves in the negative viewpoint, we inhibit our growth. When we choose to see things from a positive viewpoint, we are more open to input, change, rapid growth, and development.

Problem IX

How to present ideas to your boss.

Solution

In the Adjusting Phase, we offered a rather detailed solution to how to *sell* ideas to your boss. This solution will speak to how to *present* ideas to your boss. The difference here is that we are addressing individuals who are in the Planned Growth Phase, and presenting ideas is best done by people who are about to step over into the Success Phase. The ideas we are referring to here are more conceptual than those in the Adjusting Phase and border on new developments or new directions. They are more risky or radical and may deviate from the norms of the organization. These are also ideas that you need to get your boss's endorsement on before proceeding to develop them further.

You should present an idea to your boss in the very early stages of its formulation, before you use other resources. Rough out your idea and put it in a tight format. Write the words "Blue-Sky Thinking" at the top and bottom of each sheet. This will signal your boss that this is a very rough idea and you are using the boss as a resource to help further develop it by providing thoughts, comments, and reactions. Ask your boss to give you the names of other resources to consult on the idea. Meet with the resources and use their input to further develop your idea.

Concept

Blue-sky thinking. Despite its rather romantic title, this concept has an entirely serious purpose. Blue-sky thinking is a nonthreatening way to introduce new and innovative ideas into an organization that may not be very receptive to creative change. It is safer because it is low-risk. By using it, you get your idea sanctioned or disapproved by your organization early on. You may still go forward with your plan regardless of your boss's reaction, but at least you will know where you stand and what you are up against.

Problem X

How to disuss racial incidents and the effects of race on an issue or situation with whites.

Solution

Racial prejudice is an important issue to deal with because most blacks sooner or later will encounter a work situation where race will affect the dynamics. At best, this is a difficult problem for both blacks and whites to deal with because there is normally some confrontation associated with the resolution of the problem. Racial prejudice is a sensitive subject, packed with emotion, threat, guilt, power, and so forth.

When talking about racial incidents with whites or the effects of race on an issue, the important thing to keep in mind is that people behave on the basis of their perceptions of the world. These perceptions may or may not be correct; that should *never* be the issue, since it leads down a one-way, dead-end street. It also diverts attention from dealing with the issue at hand. That kind of disussion of right or wrong perceptions is best left for parlor-room debates. Whatever the perception, the person's viewpoint and behavior will be affected by it.

When you discuss racial incidents in the workplace, stick as much as possible to the facts as you perceive them. For example, you are trying to accomplish a task, and you have to work with a person who is displaying racist behavior toward you. It has gotten in the way of performing the task, and you need to discuss this with your boss. Open the session by clearly stating what you want from the boss. He or she needs to know whether you merely want to be listened to or whether you are asking for some action to be taken. Describe the incident as factually as possible. Then tell your boss the effect it has on you. If your boss reacts negatively to you, for whatever reason, say that you are not dealing with the boss's perception of what happened or how the boss perceives or interacts with the other person, but rather with how *you* see the situation and how it makes you feel. The least your boss can do is respect your different view of what occurred. The boss may not have noticed the other person interacting in an interracial situation.

If the discussion comes to a confrontation, and the boss attempts to shut you down, then you should relax and let the boss blow off steam. Do *not* allow yourself to become intimidated or to react hostilely to the boss. This can be accomplished by not responding when the boss blows off steam. When the boss has finished, look him or her in the eye and ask, "Can you share with me why this makes you angry?" This simple questions offers the boss an opportunity to share discomforts and feelings about the situation, and once these are dealth with, the boss is freed up to help you with your problem.

If the problem you are experiencing is deep, complex, or extremely upsetting, you may not be able to help the boss face his or her difficulties with the racial content of the situation. If this is the case and you need immediate assistance, you may prefer to say to the boss, "I don't know why *you're* upset, but let me tell you again what the situation did to me and how it is interfering with my accomplishing my job." Then repeat the incident. Give the boss another chance to deal with the problem, because it is a legitimate employee need.

The next thing to happen, in most cases, is the white boss will feel a need to take care of the problem and will become alarmed. Let the boss know you would first like to discuss what needs to be done. Maybe you as a black can handle the situation better than the boss can. Perhaps you do not want the boss to do anything except listen and be apprised of what is going on. You may need the boss to help you resolve the issue or to sanction some strategy you have developed. However, remember to state this before the conversation begins.

Concept

No-response response. Although its name may sound like double-talk, this is a very useful concept. Many times, we use it without realizing that we have done so. A no-response response is simply refusing to acknowledge some dysfunctional comments or behavior. For example, when teasing starts, we may tell our children, "Just ignore it," or, "Do not respond." The other person will be forced to cease the unwanted comments or behavior. This also works well when adults temporarily lose control. Fuel is not added to the emotional fire by responding and thereby giving the dysfunctional person additional cause to continue the unwanted interaction. This concept can be used to stop many unnecessary arguments before they begin. It does, however, take emotional control on your part to successfully use this concept.

Problem XI

How to set up an informal learning group.

Solution

Quite a few black managers in middle- to upper-management positions have a number of things in common. One of those is that during their early careers, they were members of informal learning groups. The groups consisted of blacks in the company or organization who were interested in learning how to survive and position themselves for success. Informal learning groups can be set up by one person by simply selecting and influencing at least two others to join him or her. Start with one person whom you know well and who wants to learn to accomplish tasks with outstanding results. Suggest to the other person that you should get at least a third person to join you; this will help to balance out any differences of opinion. You can meet at each other's home or apartment on a weekday night, on the weekend, or on an alternating basis. Assign someone an area of learning to be discussed at each meeting; be sure to leave time to discuss actual events that took place at work. This allows you to review what you did so that you might do it more easily or better the next time. Take the opportunity to practice in front of each other presentations you have to make at work, speeches you have to give, or budgets you need to develop. Give each other helpful input.

You may want to invite a more seasoned and experienced person to work with your group on presentations, actual problems, or hot organizational issues. The invited guest can give insight on current organizational events that you need to know about, such as reorganizations and budget preparation. Invited guests will be flattered that you asked them to help you.

Remember, you can also meet periodically at work. This is acceptable because you will be working on company or organizational business, which will help you perform better. It also gives you an opportunity to test new and creative ideas on how to accomplish tasks or how to improve your company's products or services. Agree to at least one meeting per month (at lunch) in the company's or organization's dining room. You may also want to meet after working hours at your offices, especially if you need equipment, such as computers. Perhaps you may want to train each other on ways to expedite work tasks by using new computer programs. At the appropriate time, invite others to join your group. Developing this kind of informal learning group will offer you tremendous opportunities to learn at a rapid rate.

P.S.: If you are the only black person in your company or organization, then meet with blacks from other companies or organizations; the aforementioned principles will still apply.

Concept

Self-improvement. This is closely associated with the concept used in problem V, "How to take initiative in your job." By taking initiative for self-improvement, you forever place yourself in *your* hands and not in the hands of the organization. This way, you go out and get what you need without waiting to be given it. As long as you follow this route as you rise in the organization, you will be successful.

5

Success Phase

Critical Issues

Attitudes

- Accepting the additional demands of a supervisory manager position or first promotion as a challenge
- Realizing that making mistakes or failing is not an option
- Using protective hesitation as a strategy
- Being aware of one's own blackness and its impact on an organization, various situations, and individual interfaces
- Continuing awareness of how subtle prejudice operates
- Being more sensitive to the work environment
- Seeking fewer strokes; being results-oriented
- Understanding that racist behaviors must be managed with skill, not reaction

Emotions

- Sublimating emotions
- Feeling and displaying high confidence

Behaviors

- Using communications networks (both formal and informal) effectively
- Continuing to refine and smooth personal style
- Confronting whites in a way that allows them to retain their dignity
- Continuing to set and meet goals
- Producing high-quality results

- Displaying a success affect
- Learning to manage the racism of others
- Learning to be appropriately aggressive

Job Skills

- Using higher levels of interpersonal and behavioral skills
- Using skills to resist power
- Continuing to develop multicultural management skills
- Using the organization more appropriately to get things done (i.e., learning corporate politics)

Overview of the Critical Issues

The criteria for determining success vary among individuals. We will be discussing the Success Phase from the standpoint of a promotion; therefore, if you have different success indicators in your organization, you will need to make that translation in your mind as you read this chapter.

Let us reiterate: In the Success Phase, black managers reach a plateau that is the culmination of all the learnings and experiences from the Entry Phase through the Planned Growth Phase. This becomes a cycle that begins again with each major job change throughout the career life of a black manager. Each time the growth pattern is repeated, it should take less time to complete, and the learnings will be more sophisticated. Black managers become successful when they adopt productive attitudes about the job, learn to properly use and control emotions, display more than adequate job behavior, and learn the appropriate job skills during the Entry through Success Phases.

Attitudes

Black managers who become successful are aware of additional burdens with which their white peers do not have to contend. Moving up in the white corporation, some blacks become concerned over how they are viewed by others of their cultural group. They fear that they may be seen as part of the establishment, having deserted the brotherhood or sisterhood. This is especially true in situations in which an individual is the first black to be promoted or there are only a few blacks represented in the hierarchy.

There is also the added burden of feeling responsible and obligated to other blacks in subordinate positions. Some blacks attempt to help pave the way for those other blacks who aspire to move up in the organization; this draws extra time and energy from the successful black manager. Although some whites may also want to help blacks move up, a major difference is that black managers feel a responsibility and an obligation to ensure that the black subordinates succeeds. If the subordinate fails, the successful manager usually has some feeling that he or she has also failed. This is especially true when there are few blacks in the organization. The success of one black (regardless of level) has a carryover effect to other blacks. Conversely, and even more significant, the failure of one casts a stigma on all. If successful managers ignore their cultural group, they often feel guilty that they have not paid their dues—that is, turned back to some other black the opportunity and personal help to also become successful:

> "I spend time talking with blacks about the management role I play and what it's like, so I won't be out there alone. I am careful not to get on an ego trip and lose touch with reality."
>
> "I avoid being too much 'in' with white peers. I maintain some closeness with blacks and some distance from whites so as not to be socialized too much."
>
> "As you are promoted, you advance deeper into an all-white environment. There are fewer black peers and different interactions—it creates internal stress."
>
> "Upper-level black managers are in a bind from having to give training to other blacks. You must never be on a fence about anything. I must make the brotherhood feel I'm a part of it, tell the brothers what I've done, but mostly keep in contact."
>
> "I feel obligated to spend time justifying myself to other blacks, mainly at the lower level, to dispel the thought that as blacks move up, they collude with whites and lose sight of their blackness and the problems blacks have because they have a little bit of power."
>
> "You're always being expected to work people problems. I've gotten some criticism from my boss's boss for not sharing my black-white interpersonal skills with my organization."

One of the most important attitudes of the black manager in the Success Phase is the knowledge that making mistakes or failing is not an option. With every failure, blacks know they reinforce the expectations of some whites. When a white manager fails, he fails personally.

"He couldn't cut the mustard," it is said. When a black manger fails, he or she fails for the group:

> *"A white manager found a couple of holes in my presentation, so now I make sure there are no mistakes in my work."*
> *"Blacks feel under a microscope and can't afford to make too many mistakes because we will feed into whites' negative stereotypes."*

An attitudinal result of the desire not to fail is the development of protective hesitation as a strategy. Successful black managers tend to accept this attitude as a way of life in the white organization. They remain cautious in interactions with whites, prethinking before speaking or making a move. *Smart* successful black managers have by this time learned that openness in a white organization is a luxury afforded only to whites by whites. They are cautious about identifying and using resources. Preplanning is now a normal part of the protective hesitation process and just doing the job:

> *"You cannot be open with whites. You cannot say, 'I would like that job a level above mine.' Rather, you must say you want to learn—using terms that apply to all the attributes of that job level."*
> *"I give a lot of careful thought before I make any input."*

In the Success Phase, most black managers realize that their success is in part a result of their being constantly aware of their blackness and how this impacts the white corporation; that is, they know their success depends on their remembering who they are and how they are seen by the organization. Therefore, black managers must have a good understanding of how their blackness impacts the people and the relationships in the corporation. It is not too strong a statement to say that forgetting these factors is tantamount to a *loss of survival instincts*. Black managers who forget may find themselves quite easily brushed aside and forgotten.

In the Success Phase, black managers know they must be aware of the prejudiced behavior around them and have peripheral vision in interactions with others. In other words, they must continue to be sensitive to the many cues in the environment but not respond to them all; however, they must be able to respond to those that may threaten survival or that may offer an opportunity for growth.

Successful black managers have more positive attitudes toward themselves. Blacks in this phase can look outward at the events that happen instead of turning inward and perceiving failure. They can make the system own more of the failures while they own fewer. By now, blacks seek fewer strokes from other people or the organization. Since they have become more results-oriented, the strokes come from within by knowing that a job has been particularly well done:

> *"I'm not dependent on organizational rewards or strokes, because they are few and far between; so I make my own."*
>
> *"Sometimes, the way whites tell you you've done a good job, it's two days later before you figure out you got a compliment. I don't depend on that kind of begrudging reward anymore. I know when I've done an outstanding job."*
>
> *"I know my job better than most. When I finish a job, I don't give a darn what whites say. The result shows for itself."*

The black manager has come to realize through his or her planned growth period that being successful depends on learning how to control emotional reactions to racist and/or sexist behavior. Many whites, unknowingly or knowingly, seem to push blacks' "buttons" by making insensitive remarks, thereby cutting at the blacks' psyches and making them angry. Blacks in the Success Phase learn that they cannot continue to react to others' lack of sensitivity and that they must allow others to own the consequences of their dysfunctional behavior. It takes too much energy to fight all the time. Success Phase blacks know they must learn to skillfully manage the racist behavior of others.

Emotions

By the end of the Planned Growth Phase, black managers have learned to sublimate their emotions. Anger and rage have been made to work for them as part of the overall acquired strategic skills. These feelings get channeled into something that helps produce better results; managers no longer allow emotional displays to erect barriers to their productivity. They regain a feeling of confidence in the success phase based on measurable results, and they reach a level of comfort with themselves through accomplishment.

Behaviors

As black managers move up the hierarchical ladder, they have more and more access to both the formal and informal communications networks. Since they know by now how important those networks are, there is little hesitation in tapping them, even when the source is obviously discriminatory:

> *"I take what I can, even though I know blacks aren't privy to the real in-depth, inside info which equips many whites for progress."*
>
> *"To reverse black exclusion from the communications network, I seldom pass up a chance to eat lunch with whites or stop with them for a drink on the way home. It's my chance to penetrate their data."*
>
> *"Even though I keep my ears open, I find we still don't get information until something is almost at hand, and that kind of exclusion keeps us always in a one-down position from our white peers."*

As black managers reach the Success Phase, they have generally smoothed their problematic personal style. Development of personal style continues as the environment helps shape that style. They discard behavior that proves dysfunctional and develop behavior that works well. The real crux of the shaping of personal style is that black managers find they must use more influential behavior than their white peers do. In working with whites, they have at their disposal more charismatic power than real power recognized by the organization, no matter what hierarchical level they occupy. As part of that developing style and use of influential behavior, black managers in the Success Phase have learned to confront whites in a way that does not strip them of their dignity. The dangers of hard confrontation have all too often become apparent in the face of illogical responses from whites and the prevention of closure on issues.

Black managers continue to set and meet goals. Their focus is on high-quality results. Black managers in the Success Phase behave in a manner that conveys confidence, knowledge, and the appearance of being in charge. They have now forged a track record. They have produced outstanding results and gained respect from others. However, blacks also know that in order to keep that record, they will have to prove their competence again and again:

> *"The company moves cautiously with everyone, but with blacks, they have to be sure."*
>
> *"You find yourself having to establish credibility each time you shift jobs."*
>
> *"Blacks get tested over and over on each job, often having to spend extra time sorting out the racial pieces, then figuring out what to do about it."*

The preceding remarks by black managers also point out that blacks take on most of the responsibility for learning how to manage racism in an organization. They must learn ways to neutralize, reeducate, and direct others who present barriers to their achieving success. They must also learn how to be appropriately aggressive. By this we mean, they learn to be persistent, to speak up and challenge others in an acceptable corporate manner, to push back on the organization when necessary, and to seek appropriate visibility within the hierarchy.

Job Skills

Everything has become important to the black manager in the Success Phase—dress, style, and timing. Blacks see themselves as having to develop a higher level of interpersonal and behavioral skills than white males do. As we have said, the corporation will allow whites, as part of the normal corporate system, more latitude to be dysfunctional than blacks, who are a relatively new entity in the system. Overall, strategy is a very important component of success to blacks in utilizing their job skills. All of this is important because external forces work on black managers, but not on whites, to reduce their impact on the system:

> "You have to know about the interpersonal-behavioral aspects of working with people just to survive as a black, and you must understand it to succeed. You have to be strategic."
> "Strategy and high visibility are what count. Whatever I get from the organization in terms of a reward won't be because it was right for me to get it but will be because I helped whites to see that I deserved to be rewarded."
> "You have to strategize around everything, do more of everything, and be darn sure about how you as a black are coming across. Whites have negative stereotypes about blacks that they may consider to be positive in other whites."
> "No matter what level you are on in the hierarchy, blacks are faced with not having their input accepted by whites. And you'd better have your interpersonal skills together, because blacks are always having to use whites to get things done. Whites can have potential and make mistakes, but blacks have to prove everything and can't make mistakes. You'd better learn to strategize well, too, because blacks have to do a lot more of it than whties to get to the same place."

To become successful, black managers have to learn how to resist power under some circumstances. This is necessary to offset the slave-master relationship that can potentially build in a white boss–black subordinate relationship:

> *"White people in organizations seem to be comfortable in allowing power to be used on them. As a black individual, I didn't like it. I didn't like it because I didn't know if power was used on me because I was black and seen as less-than or because I was just another person in the organization."*
>
> *"Blacks have no other choice but to challenge the boss, because things that are effective for whites are not necessarily effective for blacks. If a black has to go away and do exactly as the boss told him to do, a lose-lose situation sometimes results, especially when the black person's experience tells him to do something different. Whites very often do what the boss wants them to do. Whites are very hierarchically oriented; they can feel the pressure of power very easily."*
>
> *"I challenge the boss and have no fear because I'll give him three options: (1) I'll go home, (2) he can send me home, or (3) I'll go back to work. Most whites tend to compromise because they're the bosses. What whites don't understand is that even though they are boss, what you are really challenging is not them and their ability to reason, but instead you are challenging whether or not we have looked at all the data and options. Whites tend to get tunnel vision."*

Corporate politics in the Success Phase takes on a new meaning for blacks. *Politics* has been a dirty work in the black community because, in the past, blacks were always on the negative receiving end of other people's politics. In this area, most blacks feel used and manipulated by the larger society. However, most successful blacks come to see that politicking is the way people cause things to happen in an organization. It is the method through which people get their needs met and thus meet organizational goals. Success Phase black managers begin to recognize the need to learn corporate political strategy and to appropriately assign its misuse to the user rather than to the act itself.

Now let us return to Jack's story.

"I Did It, Didn't I?"

I'm sorry; that was my wife. She said she was running a little late; it'll be another hour before she arrives home from the city. We should be finished by then, don't you think?

Now, where were we? Oh, yeah. It's kind of hard to say just when I went into the next phase. There's really no clean cutoff and start-up point for any of this. There are a lot of indications that you're operating differently and that past behavior is refined, that you're handling things with more proficiency and without a lot of conscious thought. When you know you're operating at a different and higher level, that's when you know you've moved on to another phase in your development.

It's like I told you before: I was doing my thing, learning fast, everything was exciting, challenging. I was learning rapidly—got to apply a lot of techniques, made some mistakes, slipped a little, uh . . . had to go back and refine some more of the things I was doing.

I didn't realize it at the time, but as I became more refined at managing, the racism got more subtle. Before, people would openly challenge me. Now they challenge in more subtle ways.

Like what? OK! I put together a program whereby the black and white managers had an opportunity to have open dialogue between them, get their problems out on the table and work to iron them out—you know, the difficulties they encountered in working in a multicultural environment. One white upper-level manager wanted to know, "How do you know your program is going to work? People can't just sit and talk about those issues. They're not going to learn anything."

It was a direct challenge. OK? The unspoken message was, "You don't know what the hell you're talking about, nigger!" That one example!

Another thing people would do—instead of asking you questions, they'd just take an opposite viewpoint. "You can't do it like that; you have to do it like this!" In meetings, for instance, people would openly challenge you by simply saying, "I don't believe that." I'd make a statement, and they'd say, "I don't believe that!"

After I had established a successful track record, then . . . then when I rolled out creative things like my program, people didn't say, "Prove to me it'll work." They'd say, "How are we going to implement it? How will it work?" Not, *if* it'll work—and that's a more subtle difference.

As my public track record got better and better, they'd say, "Yeah, I hear what you're saying. I'm not sure that will work." See the difference? There was still negative prejudice operating, but it had become more subtle. The message was still, "I don't think you know what you're talking about, nigger," but it was said politely.

Man, I'm not readin' nothing into nothing. Hear me out. Let me run it down to you. I had to strategize and outthink a lot of people in the hierarchy to get my program over. I knew it was good. I had a lot of support from the ranks. People were begging me to help them with a lot of issues they were dealing with. I'll tell you what happened, and you tell *me* if I'm seeing something that wasn't there.

When my people had workshops, one upper-level boss in another department of the company wouldn't let me give workshops in his area because he figured the stuff wasn't going to work. But as soon as we started to develop a track record—as soon as I pulled together a small bunch of other upper-level managers who had tried the program and results were shared—then this guy wanted to jump on the bandwagon.

Oh, yeah! We had a lot of managers who were reluctant to attend the workshops. I sensed it, sensed an undercurrent of negativism. OK? Again, a lot of negativism was racially based stuff that was subtle. But by now, I had my act together, so I decided to take the initiative and seize upon an opportunity, so to speak.

What I did was to put on a half-day session for upper-level managers using my consulting team to discuss our program. I used both black and white consultants, and everybody had a story to tell. So we told what we had done, how we had done it, and what the results were—how we, uh . . . how we used questionnaires, which were completed before and after the workshops. And it was in company language and terms, presented in a way the upper-level managers could understand. They didn't realize that we were evaluating and documenting what we had done—keeping track of results, assessing the value to the company and in terms used by the company—*and it blew their minds!*

So at that point, they all wanted to jump on the bandwagon because they had visual proof that there were a lot of positive results. There was nothing I did or said that had made any difference before this. There had been just a few white upper-level managers who had believed I could deliver the right results. The rest couldn't believe a black manager had the potential to handle such a large project before they could see it.

Oh, in terms of how I felt about it . . . I felt damned good about it, because I felt I'd had a gem of an idea. I used my creativity, I planned, I organized, and I implemented something—and got outstanding results. That turned me on; the more I got, the more I wanted!

See, in the last phase I was telling you about, it was like being on a roller coaster. You'd be up some days, and you'd be down some days when you didn't do things right and people were telling you that you had screwed something up. It was up and down.

Whereas now it felt more like a steady climb. I'd go up, and things wouldn't drop out from under me as before. You have some plateaus, where you'll flatten out. You'll go up again—but you won't drop.

You know? During this time when you experience success, if you don't have a continuous challenge, you feel, uh . . . like—blah! It's because you've been running and charging hard, and then you have to slow down or stop.

So I guess one of the effects of being successful on most black managers is it will cause you to ask for more responsibility.

Yeah, that's what I did! I asked for more work and was given some additional personnel programs along with the people who administered the programs. Oh! Well, that meant I got a promotion. I got a title that I had deserved, which essentially . . . well, uh . . . I had been working with these people in the background anyway, even though they didn't report to me.

Sooo it's as though I had already been operating at that level long before I got the title and official responsibility. I'd been managing a budget and doing some other tasks.

You know what? It got so bad, people would come up and ask me, "Well, when are they going to promote you? You're already operating at the next level." Yeah, man! Even some of the secretaries said that; they could clearly see it.

You know, it finally dawned on me that organizations make blacks operate at the next level before they sanction it—and they do this to protect themselves. That way, they can ensure that they don't have any blacks who fail.

What it did was to make me angry; I was *very* angry over it. It was a different kind of anger from what I had experienced before. I could see my results and successes and . . . and I was angry because I didn't get rewards for my work.

But I sublimated that anger and used the energy instead to position the organization so it became embarrassing to them to not give me a reward. How? By getting unique results. Outstandingly unique results, such that nobody could deny that they were oustandingly unique results.

Since I had done that several times, the company had to do something to show they recognized my outstanding contribution—more money, a title, a promotion, or something! You almost have to force organizations to see your results! You have to strategize because your results can easily get dismissed, or the organization might not attribute a . . . uh, lot of expertise to the obtaining of the results.

You . . . you have to show the results in a dramatic way, so that it's undeniable that you got *good, unique, outstanding results*. You've got to strategize about who you're going to show the results to or how to position people so they can see the results.

That's what I did when I had the half-day session for the upper-level managers. And the most important thing I did was that . . . that *I* didn't put the results in front of them, other people did. The experts. And some of them were white. You had whites listening to whites about something that I was responsible for. See, I didn't blow my own horn; other people did. So anyway, I got some people working for me and a title, and . . . and the thing that really bothered me was the first day I had to look at a subordinate's salary and give input on how much I . . . I thought the person should get. And it hit me all of a sudden that here I was in a proper position, that I could dictate somebody's life-style.

I guess what ran through my mind was, "Does this mean that I am now on the other end of the stick—the power stick?"

See, at one time I was on the receiving end. And I'm now on the giving end! So the first thing that hit me as a black was, "Oh, my God! Am I leaving a group?" It was a strange feeling. Like, am I leaving one group—familiar, comfortable—and going to another group—alien?

I guess that was the beginning of my, uh . . . uh being stressful around, "Are you giving up your blackness? Have you now been absorbed by the system?" I really had to think through and deal with that.

The same thing happened when it came time for me to evaluate a person. The first thing that hit me was, "Wait a minute, am I going to be guilty of doing the same to other managers that I felt was done to me?" That was a struggle.

I had to think that through, too, and just deal with it. Do you understand? All of a sudden you're a supervising manager, and what does that mean to a black? Have you been absorbed by the white system? Or does it mean you're still black, or . . . or—? You have to think it through. That's a confusing feeling even though you feel good about the results you've gotten and proud of your successes.

OK, now where was I in terms of all of this? Oh! I had people working for me and a wider span of control. That had an effect on me because, even though I had gone through this last structured growth period, now what I did was to reach back in my mind and implement more of the things I had learned to do in terms of effective managing because I now had more latitude to do it.

For example, now I had to think about subordinates, their evaluations, about, uh . . . their pay, about vacations . . . uh, planning, organizing, coordinating! What it meant was that I had to do a better job of using whites as resources.

Some of them kind of reacted to my getting promoted. What do I mean? Well, it was confusing to some of them and a little threatening because now I had more power in the organization. Some couldn't figure out how I got promoted.

The only answer I've got is that it was their racism. I don't know. Well, it may not make sense, but— Let's see. How can I explain? Let me see if I can put it in words. Let me go back and see if I can put the *feelings* in words.

When I got promoted, a strange thing happened. People would step back and let me walk through the door first. They would hold the door for me. Sometimes, on the elevators, they would step out and hold the door for me to come in and then they would reenter—whereas before they wouldn't do any of these things. It was strange to me as a black to have whites do that.

It was just . . . a funny feeling. I guess what it was related to was the fact that, uh, growing up, I'd never seen blacks in a power position before. That was a new phenomenon to me.

You see, it's as though you stop long enough to catch your breath and say, "I really do have it made this time. I didn't when I came in—but I do now—because the people are showing respect for me—like opening doors and letting me pass first and so forth." *That felt good!* Man, oh, man!

But then—you . . . you get hit again with people's day-to-day negative prejudiced behavior.

For example, if you've got white subordinates and black subordinates, you've got to treat them differently. You can't manage them the same way. A white manager has to consider a person's blackness because it is part of the person and must be responded to. Most white managers say, "I treat all people the same." And they work hard to do it, too. But all people aren't the same, you know. People are different—they have different needs which must be responded to differently.

What the white subordinates will do is to immediately challenge you. Their whole behavioral pattern is one of "I know I'm smarter than you, and I'm not going to do what you tell me." Your immediate reaction is to get angry and say, "Damn, you can't act that way with me because I'm your boss." But then you don't quite know how to deal with their attitudes. You know what's behind it.

Oh no, man! Don't just take my word for it. Let me tell you just one of a lot of little incidents. I know you're gonna smile, but this really happened to me. Not that long after I'd been promoted.

I had this white subordinate who had worked for me for just two days. So he came in and told me, "I don't like that picture behind your desk. It looks depressing, and I don't see how I can be comfortable trying to have a discussion with you while looking at that." OK?

What I did was to look at him and . . . you know, I kind of shrugged my shoulders and went on and worked our meeting agenda. At that point, I knew he was trying to pick a fight with me—he *had* to take me on in a fight because he was white and he's supposed to be smarter and quicker than me, and he had to see if he could win. Except, I didn't fight him. I went on and worked our agenda.

Then when I finished the agenda, I went back to his first issue and said, "Now let's work—let's deal with your response about my picture."

I said, "This is my damn office, and I will decorate it the way I want to. If the picture is too depressing for you, then I guess you'll have to look in another direction or place your chair where you can't see it." I said, "Why did you feel the need to tell me that?"

He said, "Well, I thought maybe you'd want to know, because you might want to change the picture."

I said, "Hell, no! I'm not going to change my picture. I like it. That's why I put it there in the first place." What he made me do was verbally smack him, and when I finished, he couldn't wait to get out of the room.

I've had more bizarre incidents than that happen, and most of my black friends have, too. What I'm trying to tell you is, black managers get tested by *everybody*. Not just those above them in the hierarchy, but subordinates, peers . . . [sigh].

OK! OK! I'll give you another example! One of the white managers working with me was responsible for setting up programs to meet the different needs of women in the company. And he set up a group of managers to just . . . kind of be a resource to him. And he tried to keep me out of it. Yet he had some white outside consultants sitting in on the group. And I blew up at him! Because I asked him, "How can you *not* have me in this group?"

See, all along, the guy had been potshotting at me anyway because I was getting noticeable results with my programs and he wasn't. I'd been telling my boss that he'd been taking constant shots at me, and my boss, in essence, didn't really do anything about it because he'd never seen the guy do any of that.

Finally, this one day, we were *all* in a meeting together when the guy, with his outside consultants . . . well, he tried to push my button—you know, get me upset about an issue. I'd made a statement and he looked at me and said, "Well, Jack, you're acting just like a *white* manager would act."

At first, I didn't respond. I just looked at him. Finally, I said, "Well, Robert, I'm sorry you feel that way."

Then he made another statement, and since I didn't react to that one either, he just *blew up!* He just—he looked like—in fact, he got almost irrational, and then he realized that he was getting irrational and I was sitting there calmly with my legs crossed. Then he looked around and stopped. But then it was too late; the others had seen it.

So I've had white managers question the results that I got in terms of how important they are.

Why was my input important to Robert's piece of work? Because I'm a minority, I'd gone through a lot of learnings regarding black-white issues, and some of the principles involved are the same. Plus there were no other inside blacks on his committee. I wanted to be sure there was fair consideration for *all* the minorities.

During this time, I was busy tightening up my programs. And I was also attending a lot of outside management programs because what I discovered was, by going outside, I could get a lot of things I couldn't get from people inside.

I'd come back and use some of the techniques, and I could . . . I really had to be aware of the effect my own blackness had on the situation, because I'd roll some things out to people, like "time management," and talk about how I had my office structured and organized, and whites would look at that information and get very threatened by it.

Why? Because many of them had been around for years and hadn't tried a lot of stuff—but I did. The rookie on the block!! That's . . . that's how they looked at me, the rookie on the block. I didn't have their years of experience, and they figured I *must* be doing *something* wrong.

Oh sure! The same can happen and does to whites—but with the same degree of resentment? Tell me—whites can get help from other whites, and that explains stuff, but how did that nigger get so smart? He's got to be doing something wrong.

Sure, they did have the same opportunity I had to learn and use the material. The difference is, I went out seeking information—they weren't seeking. Maybe they didn't feel the same need I had to get outstanding results or feel the same pressures to do a superior job so that the organization would notice me and see I was a good manager.

So I guess what I'm saying is, as a black during this time, I had a strong need to ensure that whatever I did would be successful. I did not feel that failure was an option with me in anything I attempted—which meant I had to go out and get as much managerial knowledge as possible.

No way was this self-imposed pressure. Look at the situation in context. I was promoted and inserted into a white peer group—and with some of the new techniques I'd learned, because I needed them to help offset organizational racism, my white peers would look at that and get upset by it.

See, what all this would do is make them tighten up their game, because they knew they were going to be evaulated along with me and—initially, they'd look at me and make comments and behave in such a way as to say, "Well, I know I'm sharper than you, and I've got more experience; I'm white and you're black, and blah, blah, blah!"

But then I continued to get unique results that they were not getting, and they let me know in many subtle ways that they didn't like it *one bit!*

Most of the white managers did tighten up their game, and some of the managers started to use me as a resource instead of always the other way around. So . . . as you see, the more success I got, the more subtle some people's negative behavior toward me became.

You know what? One of my peers went to my boss and said that I had a problem with another individual and that I needed his—my white peer's—help. So I sat down with my boss and I said, "Look, did you ask my white peer why he didn't come directly to me?"

My boss said, "No! But I'll go back and ask." So he did, and what he found out was that my white peer said he didn't come directly to me because he didn't think I would listen. He thought I would get upset.

To me, that was racism. So my boss quite rightly told my peer, "Well, you go directly to Jack and work that out with him. Don't work it through me." And until this day, I still haven't heard from this guy.

So I went off and took care of the problem by myself. These kinds of things often happened.

Another thing . . . whites would go to my boss and say they had a problem with me. They'd say, uh, I was interacting with them in a way that they couldn't handle. In some cases, I had to confront my white peers as well as whites above and below me. But now I had to do it in a way so that they remained functional and didn't become dysfunctional.

The key to me was to take their information and get them to look at it instead of handing out a lecture which they wouldn't have listened to anyway.

One afternoon, I was working with this white subordinate on goals and objectives and setting priorities when the subordinate got dysfunctional and, in essence, said that I didn't understand the situation and this wasn't the way he was going to do it and so forth and so on.

So I made an agreement with him. I said, "I tell you what, for the next two weeks, you don't have to meet with me and I won't tell you anything. I won't give you any direction." At that point, I got a little angry and was *determined* not to interfere or direct him.

After one week, the subordinate came in with a blank sheet of paper, put his pencil down, looked at me, and said, "Jack, I'm ready to learn now."

That has happened a number of times. Once, a subordinate came in and said, "I'm ready to let you help me now, Jack. I'm six feet under and sinking fast." [Laugh.] His subordinates were about to march on his office.

It's a sad comment on the state of things for blacks in white industries, but every white subordinate I've ever had, I had at some point been forced to confront their behavior with me. Because what they'll do is try to read your experience and . . . and say, "Well, I don't know if I can learn anything from you." They're comparing your experience relative to theirs to see who is the smarter.

With blacks, it's different. With black subordinates, I had to be supportive because they were dealing with things like self-confidence and all the kinds of things I've talked about before. Sure, I've had to kick blacks about their behavior, but in a supportive way.

For example, one black subordinate of mine had a task to do, and he was going to get arrogant with it. He was going to go into a group of whites and just lay the stuff out—"Take it or deal with me!"

So before the meeting, I had him go to the board and put down his thought processes, outline them. Then we sat down and looked at it. I got him to look at what would motivate him to take that approach. When he looked at it, he realized he was meeting his own needs, not the needs of the people in the meeting.

I had to get him to understand he could meet his own needs through meeting the needs of the other individuals. That was a new way of thinking for him. You see, being a black, he had been positioned in a defensive position and had to learn to take an offensive posture.

That's right. Sometimes, as a supervisor, you have to, as we say, kick some butts—but it's different for blacks and whites. With blacks, you kick in a teaching, supportive way, whereas with whites, I just had to use raw power at times because initially they wouldn't allow me to teach them anything. How can you allow somebody to teach you something if (a) you don't respect them and (b) you don't think they're as smart as you? And that's the difference!

Now, there are some blacks who cannot be reached through a supportive position. Some blacks are dealing with self-hate. That is, their blackness is a mean, shameful burden to them, and they would like to dismiss any connection with it.

In this case, you take the supportive role first. If they don't respect blackness, they won't hear your input. So if support doesn't work, you use raw power the same as with whites who have the same attitude.

With recalcitrant blacks, you let them know the same thing you'd reveal to resistant whites: "I've got my hand on your paycheck, and you need to understand that I am your boss and you can't just dismiss or disregard me. You have to respect me as your boss whether you like me or not. I'm not dealing with your likes."

What? Oh man! You couldn't begin to dream of some of the crazy stuff people did. I had one manager come in my office and say, "Well, I've got twenty-three years of experience; how many years of experience have you got?"

What about my bosses? Well . . . for one thing, I'm careful to ask questions and make responses in a way that is not a put-down. In the workplace, I think whites usually look for signs of whether or not a black subordinate is smarter than they are.

When a black subordinate gets arrogant with the boss in a public meeting, he (or she, for that matter) is *asking* to be crushed. So what I deal with is not who is the smartest, but are needs met and has the boss said what he really wanted to say.

And if I'm ever forced to take on my boss, I always do it in a room behind closed doors so he can keep his dignity. I'm also very careful to try to get some measure of closure in a conflict by putting things in terms of his self-interest—that is, in terms of what he can get out of the issue for himself.

I discovered that as a black, I had to not only pay attention to the content of an interaction but also to the process of the interaction. I'd have to note the questions asked, how they were asked, and then ask people why they had asked me certain questions. I had to hear and watch people's interactions with me.

I became very sensitive to my environment. In other words, I had to learn to pay more attention to people's motives. OK? It became automatic. For example, in workshops, sometimes people would get uncovered because they displayed negative racial behavior, and . . . after the workshop, they would come looking for me. They'd want to fight with me and say the workshop was no good. I had to learn how to handle that.

What I had to do was get the person calmed down and get him or her to look at the data instead of fighting, because I discovered that so much was going on—until my energy was getting spread thin and I couldn't allow it to be spread out on a whole bunch of fights all over the place. So I was *forced* to . . . uh . . . be more sensitive to people and their motivations and . . . uh . . . be strategic so I could concentrate in order to use my energy on other things. I had to pinpoint hot issues and put my energy on trying to solve those for the organization.

My motivations? Did I get stroked a lot? No! I got fewer strokes than before. I think one reason for this was that I was now the peer of the group of people who gave me strokes. Since I was now their peer, they had no need to stroke me.

Promotion put me in competition with a different group of whites, and . . . and the higher up I went, the more pronounced the competition.

Oh, no. That doesn't bother me any longer. I discovered that I get strokes from my results—from the quality of the contributions I can make in my company. I got strokes from publicly taking care of hot issues.

Strokes came from my asking for more responsibility and having the organization give it. I could now see this as a stroke. Fewer people now verbalized strokes by saying, "Hey, that's a good job you've done." There's less and less of that, but I don't need it any more. Successful blacks can see that the real strokes come from the organization giving you more control of resources—both monetary and people resources.

Yeah! I *am* more confident. I made a lot of presentations because I had to sell my programs. I had to become a skilled salesperson. And *that's* the real test.

If you can stand up in front of a group as a black and sell something that's, uh . . . people will tend to—their racism may come out. They'll potshot at you, and you've got to learn how to think on your feet and outlogic them or get them to look at their own data. I had to learn how to do that, and it can be very stressful at first— *very* stressful!

Also, as you move up in the hierarchy, you have to learn how to sell programs through other people. And that's a strange feeling, too, because now I'm a level removed. Before, I did the hands-on work. I'd do the task myself. Now I have to direct other people to do the hands-on work.

No! That's not really any different from what a lot of white managers do. But man! I've seen a lot of white managers get destroyed when they moved up into the hierarchy and couldn't turn the hands-on work loose and learn to direct and delegate tasks.

But the whole company's made up of whites; there were only a few of us, and we couldn't afford to fail. We had no choice but to learn how to be good managers.

The thing that really got to me in particular was that I did not want to be insensitive to the needs of my people the way I felt people had been insensitive to me. So one immediate thing I did was to set up individualized training and development programs for each of the people who reported directly to me. You have to learn how to do this without shutting off other people's creativity. It has to be a balance between how you think it should be done and how the subordinate thinks it should be done.

So not only did I direct the tasks, but I offered development as well— opportunities to learn management skills. Man that's funny! No, I didn't discriminate.

Yeah, yeah. Blacks do have to put in a lot of extra energy. That's why even today the average or mediocre black isn't gonna go far.

Ohhh, whew! There's so much! Let's see. I had to continue to refine my ability to tap the communications network because it was even more critical that I get the appropriate data from the organization. While I was training my own people, I had to be concerned about my own training and development and continue that, and uh . . . evidently, I had to get with my boss and refine my yardstick so I'd know how I was to continue my development.

You know, there's something else I've thought a lot about that I haven't mentioned . . . uh . . . and . . . and it's about this power thing that keeps coming up in my conversation. There's something strange—let me see if I can explain what I'm thinking.

The power dynamic plays a big part in the relationship of a white boss to a white subordinate. It's like, whites are . . . accustomed to and accept having power used on them.

On the other hand, when a black subordinate has a white boss, the white boss will use the same approach as with his white subordinates, but something different happens. Blacks won't allow the power to be used on them in the same way, because blacks are trying to find out what part of the boss's behavior is racist and what isn't.

So with blacks, there is an . . . an automatic resistance to the power, while . . . while at the same time acknowledging the white individual is the boss and that you are going to respond. It's like, before you respond, you'll seek clarity as to whether you're being put in a slave-master context with the person.

OK! Everybody responds to power, but whites don't have to worry about the less-than-human feelings from having power exercised over them.

So when power is exercised over us by whites, resisting it until we understand the motivations and sense of it is like hanging on to our dignity and our right to be equally human. See what I'm saying?

You've got to learn to be corporately aggressive and— No man! I don't mean assertive, I mean aggressive!

Just like I said. You know, I'm not talking about hitting anybody. Now, that's a racist notion. You white boys have always been aggressive. I'm talking about the same type of aggressiveness—taking the initiative to get things done, taking business risks, and challenging your organization to do a better job. And we've got to be aggressive about learning how to skillfully manage the personal and systemic racism on the job.

It's a trip, man! I mean, you've got to learn how to stop being . . . being reactive! You've got to become proactive and strategic. That's what I'm talking about . . . being aggressive.

Wait, is that a car pulling up in front? Yeah, that's my wife. Good! She got here a little earlier than she thought.

You're gonna enjoy talking to her. Oh man! Does she have a lot to tell you about what it's like to be married to a black man moving up in an all-white organization. There are pressures and changes there, too. She can probably shed light on a lot of stuff I've told you about from a different perspective.

And . . . oh, shucks! That's a whole 'nother story.

Analysis of the Critical Issues

In the Success Phase, Jack's basic overall attitude was one of feeling good, confident, and positive about his ability to succeed. He had few illusions about his company or the people who worked with him. He knew that much of his success was dependent on how he approached his job and the skill with which he interacted with those around him. He was aware that he had learned many things, such as managing his anger. In addition, one of the biggest and most difficult things Jack had learned was to accept the added burden of being a *black* manager. This is very difficult for most blacks and is often another point at which the blacks who will continue to move and rise are separated from those who will remain at the lower levels of the hierarchy.

Jack was also very clear about the additional pressures placed on him when he was promoted because, unlike his white peers, he could not afford to make many mistakes or to fail. What he said to us was that a below-average or average black probably would not become a supervising manager. Jack had now become fully aware of his blackness and its impact on the organization as well as how that dictated his behavior within the organization. Because Jack was a successful manager, he had to be concerned about his motives and the motives of others as he interacted in the organization. He also had to continue to resist the people who tried to pressure him into becoming totally socialized into the white corporation. Position power brings new problems to many blacks.

Blacks tend to feel strange when they are given power. Jack shared with us his feelings of strangeness and how he had to wrestle with himself over the use of that power. Most blacks feel ambivalent about the use of power. On the one hand, the person feels good because there is a greater ability to direct resources and get appropriate organizational results. On the other hand, the person who has always been on the receiving end of power often feels guilty because of the possibility of misusing the power. Jack asked himself if whether he would be guilty of doing to others what was done to him by the organization.

What blacks must understand is that they are now in control of their behavior and that the organization is not going to *force* blacks to mistreat anyone. What needs to be understood is that it is natural to feel this ambivalence about moving from one level to the other in the hierarchy and gaining position power over those who have traditionally held power over blacks.

Few blacks have had prior exposure to or experience with being in a power position relative to whites. This should, however, be a positive learning experience. Blacks need to say to themselves, "I feel this way because this is something new and different and I have never been in this position before. I am stressed over it, but I will become less stressed as I learn how to handle my power appropriately. Power does not mean mistreatment, but rather, it is a means of getting a job done more effectively and efficiently." Over the centuries, blacks have, as a group, been on the receiving end of power and have felt its misuse. Ambivalence comes from the notion that possessing power means that you are expected to and will mistreat people. That assumption is *incorrect*.

Another burden or responsibility Jack felt was the necessity of managing blacks and whites differently. Treating all people the same is *not* really equal treatment. True equal treatment means that people should be treated according to their needs, experiences, training, and cultural background. Before reacting to this statement, whites should attempt to understand the context in which Jack was speaking. This may be the first opportunity a white or black reader has had to understand the differences in the dynamics that occur when a black is in a supervisory position. We need to understand why these differences occur; then both whites and blacks can understand that certain things need not happen if they are aware of the dynamics.

White subordinates may resent their black bosses, but those subordinates need to understand that the people above them selected the black managers and that by questioning the black managers, they are really questioning the wisdom of the whites who made the selection. Instead, the white subordinate might say, "My organization picked my boss to hold this position. So rather than react to my boss, let me see why this person was chosen, because I might learn something." This is a healthy attitude to take.

Jack talked to us about the ease with which he could now handle himself in meetings. That speaks directly to high self-confidence in the Success Phase. The process for black managers is to start out with pseudo–high confidence, dip to low self-confidence, than build real, solid self-confidence rather rapidly as a successful track record is forged. At some point the need to get external praise or strokes will get turned into the need for internal, self-generated strokes. When that happens, blacks know they have reached the Success Phase. As Jack informed us, the results obtained become the strokes.

Initially, blacks unconsciously say, "I have been taught that whites are in a power position, and to feel good about myself, I must have whites give me strokes." As confidence builds, blacks begin to say, "I don't need strokes from whites to feel good about myself." This is when blacks take more initiative and more risks. On the basis of these factors, an organization can manage blacks to be successful, or it can program them for failure by withholding strokes early so blacks never have an opportunity to gain real self-confidence. Whites cannot say that to blacks in so many words, but they can certainly act it out.

Also, Jack was beginning to deal with black empowerment. Jack thought to himself, "Don't those white subordinates understand that I have my hands on their paychecks and that they must behave properly?" Blacks need to get to a point where they can say that publicly and feel OK with it; that is black empowerment. Whites will react to it, perhaps in a negative manner, but that is another burden blacks will have to bear at this time. Whites use power on other whites and are comfortable with empowerment.

Another feature of the Success Phase is the way people approach blacks because they have attained a power position. Certain kinds of outward displays of respect that are accepted as commonplace by whites in the same position can initially feel strange to blacks. The flip side of this is that prejudiced people approach the empowered black with more and more subtle racist behavior.

In the first two phases of the developmental model, blacks have great difficulty seeing themselves in a leadership position because they have been taught whites lead, blacks follow. Blacks often apologize in some way for taking leadership or initiative of for being put in a leadership position by the organization, even if it is temporary. They may have difficulty directing whites and will tend not to be as directive as they should be because of discomfort with black empowerment.

In the Success Phase, this will still be a problem, although not to the same extent as in other phases. It normally takes a great deal of time to overcome this particular problem. Sometimes, blacks still dealing with the discomfort of empowerment will act as if they should not have the skills they are displaying. This makes them come across as being very modest. Sometimes, blacks will disregard their skills or appear not to see them. They will use a sad look or tone of voice to dismiss what is obviously clever strategy. Consistent success can alter this, but progress is often retarded because whites inadvertently reinforce this kind of "modesty" from blacks.

When blacks gain a significant measure of comfort with having and using power, they behave differently—the walk is different, more commanding; the tone of voice takes on authority; and attitudes are different. Blacks no longer ask "Mother, may I?" Instead, they make the positive statement, "This is what we are going to do."

Jack told us racist behavior becomes more subtle during the Success Phase. He told us that blacks must continue to refine their styles so that subtle prejudiced behavior does not cause them, or white people, to become dysfunctional. In other words, the burden placed on the black supervising manager at this point becomes one of not reacting to racist behavior, but skillfully managing it instead. The black manager must also make the white person understand what is acceptable and what is not in such a way that both of them can retain some dignity in the situation.

Jack was faced with subtle racism in various meetings when he was questioned by whites. He sometimes handled it directly by saying, in essence, "Can you help me understand what your core concern is, and may I speak to that?" Perhaps black managers are going to have to carry the burden of dealing with the negative prejudiced behavior of others for the next twenty or thirty years, because it may take yet another generation before enough blacks are represented at top levels in corporate hierarchies to make significant changes from within institutions.

Attaining success can really be a letdown for blacks. They may ask themselves, "Is this it? Is this all there is to it?" This happens because the black manager has been charging hard, and all of a sudden, tasks that previously required a lot of energy now take significantly less energy.

Whites need to be sensitive to blacks in the Success Phase and keep challenging them to the best of the company's ability. If that does not happen, performance may drop off because the black managers are accustomed to running hard, and everyone will wonder why these previously sharp individuals are not producing the same output.

Jack discussed with us how blacks must operate at the next level before moving officially to that level. Some whites may think this is a logical way to make sure blacks do not fail, since they are new to the corporate setting. However, blacks will not feel this is fair and may get very angry. Again, black managers are being asked to pay an additional price for the opportunity to succeed in corporations and institutions. Now black managers can get angry and refuse to pay the price, at which point they will not make it to the next level. Or they can say, "This is reality. I don't like it—I'm angry—but that is the price I have to pay to reach the next level. At least, it is for now; in the long-term future, we can hope it will not be." White managers need to say, "We in the system must change things so that blacks, women, and other minorities are given responsibility based more on potential, in the same way that white males are given responsibility." Now that leaves us with the core issue: What are the key characteristics that whites need to look at when evaluating blacks?

At one point in the story, Jack mentioned he had whites talking to other whites about his success as a black manager. It is very interesting to note that even today, whites will tend to listen more readily to other whites than to blacks, no matter how smart or logical the black may be. Jack was aware of this and used strategy to compensate for it. His approach was to be comfortable with allowing whites to speak on his behalf or to directly confront the situation. He let us know blacks need to be flexible and behave in a situationally appropriate manner.

Even when Jack obtained outstanding results, he still had to use strategy to ensure the results were properly seen by the right people in the organization. Again, this is a sad commentary, but it is something blacks must deal with because whites who do harbor negative prejudices against blacks will tend not to want to see the results blacks obtain. At the least, they will tend not to put them in the correct perspective. Therefore, blacks must be prepared to handle this as a personal responsibility.

Even though they are generally not in policy-making positions in major white institutions in this country in the 1990s, blacks and other minorities are the ones who are learning and forming the precepts of multicultural management. Unfortunately, since these people tend not to be at the top of various organizations, the skills are being learned at the bottom. Somehow, this learning must be forced to the top because it is crucial for the future. American productivity is on a downward slide. We therefore need to make better use of all existing resources, and a lot of those resources happen to be blacks, women, Hispanics, Asians, and others. If these resources are to be properly and efficiently utilized, then the managers in charge of the resources are going to have to learn multicultural management. (The issue of work force diversity and the importance of developing multicultural management skills is discussed at length in Part Five.)

Teaching people to resist power is a very delicate issue, because what we are saying is the people at the bottom and in the middle must learn how to resist power from the people at the top. Viewed in a positive context, however, it will be good for the entire institution and the people involved. We can say this because, if the people at the top do not understand multicultural management and the people at the bottom and the middle do, then resisting the power of the people at the top can prevent them from making mistakes that will violate the precepts and concepts of multicultural management.

How-To Solutions and Basic Concepts

Problem I

How to respond to a direct challenge without threatening the other person's dignity.

Solutions

Solution 1. A direct challenge can come from a one-on-one meeting, from a group meeting, or from just standing in the hallway. Use the following six-step process to deal with such a challenge:

Step 1. Relax. Do this even if you must force yourself to do so. Sit back and cross your legs if you are sitting. Do not panic. This first step is very important because the challenge may be laced with racism and you may have a strong visceral reaction. On the other hand, the challenge may simply be a deep concern on the other person's part about what is transpiring and may result in a better solution or proposal for all involved.

Step 2. Be sure you understand the challenge and the motives behind it. Let's say you have just suggested a proposal to a group and one person has challenged you. Ask questions of the challenger to make sure you understand what is being challenged. If, for example, the challenger's concern is directed at the cost and schedule of the proposal, it may be a legitimate concern, or it could be motivated by the person's negative feelings toward you. The negative feelings can be of a personal or racial nature.

Step 3. Repeat your understanding of what is being challenged and have the other person tell you whether you are correct. If the response is no, have the person repeat the concern until you reach an understanding of the issue.

Step 4. Respond to the person's concern with whatever information you have. For example, "I understand why you would be concerned about the timetable for the execution of this proposal; however, let me give you more details as to why I think the timetable is workable." Then share your information with the person.

Step 5. If the challenge continues and the person says something like, "I hear what you are saying, but I still don't think you can meet that deadline," then look at the person and say, "Since you are concerned with the cost and the schedule and I've explained why I think we can handle the schedule, will you share your *core* concern with me?" After the person has answered, repeat your understanding of the core concern. Now try to respond to that concern.

Step 6. If the person is satisfied, then fine, move on. However, if the person is still concerned, then suggest a solution that will involve the challenger. For instance, you can say, "I would like for the two of us to meet with the person who put the schedule together." Later, have that meeting; you may have to compromise or provide still more data to help relieve the concerns. If the person is acting out of a prejudiced attitude—that is, just trying to upset you or make you look bad—then he or she will probably respond to your suggestion of a further meeting with, "Oh, I don't have to meet with you. Everything is OK." This is one way to flush out dysfunctional behavior.

Solution 2. If you are pushed for time, a second solution is to say to the person who just challenged you, "That sounds like a legitimate question. However, could we work on that after this meeting?" Then, after the meeting, get together with the person and work on the issue in private. This is a quick way to defuse a challenge, and if it turns out that the concern was not legitimate, it can be handled later in private where neither party will be subject to public embarrassment.

Concepts

Concept 1: Relaxing. Throughout this book, we have stated that when you are put in a challenging or confronting situation, you need to relax.

In this problem, we make a point of asking you to consciously relax. This is very important, because if you do not relax, you cannot think clearly. If you do not relax, it is because you are stressed. If you are stressed, you will have difficulty thinking clearly or creatively. So if you feel yourself becoming stressed in a situation, that should automatically tell you to force yourself to relax *before* you attempt to respond.

Concept 2: Playback. This concept centers around the need to fully understand what the other person is saying before you respond. In this case, it was understanding a challenge being made. Understanding can be obtained by asking questions of the other person until you feel the information is clear. We have asked the reader to do this before; now we have simply put the label "playback" on it. The way this concept works is to listen to what is said, think about it, ask questions until you think you have full understanding, and then play back, or repeat, to the person what you understood him or her to say. This helps prevent misunderstandings, assumptions, jumping to conclusions, and over-reacting.

Problem II

How to operate at the next higher organizational level.

Solution

Determine what kinds of information you need in order to operate at the next level by identifying people who have a reputation for being successful and who are one hierarchical level above you. Closely observe what they do when they are being successful and take notes on their behavior. Look at whom they use as resources, whom they talk to, and how they talk to them. You need to do this with a minimum of two different people.

Hopefully, one of the people will be someone you trust and with whom you are able to have a conversation. Meet with the person and have him or her describe the difference between how people operate at your level and at the next higher level. Ask how and why there is a difference. Take notes. An alternative to this is, if you have a close friend at the next level who is someone you trust and who trusts you, ask him or her to describe the difference between how people operate at the different levels. Ask the person to put this down on paper and give it to you. It can be marked "Confidential" and may be handwritten. Please *be careful* how you use this information. Do *not* wave it all over the place.

Once you have the information, sift through it and pull out and document the common things successful people do. Now implement the behavior *cautiously* and *only* if you are getting positive feedback in your present job position. It is inappropriate and dysfunctional to use this solution if you are in performance difficulty. It would not make sense to attempt to act at the next higher level if you have not yet learned how to operate successfully and smoothly at your present level.

Problem III

How to position the organization to see your results.

Solutions

Solution 1. It is best to set goals early in your job position. Doing this makes it easy for you to show results to an organization. Essentially, then, all you have to do is write a report or give a presentation on what you did and the results you achieved. If you did not establish written goals, then the following solutions will apply; if you do have written goals, the suggestions given here can be used to refine your presentation of your achievements.

Write a short report on what you did to obtain your results. Use the following format:

Subject area
Key results obtained
Statement of problem or issue resolved
Discussion of what was done
Use of the results

Send this write-up to your boss and others involved in helping to obtain the results. Ask them for comments and suggestions on additional uses of the results. Be sure to acknowledge the assistance of others in obtaining the results.

Solution 2. Arrange to give your boss and others an update and status presentation on what you did and the results you obtained. Use the following outline:

Subject area
Purpose (of meeting)
Key results obtained

Short discussion of what was done
Use of the results

You may choose to use a large newsprint pad, pass out 8½" × 11" sheets of paper with your agenda, or use an overhead projector. Visual aids offer an impressive addition to any presentation. Influential people give added meaning to seemingly small and insignificant events by dramatizing them. Now ask for comments and suggestions.

Concepts

Concept 1: Write 'n' tell. This concept simply means that you should write a short report or otherwise document significant meetings and other things you do in order to share them with your hierarchy at a later date. Write 'n' tell differs from jotting it down, which means taking notes for your own reference. Write 'n' tell directs you to formalize information for sharing with others through a letter, a memo, or a report. This can be a very expedient way to disseminate information to a large group of people.

Concept 2: Show 'n' tell. This concept, named after the popular childhood activity, is widely used in most institutions. Simply stated, you need to periodically prepare and give a presentation to others in order to share information. Writing reports may be all that is required of you, but it does not give you personal exposure. Often, *you* can be remembered long after your information is forgotten, especially if you are able to present your most dynamic and impressive front.

Problem IV

How to initiate management of a white subordinate.

Solution

Initiating management of a white subordinate is an important problem for discussion because a black boss–white subordinate relationship is antithetical to the business norm of society in this counrty. It is the reverse of what we usually see. We were reminded of this by a black boss who was told by a white subordinate, "Not only do I have to tell my family I work for a younger man, but I have to tell them you are also black." Occasionally, we see employees avoid introducing their families to the black boss or making any reference such as "This is my boss, Mr.

Jones." Society inappropriately continues to teach that whites are the bosses and blacks are the subordinates. Therefore, in order for black boss–white subordinate relationships to be successful, the subject of race and its effects on the interaction must be opened up for discussion regardless of how uncomfortable it may be.

You may need two to three hours for the initial boss-subordinate meeting. It will help to ask the subordinate to think about a number of key questions before the meeting. In other words, give the questions as homework. The two-part process presented in this solution involves getting information from the white subordinate and giving information as the black boss. Both boss and subordinate need to think about their answers to the following questions against the backdrop of race and its effects on their interactions.

(Refer to the section entitled "Successfully Managing Subordinates" in Part Four, Chapter 8, for additional information on the black boss–white subordinate relationship.)

Part I. First, ask in what direction the subordinate wants to go. That is, what does the subordinate want to do with the job? Then, what are the top three work items in terms of priority? In essence, the question is: "If I, the boss, give you, the subordinate, a job and you are going to do something with the job instead of just day-to-day tasks, in what direction would you like to take your job?" At this point, you may need to test the racial component by looking at the answers and asking, "If I were a white boss working with a white subordinate, would the answers be different?" If they would be, then you and the subordinate need to look at and deal with the issues around the differences.

Now find out what major expectations the subordinate has of the job and the boss. The white subordinate has expectations of the job that need to be shared with the boss. For instance, the subordinate may say, "I expect to be able to go and find out what the major problems are in the work area and solve them independently," or, "with collaboration," or, "with the boss," or, "with the use of resources." These are the kinds of things you as the boss should look for. Regarding expectations of the boss, the subordinate may say, "I expect you to support me," or, "I expect you to collaborate with me, to act as a coach." You need to know what your subordinate's thoughts are on these subjects.

It is not acceptable to have the white subordinate say, "I don't have any expectations." Everyone has expectations about their jobs and the people working with them. The black boss will have to take leadership in getting subordinates to discuss their expectations and also in pointing

out the possible conflicts arising as a result of different cultural backgrounds. These issues need to be interwoven in the discussion of the
answers to the job-related questions. For example, regarding the expectations of the subordinate, the black boss needs to ask, "Would the
answers to these questions be different if I were a white boss?" Chances
are, the subordinate will say no. The boss then needs to slow the
process and probe the issue. If a black boss does not ask for the white
subordinate's expectations in the context of race, the racial element will
get acted out anyway and maybe in a dysfunctional manner. Therefore,
it is important to open the issue up and ask.

There are instances when whites are put in an awkward position
because of the racial attitudes of other whites. If race is introduced early
as a legitimate area for discussion, whites will have an avenue to deal
with problems that may arise. For instance, what does a white subordinate do when he or she sits at a lunch table and another white person
makes a racist remark about the black boss, especially if it is designed
to undermine the boss's effectiveness? Does the white subordinate sit
and say nothing? Does the subordinate defend the boss? These are the
kinds of issues the subordinate may have to face.

Ask your subordinates how they like to work. Do they like to be
given a task and left to work alone, collaborate with the boss, use
resources, or not use resources? It is important for the boss to know
how subordinates want to work because people will tend to produce at
their fullest if they are working in the manner that is most comfortable
to them. Again, race may play a part at this point, since white subordinates may want to work alone without a lot of direction from the boss
because of their attitude about blacks. This method of working may be
counterproductive to how tasks are normally accomplished. If so, then
the black boss may have to deal with that. This may not be the time or
place to work on the issue, but at least the information will be shared
up front. At some later time when it is more appropriate, the boss can
prepare to negotiate a change in the subordinates' working methods.

Ask subordinates what their major concerns are about the boss and
the job. For example, subordinates may be concerned that the boss does
not have years of experience in their work area. This is a very common
issue blacks face because of their newness to the white corporation.
Also, whites tend to be concerned with whether or not they can learn
from the black boss. The concerns will tend to be centered around
power, control, trust, and intelligence. We can guarantee you these
issues will arise.

It will be difficult for a white subordinate to raise these issues at the first meeting, so the black boss needs to take leadership in opening these issues up for discussion. At least in the subordinate's mind, there will be such questions as, "Will you offer me fair support even though I am white? Are you going to punish me for social problems I had nothing to do with? Are you going to help train me? Are you going to use reverse discrimination on me?" All of these are valid questions that must at some time be dealt with by the black boss.

Part II. In the second part of the process, the boss should give information and take into account the information the subordinate gave. As the boss, you should tell the subordinate in what direction you want the job taken and give three top-priority items for the subordinate's work area. This is a good time to discuss any differences that may exist in this area. You must be careful here not to apologize for being a boss. You need to say, "The company has put this responsibility in my hands, and I am accountable for it. I will take the leadership, and this is what I want the top three priorities to be." This is black empowerment.

The next step is to tell the subordinate what your major expectations are. For example, "I expect to be informed of problems encountered in accomplishing your tasks. I expect you to use me as a resource. I expect you to inform me of all major decisions you make."

You need to tell the subordinate how you like to work. "I like to be kept informed of the status of your various tasks. I want us to hold regularly scheduled meetings. I like to collaborate. I prefer to see work in finished form." These are the kinds of working methods that the boss needs to discuss with the subordinate. You also need to talk about the kinds of problems you expect subordinates to bring to you.

You need to discuss your major concerns with the subordinate, and those concerns to relate to the subordinate, the job, and other things, such as personal matters. If, for example, you also have black subordinates, you need to address that subject with the white subordinate, who could be concerned that you may not be fair in judgments and treatment. Discussion of these types of issues can help clear up many potential misunderstandings and leave the door open for working out such problems that arise in the future. This is an opportunity for the black boss to act as a resource for the white subordinate regarding any anticipated problems relative to cultural issues, because this is likely to be a new experience for many white employees.

The information from this meeting should be documented and shared with the black boss's boss. This can be done in one of two ways: (1) The black boss can meet with his or her boss and go over the information, or (2) the three individuals could have a meeting. What frequently works well is for the boss to first share the documented information with his or her boss, then have a subsequent meeting of the three individuals to discuss concerns. If there are a number of white subordinates in the work group, what works very well is to have the black boss's boss meet with the entire work group and discuss such issues as direction setting and expectations.

Concept

Refer to the "Concept" subsection for problem V, which discusses the concept that applies to both problems IV and V.

Problem V

How to initiate management of a black subordinate.

Solution

The first important step in a black boss—black subordinate interaction is for the black boss to share his or her company history and personal work experience at the present place of employment with the black subordinate. This provides a connection between the boss and subordinate. That is, the black subordinate will be able to identify with the boss on the basis of common experience. This is important because many blacks have a problem seeing other blacks in leadership roles in a white organization, since, as we said earlier, it is antithetical to the normal role structure in our society.

Sharing this kind of information in the beginning of the relationship starts the process of support that is extremely important when both the boss and the subordinate are black. Support is an essential ingredient because black subordinates must operate in an environment hostile to their achievement and need to know there is a reliable and organizationally empowered person who can be used as a resource. The role model aspect of the personal sharing along racial lines is also important. It lays the groundwork for the black boss and black subordinate to be connected for that necessary support. If black subordinates feel that the black boss is a part of the white establishment—that is, that the black boss is placing them in a less-than position—the subordinates will relate to the boss as if he or she were white. The black subordinates may then use protective hesitation and may sometimes behave in a dysfunctional manner fueled by anger.

Three major issues are operative here that need to be mentioned before we move to the solution. Keep these issues in mind as the solution is implemented. The first issue is black self-hate. We will not attempt to explain this concept fully here because it is treated separately in Part Four, Chapter 7. Suffice it to say blacks tend to project their group-identified shortcomings onto other blacks. This is usually done unconsciously. Self-hate exists as a result of the culturally assigned roles given to blacks over the centuries and the fact that many blacks have unconsciously accepted those roles, together with their secondary status in the larger community. This also makes it easier for many blacks to project their personal shortcomings onto other people whom they see as being the same as or less than themselves.

Second, there are black-to-black power dynamics. White males are still seen as more powerful, and the society continues to teach and reinforce this precept. Some blacks have difficulty seeing blacks in power positions and are reluctant to take direction from other blacks. The thought is, "You're not supposed to be here doing this because you're black like me and blacks are powerless."

The third issue centers around fear that black bosses have sold out of the black brotherhood and sisterhood to the white organization. This can cause a black subordinate to be angry and cast the black boss in the same light as a white boss. There can be suspicion and doubt that would cause the black subordinate to try to undermine the authority of the black boss. In many cases, the feelings of a black subordinate would be more intense toward a black boss than toward a white boss because of a feeling of betrayal by the black boss.

This solution uses the same basic approach as the solution to problem IV, and the same types of questions are asked; however, the dynamics are different. The dynamics operating with the white subordinate and black boss are *inter*cultural; with the black subordinate and black boss, they are *intra*cultural. Black subordinates need the additional reassurance that they will get support from the boss.

(For additional information, refer to the section entitled "Successfully Managing Subordinates" in Part Four, Chapter 8. Although that section focuses on the black boss–white subordinate relationship, much of the information provided there will also prove helpful in managing black subordinates.)

Part I. Ask subordinates in what direction they want to go. Now ask the same question you asked the white subordinates: "If I were a white boss, would your answers be different?" Look at the significance of doing this by considering the following example. Suppose a black subordinate wants to depart from normal procedures in accomplishing tasks. The black subordinate may be reluctant to try something new because he or she may feel the black boss does not have the organizational clout to support the change.

Find out the subordinate's major expectations of the job and boss. Again, ask the same series of questions as in the preceding solution. Expectations exist whether people want to discuss them or not, so pull them out by taking leadership in opening up issues. This probing can set the stage for building a high level of trust and establishing a supportive boss-subordinate relationship.

Ask how the subordinate likes to accomplish work tasks. This discussion can give black subordinates the opportunity to free themselves up in relation to work procedures. Often, black bosses can make an easier connection with some of the creative methods black subordinates have to use to offset resistant forces that white bosses have never had to consider or deal with. This offers further support to black subordinates in maximizing their task performance.

The boss should ask subordinates about their major concerns. Somehow, the black boss needs to talk enough so that black subordinates are comfortable in openly discussing their concerns with him or her. Perhaps black subordinates have some of the same concerns as white subordinates would have in terms of the boss's experience in the job and the boss's ability to train and coach. Black subordinates may be concerned over whether or not the boss has any real power or influence to get things done, whether they will get fair treatment or whether whites will be favored for the good jobs, and whether the boss has sold out. The boss may need to take leadership in drawing out these concerns.

Part II. In the second part of the process, the boss takes into account what the subordinate has said and discusses the direction that the boss would like to see the subordinate take in his or her job position. If the black subordinate is working on some power issues with the black boss at this point, an argument could ensue. If it does, it will have to be worked through. One approach to this is for the boss to start where the subordinate is, relative to personal and organizational growth, not where the boss is. The boss can help subordinates deal with their thinking processes and change their perceptions, instead of laying out heavy organizational power. Use power only if other options fail, because a black subordinate will react very negatively to this, especially from another black. Therefore, carefully work through the differences.

The boss should tell the subordinate his or her major expectations. Work these through also.

Then the boss should tell the subordinate how he or she likes to work. Be careful about the power dynamics.

The boss needs to discuss his or her major concerns with the subordinate. For example, if black perceptions about black bosses have not been discussed, this would be a point at which the black boss needs to take some responsibility and leadership in this area. The major concern is how the black subordinate and the organization will see the black boss–black subordinate relationship. We can guarantee this will be a concern whether it gets voiced or not. The subordinate will anticipate that the organization will expect the black boss to be unfair and give a disproportionate amount of support and attention to black subordinates. This anticipation of expectations will be correct, especially if the boss *and* subordinate have both personal and organizational power. The key question for all becomes, Will the black boss be as fair with whites as with blacks?

At the same time, the boss can be assured that black subordinates will wonder whether they are getting a fair deal because the black boss is trying to prove to the organization that as a boss, he or she can give white subordinates fair treatment. Unfortunately, it does happen in some cases that black bosses are so concerned about how the organization views their treatment of whites that they tend to give less help to black subordinates. Here is the opportunity to set the stage for a good working relationship and ensure that it does not become antagonistic or hostile. As with the previous solution, document the session and use the same options in sharing the information with the boss's boss.

Concept

Open, up-front discussion. Throughout the solutions to problems IV and V, the key approach was to confront issues in an open manner, seeking honest input on feelings and reactions. One possible drawback in using this concept is once an issue is honestly addressed, you *must* work on it until there is closure. Discuss it enough right away to reach a resolution, or set some definite future date to complete the discussion so both parties can become comfortable with the issue. *Caution!* Do *not* probe in depth on personal values or private issues with the other person. Keep the discussion related to solvable problems that either facilitate or impede work tasks, especially in the racial context.

If you are not prepared to work an issue to closure or to some mutual understanding, then it is best not to open it up for discussion in the first place. If there appears to be a serious problem that can be a hindrance in the other person's relationships, you may consider engaging a professional third-party consultant to help deal with the pertinent issues. We repeat, do *not* open up a person to a painful experience when you have neither the skill nor the time to get closure on it.

Problem VI

How to develop a personal job strategy.

Solution

The development and implementation of a personal job strategy in the Success Phase is extremely important. Since success has been reached, using a personal job strategy is a way to ensure success. This solution deals with the principles involved in developing that strategy.

There are four overview pieces in the solution: (1) Be clear about what you want, (2) be clear about how you operate, (3) develop a plan and a strategy, and then (4) implement the plan.

Five steps are involved in developing the job strategy:

1. Develop personal goals in the areas of job and home. Think in terms of one-year, two-year, and five-year goals. In the job area, there are three basic categories:

   • Growth and development—learning how to do your job better and expanding your skills
   • Task accomplishment
   • Management of people and resources

   The goals for home will be centered around how you plan to integrate home with work; what you want for the future—new house, car, land; more education for self or family; and investments, financial planning.
2. Develop a vision of what you would like in the future. You need to actually see your goals brought to fruition.
3. Develop and be clear about your philosophy of operation. This

means you must develop a set of personal beliefs and values about how you do things. You need this philosophy for both job and home. It should include the same categories as listed in point 1. For example, your philosophy on management of people might be that people will produce at their maximum if they are in a job that meets their needs so they have high interest and high energy. Another example might be, if you find out what people's needs are and match them to the right job task, then they will perform at their maximum.

4. Identify both power figures and resources. Develop a sponsorship-type relationship with one or two power figures. Be sure you make periodic use of resources relative to hot company issues.

5. Define your implementation strategy, which means your plan or technique for achieving some end. The substeps to this are:

- Define a plan for managing the working relationship between your boss and you. How will you ensure that you get optimum results when you interact with your boss?
- Set priorities for your job and home. For example, under the category of "home," you may have to decide whether you will save money first for a house, car, or investments.
- Develop action steps to meet your goals.
- Set dates for implementation of each action step.

When you finish your plan, share it with your mate or a trusted peer or friend for input. When corrections are made, put the plan into action.

Problem VII

How to ensure that appropriate communication takes place between the appropriate people.

Solution

In many organizations, a lot of very important business is handled verbally by many different people in different departments. This approach does work after a fashion but can easily lead to misunderstanding, misinterpretation, and conflict. One very simple way to circumvent this is to write short summary memos. To help ensure that these memos will be read, restrict them to one to two pages.

Write a memo to sum up your understanding of the results of important meetings with an individual or a group of people. This will give you an opportunity to make sure that you correctly understand what transpired at the meeting. Send the memo to the person you met with; in the case of a group meeting, send the memo to the person who conducted the meeting. Be sure to send a courtesy copy (cc:) to your boss, subordinates, peers, and others involved with you in the project or task. By sending a copy of the memo to your boss and subordinates, you will help keep them informed, and they will greatly appreciate it. If your understanding of the meeting results is not correct, people will let you know, either verbally or in writing. As a result, misunderstanding, misinterpretation, and conflict can be avoided right at the outset. We are certainly not asking you to do this for *all* your meetings, but do it for the ones that really count; you be the judge as to which ones they are.

Keep the memos simple by choosing a straightforward and simple format. You will then not be reluctant to write it, and the reader will not be reluctant to read it. Figure 5-1 shows a simple format.

Problem VIII

How to successfully manage your time.

Solution

This is a short, quick, and easy approach to managing your time. Setting the proper priorities is essential to time management. The best way to set priorities is to know how you presently use your time so that you can reorder the things you do.

Step 1. Determine how you use your time for a two-week work period (or longer). Develop your own personal record sheet to include (1) starting time, (2) your location, (3) originator, (4) action (such as interruptions of me/by me, phone, or meeting), (5) individual(s) involved, (6) topic involved, and (7) reason for action. To make this easy, keep track of the time to the nearest five minutes.

Step 2. Analyze your personal record sheet by category by totaling the time spent on interruptions, phone calls, meetings, etc. It will be helpful to do this on a percentage basis, but it is not necessary to do so.

Figure 5-1. Simple memo format.

Subject:

Opening Statement:

   For example: This is a summary of my understanding of the meeting held on (date) concerning (subject) and attended by (names).

Key Points/Decisions/Agreements:

   List these in a way that will divulge who is responsible for doing what, how they will do it, and by when they will do it.

Closing Statement:

   Several examples include:

- Please contact me if we need to discuss this matter further.
- I will contact you in a few days to determine whether we need to discuss this matter further.
- The meeting was great; it cleared up a lot of unanswered questions. As a result, the project is on track and we are off and running.

Also add any other relevant information at this point.

This analysis will give you an immediate picture of how you use—and waste—time. Now let us work to change how you use your time.

Step 3. Develop a weekly or biweekly schedule of standard meetings you cannot change (such as weekly staff meetings with your peers and boss). If you have the use of a secretary or an administrative assistant, have him or her do this for you.

Step 4. Use the time remaining from step 3 to select some quiet thinking time in chunks of at least two hours, twice a week. This becomes your personal time, which a secretary or an administrative assistant cannot schedule for any other purpose without your permission. This helps you get the things done that require your personal attention. If you do not control your time, then time will control you in doing your job.

Step 5. Develop an "interrupt list," which will include the names of people for whom you would interrupt a phone call or meeting. If possible, have someone answer your phone and screen your calls according to your interrupt list. If you cannot have someone answer your phone, use your interrupt list to screen your calls by asking whether you can get back at a later time to those callers not on your interrupt list.

Step 6. When scheduling a meeting, give yourself fifteen to thirty minutes to prepare for the meeting. Give yourself fifteen to thirty minutes after the meeting to prepare a memo, make notes, or do any necessary follow-up before moving on to other work items.

Step 7. Take a few minutes to develop a short list of criteria that will help you and others to set appropriate priorities. Again, if you have a secretary or an administrative assistant, have him or her participate in developing the criteria. For example: You will give top priority to those tasks that are time-sensitive or that your boss asked you to do. Do not work on something that you can delegate to others. Remember, you can delegate work items to others even if you do not have people working directly for you. You can always delegate work to others in staff roles such as personnel, finance, or budgeting offices or to specialists such as computer analysts. They will be happy to help you if you ask them. Remember, practice makes perfect.

Part Three

Beyond Success: Job Mastery, the New Frontier

Part Three deals with job mastery and is addressed to those organizational leaders who are near or at the top of their organizations and those who aspire to be.

Job mastery phase black managers are those who have developed beyond the developmental model to the advanced skills, attitudes, and emotions required to move beyond the middle-management levels in organizations and break through the "glass ceiling." These are the individuals who emphasize the positive rather than the negative, who see "opportunities" where others merely see "problems."

Job mastery for black individuals at the top of a major white corporation is a new frontier and means many things, not the least of which is an intense and rigorous mental metamorphosis. *How* these managers think now becomes just as important as *what* they think. The "how" is entrepreneurial. Top-level managers "own" the company or organization and are therefore responsible for its well-being and excellent results. At these levels, job mastery success consists of being "in," competing intellectually with others to protect and grow the organization, building a power base that can facilitate the use of a wide range of strategically chosen behaviors and responses, and being able to see and use winning possibilities and opportunities.

A common indicator of success for all managers is the additional responsibilities and material benefits they are given. For those who have moved beyond this success, the rewards become more internal. These rewards are based on setting one's own high standards—never mind what others might ask, seek, or allow—and obtaining quality results because of these

We give special thanks to corporate managers Henry Brown of Cincinnati, Ohio, and Lloyd Ward of Stamford, Connecticut, for their invaluable help with Part Three.

223

high standards. The platform for these standards is personal integrity. Without these factors in place, black managers at the top level merely hold a position but are not in job mastery.

For black individuals at the top, job mastery means being driven toward personal leadership and a commitment to personal growth and challenges. It means seeking to attain the unattainable, to realize possibilities, and to challenge oneself beyond today's capabilities. It means being able to develop a vision, to articulate that vision to others, to set high standards, to excite, to encourage, and to make things happen.

Our interview with Jack stops at the Success Phase of the developmental model because Jack will repeat this model until he makes it to the top of his hierarchy. Each repeated cycle will mean a gain in knowledge and skill, and each promotion and increase in responsibility will significantly decrease the time spent in each phase.

If we were to interview Jack today as a black leader functioning at the job mastery level, we would see a very different Jack. He would have grown tremendously in terms of attitudes, emotions, behaviors, and job skills. We do not want to give the impression that the life of a top-level manager is a bed of roses, for it certainly is not. Corporate America is a tough, competitive, and all too often "dog-eat-dog" environment. It pays to be able to acknowledge that fact. It makes heavy demands on everyone; the expectation is that results will be delivered—regardless of color or gender. There are no free rides. However, Jack's critical issues would be significantly different, and he would have developed quite a different mind-set in job mastery. Jack would continue to deal with the "isms" on his job—racism, sexism, classism, ageism—but his power base and responses would be different.

6

Job Mastery Phase

Critical Issues

Attitudes

- Believing in oneself as someone with something special/unique to give
- Being motivated by self-interest
- Having a "can-do" mind-set
- Having a "can-win" inclination
- Taking charge
- Being self-reliant
- Always seeking the next challenge
- Having feelings of ownership with respect to the organization's welfare and output
- Feeling a responsibility to lead
- Being personally involved in the business
- Seeing problems as challenges and opportunities
- Trusting subordinates' responsiveness to delegation
- Being unwilling to deal with inconsequential data
- Recognizing the importance of the use of personal time

Emotions

- Having a high energy level
- Displaying excitement
- Feeling proud
- Having periodic anxiety/apprehension
- Experiencing periodic disbelief in the results of personal achievements, living standards, and demands

Behaviors

- Displaying high self-confidence
- Showing business professionalism
- Having high expectations
- Having a positive disposition
- Taking calculated risks
- Being focused
- Displaying organizational competence
- Taking initiative
- Displaying sensitivity to people needs
- Keeping in touch with lower-level people
- Stepping over hurdles

Job Skills

- Using highly developed people skills
- Using resources well
- Having political aplomb and expertise
- Performing as a leader
- Freely using power, both personal and organizational
- Having a smooth interpersonal style
- Being conceptual
- Being visionary
- Directing and delegating with ease
- Having strategic focus
- Networking effectively

Overview of the Critical Issues

As we take a look at the characteristics of the black managers who have moved beyond success into the organization's job mastery leadership position, we must remember that their attitudes have undergone a critical shift. Their emotions are different, and their behaviors are an essential part of the managers' power base. Their job skills are now more conceptual and people-based; that is, they work from ideas and concentrate on motivating others to move the business ahead.

Attitudes

By the time black managers have gained access to the top levels of their organizations, they have undergone rigorous mental exercises and change. Tremendous personal growth must have occurred because of the different demands made on managers at this level. By now, the black managers have a mental picture of what success looks like and can see themselves in that position and functioning successfully in that role. A positive attitude about success has been developed—i.e., they now feel they have earned it through their unique personal abilities and contributions.

They can define what success looks like for them and articulate it, not only in terms of material gain but as it satisfies their need for personal accomplishment and fulfillment. A job mastery manager's attitude has become, "I can accomplish whatever I set my mind to do."

This self-confident attitude is based less on arrogance and more on a "can-win" orientation. It is a product of knowing that success depends on their ability to take charge, rely on themselves, and plan for success—never leaving anything to chance. At this level, success attainment is consciously planned. They have a clear understanding of how the organization operates, how their bosses operate, what they do best personally, how they as individuals operate most effectively, and when something is or is not in their best interest. They have clearly learned when to fight and when not to.

Black managers in leadership job mastery have given up the concept of "How can I continue to climb to the top?" and have moved to "How does an individual parachute onto the top?" They find themselves in the position of always seeking the next challenge. They have a burning desire to grow beyond their current capabilities, to stretch themselves as far as possible. They will, if not challenged enough on the job, look for growth opportunities and challenges outside the job. Many black corporate leaders are active in community and political affairs, not just for public relations reasons but because of the additional growth opportunities and challenges that such pursuits offer.

The feelings of ownership and personal initiative are key characteristics of black corporate leaders in job mastery. They feel that the company belongs to them and that its welfare is their personal commitment. They feel both an obligation and a responsibility to lead. Blacks have, by this level, come to understand that they cannot be a renter in the organization and be effective. They must, as top-level bosses, have ownership in the company and be active players in running it. They must be players in the organziational dynamics of the company for its welfare as well as their own. Riding the fence or doing nothing has high costs for both the organization and the black managers. They must be personally involved in the business.

At the leadership level, black managers learn to deal in what is possible—not merely in what is asked for or expected, or in the reality of what currently exists. They have learned to be self-reliant and trust their instincts. If events do not match the expected outcome, they have learned to move quickly and recover. When things get rough, they use their own personal standards to provide them with what it takes to keep going.

Their first concern is with what they can personally control or influence. By now, black leaders in job mastery are acutely aware that the organization will watch closely to see how they handle themselves. They neither act nor react until all relevant facts are known. They feel confident that if there is a fire, they have a fire extinguisher—i.e., they beieve that no matter what, they can turn a potential negative into a positive. Most black organizational leaders seem to have adopted the attitude that organizational life is like a soap opera: Tomorrow there will be a new twist, so one does not worry too much about day-to-day crises.

Another key issue and difference between lower-level black managers and top-level black job mastery leaders is the leader's ability to regard problems as challenges and opportunities. They have had to learn how to envision (see) beyond the bosses and the organization in order to anticipate possible business difficulties and seize upon possible opportunities to help the organization problem-solve. This is particularly true in regard to the company's people issues. Stereotypically or not, most organizations expect blacks to be more sensitive to people issues and to come up with solutions. It has become increasingly critical for top-level black managers to be aware of and be ready to use their cultural sensitivities to people. This more humanized method of management is one of the skills many organizations are counting on from their top-level minority managers, whether they articulate this objective or not. Fortunately, most blacks who make it to the top levels believe that work output is driven by people and that people make the difference between failure and success, particularly their own.

Solving the organization's hot issues becomes a major focus for blacks at the top. Challenging the status quo and encouraging people to seek creative solutions to traditional problems is one great strength top-level black job mastery leaders bring to the corporate arena. They know they must be seen as making the kind of waves that propel the business forward. When they do not, white top-level bosses openly ask, "What good are they?"

What lower-level black managers fail to recognize, and top-level black managers must, is that white executives expect their black managers to challenge business tradition and the organization's power figures—the bosses. They expect blacks to infuse the organization with new energy because today's businesses realize that homogeneous thought leads to mediocrity. In today's world market, mediocrity means death for a business.

Black managers at the top trust their subordinates to be responsive to their delegation regardless of the subordinates' views on race or gender issues. They spend little time dealing with others' opinions of their qualifications. They consider that they have the support of the top executives and would not be there if it were otherwise. Their use of time is a matter of strategy, and they regard time as too valuable to waste on changing the personal attitudes of others. They learn very quickly what white executives have known all along—teamwork is not a democracy. Someone will and must lead.

Emotions

For black managers in a leadership position, job mastery is full of high expectations, energy, and excitement. It is a new world at the top for blacks—a world of unexpected wonders and, yes, shock and surprise.

Most blacks in America never really expect to be a part of the world that they see on television and in the movies—the world of high-level decision makers, movers, and shakers. Those who get there experience culture shock. There is a tremendous feeling of pride and sometimes of unreality. The question invariably runs through their head, "What am I doing here?" That can also bring on feelings of anxiety and apprehension. It is a mixed bag.

On the one hand, black managers in the Job Mastery Phase are taken aback by what most companies consider the usual perks. There is a feeling of specialness that comes from being surrounded by power and comfort about which most people never know.

On the other hand, racism produces some feelings of anxiety and apprehension:

"Is this all a dream?"

"Will I somehow make a monumental mistake and have this all taken away from me?"

"What does all this mean? Am I still black? How will other blacks relate to me now?"

"This is lonely. There are not many blacks I can talk to . . . who would understand what I feel, what I face."

"Where do I fit? How do I fit? I can never be white, but I no longer have the same needs and dreams of other blacks."

These anxieties are realities for top-level black managers. The emotions are based on real-life situations relative to their change in vision, needs, and professional and social positions, which thereby place a strain on identifying with their ethnic group. There is no question that while the preponderance of their peers are white, they are not truly part of the "white club." The subtle differences between blacks and whites invariably get played out such that there are always reminders of who they both are. Even close friendships with whites cannot totally erase this. Therefore, the periodic apprehensive feelings are valid.

Most top-level black managers form one or more relationships with a peer-level black professional. If no one is available in their own company—which is very possible—it is important to have someone in the community or in another company to talk to who can respond from the same cultural base. This form of networking is commonly referred to as "a sanity check." It is often an additional means to keep from being totally isolated from the black community.

The really strong black job mastery leaders make themselves as visible as they can in the black community by participating in black community events. They also make themselves visible to lower-level managers within their organization by hosting events that provide them with opportunities to dialogue with other blacks.

For top-level black managers, there are also periodic flashes of disbelief in the results of all their hard work and careful strategy. There are periodic flashes of disbelief as they experience other people's responses to their position power, as they watch subordinates defer to them. As corporate courtesy is extended and people jump to meet their needs, the question flashes through their mind, "Is this *me*?"

Disbelief often extends to the change in living standards, expectations, and demands resulting from the new position. The social front that many blacks are taught to disdain is a normal part of doing busienss at the top levels. Appearance is important. For some blacks, this can cause inner conflict and a major shift in values. It also serves to further distance these black managers from other blacks—which, for some, can be a painful, if private, transition.

Behaviors

Successful black managers in the upper levels of organizations are usually easily distinguishable by their use of personal style and charisma. They have developed an affect that says, "I'm in charge." It is reflected in their dress, their body language, and their smooth interpersonal style. There is an air of high self-confidence and business professionalism, even in moments of stress. They display high expectations—both for themselves and for those around them.

In job mastery, no learning is lost or wasted. Top-level black managers will use all previously mastered successful behavior, but in a smoother, more creative manner. For the most part, their disposition is positive, particularly when working with their people. For top-level black managers, taking calculated risks is a part of the territory in which they operate. They capitalize on all their past successful experiences to push the organization in new or different directions. They are focused in their positions—i.e., they know what they are doing, where they are going, and what it takes to get there. They quickly learn the culture and fully understand how the organizational system works, such that they know how and when to push innovative ideas and new directions. They are also sensitive to the timing that keeps them in the risk-taking arena. They are aware that they must take strong and visible leadership positions. This means that besides thoroughly learning the business, they must also display organizational competence and get the work done.

It becomes imperative that they be willing to take the initiative to help the organization resolve its hot issues. This shows the organization that they feel ownership and responsibility for the company's welfare. In addition, it justifies the faith their bosses have that they will be active players in the organization.

A glaring difference, in our experience, between black and white organizational leaders is that top-level black managers are much more attuned to the people aspects and issues of running an organization than their white counterparts. Whites tend to have been taught to consider production as their top priority, with people as merely the instruments of that production. Blacks, on the other hand, tend to have more sensitivity to people; top black managers tend to use people well because they know that people make the difference. They are more sensitive to the fact that people have feelings, job needs and aspirations, fears, and a cultural base with differing values, expectations, experiences, and perceptions.

Something that struck us as being significantly different about the way top-level whites and blacks tend to operate in an organization is the ease with which black executives talk and relate to all the people in the organization at various levels. There is also a greater willingness to be open, be informative, and allow people to get to know them. These black managers show more respect for the people in the organization at all levels and are more willing to give subordinates the freedom to share their ideas in order to help produce better results.

One way they demonstrate the value they place on people is by protecting and nourishing relationships. Job mastery black leaders seem to have no trouble keeping in touch with lower-level people. Contrary to what you might expect, they do not pretend to know everything. Instead, they position themselves to learn from anyone. They listen to and question diverse people with different perspectives that can lead to other possibilities. One of our more interesting examples is of a black vice-president of a large corporation who seemed to know everything that went on in the organization before anyone else. He was always prepared for whatever move his company made. It was puzzling to his bosses how he could anticipate their needs. In investigating how he operated, we found that he had exceptionally good relationships with the people in his company, who looked out for him and kept him informed about things they heard or read. He was never too busy to spend five minutes talking to the doorman or inquiring of the maids or janitors about themselves and their families. He offered them assistance if they had problems. He was on good terms with all his bosses' secretaries, treating them more like respected individuals than like staff help. No one was so trival a cog in the machinery that he would not periodically give a quality moment of his time. He made it a practice to talk *with* people, not *at* them. As a result, the people in his organization returned his respect. They were anxious to cooperate with him and help him to be successful. They felt he represented them and would help them meet their success needs.

This manager certainly represents the best of what can be accomplished when you make all your people feel a part of a team, when you encourage everyone to feel ownership in the company. It defintely shows how one can build a power base and gain loyalty from others. We have found that to the same or a lesser degree, all top-level black managers exhibit this tendency to involve various levels of the hierarchy in the company business.

Another common behavior seen among top-level black managers who have achieved job mastery is the ability to step over psychological hurdles and barriers. They face such obstacles and move to deal strategically with them. Job mastery managers are forced and driven to problem resolution because they know that in most instances, "the buck" stops with them. They have the wisdom to understand that since they are among the few who hold positions, all eyes are on them. They do not waste time worrying about whether or not the system is fair; rather they concentrate on how they can most effectively operate within it.

Job Skills

Black managers who have learned job mastery leadership skills know how to use the system to meet both career and personal needs. We have already discussed how they use highly developed people skills to nourish relationships at all levels of the organizational hierarchy. They use those same skills to establish personal relationships with influential "movers and shakers" in the organization. They position themselves to get advice and counsel from their bosses and, most especially, from one or more sponsors. They position themselves under the wings of those sponsors. Top-level black managers freely socialize with those at and above their levels. They invite themselves to high-level meetings, on trips with officials in the company plane, and anyplace else they are normally not expected to be. They do all this to get training and exposure to those who, in the future, will be responsible for their advancement.

Black job mastery leaders have learned that *politics* is not a dirty word or something to be feared. They have developed political aplomb and expertise. They understand that in order to perform effectively as leaders, they must be comfortable with using both personal and organizational power, as well as the power of others. They have the skill to push back on the power of others, using a smooth interpersonal style, which allows people to keep their dignity. They have learned how to present options, along with the pros and cons of ideas and situations, in an objective way. They may be no less emotional about a situation, but they have gained the kind of flexibility of style that better suits their environment.

An extremely important job skill for black leaders is to be both conceptual and a visionary. Since nine times out of ten, they are alone at the top, they must deal conceptually with the organization's needs, develop visions, and articulate them to others. They must set objectives, develop viable plans, direct, and delegate to others in order to implement those plans. They do not have other blacks surrounding them to shore up sagging spots as do whites in the organization. Literally, they are expected to be a "jack of all trades and master of all." This is the burden they bear as pioneers.

These black managers are also aware that they must maintain a strategic focus on the work at hand. Since they bring a different perspective to communications within the organization, they must know how to use their resources well and network effectively. In their case, networking is important to both their survival and their success. Race is still a key factor in the life of black managers, no matter how high their position in the company. As such, these true masters of leadership always factor that into any strategic move they make. There are some fundamental differences between America's diverse ethnic groups, but black job mastery leaders know that open two-way dialogue is the most effective way to produce effective teamwork.

In summary, top-level black managers in job mastery:

- Have dreams and develop a vision
- Articulate their dreams to others
- Commit to a dream, goals, objectives, values, etc.
- Use judgment
- Garner respect (not necessarily love) from people
- Recognize, know, embrace, and effectively use power
- Use their creativity and the creativity of others
- Get people to follow them and draw people to them emotionally
- Are intuitive and trust their gut reactions
- Accept responsibility for themselves and others
- Set high standards and feel challenged
- Display high energy, focus, dedication, and purpose
- Display integrity
- Perform well under stress
- Display job knowledge and competence, especially on their own level
- Know their people and treat them as valuable resources
- Motivate and reward people
- Develop subordinates
- Develop a success style
- Take ownership for their organization and set examples for others
- Take charge of and continue their own professional and personal development

Key Principles of Job Mastery for Leaders

The key principles presented in this section refer to job mastery for minority *leaders*. We are very much aware that people other than leaders may also reach a state of job mastery—for example, those who have worked in the same job position for many years. Individuals such as these may be satisfied to be the *experts* in a certain field or area and not care about leading an organization or others.

These principles of job mastery were developed from our interviews and operating experience with individuals who have become successful leaders in major organizations. We sincerely believe that these principles are fundamental truisms that are adhered to by individuals who have attained job mastery. Our purpose in sharing them with you at this point is to help set a personal standard by which you as a leader should operate. For you, these principles will become one of the keys to obtaining the success you desire.

Have a Clear Vision of What You Want to Accomplish

The first step in developing a clear vision of what you want from a job, your life, family, or social environment is to visualize, or construct a mental picture of, what you want so you can develop a plan to successfully go after it. For example, if you want to become the head of your organization (general manager, operations manager, chief executive, etc.), you must spend some time "daydreaming" and actually see yourself performing in the desired job role. You must see yourself conducting meetings with your staff to set directions that will lead to increased organizational profits or better service. You must see yourself accepting the rewards for excellent performance—a pay raise, new assignment, promotion, or company perks. The ability to do this sets leaders apart from those individuals who cannot or will not visualize themselves in their sought-after roles and positions. You cannot attain that which you cannot "mentally see." In the absence of a clear vision, you are literally at the mercy of your organization to give you only what it thinks you deserve and want.

We strongly recommend that you use as a "sounding board" individuals who are very close to you, who can understand your needs and desires, and whom you can trust. As you develop your vision, this will give you an opportunity to ensure that you have not overlooked any important areas and that you are thinking big enough. If you are going to develop a vision of what you want, develop one that is big enough to stretch you into new growth areas; make sure that you "dream big dreams."

As you work to develop a clear vision of what you want, do not overlook the opportunity to make maximum use of your relationships with your bosses. Individuals in job mastery know how to utilize the strengths of their bosses regardless of whether or not they "like" them. Because of the nature of racism, stress, anxiety, and threat tend to be present in the relationship between strong, sharp minorities and their bosses. This cannot be eliminated; it can only be reduced to a manageable level. Therefore, whatever the quality of your relationship with a boss, you need to identify his or her strengths and use them to help develop your vision. Ask a boss to share his or her experiences and thoughts about existing opportunities and any other creative ideas.

Be Clear About What It Takes to Succeed

We define success as attaining and realizing a clear vision. You can plan to be successful. If you do not *plan* to be successful, then you place yourself at the mercy of random events in your life that may or may not lead to success. Leaders have a clear vision of what they want and where they intend to go. The vision must be clear enough so they can articulate it to their followers. In conjunction with the clear vision, leaders have a positive attitude about getting what they want which is used to enroll others so they will "follow the leader" to realize the clear vision. Planning follows, which must be workable and includes goals, objectives, and strategies that involve others in developing and defining the plan. Implementation is the simplest part of the process. Leaders monitor the process and make changes in the plan if necessary.

Move Away From Unfulfilling Job Positions/Roles and Life Events That Cause Untenable Physical and Mental Distress

Very often, we talk with minority individuals who do not possess job mastery and operate under a lot of stress in their job positions. They seem to be clear about what they want but are hesitant to act to change their predicament. In other words, they act like victims and not like leaders. However, those individuals who operate at the job mastery level have enough self-confidence and personal drive to physically move out of job positions/roles and life events that causes distress. They are patient, but not too patient. They are only patient long enough to develop strategic approaches to relieve themselves of their physical and mental distress.

They accomplish this by informing their bosses of their dissatisfaction or their changing wants and needs. They negotiate increased job roles or new assignments, and they keep their career plans updated to ensure that they are on the track *they* want to be on, not a track that others may select for them. They tend to have ongoing conversations with their bosses and influential people in the organization. With their desires known, others then tend to look for job positions that offer personal and organizational growth opportunities for them. Those individuals in the top level of the job mastery arena take charge of their lives by including their families in discussions on their changing needs and job opportunities. Taking charge means they do not accept dead-end jobs and roles that do not allow them to use their maximum potential. Instead, they ask for and seek opportunities that will fulfill their need to operate at peak efficiency. This kind of behavior signals to the organization that they want to contribute as much as they can to help the organization produce at its maximum.

Understand What It Takes to Be a Leader

Leaders go forth in front of others to steer a group in a meaningful direction and endeavor. Leaders have clear vision and the persistence, stamina, determination, endurance, fortitude, tolerance, and courage to act to bring their vision to fruition. They are risk takers, and they have the behavioral flexibilty to be team players when it is required or individual players when circumstances dictate it.

Leaders are conceptual, committed to success, and motivated. They have high energy, handle stress well, exercise good judgment, provide counseling and coaching to others, have good and productive interpersonal relationships, understand business needs and know how to meet them, influence others to perform well, develop others, delegate well, surface and resolve conflict in a constructive way, and develop a "can-do" attitude in people.

> The challenge of black leadership in a white culture is not so much taking leadership action, but rather getting followership response. In general, the majority culture tends to not have leadership expectations of minority constituents. We are

expected to be managers, followers, doers—not leaders. This is both our biggest challenge and our biggest opportunity.[1]

Be a Role Model and Set an Example for Others

Minority leaders in the job mastery category are well aware that they are automatically seen as role models. We say "automatically seen" because there are so few minorities in high-level corporate, government, or public service positions. Therefore, they stand out as individuals who are somehow different. They are admired and seen as persons to be imitated. Even if these leaders are so modest that they do not wish to be viewed as role models, others will regard them that way nonetheless.

This places a heavy responsibility on those individuals who have achieved job mastery. They have the responsibility to behave in a supermoral way and to help others achieve at their maximum potential. They seek and use opportunities to be visible so they can set public examples of how to be successful.

Develop and Display Self-Confidence and Personal Charisma

Self-confidence—the belief that you will behave effectively through the use of your own powers and abilities—is essential to display when you ask others to follow you and your directives. No matter how smart individuals may be and how quickly they may be able to think, people will not follow them if they do not display self-confidence. The display of self-confidence is an unspoken behavior that causes others to trust and believe in leaders. It may be the way they hold their heads, the way they stand "ramrod straight," or the way they move—quickly and with purpose. It may be the way they smile and invite others to join in a conversation. Basically, it is the projection of a positive self-image—an image that says, "I am somebody."

Personal charisma adds one more dimension to the ability of leaders to get others to follow them. It is the enchantment or magnetic attraction displayed by a leader. It is that quality which causes people to stop talking, look up, and acknowledge an individual when he or she enters a room or approaches others in a group setting; it is that quality which causes others to listen, ask questions, and allow themselves to be influenced by an individual.

1. Lloyd Ward, Cincinnati, Ohio, interview with the authors, May 6, 1989.

Those who possess job mastery have self-confidence and charisma; people who have those attributes make others feel good about themselves even though they may not have self-confidence.

Energize High-Level Decision Makers and Get Them to Produce Excellence in Whatever They Do

Individuals who possess job mastery exercise their ability to capture the attention of high-level decision makers by speaking, behaving, managing, and leading from a positive perspective and with a positive attitude. Instead of saying, "We have a problem," they say, "We have an opportunity to make a positive difference in this organization." Under these circumstances, the high-level decision makers listen and pay attention to the individual making this statement. The leaders' subordinates will join in efforts to make that positive difference.

These same leaders have the ability to simplify complex issues for others, including their bosses, who can then act in a way that brings positive results to an organization. They simplify the complex issues by showing visually how the actions of various organizations and persons interact to produce difficulties that prevent an organization from realizing its full potential to positively affect bottom-line results. Once the visual picture is developed on paper, other people can quickly see specific areas of the business needing to be changed. This approach helps to enroll others in the process of identifying the appropriate tasks required to "fix the situation."

When high-level decision makers see this happening, they provide the leaders with the necessary resources so they can make a significant difference in the organization's business.

Take Big Risks and Win

Leaders in the job mastery state have learned how to take big risks and win simply by sharing the risks with others. Being a leader does not mean that an individual must always shoulder the entire burden and stress associated with taking big risks. "Smart leaders find others who share their vision, enthusiasm, high energy, and business savvy; the leaders then enroll them in a sequence of events to make things happen. Once they enroll others in a project, leaders use their personal creativity and innovation, along with that of others, to invent, improve, and market products and change the way business is conducted to improve bottom-line results."[2] By enrolling others and using their skills, leaders not only improve the odds that a project will be successful but also are able to reduce their personal risk because the others share the total risk associated with the project. When the project results are in, the entire team shares the glory.

Important Job Mastery Behaviors

To achieve job mastery, you should be able to exhibit the important behaviors characteristic of organizational leaders operating at that level. The following list provides concrete examples of such behaviors:

1. *Write proposals on ideas and suggestions.* This helps you to clarify and be concise about your ideas and suggestions. Send them to your boss and/or influential people in your organization.

2. *When you have to write a report on an event or a project, or information for decision making, write it in layers.* Each layer is really a stand-alone report directed to different audiences. The top layer is a one-page executive summary for high-level individuals and contains only the information they need to act or to be informed about a subject. Therefore, this layer consists of a brief summary and key facts. The middle layer is a report for the managers of the people who did the actual work on an event or project or for those who gathered the information for the decision. It contains background data and the written information from which the brief summary was made for the top layer. The bottom layer is a detailed report with attachments containing all the pertinent data associated with the event, project, or decision. It must contain all the information from which the middle and top layers were prepared. Recipients of the report can read as many layers as they need to meet their information needs.

3. *When peers or subordinates produce outstanding results on a job, praise them in writing.* To keep your boss informed, be sure to send him or her a copy. People appreciate being told they did a good job. It is motivating to them, and it makes them feel good. As a result, their productivity will improve.

4. *Teach the business to employees.* Make sure they know how the business operates, who sets product and profit targets, how products

2. Lloyd Ward, Cincinnati, Ohio, interview with the authors, May 6, 1989.

are made, how they are marketed and sold, who the influential people are, how decisions are made, how profits are determined, etc. For example, employees in manufacturing may be able to affect the results in sales if they know how the product they manufacture is marketed and sold. Informed employees are positioned to be creative, innovative, helpful, and more productive.

5. *Develop criteria for success for your job position and your subordinates' job positions; share those criteria with them.* When your subordinates become aware of the criteria, they can and will act to help the organization achieve success. This helps enroll them in a process that allows them to operate at peak performance.

6. *Keep a personal development file to document your learnings.* This becomes a personal diary of leadership and management learnings. Date each entry; list the information you learned and the name of the person who informed you. Review the file every three months.

7. *Attend at least one major training or development event per year outside your company.* This gives leaders a chance to get away from the pressures of the work environment in order to meet other people and learn new things. It lets them see how they compare, in terms of skills and experience, with peers from other organizations. More important, it provides an opportunity to learn and become familiar with new management techniques. The experience can be motivating and can trigger creativity and innovation, which can then be applied to ''back-home'' work situations.

8. *Develop a list of leadership and management books, audiotapes, and videotapes. Purchase the most important ones.* Assemble a list from the latest group of leadership and management books, audiotapes and videotapes. This information can be obtained from the library, bookstores, or book and tape clubs. Purchase the important items and make them available to your staff. It helps to have a selection of books and tapes in your work area so they are readily accessable to people in your organization. Distribute summaries of books and tapes to subordinates. This action sends a message to your organization—i.e., it is important to read, watch, and listen to learn new and different ways of getting things done.

9. *Add a leadership development item to your staff-meeting agenda.* Assign subordinates topics to present to the entire group on a periodic basis. Ask subordinates to review what they learned from courses and seminars they attended on company time. Have them select topics from

the latest management books and discuss how the principles can be used in your business. Relevant topics include how to: (1) write one-page memos, (2) get the most from a diverse work force, (3) improve profits, (4) get people to be creative and innovative, (5) have more effective meetings, (6) work best with bosses/ subordinates, and (7) develop a business plan for individual organizations.

10. *Assemble an "informal group" of peers and others off of whom you can "bounce" ideas.* Put together a group of five to seven trusted peers and others with whom you can share thoughts, creative ideas, innovative approaches, and plans. Ask for their input and reaction; consider them as you develop your ideas, approaches, and plans. This allows you to multiply your expertise because each of the people involved brings his or her own brand of skills and experiences to bear on what you present to the group, which will greatly improve the quality and content of what you present to them.

11. *Develop and implement a business plan for your area of responsibility.* Include your subordinates and boss in the process of developing a business plan for your area of responsibility. Decide on a format, delegate pieces to others, prepare a draft, and review it with your peers in other areas. Make sure that the plan fits with the business plan for your boss's larger organization. When the plan is implemented and properly monitored, it will ensure that everyone in the organization is working to move the profits and service in the direction that will realize the vision set forth in the plan.

12. *Assemble a list of developmental candidates in your organization.* Review the performance and assess the potential of the people in your organization; then select the top 10 percent to 15 percent to put on a development list. These people should be the fast, outstanding subordinates in your organization. Creating development plans for them ensures that they will get the appropriate type of management and work experiences to promote their further growth. They then become more valuable to the organization because they are the future leaders. Review the list and personal plans every three months.

13. *Network effectively with others.* Build relationships with bosses, peers, subordinates, and others by networking with them. Set aside time, either at work or after work, to meet with others to solicit information, give information, and obtain input. Do this on a a regular basis. When minority leaders rise beyond the middle levels in organizations, they (1) tend to lose touch with those who can tell them what is really going on in the organization and (2) get lonely because the circle

of people they talk to each day becomes very small. Chances are, they will be the only minorities in the group. It is therefore imperative that minority leaders make a conscious effort to tap into the informal information network. Go on coffee breaks; have breakfast, lunch, or dinner with others; play sports or attend sporting events, plays, or community events. Most of all, these activities make leaders feel good.

14. *Influence the business of the company or larger organization.* Always be on the alert for opportunities to influence the business of your organization. Take the initiative in affecting the way products are developed, manufactured, marketed, or sold or the way service is delivered. Spread your influence across organizational lines. Minorities in the job mastery stage have the appropriate skills to influence how people in other organizations conduct their business. This enhances their value to the total organization.

Part Four

Critical Guidelines for Success

The four chapters in Part Four focus on critical guidelines for the successful black manager. As we promised in the Introduction, this part of the book illuminates the concepts and key principles used to implement effective behavior in order to overcome difficulties.

The guidelines presented in the first three of these chapters consist of strategies involving the internal, external, and environmental systems in which blacks must operate. The internal system deals with your intrapsychic understanding of yourself—how and why you think and operate as you do. The external system relates to the outside stimuli that impact both you as an individual and the interpersonal relationships in which you are involved. The environmental system deals with the setting in which you operate. We have identified concepts and principles in each system that are necessary to attain success.

The fourth chapter in Part Four presents guidelines regarding a number of other issues that are vital to the success of black managers in the white corporate world, including building effective, relationships, sustaining your presence in the marketplace, information gathering, and career planning.

Throughout Part Four, we discuss those problems and issues that have been most frequently identified by blacks as needing to be addressed and those that Jack portrayed in his narrative.

7

Internal Strategies

This chapter examines a number of key factors that affect how you operate, and it presents strategies for managing those factors to minimize dysfunctional behavior and maximize success in a corporate setting. These factors include creating an effective personal style, learning to manage rage, getting a handle on your new job, resisting power when it is inappropriately used on you, learning to evaluate yourself, setting your sights higher, establishing the principles of your operating strategy, and resisting black self-hate.

Effective Style

For the purposes of our discussion, we define *effective style* as a person's manner of successfully expressing himself or herself in writing, speaking, behaving, and personal appearance. In this section, we discuss two major aspects of effective style: appearance and behavior. Appearance involves dress and grooming; behavior involves primary and backup patterns, both of which are displayed in verbal and nonverbal communication. All these factors are important. There is a popular cliché today that says, "You never get a second chance to make a first impression."

Appearance

Let us start by exploring appearance. When you first see a person, you rapidly note such things as dress—colors, style, and fit of clothes; and grooming—whether the hair looks combed, the face is shaved or makeup is skillfully applied, clothes are pressed, and shoes are cleaned and shined. Everyone is automatically perused with regard to outward appearance; in the case of blacks, however, personal appearance is judged even more stringently. Corporate managers are very sensitive to the pictures presented by blacks and the stereotypes into which these pictures feed. Does the person wear a suit and look as if he or she were about to conduct serious business? Does the person wear a beard and unkempt hair, slacks, and an ill-fitting shirt? Does the person have braids, no makeup, and overly flashy or too tight clothes? Does the person present the picture of a militant, someone out for play, or someone with a careless attitude about himself or herself who would thus be less than serious about the job? In most American companies and organizations, the new looks and fads do not go over very well. They cause people to judge you as flighty, unstable, and not serious.

Personal appearance determines immediately whether or not you are seen in a serious light and whether or not you feed into the negative stereotypes of the larger community. First impressions are hard to overcome; very often, they are lasting. Showing up on the job dressed inappropriately gives some whites the impetus they may need to pull out their negative stereotypes and run a checklist against you. On the other hand, appropriate dress can add to the individual's total charisma, particularly for blacks. It can help provide a mystique, a smoothness, and an attention-getting charm and enhance your ability to draw people to you and make them comfortable. It helps to assure people that you are in control of yourself and the situation. Think of your wardrobe as an investment in your career. Dress in a way that will make you stand out as a leader. People will tend to be more attentive to you, more trusting, and less prone to stereotyping.

Some blacks have a problem with dressing appropriately because they feel it is yet another way in which whites try to socialize blacks into conforming for the purpose of further subjugation. As blacks move into all-white organizations, a certain amount of socialization will and must occur. A degree of socialization is necessary in any organization to ensure that its members all pursue the goals and objectives that are in line with the success of the organization. What many blacks fail to do is connect an effective style to the organization's goals as well as their own goals. If there is no career interest, then style is not a concern. But if blacks have high aspirations with regard to their careers and personal lives, then effective style is extremely important in meeting those goals. Conformity, to a degree, then becomes a means of attaining goals rather than a sellout. Being well groomed does not necessarily mean a short haircut for a black male manager. Afros are fine if they are well taken care of and neat.

For example, we worked with a young black male from a small town. He was bright and sharp in his thinking and very creative in his ability to execute a task. However, he dressed like a farmer, and his hair always looked as if it needed combing. It immediately became obvious that he was dealing with issues related to his self-image. He did not present himself to others very well, and it was very difficult for them to listen to him. The picture he presented of himself caused whites in his environment to question his competency.

Another example is the college-kid appearance some blacks try to keep after entering a corporation. These individuals continue to wear sweaters, open collars, jeans, and so on. Their stance is that the organization should accept them for who they are, not for how they dress. These blacks have not stopped to consider that college is a learning institution where informal dress has become appropriate, but the "uniform" that identifies a white-collar professional in the work force is not the same as that of a college student. Continuing to dress as college students conveys to the other members of the organization that they are trainees, not full-fledged members of the professional ranks.

Even in institutions where dress tends to be less formal and more relaxed, certain rules still apply. In order to remove appearance from the checklist a racist may use to evaluate them, blacks need to stay away from the jeans and rumpled shirt look and avoid being untidy or wearing ill-fitting clothes. There are many well-fitting, sporty garments to choose from, and there is never an excuse for being unkempt. A rule of thumb is to ask yourself, "What picture do I want to leave in the minds of the people who see me? What kind of first impression do I want to make?" We recommend three very good books written by John T. Molloy that discuss appropriate dress in more detail, and they examine some of the effects of race and gender on personal appearance and dress.[1] The following are several key points to assure yourself of a successful appearance:

Pointers for a Successful Appearance

1. *Find a good barber or hair stylist and invest in a flattering, appropriate success haircut and style.* Keep beards, mustaches, and long hair neatly trimmed.
2. *Learn your organization's dress code and dress appropriately.* Know

1. *Dress for Success* (New York: Warner Books, 1984), *John T. Molloy's New Dress for Success* (New York: Warner Books, 1988), and *The Woman's Dress for Success Book* (New York: Warner Books, 1984).

what is appropriate to wear for the occasion. This is an important element in a charismatic person's total effect. The traditional dress uniform for high-level corporate meetings is a blue suit with a white shirt or blouse. This will have a greater influencing effect on your audience than anything else you can wear. Incidentally, the red "power tie" or scarf is still appropriate.

3. *Know what you want to convey to others.* Select a suit, dress, jacket, pants, and accessories so that the colors, fit, and design present the kind of picture you want to convey to others.
4. *Remember that your dress tells people how you expect to be treated.* If you dress like a college student, you will be treated like a college student. If you dress like a professional, people will respond to you like a professional.
5. *Set yourself apart from your peers by the way you dress.*
6. *Consult with professionals or with friends whose dress marks them as leaders.* Take a knowledgeable friend shopping with you.
7. *Select clothes that make you stand out as a leader.* Remember, a person's blouse, shirt, and tie or scarf can be seen at the open collar of a lab jacket, and skirts, slacks, and—especially—shoes can be seen below a lab jacket.
8. *Plan and purchase your wardrobe as an investment.* Resources can help in determining what is appropriate for you, what to buy, and what it will cost.
9. *Learn to match colors.* Those who consider themselves hopeless should rely on someone else's expertise. Keep matched clothes together in your closet so you will not have to wonder what matches.
10. *Wear nice shoes and keep them clean and polished no matter where you work.* Never get caught with dirty, run-over, or beat-up-looking shoes. Shoes indicate one's power status. Powerful people never wear dirty, run-over shoes. Take a hint from the men and women in our armed services.

Behavior

The second important area of effective style is behavior. People display two behavioral patterns on the job: primary and backup. A primary behavioral pattern is the basic way of behaving we each use under normal conditions in both verbal and nonverbal communication. This includes how we talk, act, move our bodies, etc. When extraordinary situations, such as confrontation, occur, we may use a backup pattern of behavior with a different display of verbal and nonverbal communication.

It is important for blacks to be clear about how their behavior is seen and how it impacts others. Just as we are immediately judged by others on our personal appearance, we are further judged on our behavior. If your primary behavioral pattern is offensive and dysfunctional to others, you will, of course, be negatively evaluated. This happens in any case no matter who you are, but if you are a black person interacting with a white person who has prejudged notions about you as a member of a less-than group, you will reinforce those negative attitudes and stereotypes. Therefore, to do well in a predominantly white organization, it is critical that blacks develop a pragmatic verbal and nonverbal primary behavioral pattern that is appropriate to corporate settings.

Let us look at a couple of examples. A black manager may have a primary behavioral pattern of shaking a finger in the face of the person to whom he or she is talking. Or a black person may have a constant unconscious frown on his or her face. If done by a white manager, this behavior might be irritating, but if done by a black manager, additional negative connotations will be attached to the behavior. The black manager may be judged militant, hostile, or threatening.

Whites sometimes attach a lot of significance to habitual unconscious nonverbal or verbal primary behavioral patterns of blacks. Whites are also unaware of cultural behavioral habits. This is why it is of paramount importance to, first, be aware of your behavioral patterns and, second, be willing to develop functional behaviors appropriate to the environment. Consider what you want people to think about you when they leave your presence. That will tell you the kind of behavioral pattern you need to establish.

Since environments are dynamic, behavioral patterns should also be dynamic. If the environment changes and your established primary behavioral pattern continually gets you in trouble, the smart thing to do is to change the pattern to one that helps you meet your goals. We are not suggesting that you adopt a behavioral pattern that is uncomfortable for you. Instead, we are talking about modulating your behavioral style or learning a different behavioral pattern that is more appropriate to the new environment and that is strategically organized and developed to get you what you want. In other words, be flexible.

To sum up what we have thus far discussed, allow us to use an analogy. If you were going to participate in a formal traditional wedding, you would not appear in blue jeans and a gaudy shirt, nor would you shout loudly at the guests. Instead, you would dress meticulously in the appropriate garb and put on your best, most cordial behavior. This is all we are saying about the corporation. Hang on to your blackness, but do what is appropriate to the situation and environment. Conventionality gives order and purpose to our behavior and prevents us from performing in a chaotic manner.

The following is a list of key principles that are easy to follow and that will help you develop a successful behavioral style in your organization:

1. *Behave in a personable and friendly manner.* Use charisma; it can help to create a relaxed and trusting atmosphere. For blacks, charm goes a lot further than being impersonal, aloof, or coolly businesslike.
2. *Start a conversation.* Show interest in others. Most people are receptive when you show interest in them.
3. *Use humor.* A joke or quip can cause others to relax. Avoid ethnic humor, especially in the workplace.
4. *Show confidence in yourself.* Stand and sit erect, look people in the eye, and speak in a self-assured tone by keeping the volume of your voice constant.
5. *Show high self-esteem.* Speak confidently but avoid developing an air of arrogance. Never indulge in self-abasement for any reason. Show that you have a good opinion of yourself.
6. *Display a relaxed affect.* Sit back and allow your body to relax without slouching; avoid worry and tension lines around your eyes and mouth. Concentrate on what is happening around you.
7. *Be flexible in your behavioral patterns.* Learn more than one style of behaving and know when to use each style appropriately. Learn to be assertive (gently, confidently pushing back) and aggressive (vigorously taking the initiative to make something happen).[2]

2. We personally dislike the term *assertive* because we feel it only came into popular use after blacks and women joined previously all-white male organizations. When organizations had only white males in professional roles, the word *aggressive* was a positive and acceptable term for people taking charge. However, when blacks and women joined the professional ranks, they were expected to take charge but in a nice way by gently influencing others. Therefore, the term *assertive* gained popularity. We are stuck with the word *assertive*, however, and the supposed difference between *assertive* and *aggressive* today lies in the degree of hostility and combativeness involved.

8. *Read the style of your audience.* Develop the art of reading cues and respond with behavior that will meet both your needs and those of your audience.

9. *Copy the styles of other people.* Learn how to copy the behavioral styles of others to get your needs met. When you see someone behaving in an outstanding manner that gets that person what he or she wants, copy the behavior.

10. *Time your behavior.* Some people have natural timing. If you do not, be sensitive to the cues that tell you that a given behavioral style is getting you nowhere; then change your style.

11. *Display high energy.* Allow your enthusiasm to infect the people around you; walk fast at work. Let your personal excitement be reflected in your tone of voice and facial expression.

12. *Be sensitive to others.* Be aware of the needs of others and behave appropriately. Learn to be sensitive across cultural and gender lines.

13. *Show respect to others.* When you give respect, you tend to get respect. Freely use your cultural abilities to relate to all people at all levels and ages.

To help you focus on, build upon, or improve your overall style, we strongly recommend that you use the "Effective Style Assessment Checklist" (Figure 7-1). Make a copy of this form and complete it. Then make a separate form showing how you could enhance your style and appearance. Review the information to get a clear picture of your style; decide what you like, what you dislike, and what areas you need to improve. Use the form as your road map to develop and improve your style. Periodically, update the form. Be sure to date it so that you will know which is the latest copy.

Management of Rage

Little is ever said about black rage. Whites are afraid to discuss it openly, and many blacks deny it exists. Two of the few authors who have dared to expose and candidly discuss this volatile issue are Dr. William Grier and Dr. Price Cobbs, in their book *Black Rage*. Admittedly, the concept is a difficult one to face and explore because of the strong implication of violence associated with it. However, we would be remiss in our task if we did not give this subject some attention and attempt to provide a positive perspective on a condition that we all know exists.

Figure 7-1. Style assessment checklist.

Date:_____

I. Appearance in the Workplace

  A. Clothing

    How do you feel about clothing, particularly dressing for your job?

    _____

    _____

    _____

    Describe your normal working clothes.

    _____

    _____

    _____

    Taking into account the colors you normally wear, how do you match your colors?

    _____

    _____

    _____

    How much do you think your dressing habits are affected by the dressing habits of your peers?

    _____

    _____

    _____

    In dressing, which of the following factors do you pay attention to?

    ☐ Fit   ☐ Personal taste

    ☐ Style for the situation   ☐ Popular styles

(continued)

Figure 7-1. (continued)

B. Grooming

- Is your hairstyle flattering to you?_____
- Does your face look neat: clipped mustache, shaved face, trimmed beard, or flattering makeup?_____
- Are your clothes pressed and neat?_____
- Are your shoes clean and shined (not run over, beat-up, or showing "skinned" heels)?_____

When people first see you, what picture do you think you leave in their mind?

_____

_____

_____

How do you want people to view you on first glance?

_____

_____

_____

II. Behavior in the Workplace

A. Primary Behavior Pattern

Under normal circumstances, what is your behavioral pattern with respect to the following factors?

Facial expression _____

Body position _____

Position of your hands _____

Speech pattern _____

B. Backup Behavior Pattern

Under stress or time pressure, what is your behavioral pattern with respect to the following factors?

Facial expression _____

Body position _____

Position of your hands _____

Speech pattern _____

III. Effective Style Assessment Checklist

When I consider my style and appearance, I need to improve by doing the following:

1.

2.

3.
   .
   .
   .
   .

Very seldom do we make all-inclusive statements, but we will say that all blacks are angry in America—regardless of whether or not they act out that anger toward whites. In American blacks, most black rage is turned inward and sometimes comes out in self-destructive ways, as we will discuss later in this chapter. As we defined *black rage* in Part Two, Chapter 3, it is the furious anger born out of a person's blackness and all that means in our society. Black rage is the logical reaction of blacks to racism. The anger is the product of being and feeling powerless, less than whites, systematically discriminated against, and frustrated.

Jack, in his narrative in the Adjusting Phase, gave a good example of how this black rage mounts and surfaces in blacks in the work environment. He also pointed out what kinds of prejudiced behavior trigger the anger. Jack told us how he was frustrated in his efforts to grow and learn. He talked to us about how this frustration and anger surfaced and how he became dysfunctional in his interactions with others. His behavior became more and more inappropriate, until he realized that he had just two options left—he could either learn to manage his emotions and channel that energy into something constructive, or he could leave the company. Today, more blacks are opting to leave the company, and many of these men and women are choosing to pursue their own entrepreneurial endeavors.

This brings us to the management of rage—what is it, and how is it accomplished? We define the *management of rage* as the ability to control the vast amount of anger that blacks feel and to cope with the other emotions that are associated with that anger. Here are seven key principles for managing rage:

1. *Rage is inevitable for blacks.* Given that blacks for hundreds of years endured racial prejudice and discrimination, it would be ludicrous to believe that all is well and calm and that blacks are not angry. Rage is the natural reaction of a persecuted group to another group's ability to act out with power, authority, and desire its hostility and prejudice. Therefore, it is fruitless to deny that the rage exists and think that denying it will make it disappear.

2. *Do not block your anger.* Since rage is inevitable, do not block the internal anger. Particularly in white settings, blacks tend to bottle up their anger. Evidence of this bottled-up anger is a prevalence of hypertension and heart attacks among blacks as a group.[3] We are not suggesting that you should riot or in any other way exhibit inappropriate behavior. We are saying recognize the rage and understand what it is and why it exists. Your black rage can be a source of strength and energy if you allow yourself to freely experience it.

3. *Rage can be cathartic.* Rage can have a cleansing effect because it is a built-in pressure-relief valve that when used appropriately, prevents the invididual from exploding from within. Much of the harm we do to ourselves and others is a result of pent-up anger, frustration, and resentment. What most often happens is that the rage we experience and yet deny leaves us feeling crazy. Jack brought his phenomenon to our attention in his narrative. This is a frightening experience. The feeling of going mad can end when we accept our honest feelings of anger, realize they are justified, and know there are ways to deal with the emotions constructively.

Initial release can come in many ways. Some blacks discuss their feelings with their mates or close, trusted friends. Sometimes, strenuous activity, such as exercise or sports, may help. A hobby can bring great relief, as can doing strenuous work around the house.

3. William H. Grier and Price M. Cobbs, *The Jesus Bag* (New York: McGraw-Hill, 1971), p. 183.

4. *Rage can be managed.* It is possible to control anger and cope with strong emotions if you understand where they come from and that you should not block them. Allow them to be cathartic. Rage can be managed when you feel OK with your emotions, understand them, and know you need not misuse your feelings by hurting someone or yourself. Rage is raw energy, like fuel in a car, and can be used as such to drive you to problem resolution. The strength and energy generated by the rage can be harnessed and used strategically to confront and resolve major issues. It can physically drive you to address those issues and correct an intolerable situation you may be experiencing.

5. *Use rage as a strategic constructive tool.* As we said, rage can be a source of strength for blacks. When you feel rage internally and you are managing it because you understand why you have it, where it is coming from, and what it is, then you can let it surface in a controlled way. Believe us; it will get the attention you seek. You can do this without turning people off, frightening them, or jeopardizing your career.

As an example, let us take the case of a young black manager who administratively reported to one boss but, in addition, performed tasks for another functional "boss." In essence, this black manager was responding to the directions and needs of two different people. He had two full-time jobs in this situation and was constantly being asked to do more. The two white bosses normally did not talk to each other about what the black subordinate was doing for each of them. Both bosses wondered why their black subordinate could not handle more tasks. The black manager tried to explain that he was doing work for two people. The two bosses never seemed to get together, and the black subordinate was never able to get them together, either. Finally, one day, out of utter frustration, the black manager became so angry and so filled with anxiety and emotion that he could not stand it any longer. Literally pounding the table of one of the bosses, he shouted, "Damn it! It's not fair! I can't and won't take this anymore!"

In this example, the black manager used his rage, without attacking the other person, to get one manager's attention. As a result, he made his boss understand that something must be seriously wrong, because he did not normally behave this way. The boss figured it would be wise to stop and really listen to determine what the problem was. Once the black manager had his boss's serious attention long enough, he was able to explain the situation. The white boss said, "Oh, I guess you and I had better go talk to the other guy. I didn't know we were putting that much pressure on you." The black subordinate had tried to tell the boss before, but the boss would not listen. On the basis of the information we have already covered, we can speculate about why the boss failed to listen. The black manager finally allowed his rage to surface so that he could force his boss to face the issue of what he was doing. He was able to use his anger strategically and constructively to get the boss's attention so the white manager would slow down, listen, and help change the untenable position in which he had helped to place the subordinate.

6. *Do not personalize your anger.* Do not direct your anger toward a specific individual but rather toward an issue. You gain nothing by berating a John or Jane Doe but may gain a lot by attacking Doe's dysfunctional or inappropriate behavior. If a person has exercised bad judgment in a situation involving you, you need to direct your rage toward the person's judgment—not toward the person's character and dignity.

7. *Rage can lead to creativity.* Anger is not a natural state for anyone, and it takes a lot of effort and energy to sustain it. Usually, when anger cannot be released, it is either turned inward to eat away at the individual or builds until it erupts in explosive, dysfunctional ways. When they accept anger as a logical reaction to unfair personal and systemic racism, individuals can plan to use their anger as fuel—as energy that will enable them to become creative and innovative in seeking solutions to resolve the situation that is producing the anger.

Jack, in his narrative in the Adjusting Phase, presented us with examples of his creative thinking after he became enraged over the situation in the personnel office. Despite his company's protestations about its inability to find qualified blacks, Jack realized that white individuals in his company were not looking in places where blacks could be found. Rather than vent his anger onto the recruiters, Jack found ways to make himself an example by recruiting more qualified blacks than the company could use. Jack also became enraged over the insensitive manner in which the company responded to its black employees, so he reorganized the office and found creative ways to improve the situation. He was able to do this because he was fueled by his anger.

One very important technique to use in managing rage—as well as ensuring that your actions and goals are realized—is to develop an individual strategy process. The block diagram shown in Figure 7-2 illustrates how to develop an effective individual strategy. Try it out. First, focus on a situation that has produced frustration and anger for you. Using your anger as fuel, just as you would put gasoline in your car, focus that energy into building an individual strategy.

Figure 7-2. Process for developing an individual strategy.

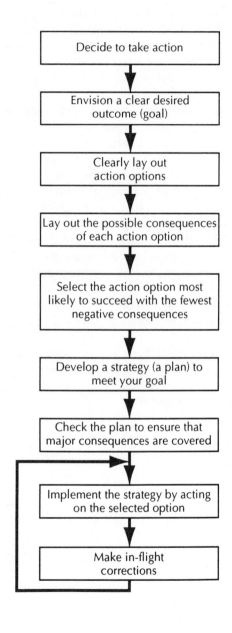

Getting the New Job Together

It is of the utmost importance for blacks starting a new job to begin in the right mode and direction. As a black, you cannot afford the luxury of waiting for the informal communications network to help you get started or for your peers or your boss to know what to tell you to do. They may not be skilled in multicultural management. The principles we discuss in this section also apply when you move from one job area to another within the same company. It is important to have a documented plan to give yourself a purpose and direction before you dive into your job tasks. There are four basic principles:

1. *Obtain preliminary information.* When you have several pending job options or when a transfer is imminent and more than one job area may be open to you, you may want to ask the following questions of each potential boss. It is important to do so in order to have a clear understanding of what kinds of things you are looking for, what the job is all about, and what direction you desire for the future. Your new job needs to be a step toward reaching your overall goal:

- What are the major tasks to be accomplished?
- What are the hot organizational issues and concerns in the job area?
- What is your timetable for my accomplishing the major job tasks?
- What do you personally want me to do with the job?
- What skills and positive characteristics does one need to be successful in this job position?
- What skills and characteristics do you see me bringing to this job position?
- What will the things I learn in this assignment permit me to do in my next assignment?

These questions are the key to beginning your new job because they will provide you with all kinds of preliminary information that can be used to develop a "joining-up checklist."

2. *Develop a joining-up checklist.* Use Figure 7-3 to lay out the steps you should use in setting up your job. For those of you who are more experienced and regard Figure 7-3 as being too elementary, we suggest you use Figure 7-4. Perhaps a combination of the two charts would be appropriate for some of you.

Figure 7-3. Joining-up checklist.

Area	Discussion Topic	Action
Job content	• Core mission of your organization • Major tasks • Hot job issues and concerns • Your organizational role • Status of present work in job area	(Use this column to list your action steps.)
Management of job	• Boss's expectations • Success factors for the job • Setting goals and objectives • Setting priorities • Identifying resources • Relationship with other organizations	
Management of people (self and others)	• Identifying and meeting key people • Developing evaluation criteria • Identifying adversaries and supporters	
Training and development	• Personal training and development needs • Training and development resources • Documenting your plan	

Figure 7-4. Job plan.

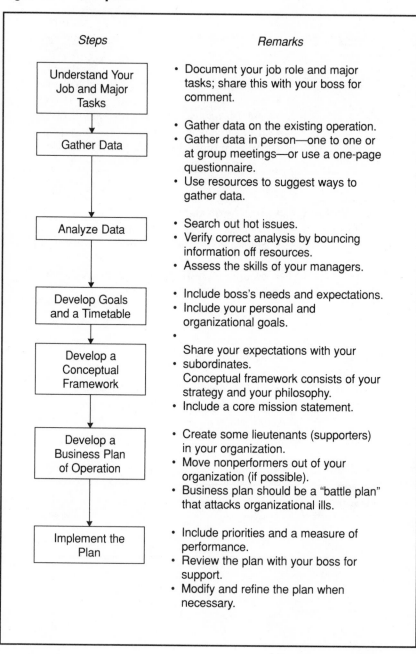

3. *Develop a job implementation action plan.* Consider all the preliminary information you gathered and, after making the joining-up checklist and checking off the items on that list, develop a job implementation action plan. In other words, take all your information, organize it, and develop a strategy in order to implement some action to start performing the job tasks, whatever the job is. Part of the action plan has to include some way of expanding or refining your existing job so that when you leave the job, it will not be the same as it was when you started it. We leave the action plan up to you, since it must be specific to your needs; however, remember to include a timetable. It should be a step-by-step plan with dates that shows how you are going to start to perform in the new job. For example, step 1 might be to identify the tasks you need to perform in the next two weeks; step 2 might be to plan and organize in order to perform the tasks by the end of the third week; and so on.

4. *Seek a sponsor.* If you already have a sponsor and you have merely moved from one job area to another, you can continue your relationship with the existing sponsor or develop a new sponsor. If you have moved into a new job area and you do not have a sponsor, it is to your advantage to develop one, as we have stated in previous chapters. (To review the specifics of developing a sponsor, we refer you to the solution for problem VI in Part Two, Chapter 4.)

Resisting Power

In the context of our discussion, *resisting power* is defined as a black manager's pushing back on someone who is in a position of power (i.e., a boss or a top-level manager) when the situation is viewed as one that violates the value system or integrity of the black individual, will negatively affect the career of the black individual, or could come back to haunt the black individual, the boss, or the higher-up. Resisting power is a touchy issue for blacks because the boss has the ability to punish subordinates by giving them bad evaluations and dead-end assignments. In resisting power, it is performance that counts—not knowledge of how to do it.

With this definition and explanation in mind, let us look at why resisting power is important for blacks. Take into account the historical plight of blacks in this country and to their position in society. We know that blacks have been regarded as second-class citizens, and as a result of the long-standing propaganda and consequent discrimination, most blacks have at some time bought into some pieces of this negative stereotype. Blacks have to push back to challenge white managers' negative stereotypes. When this is done effectively in the workplace, the bottom line is, of course, greater productivity and efficiency. Pushing back eliminates a lot of dysfunctional behavior between managers of different cultures that would cause a decrease in productivity. What we are saying is, if white managers hang on to their negative stereotypes about blacks, it will cause them to give blacks smaller jobs, have lower expectations of blacks, and deny blacks opportunities to use their expertise and creativity. Therefore, there will be black managers who are not working at their maximum potential. That affects the productivity and efficiency of the total organization. There are five key principles associated with resisting power:

1. *Effective leaders at one time or another resist power.* They use the concept as a strategy in accomplishing tasks and resolving issues. If you desire to be an effective leader, you *must* learn to appropriately resist power. Effective leaders do not give in to people who use intimidation as their primary style of interacting.

2. *There are two kinds of resistance to power.* When individuals push back, they use either *immediate* resistance or *delayed* resistance. Immediate resisting of power occurs at the time when a stimulus in an interaction causes a reaction. Delayed resisting of power occurs during an interaction subsequent to the one in which the initial stimulus occurred.

Everybody, no matter what their level in the organization, will be told on many occasions to, in essence, "Shut up and draw." That means, do only what the boss tells you to do, no more and no less. In the case of a black manager, this kind of order causes automatic, often immediate, resistance. This happens because such situations involve the black individual's self-concept, which plays a big part in his or her primary and backup behavioral patterns. Take Jack as an example. When his boss said, "Go over there and do this job just as I told you to do" (i.e., "Shut up and draw"), Jack did not have to use any of the expertise he had developed in school or through his years of experience. He reacted automatically.

If you're a black, you are going to try to protect your self-concept. You will say to yourself, "I *am* somebody, and if I am somebody, I can think on my own. I need the boss to tell me what end point he or she is trying to reach and let me use my own expertise and creativity to figure out how to get to that end point." Depending on where the black manager is in the four phases of development, he or she may externally resist power by saying, "Wait a minute. Can't we discuss the end point that you're trying to reach by taking that approach?" This would be immediate resistance to power.

Some managers have a primary behavioral pattern of intimidation to get people to respond to them. When a very strong upper-level white manager uses intimidation on a black manager, it is often done rapidly, or it may be done in a situation involving other people. The black manager will tend to react internally but will not externally display resistance to power. The black will take in the message, go away and think about it, analyze the situation, and decide not to do what he or she has been told but instead to go back and reopen the issue. Blacks have to resist power when they do not understand why they were told to "Shut up and draw."

If the intimidating white manager is one level up, then it is relatively easy to come back in a one-to-one setting and engage that person in conversation. If the manager is two or more levels up, the black should use a database to develop an alternative way of accomplishing the task. In this case, resistance should be based on data analysis. The black manager should first gather data, analyze the situation, and then come back and resist the power of the upper-level white manager. It can be done very smoothly by saying, "I understand you want me to do X, Y, and Z. However, have you considered the risks involved? Do you really want me to do it this way? If you do, I will. But recognize that I'm not in agreement with it even though I will do it."

Those blacks who do not resist power will become intimidated and not fight back. This will have a detrimental effect in terms of continued low self-concept and reduced productivity.

3. *Use the concept of resisting power only when logic and explanation fail.* This is a good rule of thumb to remember. We must be candid with you: Resisting power can have negative consequences for blacks. When you sense that you may need to resist power, first try using logic to explain your position on an issue or a problem. Introduce facts and figures. Only if this fails should you use the concept of resisting power.

4. *Depersonalize the resistance to power.* Focus your resistance on the task or issue and not on the person involved in the interaction. It is inappropriate to exclaim, "Are you crazy?" or get angry and scream, "Have you lost your mind? Do you think I'm incapable of knowing how to do my job?" or make any other personal attack on the individual. You should not strip people of their dignity.

5. *Resisting power is triggered by external events.* You will resist power when you feel rage or when you feel in a less-than position. When you cannot separate the boss's directions from his or her racism or sexism, you will react and resist power. When you have been positioned so that you cannot use your expertise or creativity to do your job, you will feel it necessary to resist the power of others. There are times when you may be asked to take some inappropriate action that protective hesitation tells you not to take; then you will resist the power of the person who has attempted to intimidate you. You will resist power when all options in a situation have not been considered and when you strongly feel you are right or when you substantially disagree with someone in a power position. You must resist power when you could potentially be labeled a follower or a weak leader. You may also have to resist power in order to push or sell one of your ideas.

Self-Evaluation

Self-evaluation is especially important *against the backdrop of race or sex.* Its purpose is to help you (1) find out where you are relative to your goals; (2) evaluate yourself against some preset organizational standard of performance; and (3) assess your personal growth and development, which includes the impact that the organization has made on you, as a black, as well as the impact that you, as a black, have made on the organization. This information will position you to determine your future direction. Self-evaluation can also be helpful to you when used as a yardstick to measure the distance that remains to meeting your goals. The results of self-evaluation can help build self-confidence as a black and increase self-esteem.

Because you are black, you should evaluate yourself with a different cultural reference viewpoint from that of the dominant culture in a typical organization. Self-evaluation is a legitimate system of performance counseling that is not used very often. It is helpful to perform self-evaluation because the odds are you know a great deal more about yourself than anyone else does. You know what your needs are, what you want for yourself, what your skills and abilities are, and what motivates you. The system of self-evaluation should, however, be integrated with the official formal organizational evaluation that your boss gives you.[4]

4. Lois Borland Hart, *Moving Up! Women and Leadership* (New York: AMACOM, 1980), p. 119.

Self-evaluation should occur at least every six months. It should be done at transfer time and before a formal assessment by your boss. Anytime you feel you want to test yourself to see where you are in terms of your personal development, stop and evaluate yourself. Also, do it anytime you need to answer the following questions:

- Where am I rated in terms of my job performance?
- Where am I located in the four-phase black development model?
- Where am I with myself—i.e., am I comfortable with my black-ness or femaleness?
- Am I on a fast or normal track of movement toward increased responsibility within the organization?

There are five key principles to remember in self-evaluation:

1. *Obtain internal information on your job performance.* Make your own judgments on how well you are performing your job. Ask yourself, "What are my areas of strength, as I see them? What areas need development?" Much of this is based on how you feel about yourself. Do not deal with what is right or wrong. Jot down notes that answer the questions strictly from your perspective and from your perceptions of yourself in your working environment. Include your perceptions of how you operate as a black in a white setting. Then relate these to relationships with bosses, peers, and subordinates (if any) and to your own control over your environment in terms of how you get your needs met in order to work most efficiently and productively.

2. *Obtain external information on your job performance.* Ask yourself, "What is the gist of the latest information I have received from others in the organization? Is it positive, negative, or neutral?" What specific things have others asked you to improve on? What suggestions have they made to you? "Others" can be peers, bosses, and subordinates. Try to weed out the racist and sexist pieces. You need to ascertain what is legitimate feedback and what is inappropriate.

3. *Test where you are relative to your personal job goals.* By this time, if you do not have personal training and development goals, we are sure you will at least have thought about some. We suggest that you stop now and jot down at least five of these goals. If you do not have goals, you cannot do a good job of self-evaluation. Assuming you have already developed some personal job goals, find out where you stand relative to the accomplishment of those goals. Remember, you want to be able to test where you are relative to where you want to go.

4. *Test where you are relative to your organizational goals.* If you are confused about the difference between personal job goals and organizational goals, let us look at an example that illustrates the difference. A personal job goal might be: "Within three months, I will develop an effective personal interactional style. I will know I have accomplished this goal when I do not receive any negative input on my style for a three-week period." An organizational job goal might be: "Within three months, I will develop a new set of procedures to accomplish one of my major job tasks. This will be evidenced by more efficient and productive completion of the job."

5. *Document your evaluation.* Make a copy of the form shown in Figure 7-5 and use it to document your self-evaluation information. Run the information past a trusted friend, spouse, or peer. You may also use your boss or sponsor. However, if you do use your boss, you must have a good relationship so there will be no misunderstanding or misdirection from the boss. If the boss is racist or sexist, you should not run this information past him or her. You may decide to share your information with your sponsor. Remember, you cannot use every sponsor for every need; you may have to develop different sponsors to meet different needs. Sponsors, too, can be racist and sexist. Be sensitive and use good judgment when sharing information about yourself with others. Periodically, update the worksheet; review it at least every two months to ensure that you are on track to improve yourself.

Setting Your Sights High

Complacency is a form of living death for blacks and other minorities that affects not only the individual but the group as well. It certainly satisfies the racists who insist that blacks are happy with their present status and that the "agitators" who would like to cause friction should leave blacks alone. It also satisfies sexists who feel that women belong in the home, caring for children. Minorities need to thoughtfully and continually set their sights higher throughout their work lives if they are to be successful.

Set your sights higher when you find yourself stuck in any of the developmental phases. Even the Success Phase demands more success. Set your sights higher when you find yourself accepting less than what you desire or less than what you feel you are capable of achieving. If

Figure 7-5. Personal-planning worksheet.

Date:_____

Part A: Developmental Needs

1. I see these as my:

Areas of Strength

Areas Needing Improvement

2. I want to sharpen my skills (strengths) in these areas:

These are the resources I have identified:

Names   Skill(s)

3. I need help in developing these skills in my areas needing improvement:

These are the resources I have identified:

Names   Skill(s)

4. I will develop these networking opportunities:

5. I will access a mentor/sponsor and develop a relationship:

Names   What I Will Do   By (Date)

6. These are the development needs I would like to address next:

(continued)

Figure 7-5.   (continued)

Part B: Goals and Objectives

These are my personal goals in the company:

This is my tentative game plan (include a date):

These are the resources I will use:

Name   Kind of Help Needed

These are my career goals in the company:

This is my tentative game plan (include a date):

These are the resources I will use:

Name   Kind of Help Needed

you are the type of person who feels a strong group alliance and a need to be a role model for other minorities struggling to achieve success, and you are angered by the plight of minorities in business institutions, then you have an additional reason to set your sights higher. Former Mayor J. Kenneth Blackwell of Cincinnati, Ohio, speaking at the Second Annual Salute to Black Achievers on April 17, 1980, summed this up by stating, "The human condition is not a spectator sport; either act or be acted upon."

Many great people have encouraged us to start by having a dream. This makes sense because how can you experience desire without a dream? Setting your sights higher is the first step toward fulfilling a dream. Not only must you have a dream, but you must have a strong desire to make the dream come true. You must want to be successful.

You should set goals, develop a plan of attack, and implement the plan. Setting goals is important because, without this step, you cannot be clear about what you are trying to achieve.

When you develop a strong desire for success or when you sense that your self-concept is lower than your skills level, raise your sights. In setting your sights higher, there are five key principles to remember:

1. *You must have a very strong desire to succeed.* If the desire to succeed is not present or if complacency has struck, blacks will find advancement nearly impossible. Success and advancement are seldom automatic; they require effort. All blacks are not going to succeed any more than all whites. Some people decide they do not want the hassle of being a leader or manager. If that is where a person is, that is fine. But if you are a person with a burning desire to succeed, you will seek to set your sights higher. You need to periodically fuel your dream in order to begin your plans. Sit down and fantasize as you did when you were a kid. Think about what you will be doing when you have reached your goal. Detail everything in your mind so you have a complete picture of yourself in the situation. Picture the person you are talking to, what you are wearing, whether you are sitting or standing, and so forth. You must feel, touch, and taste the dream. Now savor the positive emotions you feel. If you do this often, it will increase your desire to succeed and build up your energy level. You will surely depress yourself and lower your energy level if you allow yourself to believe you must not or cannot dream. Everything is set against your being successful when you are unable to set your sights higher. If your dream is a part of your day-to-day reality, you will be more likely to make it happen.

2. *You must have the proper attitude.* Former Mayor Blackwell of Cincinnati also stated at the previously mentioned meeting that his grandmother always told him, "Your attitude determines your altitude." In other words, your attitude determines how high you rise in any endeavor. If you are black with a negative attitude working in any predominantly white institution, your attitude will ensure that you will not succeed.

For example, we have an acquaintance who is a black assistant principal working at a predominantly white high school. He is bright, energetic, and next in line to become principal in the school district. In talking and working with him on some projects, we found him to have a very negative attitude about himself, the system, and his ability to get things done. He sees injustice, but rather than positively attack it head-on, he complains about it, tends to be angry much of the time, acts disgusted, and frequently strips people of their dignity. His coworkers will not help him solve problems. He is working to achieve failure by refusing to believe in his dreams and therefore cannot set his sights higher. He wants to be principal, but his negative attitude is ensuring that he will not be chosen. We can assure you that developing a proper attitude will have a profound and positive impact on setting your sights higher and achieving success.

3. *You must take risks.* If you are not willing to take some degree of risk, then it is difficult to set your sights higher and achieve success. You will not push to resolve some of the hot issues that may be facing you in your organization. Different people are willing to take different degrees of risk. If you are serious about setting your sights higher and you have a low tolerance for taking risks, you need to use role-modeling techniques to draw the essence of how other people take risks and role-play that.

4. *You must have a major goal to achieve.* You need to define a major goal because it gives you something to race toward in order to achieve success. You do not want to be all over the place, racing in many directions, depleting your energies, and diverting your attention.

5. *You must have an action plan that can be implemented.* It is obviously a waste of time to develop an action plan that you cannot implement. Be realistic about what you can and cannot do. You must be careful because you want to be sure you are taking a risk and not choosing goals that are too easy to achieve. Goals that are too easy are not really going to achieve anything because they will not challenge you or give you an opportunity to grow. One way to test a goal is to ask whether it stretches you. Does it create some anxiety, and does it have growth potential for you? Think about your hardest but most enjoyable course in school; the educational level or type of course does not matter. Remember the feeling of anxiety that you had in the pit of your stomach after about the second week in the course? That is how you should feel about your goal. If you do not, then it is not difficult enough, which means you are not setting your sights high enough.

Establishing the Principles
of Your Personal Operating Strategy

One tool we have found especially helpful in setting your sights higher is a list of the principles of personal operating strategy, which we will present for your use. Many of us go to work without a conscious thought about how we will approach and perform our job roles. Although few of us would travel by car from New York City to Los Angeles without a road map, we sometimes approach our job roles without a "road map." It is possible to travel from New York to Los Angeles without a map, but it will certainly take more time and effort because you will be "traveling blindly" and at the mercy of state highways. Even if you have traveled the roads before, conditions change, which may necessitate your constantly reevaluating your route without the benefit of knowing your available options. Having a road map allows you to plainly see the route options available to you. You can then select your route according to your needs at the time. You may be in a hurry and want to take the shortest route, or you may be on vacation and want to see the sights without regard to time. Developing and using a "personal operating strategy" is like having a road map that will illuminate the available options and help you make decisions that will enable you to achieve success in your job role.

There are rules that apply to the formulation of a carefully thought out plan to be used in the performance of your job. Essentially, the principles of personal operating strategy are the "road map" to one's successful operation in the work force. Personal operating strategy defines the way you conduct yourself in your job role. For example: Will you wait to be told what to do, or will you exercise initiative and seek information from others about the needs in your organization and then decide what to do? Will you shun your boss or try to develop a relationship with him or her? Will you take a risk and suggest a new product or be satisfied with working only on existing products?

A *good* personal operating strategy needs to be designed to get what you want and need from your job and career. You will not be successful in your job role by happenstance. Instead, success will come to you when you execute a well-thought-out plan of action. Your personal operating strategy should be aimed at success (however you define it) and should reflect the values and attitudes that you bring to the workplace. Again, these principles are rules that you would use to develop a personal way of operating in your job.

We will look at seven principles, which reflect those we see used by successful individuals. These principles form a basis for you to use when sitting down and mapping out the principles of *your* personal operating strategy. You may want to use these seven, or you may want to rewrite or add to them to make them apply more personally to you:

1. *Look for and use opportunities to control or influence the outcome of events.* Unfortunately, far too many black people operate from a victim's mind-set. That is, many minority managers tend to behave as though events and circumstances control them instead of deciding within themselves that they can have management control over events and individuals in the workplace. To focus yourself "in the victim's mode" will ensure that you will not be successful. Instead, for those upcoming events that are of major importance, sit down, take a piece of paper, think about the plan of attack that you are going to use, and write it down. Examine the plan, question it, and revise it; you may even want to "bounce it off" a trusted friend or adviser. This helps increase the odds that the event will turn out positively and that you will get what you want.

Sit down and list the three to five key individuals who are involved in the event and then write a brief psychological profile of each one, addressing the following: Are they power brokers? Are they weak or strong managers? Are they the kind of people who control events, or do they tend to see themselves as victims who are controlled by events? Once you have identified the people who will be involved in the event and understand their psychological profiles, you can start thinking about the events you will be involved in with these people before the main event. Use (manipulate) the events to find out where these individuals stand on the key issues associated with the event; you can also use the opportunity to let them know where you stand on the key issues. This course of action will allow you to get maximum use out of these people, who will also appreciate your involvement with them before the main event takes place.

At this point, let's look at an example. Let us suppose you are in charge of an interdepartmental cost-cutting team effort, and you are about to have your first meeting. We are asking you to identify the three to five influential and powerful people who will be involved with you in the group effort. After you have identified those people, develop a psychological profile of them: Are they helpful? Do they like to work as a team, or would they rather work individually? Are they weak or strong managers? Are they highly competent? Are they conceptual thinkers? Etc. Identify the strongest skill and talent possessed by each of the individuals. Before the kickoff meeting of the cost-cutting effort, decide which people you are going to approach to see whether they will support the direction in which you would like to take the team. You can do this by having lunch or an after-work drink with them or by playing tennis with them. Select a semisocial event to engage them in a discussion about the cost-cutting effort. In this way, you can start to position people to get your desired outcome at the first meeting. But be flexible; be willing to plant the seeds of your ideas with the people you think would be interested and who could help you influence the outcome of events.

2. *Maintain high integrity in your dealings with others.* The world seems to have moved toward clearly "cutthroat" business practices and a "me" attitude: "Let me get mine; I don't care whether or not you get yours." We have permitted normal business practices to deteriorate into something that is geared toward insensitivity and the slow breaking down and whittling away of people's morale. Nonetheless, integrity is just as important a value trait today as it has always been. The excuse that "Someone has gotten away with something; therefore, why can't I?" cannot hold water. This holds particularly true for the minority individual, who is under constant scrutiny and who must be a better-than-average performer to prosper. Consequently, it becomes extremely important for a black to maintain integrity—to build his or her name. When you display high integrity in your dealings with others, you really get people's attention and start to build a very positive reputation for yourself in your organization. Sometimes, reputation will take you a lot further than you could go based solely on your work output.

3. *Know what you want, when you want it, and how you want it.* That sounds very simple, but in most cases, we find that it is not simple. In conducting business, many of us have some vague idea of what we want, but very often, we are not clear about it. When you have an idea or you think you have an idea of what you want, write it down and look at it. Now it is out of your head and in front of you. You can see whether or not it makes sense, is attainable, and is truly what you want. Review it, modify it, play with it, and change it until you are satisfied.

Be clear about when you want something. If you have a project, jot down the time line for key events, the tasks involved, and the people responsible for completing the tasks. Share when you want it done and how you want it accomplished with the people who are involved in implementing the project. "How you want it accomplished" does not mean you should stand over other people and dictate to them every little detail every step of the way. But do be clear about how you want the events of the project arranged and how major aspects of the project are to be completed.

Returning to the example of the cost-cutting meeting, be clear about what outcome you want—that is, what will the results look like? What role will each team member play? Make your timetable workable and public. Be clear with yourself and others involved about how you expect the project or work tasks to be completed by each member and how the parts will fit together when completed (process, procedures, techniques, etc.).

4. *Prethink and preplan your activities to increase the odds of success.* Many people pride themselves on being able to think on their feet in any given situation. Although that is indeed a highly valued skill, to do that constantly or as a regular mode of operation is to keep yourself continually at risk of not being successful. The very best thing to do before any important event is to prethink and preplan your actions. What we are essentially saying here is, "Open your mind to laying out the scenario of key events before you get there." If it is a meeting, think about who is going to be there, what the various people's roles will be, and how people are likely to respond to the data that will be shared around the table. If there is a piece of the meeting that is very important to you, then, in considering a scenario for the meeting, plan what you are going to say and do and develop a strategy to move the meeting and the people. Try to anticipate the actions and responses of the important people at the meeting. You can do this if you have taken the time to understand the powerful and influential people who will be in the room. You might see it in your mind as a chess game. When you play chess, you think about your move, how your move is going to affect your opponent, and how it is going to affect each of the pieces on the board. If you take the time to do this prior to the important event, you will definitely increase your odds of success. In this way, you can also stay proactive, not reactive. You will be on the offensive instead of the defensive.

Periodically, we run into people who say that if you are highly skilled and competent and know what you are doing, you don't have to do a lot of prethinking and preplanning of your activities. Preplanning and prethinking are extremely important strategies for minorities because of the institutional and personal racism with which they are still faced. So to help disarm negative situations, it is smart and extremely important to prethink and preplan your major activities.

5. *Treat others as you would like to be treated; give praise and rewards when they are deserved and punish others only when all other options fall.* Often, people ask us to tell them how they should behave in certain situations, which can range from a career development discussion to how to best conduct a very important meeting. In the absence of any

other specific information, we rely on the "golden rule": Treat others in the same way as you would have them treat you. In other words, picture yourself in the other person's situation; then respond in the same way as you would want him or her to respond to you. If you use this as a rule of thumb, you will almost always be in a win-win situation with others.

Also, be willing to give people praise and rewards. Now, we are very clear that white corporate America tends not to do this. However, it has been our experience that to get people to joyfully perform their jobs, praising them is very important. People—white or black—don't like to do a job day in and day out and never get any verbal praise (what is sometimes called "strokes") for it. When you give people verbal praise, especially public verbal praise (praising individuals in front of others), you increase morale, which can motivate people to do even more and perform at a higher level. Punishment rarely works. Even animals don't respond positively to punishment. If you constantly punish a dog, it becomes mean—not obedient. Punishment also creates resentment and anger. When appropriate, correct the dysfunctional behavior. Reserve punishment *only* for those times when you have no other option available to resolve a conflict.

6. *Identify your adversaries and supporters; use your supporters and interact with your adversaries only when necessary.* By *adversaries*, we mean those individuals in your workplace who tend not to support you, tend to pick fights with you, and basically tend to disregard you. *Supporters* are individuals who like to be helpful to you and will give you the kind of resources and information that you need to successfully perform your job. Basically, this principle tells you to develop a personal operating strategy that clearly distinguishes your friends from your enemies. You really need to do this periodically when you are at home. Take a piece of paper and draw a line down the middle of it; on one side, list "Adversaries," and on the other side, list "Supporters." Keep this list at home and look at it every three months. This will help you refine your ability to identify adversaries and supporters. Identify the kind of support next to the names of your supporters. In other words, do they give you monetary resources or people resources? Are they good listeners; can you bounce ideas off them? Are they good at helping you work out corporate strategies or plans? This list will also allow you to keep yourself updated. Frequently, circumstances change, and a former adversary may become a supporter for some reason. You need to be clear about when that has happened, how it happened, and what kind of support you are now getting from the person.

As far as supporters are concerned, identify those areas in which they support you and use them for that particular support. As far as adversaries are concerned, basically stay away from them until it is necessary to interact with them. Then be jovial and personable with them. You do not have to be aloof or arrogant, but conduct your business with the least expenditure of energy, with professionalism, and with respect. Then move on quickly. Sometimes, adversaries tend to push your "emotional button"—that is, they involve you in an argument or debate so that they can go away and say, "See how that individual reacted negatively to me." This often happens to the supersharp minority individual who produces above-average work. Some whites appear to enjoy emotionally upsetting blacks. Be careful and do not get suckered into an emotional situation where you end up fighting unnecessarily. If you have to interact with an adversary and the adversary picks a fight, look at the person and say, "Perhaps now is not a good time to work this issue, but we do have to work it out. I'll tell you what; I will contact you later. Thank you." It may be easier to interact with an adversary through a note telling him or her what you need and by when. Sometimes, a note is much better than a personal interaction because it removes any behavioral emotionalism that can occur when you are talking to a person eyeball to eyeball.

7. *Look for and use opportunities to make others look good.* There is nothing in the world that a boss loves more than a subordinate who can make him or her look good. Make your boss look good, and he or she will have high regard for you and utilize your talents and skills. Generally speaking, making others look good is a skill that can bring you a lot of success. It keeps you in control of others. It helps you to program others to meet your needs and be supporters.

One of the characteristics of a good leader is to give credit to others when they help him or her reach goals and objectives. If it is done publicly, people will want to follow you and work for you as a leader. The most powerful leaders are individuals who seem to lack a sense of ego and tend instead to give others opportunities to look good. Dr. Martin Luther King was a classic example of this behavior.

Leaders and bosses win by surrounding themselves with sharp, highly energetic, dedicated people whose work output and behavior very quickly reflect back onto the leaders and bosses. Subordinates win because they get to use their talents and skills to influence and control events. Essentially, what we are saying is that you look good when you allow other people to shine rather than putting yourself in a position where you say, "Look at me, look at me, look at me."

Resisting Black Self-Hate

In this section, we introduce the issue of resisting black self-hate but will not attempt to explore the issue fully, since that would require volumes. Several fine books that can help further enlighten you on the subject and related areas are listed at the end of this chapter. The key principles we give for resisting black self-hate represent some of the things that blacks can do to offset the destructive forces of racism on their self-respect and on their building a positive self-identity.

When a black person wants to be identified with the white majority and accepted by whites as a member of the white majority, then that black person has succumbed to a condition called black self-hate. How much a person is affected by this condition varies with the intensity of the feeling and the subsequent behavior associated with rejection of the person's own group. A person experiencing black self-hate will actively seek relationships and friendships with white individuals while avoiding, when possible, ties with other blacks. For example, the person might choose to live in an all-white community, limiting contact with other blacks. This may include joining an all-white church, participating in functions and activities that other blacks seldom become involved in, and making friendships with whites who have limited experience with and exposure to other blacks.

Total acceptance by whites is seldom possible because the majority of blacks cannot hide the color of their skin or other distinguishing features. Whites cannot truly dismiss these differences, nor can they help projecting social prejudices, many of which they may honestly be unaware of. After all, no matter how much a black person conforms to white cultural practices and values, the individual is not white by cultural upbringing. The differences may be subtle for some blacks, but they do exist nonetheless.

There are two sides to the difficulty for blacks who experience black self-hate. Other blacks greatly resent blacks who reject their in-group. For many blacks, this rejection is seen as the ultimate affront. They, in turn, will discriminate against blacks who deny their blackness. On the other hand, all blacks grow up in this society rejected by the majority—having their dignity, character, and self-worth questioned and attacked. Blacks suffer ridicule, deprecation, contempt, and discrimination at the hands of whites. To defeat self-hatred, it is necessary for blacks to deny what society has trained them from birth to believe.

Some blacks are so hurt and have suffered so inside that they buy into the stereotypes whites have about blacks and, in a desperate attempt to salvage self-respect, try to separate themselves from the hated group and identify with whites. These blacks show contempt for themselves and other blacks and often betray their in-group in order to get closer to the majority group. The self-love that should be everyone's right gradually turns to self-hate. These blacks mimic what they think is white and behave in a way whites desire. They believe the dominant group is right and accept the existing state of things. They feel deeply and inwardly ashamed of being black. They possess qualities they despise and feel self-repugnance as well as repugnance for other blacks, who surely also possess these qualities. Blacks who have black self-hate believe that the lower the economic status, the more of these hated qualities must be present. They feel, "Those lower-class people just make it hard for everyone else."

Now, let us look briefly at a few of the reasons why black self-hate occurs. Until very recent history, most American blacks were inadvertently, or purposely, raised by their families to feel handicapped by their blackness. The intent was not vicious; rather, it was done as a way of passing on knowledge of how to survive and gain some measure of success in a hostile environment. There were many things in the environment young blacks had to "overcome" to be successful in the "white man's world."

Blacks continue to find themselves having to "overcome" the handicap of language, when, in fact, English is not spoken well by most Americans—black or white—who are influenced greatly by family, neighborhood, and regional dialects. Physical appearance is a handicap to "overcome" because the American standard is white skin, blue eyes, and blond hair with thin, regular features. Normal self-pride, assertiveness, initiative, and aggression become handicaps for blacks to "overcome" if they surface because whites prefer blacks to be passive. Blacks are forced to sublimate and camouflage their natural feelings and personal aspirations. These are only a very few of the handicaps blacks face through no real fault of their own. Is it any wonder, then, that many blacks fall victim to black self-hate and seek to strongly identify with those who are seen as so much more perfect?

Blacks who have been born with light skin and straight hair have better opportunities to identify with whites because whites often reward those blacks for their similarities to the dominant group and further reward them for their attempts at assimilation. These are the blacks most frequently accepted socially, for educational opportunities, and for promotions. The delusion for many is that fair-skinned blacks and assimilated blacks will always be rewarded, but even if this sometimes appears to be the case, there is a stopping point—a ceiling. The person is still black and will never be white.

Black self-hate is a complicated issue, deeply rooted in our history. It is not easily overcome, nor is it a simple matter to handle or resolve. Some people are too deeply hurt for this book to help and may need personal professional assistance. However, for those who may merely need insight into the problem, we offer three key principles that can help a person begin the process of resisting black self-hate:

1. *You must recognize the condition of black self-hate in yourself.* One way to check this issue is to *honestly* answer the following questions:

- Am I at ease—that is, accepting of myself and my identified cultural group?
- Do I often feel ashamed and embarrassed by other blacks when they violate some rule or some value I hold, especially if whites witness that behavior?
- Do I then want to assure whites who have witnessed the other person's behavior that I am different and seek to prove that?
- Am I comfortable thinking about and discussing race?
- How do I relate to members of my own race?
- Do I feel more comfortable relating to members of another race?
- Of what race are the individual with whom I feel most comfortable? Whom I trust most? From whom I want to get most of my input?
- Do I use my cultural experience, or do I discount it?
- Do I tend to identify myself more with whites?
- Do I deny racial issues exist, or do I admit they exist but do not apply to me?
- Do I demand that others treat me appropriately as a member of my cultural group, or do I want to be treated as someone who has no cultural group affiliation?
- Am I very concerned that whites feel comfortable with me?

To recognize the symptoms of black self-hate, you need to think logically about your attitude and behavior. Are you behaving the way you want to behave or the way you feel white managers want you to behave? You also need to look seriously at where your present attitude and behavior are taking you. Are you really getting the kind of results you need and want without making severe sacrifices in terms of your self-esteem?

Blacks experiencing self-hate tend to have blind faith in white organizations as well as in white individuals because they want to believe most whites have blacks' best interests at heart. These blacks accept the white viewpoint unquestioningly because they have bought into white stereotypes about blacks, so they do not seek black input or listen to it when given because the information is not valued. They tend to separate themselves from the black group and often become arrogant in the presence of both blacks and whites. In order to gain acceptance, these blacks tend to see themselves in intense competition with whites to prove themselves superior.

This method of seeking acceptance is dangerous because black self-hate has two stages. In the first stage, blacks feel they are better than all other blacks and behave in that manner. If they are successful in this, the second stage is to move to feeling smarter and better than most whites. Once whites sense this, these blacks are in danger of getting shoved aside in the organization, and other blacks will help by further isolating them.

2. *Understand what black self-hate is and why it exists.* Acting white when you are black is a contradiction and puts you in an ambiguous position. Whites do not appreciate that kind of behavior from blacks or identify with it as much as blacks who behave that way believe whites do. Whites very subtly punish blacks for the transgression into their group, even though whites cause blacks to behave like whites by appearing to reward the behavior. Whites expect blacks to behave like blacks, whatever that means to them in their context. Whites may try to mold a black's behavior so that the behavior is comfortable to whites. However, this does not mean that whites are going to accept the black totally in the same way as another white would be accepted. There are cultural and physical differences that cannot be ignored. Therefore, whites often put blacks in an ambiguous position, which is confusing to the person experiencing black self-hate. If you understand black self-hate and its pressures, then you can understand what is happening when a white manager tries to operate with you in this way. You will be able to see that what may initially appear to be rewards are actually not, and you will be able to deal with this.

Sometimes, white managers tell blacks that they are different from other blacks in order to manage their behavior and become more comfortable. In this manner, whites are able to control blacks so that the whites can feel at ease and not feel threatened in any way. Nearly all blacks have at some time experienced this type of interaction with whites. For some blacks, this experience triggers black self-hate and its characteristic behavior. These blacks want to be different from those held in such low esteem.

3. *Recognize and actively use a black support structure.* Have a person from the black support structure help you explore reasons why you bought into black self-hate. This may be touchy for some people, but you do need to do this with someone you trust and respect. You must also keep informed about what is occurring with other blacks in the organization. Of course, you do need to establish a reputation with powerful whites, but do not get totally wrapped up in establishing your reputation and do not do it to the exclusion of keeping in touch with other blacks. Interact with other blacks so you can keep a realistic picture of who you are and where you and other blacks are going in the organization. Find some brothers and sisters in the organization with whom you can have day-to-day contact. These individuals should preferably be at your level with at least two more years of experience than you have so they can share their experiences with you on how to survive and succeed.

You need to develop a framework in which to view yourself as a black so you will not be dependent on whites' viewpoints of you. You need enough information to define yourself as a black and be comfortable with your definition. Develop different behaviors in your organization; become flexible. Do not act white—that is, do not mimic your perceptions of whites and try to make your behavior indistinguishable from theirs.

In the 1990s, most organizations operate on the principle of teamwork in a diverse workplace. Businesses and technologies are so complex and the world market so competitive that one person cannot run the whole show the way Henry Ford did when he developed his Model A automobile. Black self-hate is an insidious crippler that prevents blacks from optimizing their contributions to the workplace. Because of it, too many blacks will never develop their creative potential, and too many will ultimately lose their souls trying to be accepted by the dominant culture, which will never recognize the price these people paid.

The Neoconservative Black

As we have said previously, people who work in corporations and large organizations tend to be molded to fit the stereotype of a corporate businessperson. We have also stated that to a degree, there is nothing strange or wrong about that. It is necessary to focus people toward the same goals, to ensure continuity, order, and purpose. When conformity begins to stifle initiative, creativity, cultural behavior, and personal individuality—in fact, all the things that have enriched our country and our business—then conformity and socialization have gone too far. A number of professional blacks today have sought to integrate themselves so fully into the business mainstream as to be indistinguishable from any group of people. "We are all just people," they say. "There's no real difference between people. We are all just human." Wrong! Each of us is much more than that, as will be seen in Chapter 11, where we discuss the value and importance of cultural diversity in the workplace.

Black individuals who display the above attitudes and behaviors are referred to as "neoconservative blacks"—an additional wrinkle to the concept of black self-hate. They have not learned new skills and technologies to *add* to their own cultural knowledge base but have instead attempted to sublimate their cultural uniqueness and replace it with their idea of a mainstream white corporate ideal. Herein lies much of the confusion and decrease in contribution and productivity of many blacks. They cannot bring a different insight and perspective to bear on organizational issues and problems. In attempting to be "just like everyone else," they lose their identity and are neither white nor black.

How do we recognize black neoconservatism? Here are some of the issues with which these individuals deal:

• *An unshakable belief in the "Protestant work ethic."* These individuals firmly believe that job success is based solely on personal competence and that only through their own efforts (great intelligence, superior education and training, impeccable background, hard work) will personal gains and successes be achieved. They deny that gender or race ever play a part in what they do. If one does not make it, it is because he or she did not work hard enough; did not go to the right school; or perhaps, really was incompetent.

• *"Blending in is important."* Neoconservative blacks insist that problems arise for blacks in corporate America because some blacks make waves. Whites do not like that. "Do your job and don't call attention to yourself within the system," they say. "Tell your bosses that everything is fine; if you do have a problem, then quietly fix it yourself." These blacks tell you that complaining will be seen as hostility. If you do not go along with the corporate agenda, you will be seen as uncooperative.

If you push back on the organization or bring in radical ideas, you will give blacks a bad name in business. "Just do your job and bring in results," they say, "and everything will work out fine."

• *"If you do not make it, it's your fault."* Neoconservatives like to place guilt firmly at the feet of the victim, where they think it belongs. This mentality stems from old European ideas of social welfare, which hold that unsuccessful lives are a result of personal defects (except for war widows and their children, who are victims of circumstances not of their making). These blacks feel if you do not have what you need to survive and be successful, it is because you are too lazy to work for it like the rest of us. And by the way, racism or sexism has nothing to do with it.

• *"Conform to the system if you want to succeed."* These individuals take a great deal of pride in how comfortably they conform to the system. "Your success depends on how well you can fit in and follow the rules and regulations set down by whites." Their greatest accomplishment is how well they have merged—Madison Avenue blue suit, expensive leather briefcase, impeccable manners and speech. Outwardly, there is not necessarily anything wrong with that, but many times, this behavior and these trappings also reflect the mind-set—the homogeneous thinking—of the black individuals and . . . Well, you get the picture.

• *"Racism is no longer a real deterrent to success."* Many neoconservative blacks believe that blacks who are not successful use racism as an excuse. There is a continuing denial of the short- and long-term effects of racism and insensitive intellectualizing by many black academics and intellectuals. They believe the reason blacks, as a group, do not become a part of the mainstream has less to do with race and more to do with other factors such as socioeconomic leverage and a desire to succeed.

It is interesting to note that a preponderance of these ideas come from the more privileged blacks who have had opportunities and doors opened for them to attend top-named schools and to work in prestigious organizations. Many whites have not had such opportunities. These blacks extrapolate their isolated and insulated experiences to blacks who are not advantaged and who are operating in a hostile environment with fewer skills and opportunities and no chance for doors to be opened for them. The average black does not have the same life opportunities as the average white.

• *"You've got to look out for yourself."* There are a couple of popular sayings among young blacks working on Wall Street: "It doesn't matter if you are black or white, as long as you can make green," and, "The only color Wall Street sees is green." Yet look around. How many blacks are at the top levels of these organizations wielding power and influence? "No matter; one must look out for oneself. We get promoted on merit, on how much revenue we can bring to our organizations. I can only look out for 'me.' " Neoconservative blacks never see the white "good old boy" network coaching, encouraging, and giving a helping hand to young whites who rise in these organizations. The "me" generation does not exist for whites in business to the extent that the "me" generation exists for these blacks. Since blacks are not in the white "good old boy" network, they seldom get the kind of networking, coaching, relationship building, and support that it takes for anyone to advance. If someone black falls, that's just too bad. It makes a way for me. But it never does. What it does do is cause many blacks to sacrifice their personal integrity and identity for the sake of carving out their little piece of territory. Blacks cannot afford to be members of a "me generation." Whites accomplish nothing alone, and they still own the American marketplace (at least for the time being). It is ludicrous for blacks to think that each individual can make his or her way independently of the help of others.

This kind of black self-hate affects not only the individual but those blacks around him or her. For black Americans in today's marketplace, there are no private choices or individual destinies. What each of us does or does not do to push the political and economic systems in which we operate will intimately affect out collective choices and destinies.

Recommended Reading

Although these titles are all included in the suggested readings, they are worth singling out here for their special value in dealing with black self-hate:

The Nature of Prejudice, by Gordon W. Allport
The Jesus Bag, by William H. Grier and Price M. Cobbs
Black Rage, also by Grier and Cobbs
Black Experience: Analysis and Synthesis, edited by Carlene Young

8

External Strategies

Chapter 8 presents guidelines for managing key relationships with others in the working environment. The chapter opens with a review of the unique challenges facing black managers as they seek success in the corporate world. The following sections discuss strategies for handling your relationship with your boss, your subordinates, and others in the organization; making effective use of the resources available to you; reading verbal and nonverbal cues to obtain critical information in the workplace; and improving your confrontation skills. The chapter closes with a section on developing your leadership skills so you will become able to function in the "leadership mode" rather than the "maintenance mode."

The Unique Challenges Facing Black Managers

In addition to the challenges that all individuals—black or white, male or female—face when they enter management positions, blacks face a number of unique challenges that are directly related to their blackness and are therefore not faced by whites. For example, blacks have to work with people who have negative sterotypes about them and have to struggle to not accept the sterotypes. Although these challenges were discussed extensively in Part Two, it is worth summarizing them in the context of this chapter because they have a powerful effect on black managers' relationships with others in the corporate world. These exclusively black challenges include joining up quickly to an organization, planning for success, finding mentors and sponsors, resisting oversocialization, developing productive working relationships, understanding the impact of your heritage, and learning to manage the racist behavior of others.

Joining Up Quickly to an Organization

Because blacks are not an accepted, traditional part of the organizational system, they will be closely scrutinized and will have to fight an uphill battle against the entrenched sterotypes of whites. Whites will tend to inadvertently exclude blacks from the networking process, forcing them to learn organizational norms and values through trial and error. Therefore, if they are to keep abreast of their white peers, blacks must join up quickly to an organization and begin producing results immediately. The longer it takes black managers to "get up to speed," the further behind they will fall.

Planning for Success

Another unique challenge facing black managers is to develop a plan that provides for both success and job growth because these results are unlikely to occur naturally for blacks after they join an organization. Instead, black managers who do not plan will find themselves at the mercy of how the organization views their abilities and how far it may be willing to permit blacks to advance at any given time. By planning effectively, black managers can greatly increase their odds of success advancement. In short, blacks cannot afford the luxury of *not* planning.

Finding Mentors and Sponsors

We keep harping on the importance of obtaining mentors and sponsors because we cannot remind black managers often enough that no one advances within the organization without help from someone above him or her in the hierarchy. Mentoring of blacks tends not to happen naturally in corporate America, since upper-level white managers are usually unable to readily identify with, and recognize potential in, blacks. Therefore, blacks must take an active role in making sure that higher-ups see them and positively evaluate their accomplishments. If we assume that everyone starts out relatively equal in terms of talent, experience, and education, then mentoring will be the determining factor in who makes the grade at promotion time.

Resisting Oversocialization

One of the most dangerous phenomena in corporate America is "groupthink." The best and most creative solutions cannot be developed when everyone dealing with an issue or a problem thinks alike about the situation and has the same experience and perspectives. As a black manager, your different perspective, social skills, and life experiences bring added value to the organization. Therefore, you must learn to resist total organizational socialization that would force you to give up that added value.

We are not saying that socialization is entirely bad, for black managers must become socialized enough to function efficiently within the organization. Socialization only becomes counterproductive for blacks when it goes too far—when their attitudes, norms, values, behaviors, and input so closely mimic those of their white peers that they have become white in all but skin color and have therefore discarded precisely those unique qualities that made them valuable to the organization in the first place.

Developing Productive Work Relationships

Because teamwork and the use of resources are essential to operate successfully in most organizations, black managers must develop productive work relationships. The unique challenge for black managers is learning to work effectively with people whom they may not necessarily like or greatly respect (which runs counter to the black cultural norm) and with people who may even be prejudiced against blacks. The solution is for black managers to focus on the basic purpose of a work relationship—facilitating the exchange of vital information so both parties can accomplish their job tasks.

Understanding the Impact of Your Heritage

Always be aware of the impact of your blackness in the workplace. Many black managers look at us quizzically and say, "I don't think my blackness impacts my performance, but maybe I'm wrong." Or, "Show me the impact, I just don't see it." So we tell them to gather their own evidence. "Do you believe the average white manager in your organization has stereotypes about blacks?" Once they reply affirmatively (and they always do), we ask them to list some of those stereotypes. The first three or four things they rattle off will be negative. Then we say, "How, then, can white managers be fair with you if their most common stereotypes are negative?" Their eyes widen, and they say, "Oh, I never thought about it like that."

Black managers get into the most trouble in white organizations when they forget or fail to realize the impact of the fact that their culture differs from the organizational norm. Blacks must remember that any-time they work with whites, the interactions always contain a racial component and that they are constantly fighting negative stereotypes about blacks that cause whites (even if they are not consciously aware of the sterotypes) to behave inappropriately toward blacks.

But awareness of the differential consequences of being black in a white organization is not enough. Black managers must learn to actively manage the impact of their blackness—by which we mean they must take a positive attitude toward racism. Although that may sound crazy to you because there is nothing positive about racism itself, racist behavior can give you an opportunity to operate creatively in the organizational setting by using other people's prejudices to your advan-tage. For instance, when a bigoted white offers you help because he or she perceives you, as a black, to be in a "less-than" position, you need not concern yourself with the person's motives. Instead, allow the individual to teach you as much as he or she is willing; then take that learning and run with it.

And finally, black managers must learn to recognize their own negative stereotypes about whites and avoid making assumptions about whites based on personal prejudices.

Learning to Manage the Racist Behavior of Others

In the early 1970s, a white manager who later became a friend of ours worked in a *Fortune* 500 company and took his boss seriously when he said, "Our organization will find, recruit, train, and develop black technical people." At the time, our friend had no idea how to repond to his boss's needs, so he consulted an internal development specialist and decided to hire outside consultants to conduct racial awareness training sessions for his managers.

After attending one of these sessions, our friend realized that some of his managers had truly racist attitudes about blacks and believed they could not do good technical work. He also realized that although he didn't know how to change the *attitudes* of these white employees, he could use the existing pay and assignment system to manage their racist *behavior*. White managers who failed to behave toward their black subordinates in a way that was conducive to their growth, development, and optimal work output got no pay raises and were passed over for choice assignments or even demoted. Our friend is a good example of a manager acting with integrity as he learned multicultural management and taught it to his subordinates.

Since white managers are not the targets of racist behavior, they can survive and succeed in a white organization without learning to manage racist behavior as part of their repertoire of job skills. Blacks seldom can because racism tends to interfere with the proper performance of their jobs. It is therefore critical that blacks develop strategies for dealing effectively with racist behavior and demand that their managers help them do so.

By the year 2000, the majority of new people entering the work force will be minorities and women, which means that whites will be managing more blacks, women, and other minorities. To ensure maximum productivity, efficiency, and teamwork on the part of *all* their employees, white managers must recognize the occurrence of certain prejudicial acts that interfere with the job performance of blacks, accept their own responsibility for training blacks to manage racist behavior, and learn how to manage the racist behavior of other whites. Today, in fact, we see an ever-increasing number of white managers who require their minority employment to manage the racist and sexist behavior of others.

How can managers, both black and white, learn effective strategies for managing racist and sexist behavior in the workplace? Since these strategies are not taught in educational institutions, the knowledge must be acquired through on-the-job training. Minority employees can learn the strategies from successful black managers as well as from white managers who understand the techniques of multicultural management.

Racism still prevades all facets of life in America including the workplace. If racism is not neutralized in the workplace, over a period of time it can help cause blacks to be unsuccessful in their jobs roles. Remember, racist attitudes do not cause problems. It is the resulting behavior of individuals acting out their racist beliefs that causes problems.

There are six key principles that blacks must use to manage racist behavior that interferes with their professional effectiveness:

1. *Understand that you must manage the racist behavior of others in order to be successful and that you are not the only black manager to have to learn to do this.*

2. *Realize that you do not have to deal with this situation alone.* You will

find that other black managers, both in your own organization and in other organizations, as well as some white managers, are willing to help you develop ways to respond to the dysfunctional racist behavior of others. Ask others to share how they manage racist behavior.

3. *Allow yourself to recognize racist behavior in action.* The first step toward managing racist behavior is allowing yourself to see that behavior for what it is. If you refuse to do so, you will not grow internally. Furthermore, your advancement opportunities could be curtailed because upper-level white managers may assume that your passive acceptance of the racist behavior directed at you means you will be unable to deliver results in a position that requires managing white subordinates.

How do you recognize racist behavior? Watch the whites in your organization and notice which of their behaviors are the same toward both blacks and whites and which of their behaviors are different. Pay attention, too, to your *visceral reaction of discomfort,* which can tip you off to subtle racist behavior with which you must deal.

4. *Take a risk and confront dysfunctional racist behavior.* Push back appropriately when someone's racist behavior negatively affects you. You do not need to call attention to the behavior but should instead focus on eliminating the negative consequences of that behavior. You could say something as simple as, "Before we move on, I would like to add to what has already been said; perhaps all of you did not hear me when I first spoke." Since not everything is worth fighting for and you don't need a reputation for argumentativeness, pick your fights judiciously.

5. *Understand the black-white dynamics that occur between individuals and in groups.* Both whites and blacks can have negative attitudes toward each other, and there are some differences in style between whites and blacks. When whites and blacks interact individually or in a group setting, either negative attitudes (usually those of the majority toward the minority) or style differences may cause conflict that hinders task accomplishment.

Although blacks in a white corporate setting sometimes tend to forget or undervalue their cultural learnings, they have historically been taught how to "read" the body cues and actions of whites. When conflict arises, blacks must reach back to their culture and use their "reading" skills to understand how whites' negative attitudes get "played out" via dysfunctional behavior. Once the black-white dynamics of the interaction are understood, appropriate responses can be developed to get positive results.

6. *Apply effective techniques for managing racist behavior.* The following list presents ways to manage racist behavior. Each includes one or more specific techniques used by black managers to become successful in white organizations:

- Manage racist behavior by strategy.
    - —Recognize racist behavior and implement a plan to neutralize it. Be proactive rather than reactive.
    - —Use effectively controlled anger as a tool for achieving results.
    - —Sell only carefully thought out ideas that you have checked with trusted resources, to ensure that you have provided for contingencies and hve not overlooked anything.
    - —Learn how to approach people tactfully, sensitively, and in a way that avoids unnecessary conflict.
    - —When whites are illogically resistant, lay out relevant data and let them think they came up with the idea. If your idea is accepted, chances are you will eventually get credit for it, since you will be the one who knows how to develop and implement it.
    - —When appropriate, confront whites directly or imply that their behavior may be a part of the problem. This will force them to examine their dysfunctional behavior.
    - —Present your ideas in terms of whites' self-interest.
    - —When using whites as resources, show your appreciation by giving them a stroke or sharing useful information.
    - —To elicit a positive reaction from whites, be friendly and sociable.
    - —To avoid creating vengeful enemies, confront whites in a way that allows them to keep their dignity and save face.
- Manage racist behavior by controlling the behavior of others.
    - —Manage through others. This may enable you to accomplish a task more effectively, especially when dealing with whites who listen better to other whites or to a select few blacks with whom they are comfortable.
    - —To prevent dysfunctional behavior that results from insensitivity or ignorance, tell whites how you expect them to behave in a given situation.
    - —Manage racists with personal style and charisma, which will tend to calm them down and stop display of racist behavior.
    - —Be careful in using organizational resources, so they do not negatively evaluate you. When using whites as resources,

couch your need in organizational rather than personal terms. Never approach a white resource by openly discussing your personal deficiencies.

- Manage racist behavior by controlling yourself.
  —Watch and listen to whites in order to learn white organizational norms and duplicate their behavioral approach. Once you understand those norms, you can decide whether to follow an organization's cultural norm or strategically discard it to accomplish an organizational task more efficiently, especially in the face of racist behavior.
  —In dealing with whites, be careful about what key organizational issues you discuss and how you phrase your needs relative to hot issues.
  —Particularly in a critical interaction, be sure you have all relevant information before stating your position. When you lack the pertinent facts or sit on the fence, racists can easily control you.
  —Do not depend on organizational rewards. Whites tend to not expect or give public strokes and rewards. Since the reward is often inherent in the accomplishment, generate your own strokes.
- Manage racist behavior by using organizational norms and values.
  —Ask for more work, which will cast you in a favorable light while shattering negative stereotypes about blacks.
  —Put information in writing. This standard organizational practice allows you to share your experience and expertise with others and can thereby help defuse any negative input about you.
  —When appropriate, ask key questions indirectly, to avoid giving racists a reason to react negatively to questions perceived as threatening or irrelevant.
- Manage racist behavior by using the communications network.
  —To ensure that you and your expertise are known by the right people, develop productive relationships with powerful people in your hierarchy.
  —Eat lunch with whites to get information from their formal and informal communications networks and make personal contact.
  —Eat lunch with blacks to share information, keep in touch with the grapevine, relax, and replenish your psychic energy.
- Manage racist behavior by using the power of your boss.
  —In dealing with a potentially racist white, simply say that your boss instructed you to use him or her as a resource. The

individual, knowing you will report any dysfunctional behavior to the boss, will tend to meet your needs.
- Manage racist behavior by using the power of your organizational position.
  —If your job carries some organizational power, use that power to get information from racist individuals. Even if you do not hold a higher position than the whites, they still have to acknowledge the power associated with your position and will respond accordingly to your needs.

Building Relationships

This section deals with the importance of building relationships as part of a major effort to plan for success in the workplace. It is extremely difficult, if not impossible, to become successful in the business world if you do not have good working relationships with the people who make career decisions in your organization. It is our experience that important, fast-moving black managers have rewarding relationships with the powerful decision makers in their organization. They have mentors, sponsors, and supporters who are personally aware of their job performance. These black individuals have worked to build the kind of relationships that position others to advocate on their behalf at crucial times. For black managers, the key relationships are those with their boss, their subordinates, and other important individuals in the organization—e.g., mentors, peers, and subordinates (other than their own).

Before we begin discussing the various types of key relationships, we want to share two important insights about the relationship-building process in general:

1. *Building relationships, especially with whites, allows whites to become more comfortable with a different culture.* Blacks accomplish this by providing reliable data and by allowing whites so see them as individuals and not *just* as members of a different ethnic or cultural group. In other words, the relationship-building process can help whites learn to individualize black managers within the black culture.

2. *Building relationships is nothing more than a "bartering of needs."* We find that in a tight economy, many companies and individuals are reviving the barter system to provide themselves with goods and services. We see a lot of this in various departments in large organizations.

Because these organizations must account for employee work effort, departments cross-charge each other for services rendered. In many cases, however, services are bartered rather than cross-charged. Exchanging services between individuals to meet personal needs is simply an extension of the barter system.

An astute manager realizes that everyone enters an organization with legitimate personal needs, both physical and psychological. The astute manager also has the skill to spot those needs and move to meet them. For example, a boss may realize that a subordinate is motivated by occasional strokes for a job well done. It does not cost the boss anything to tell the subordinate that he or she has done well. The effort that the boss expends in complimenting the subordinate will be more than repaid by the subordinate's renewed energy for the job.

A good friend of ours, who is a black manager in a large company, is very personable and able to work quite effectively with anyone. We have seen him mellow some of the most obviously bigoted people in his organization. We noticed that he does so by very quickly identifying one of the individual's key personal needs (one to which he is willing to respond) and fulfilling it. The individual, having had the key need met, becomes more willing to cooperate, even though he or she may have negative feelings about blacks.

A white manager may simply have a need to have black managers speak positively about him or her. A cold, impersonal manager may want to have warm, friendly interactions with his or her subordinates. This type of manager would tend to be more responsive to subordinates who are personable with him or her. The subordinate who knows how to satisfy this psychological need will be rewarded with more support and attention than others receive from the impersonal manager.

The Boss-Subordinate Relationship

When we conduct workshops, seminars, or lectures across the country, a common thread runs through all the events. Blacks and other minorities consistently ask questions and express concerns about their boss-subordinate relationship. This is a key working relationship, which can produce results ranging from outstanding to total chaos.

The relationship-building approach we present in this subsection represents good management for *all* managers. However, *not* using this approach has greater negative consequences for minorities, particularly blacks, because of how they are normally perceived in white American organizations as a result of racism. The material in this subsection is especially useful when employed in bicultural boss-subordinate relationships. It can help blacks share essential information with their white hierarchy in order to answer the key question so often asked by white managers: "Now that I've been made aware of black issues, what can I do to make a difference?"

Attitudes in Boss-Subordinate Relationships

Regardless of whether the boss-subordinate relationship is a new one or an existing one, it is essential that workable interactions be developed. Pairs in a boss-subordinate relationship do not have to be friends but should at least have mutual respect. Attention must be given to identifying job needs that bosses and subordinates have of each other and to deciding how to meet those needs. If pairs in this relationship have positive adult attitudes, positive results can be obtained despite the presence of sexism and racism. Blacks should separate whites' interactional style from their knowledge. Even racist individuals have data and expertise to share.

Blacks tend to respond well to stylish and open people, bosses as well as peers. Some people are neither stylish nor open, and blacks tend not to respond as well to them. This normally leads to unfortunate consequences for both boss and subordinate, preventing optimum use of each other's talents. Effective boss-subordinate relationships are essential because of the importance of bosses to the growth, development, and work results of subordinates.

Since the closest relationship for a minority manager in his or her job is the boss-subordinate relationship, it does not matter whether the members of the pair are blacks, whites, males, or females; the relationship can be a productive one. Other work relationships stem from this core relationship. If this boss-subordinate relationship is a good one— no matter whether the boss is racist or sexist—it makes other relationships easier to deal with because the subordinate has the support of the boss.

Relationships of any kind are built on getting to know the other person. It is important to understand the boss. The more you know, the better the relationship can become. You do not have to be friends with or like the other person to have a good *working* relationship. Unfortunately, blacks tend to cling to the cultural need to like and feel comfortable with the people with whom they must work, especially the individuals with whom they must closely operate on a long-term basis. In the business world, this is a luxury, since blacks cannot usually pick and choose their coworkers. White managers tend to acknowledge this fact and operate quite smoothly without always liking the people with whom they must interact. Blacks must also develop this skill. It becomes an addition to your repertoire of job skills and does not necessitate your giving up being black.

And finally, white bosses should be aware that intimidation is not an effective way to build relationships with minorities. Oddly, some managers believe intimidation causes people to produce at their maximum. Actually, the opposite occurs with minorities: Intimidation tends to kill their initiative and creativity. When whites use intimidation on blacks, a racial dimension is added to the interchange, regardless of whether or not the whites are consciously aware of the racist overtones. White managers need to realize that this will occur even if the use of intimidation is their primary operating style with all subordinates, white as well as black. Since the times of slavery, intimidation has been the expected form of behavior used by whites in controlling blacks. Therefore, when intimidation is employed on blacks, it tends to raise questions about the prejudicial attitudes of the whites involved in an interaction, and blacks will assume the intimidation results from racial prejudice. In short, if "management by intimidation" is a white boss's customary way of behaving, he or she needs to understand that a black subordinate will respond in a negative way, either overtly or covertly.

Making the Boss-Subordinate Relationship Pay Off

In working with black and other minority managers across the country, we have found the following ten key principles to be effective in cross-cultural boss-subordinate relationships. Using these key principles will produce positive results if the subordinate has an appropriately positive attitude about his or her boss, as discussed in the preceding subsection.

1. *Understand what your boss wants to do with his or her work unit. Understand his or her goals and expectations and how your job performance will be evaluated.* As a subordinate, if you understand the direction in which your boss wants to take his or her work unit, goals, organizational needs, expectations, and criteria for job success, you will greatly improve your chances of success. A boss-subordinate team can be a powerful factor in producing excellent organizational results. Bosses and subordinates should exchange the above information about each other. The quality of the work output from the two people is directly

proportional to their knowledge of each other and their understanding of each other's job needs.

2. *Learn multicultural management techniques.* At this point, it is obvious that whites cannot effectively manage minorities—especially blacks—in the same way as they manage other whites. Cultural differences do affect how people should be managed. People of a different culture can bring unique and creative ways of looking at problems and solutions that people of the majority culture might not consider. We have found that better problem solutions and decisions result when you have a multicultural team. It is therefore important that bosses and subordinates from different cultures learn multicultural management techniques. Both whites and blacks usually find that these techniques are useful for managing *all* people.

3. *Appropriately resist the power of the boss in the relationship.* Since we have established that people of different cultures need to be managed differently and they may approach problems differently, disagreements will arise in boss-subordinate relationships. When these disagreements surface, both bosses and subordinates must resist the power inherent in the boss's organizational position. By pushing back on each other in a respectful way, the best skills of both people can be used to develop better solutions, decisions, or approaches to organizational problems, issues, concerns, and opportunities. The two people in the relationship must be patient enough to learn how best to push back on each other constructively and respectfully. They must develop a healthy respect for each other's talents and skills, even if they do not like each other. Remember, a subordinate pushing back on his or her boss in a meeting with other people should not strip the boss of his or her dignity.

4. *Allow your thoughts and actions to be appropriately shaped by your boss.* Contrary to what some subordinates may think, every boss has something positive to share with subordinates. Even if a boss seems to be semiretired on the job, he or she still has experiences, skills, and abilities that can help improve a subordinate's results. Everyone's boss has done something positive as least once in his or her career. Find out what he or she has done well or is good at doing and use it to influence your thoughts and actions.

5. *Manage your boss so that he or she will not overmanage you.* Most bosses will not tell subordinates that they expect subordinates to manage them. Operating in their boss's role, they do not want to waste time overmanaging subordinates. Manage your boss by first understanding your boss's needs in a given situation. Then move to meet those needs

in a timely fashion. If, for example, your boss delegates the writing of an important summary report to you, find out whether you need a draft. If so, when is it due, to whom will it go, what should it contain, what reaction should it engender in the reader, and when should it be completed? Sharp subordinates will manage their bosses by keeping them updated on the progress of the report and making them aware of any difficulties in writing it. If you do not do this, your boss will constantly check with you on your progress. He or she may do this to the point where you feel your boss does not trust you to complete the task. If he or she implies that you are not making sufficient progress, you may even feel that the boss is being unfair or behaving in a racist manner. Remember, outstanding managers manage up the hierarchy as well as laterally and down the hierarchy; average managers manage only in a downward and lateral fashion.

6. *Remember, bosses are human and can make mistakes.* We continue to meet blacks who believe that people become bosses because they are knowledgeable and tend not to make mistakes. All bosses are not necessarily knowledgeable, and they certainly do make mistakes. At times, everyone makes mistakes. When your boss makes a mistake, as it relates to you and your job position, give him or her some margin for error, forgive him or her, and move to help correct the situation. It is to your advantage to forgive your boss. It is inappropriate to put a boss on a pedestal; when you do, there is no room for him or her to make the inevitable mistakes.

7. *Use step-level counseling.* Step-level counseling, as explained in Chapter 3, is an opportunity to obtain counseling from a member of the hierarchy at least one level above a subordinate's immediate boss. This counseling allows the subordinate to get the benefit of the boss's boss's experience, skills, expertise, and knowledge. It also allows the boss to appropriately reach around a subordinate to get to know all the people in his or her organization on a personal level. In a multicultural organization, step-level counseling helps to prevent racist supervisors from mismanaging blacks and other minorities. Although the sessions are not programmed to have a subordinate "tell on" his or her boss, there is an opportunity for the boss's boss to also find out how subordinates are progressing under a particular supervisor.

8. *Be proactive and use initiative; complete tasks before you are asked to do them.* If you know that your boss will ask you to perform a task, complete it before you are asked to do so. Bosses value subordinates

who can meet their supervisory needs. A minority subordinate can raise his or her worth with a supervisor by anticipating and meeting the boss's needs. If you happen to be in a meeting with your boss or if you overhear someone ask your boss for information that he or she does not have and you know where to obtain it, get the information to your boss before you are asked for it. This action will also help to set you apart from your peers. Initiative is a highly valued skill in a subordinate when he or she operates across cultures.

9. *Volunteer to do part of your boss's job when he or she is overloaded.* Another way to show initiative is to volunteer to do part of your boss's job when you detect that your boss is overloaded. Do this even if it overloads you temporarily. This action will make your boss look good because it will appear that he or she can produce information quickly even when overloaded. Do this when you hear your boss talk about his or her priorities and about things that need to be done but that he or she cannot quickly accomplish. If your boss tends to treat you as if you were in a "less-than" position, think what this will do to him or her. Your boss will have to start seeing you in a more positive light.

10. *Use an operational profile of your boss in the performance of your job role.* An operational profile of your boss is a set of useful data that detail the way your boss performs in his or her daily job role. If you possess and use this data, your organizational life and job results will noticeably improve. Usually, when we introduce this concept, people tell us that their bosses do not respond the same way in all situations. Although that is true, the data can reflect a boss's primary response—i.e., how he or she behaves in most situations. If you have an idea of how your boss will generally respond, you can then tailor your behavior to position you and your boss for maximum positive results in your job role.

A very effective method of gathering information about your boss is to use the standard form shown in Figure 8-1. You, as a subordinate, should complete the form. Then decide whether you want to share all, some, or none of it with your boss. Or you may wish to use the form as a personal guide to improve your relationship with your boss. This must be a personal decision based on your current relationship with your boss and your assessment of the risks involved. If your personal goal is to improve your relationship with your boss, then you may wish to use the form to open a dialogue with him or her. Modify the form to fit your need for information. If you have subordinates, we encourage you to ask them to complete the form on you as a boss.

(Text continues on page 306.)

Figure 8-1. Profiling the boss-subordinate relationship.

Date: _____

I. Describe your present relationship with your boss by placing an X
at the appropriate point on the following scale:

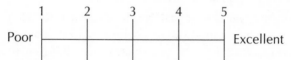

II. Sit back and view your present relationship with your boss
independently of how you think your boss may view it. Next, be
open and honest with yourself as to the concerns you have about
your relationship. Put them on the table where you can look at
them, deal with them, and discuss them with your boss. This will
improve your relationship, and you will be able to produce better
results. Even if you do not wish to discuss this section with your
boss, you still need to be clear about just what bothers you so you
can help yourself grow and develop in your job.

A. As I think about my present relationship with my boss, I can
readily identify the following three to five key issues,
problems, and concerns:

1.
2.
3.
4.
5.

B. As I think about the preceding key issues, problems, and
concerns, I wish my boss would start doing the following:

1.
2.
3.
4.
5.

C. I wish my boss would stop doing the following:

1.
2.
3.
4.
5.

III. As I think about my present relationship with my boss, I can clearly identify the following three to five things that are helpful and productive in our relationship:

1.
2.
3.
4.
5.

Sections II and III are important because they clearly identify exactly what you want from your boss. They also identify what you believe is important to improve the relationship so you and your boss can produce better results. In addition, they clearly identify what you like about the relationship with your boss.

IV. Part IV contains three very crucial questions. If you answer no to any of these questions, then you need to meet with your boss to generate the answers. You may use a regular meeting, or you may need to call a special meeting to get the data.

If you answer yes to any of the questions, jot down your answers and either send them to your boss or discuss them in a meeting with him or her. You need to do this to find out whether your perceptions are correct.

Please answer yes or no to the following questions:

1. _____ Do I understand my boss's organizational goals, needs, expectations, and criteria for success as they relate to the job?

(continued)

Figure 8-1.   (continued)

---

2. _____ Do I understand how my boss works best, and does he or she know how I work best?

3. _____ Do I know and understand my boss's list of priorities and his or her criteria for setting them?

V.   In Peter Drucker's book *The Effective Executive*,* the following seven things you need to know about your boss are listed. We believe the answers to these questions will be extremely helpful in creating a more productive relationship with your boss.

My boss (check off the best description):

1.   ☐ is a reader

     ☐ is a listener

2.   ☐ is political

     ☐ is nonpolitical

3.   ☐ likes to work in a team

     ☐ prefers working alone

4.   ☐ likes to see figures and calculations

     ☐ likes to see only the results

5.   ☐ is people-oriented

     ☐ is task-oriented

6.   ☐ seeks to define workers' strengths and weaknesses

     ☐ does not consider this an issue

7.   ☐ likes to be kept abreast of projects

     ☐ only wants to be advised when there is a problem

The Effective Executive (New York: Harper & Row, 1966), pp. 93–99.

To discover how your needs can be met, you must look at how your boss operates. You need to identify the type of boss you have. For example, if you give your boss fifty pages to read and he or she is a listener, your need will not be met. You would get a better response if you were to outline your data and discuss it with your boss face-to-face. If your boss is nonpolitical and you are trying to sell something that is political in nature, then you are wasting your time trying to get your boss to sell your idea to the organization. Your time would be better spent by asking your boss to identify the resource who could help you sell your idea.

VI. The following two items are also taken from Drucker's *The Effective Executive.*

1. List your boss's strengths and how they may be used.

2. List those things the boss does well.

Everyone does something well. *Seek it out.* No matter how incompetent a boss may seem to be, if the individual has not been fired, then he or she must be doing something right. Seek out and learn to use whatever your organization likes about your boss. Do not get wrapped up in nonproductive attitudes such as, "I do not like my boss because he or she is racist or sexist, and I cannot work for him or her."

VII. If I had the total freedom to give my boss one message, I would say:

The last statement can act as a summary to capture the essence of what you would like to see in the relationship with your boss.

Performance Evaluation: Opening Up the Possibilities in the Boss-Subordinate Relationship

We now turn to one of the key aspects of a bicultural boss-subordinate relationship—how the boss can use the performance-evaluation process to maximize this relationship so it will yield the greatest possible efficiency and productivity.

Performance assessment has traditionally been characterized by the following three factors:

1. *The assessment is focused on the subordinate by the boss.* Although others may also be included in the performance-evaluation process if the boss and/or subordinate choose to get additional data from other people, the center of attention is on the subordinate. What tends to happen is that a person starts working for a boss and does *not* discuss job roles, expectations, evaluation methods, etc. This places the minority at a disadvantage because he or she does not know what is in the boss's rule book or how his or her performance will be assessed. What happens to a minority if the boss does not know how to manager minorities or is uncomfortable with them? After all, management courses do not teach or prepare white managers to deal with minority interactional dynamics. If the focus is totally on the subordinate, there will be no discussion of shared responsibility to learn what the subordinate does well and build on that or to strengthen the areas needing development. The feedback will be mainly negative in terms of pointing out what has been done wrong. We propose that the focus be placed instead on the boss-subordinate *pair* as an *entity*. (We will discuss this approach in detail later in this subsection.)

2. *The assessment is focused on how well the subordinate's performance fits the organization's behavioral model and methods of operating.* Remember, organizations have informal models of how their members are supposed to behave, interact, and produce results. Therefore, the performance-evaluation process is going to be based on that model. Since such a model is informal, the subordinate may not understand it—especially considering that the model is based on white cultural values and norms. Whites share this common experience of values and norms; blacks do not. As a result, because the cultural norms of American organizations are derived from the white culture, whites adjust to the organizational setting far more easily than do blacks, Hispanics, and Asians, who come from different cultural norms and perspectives. Minorities, lacking the

common experience shared by whites, will naturally have greater difficulty trying to figure out the organization's informal behavioral model.

3. *The assessment is focused on deficits in the subordinate as seen by the organization and the boss.* Unfortunately, subordinates often share this view of the performance-evaluation process. However, performance assessment needs to be regarded as an *opportunity* to evaluate the boss-subordinate *pair* as a resource entity. This is important because the boss's attitudes about subordinates and his or her way of operating can influence the subordinates' performance and productivity. It can also influence the subordinates' creativity and initiative. Hence, the focus needs to be placed on improving the effectiveness of the entity, not just that of the subordinates.

What is the "entity" to which we refer? Picture two individuals separate from each other. Both individuals have different sets of skills and experiences that they bring to the job and relationship. Each person separately may perform *adequately* in the job; however, if the two people *pool* their separate skills and experiences, each gains the use of the other's resources. They complement each other, and the pair becomes greater as a whole than the individual parts. By cooperating or working as a boss-subordinate *entity*, the individuals can—to a greater degree—meet the needs of their organization as well as build a smoother and less stressful working relationship.

To provide a wider range of skills in the experience base, it is especially helpful if the boss and subordinate do not share the same experiences and job skills. For example, since blacks have not been in organizations in critical numbers for very long (about twenty years) relative to whites, blacks have not been totally indoctrinated with traditional management norms. The issue of "pushing back" on the organization is a case in point. Whites tend to "push back" on organizations less than minorities. The norm for whites is to rapidly "get in step" and "join the team." The ability to "push back" on an organization is a positive skill and opens the organization up to creativity. On a project, the boss and the subordinate can look at the job in terms of the specific tasks to be done and decide who is going to do what based on each individual's skills and experiences. Each can go do his or her part, come back together and talk about the project, put the parts together, and share their individual skills. This can facilitate completing a lot of work very quickly. It also helps in creating a highly productive, smooth-running relationship between boss and subordinate.

Unfortunately, there will be some case where the boss will not collaborate with a subordinate—that is the style he or she has bought to the organization, and it will not be changed. However, the same principles still apply. Instead of working these principles openly and directly with your boss, you will have to privately assess your boss and work the principles on your own.

As you look at performance assessment, there are various domains associated with performance and managerial styles. *Domain* refers to such areas as creativity, the need for approval, risk taking, technical knowledge, thinking, management skills, synthesis, and action. In the traditional performance assessment, differences between the boss and the subordinate in each of these domains would tend to be viewed as a performance deficit on the part of the subordinate. This comes from the assumption that variations in capabilities between a boss and a subordinate represent a lack of competence on the part of the subordinate.

For most managers, this is an inappropriate assumption. *Capability is not competence!* Very competent individuals lack capability in specific areas or domains. In coaching subordinates, the differences in capabilities between the boss and subordinate becomes possibilities for the resource entity to maximize opportunities and capabilities. The differences represent a possibility for improvement as opposed to a deficit. If the subordinate is particularly strong in one area or domain—i.e., risk taking—and the boss is a low risk taker, the entity can accomplish what would be difficult for an individual alone. Extending each other's capabilities, the high-risk-taking subordinate can perform some tasks that the boss is reluctant to attempt. It may be that the boss takes the subordinate to a high-level meeting and allows the subordinate to present data to the group. In this case, the boss may extend the subordinate's capabilities by providing information to the subordinate about the possible consequences of the risk, thus providing for strategies to lessen the risk. To do this most effectively, the boss and subordinate *must* be willing to collaborate and complement each other. Again, in cases where bosses absolutely refuse to cooperate, subordinates must be prepared to work this issue alone.

What are we talking about? *Possibilities!* We are speaking of what is possible in the boss-subordinate relationship, as opposed to having a boss evaluate the subordinate against some possibly ineffective informal system. This view opens up the following possibilities:

1. *The bigger the difference between the boss and the subordinate, the better off they are as an entity.* This is the basis for complementary staffing.

The complementary-staffing concept means assigning people to organizations in such a way that the people extend or complement each other. For example, a highly conceptual boss should have some subordinates who are hands-on managers or employees. In this way, an organization can provide itself with a total set of necessary skills and experiences to meet organizational objectives. We have taken the concept of complementary staffing a step further to produce a boss-subordinate entity that possesses all the skills necessary to produce the appropriate organizational results.

2. *Putting the subordinate into a new environment (job design) now becomes an opportunity, not a test.* Minorities are constantly told that they are getting a new assignment to *test* whether they can perform well in the new job. This creates a negative mind-set in the individual and in the organization. Instead of testing people, we can put them in a job because it provides a new and different *opportunity.* The testing of minorities always keeps them in a one-down position, as if previous track records have no value from one job to the next. This is one source of stress and frustration for minorities because the message is, "No matter how well a job is done, there will always be some doubt about job competence." For minorities, this is like being in school forever; when will they be regarded as knowing enough to graduate and join the world?

3. *There is no risk in possibilities—it is only a conversation!* Although there are risks in testing, there are no great risks in addressing the possibilities in the boss-subordinate entity because the agreement is for two people to use complementary skills to meet an agreed-upon objective. This is a win-win situation. Testing carries with it the negative connotation of failure. The success/failure factor creates stress. The concept of "possibilities/opportunities" removes the failure factor and replaces it with the learning experience between the boss and subordinate.

4. *A boss should not push a subordinate to learn a new behavior; instead, he or she should identify the opportunity and allow the learning to take place.* This approach treats an employee as an adult with a mind capable of exercising good judgment and accepting new challenges.

5. *Delegation can be executed with a better understanding of the need to pass along authority as well as responsibility.* When a boss delegates to a subordinate, it should be seen as an extension of the boss's own skills, which adds to the subordinate's authority and responsibility. This again takes the process out of the realm of testing and places it in the realm of

giving the boss and subordinate opportunities to extend the entity so it will become a greater provider of skills and experiences to meet organizational objectives. To help facilitate a boss-subordinate pair's starting to work as an entity, take a look at Figure 8-2. The optimum situation is to take this chart, sit down with your boss, and together determine where each of you is located on the scale for each of the domains. Modify or add to the list of domains; use those which pertain to your specific organization. Make a verbal contract to complement each other

Figure 8-2. Domains of managerial capabilities.

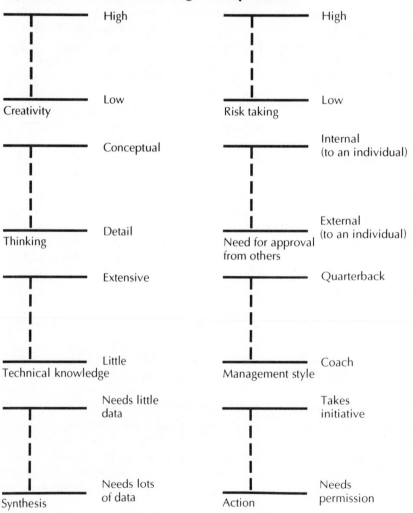

in specific areas. Some areas you agree on may be areas you dislike handling and will be relieved to delegate to someone more willing to handle them. This is an excellent way for an entity to operate—that is, being collaborative instead of operating in an adversarial mode. An entity can better focus on organizational goals and objectives, and you will *learn* from each other. This also keeps the boss-subordinate pair from focusing on each individual and making inappropriate deficit assessments.

One very effective use of the results obtained from assessing the domains of managerial capabilities is to apply them to task execution using the form for scheduling tasks presented in Chapter 3 (Figure 3-3). When the boss-subordinate entity is clear about the shared capabilities, then that form becomes a handy tool for charting progress and rapidly accomplishing tasks without duplication or misunderstanding. These tools are designed to facilitate a comfortable and smoother working relationship between bosses and subordinates. However, we have found a by-product of this concept to be the growth of mutual respect and cooperation between bosses and subordinates.

Successfully Managing Subordinates

This section deals with planning, organizing, motivating, and controlling subordinates. The focus is on the black boss–white subordinate relationship. Black bosses initially tend to feel anxiety and stress about the use of managerial power because, as a cultural group, blacks have been on the receiving end of the power spectrum. There are a number of issues that may concern black bosses: (1) ensuring fairness to both white and minority subordinates, (2) the possibility of mistreating people the way the black boss was mistreated, (3) feeling uncomfortable because of the newness of being in charge of whites, (4) the possibility that whites will not take direction from and support a black boss, and (5) the possibility of white subordinates' making negative comments about the black boss's managerial style.

It has been our experience that if people in an organization feel "freed up," they tend to give their best. They work long hours and produce high-quality work. By *freed up*, we mean that if managers position their people to take ownership and responsibility for the products or services and to feel as though they have a say-so in the final outcome, they consequently work harder. If they have definite and viable goals and objectives, they are motivated to do their best. We have found that people produce at their maximum in this kind of work environment. They drive the output of an organization. For example, if the organization makes dishwashers, then the people drive the process of assembling dishwashers and suggest ways to make dishwashers in less time, thereby directly reducing the cost of production.

Black managers who manage whites not only have to display competence and produce results in their job roles; they also have to concern themselves with organizational scrutiny because they are black. People in the organization watch the behavior of a black manager to see signs of fair and equitable treatment of all his or her subordinates. This creates additional stress for the black manager, and if that stress is not properly managed, it can become a burden that leads to loss of productivity. A key to managerial effectiveness, particularly for the black boss, is the development of personal goals, organizational goals, and a business plan. With these in hand, the odds of success increase significantly. Goals and a business plan position a manager to assume the role of a teacher and get rewards from seeing subordinates become successful through his or her help. The boss will be seen by the organization not only as a producer of excellent results but also as a developer of people.

Information You Need to Know About Your Subordinates

The following list shows the basic information you should have about your subordinates. Although it is certainly possible to manage people without this information, for a black boss, knowing this information makes it easier to manage subordinates for organizational success. Possessing this kind of information about subordinates helps to circumvent prejudice and racist behavior from individuals and organizations and positions black managers to increase their odds of success in the marketplace. In addition, it is "just plain good management":

1. *Personal philosophy about life.* This information allows a boss to understand what motivates and drives a subordinate to accomplish job tasks. It also provides an indication of a subordinate's potential for growth. If, for example, a subordinate believes that the purpose of life is merely "to earn money to provide for his or her family's welfare," then the subordinate will probably not exercise a lot of initiative and complete a large number of tasks. Instead, the person will plod along at a leisurely pace. However, it may be possible to position the person to change his or her philosophy, which will subsequently result in a positive change in the job output. If a subordinate believes the purpose of life is to "improve the human condition for the betterment of human-

kind," then that individual will probably exercise initiative and tend to be aggressive in his or her job role.

2. *Personal philosophy about people.* A person's philosophy about people is important to know because it drives the way he or she relates to others. If a person believes that people are basically dishonest and will do whatever they want to do, then the individual will tend not to value others. He or she will probably not have good interpersonal relationships, thereby making it difficult to accomplish tasks. Although philosophies are not cast in stone and can change, it is helpful for a boss to know where to begin with a subordinate. This information can then help the boss manage the subordinate in a way that will yield maximum productivity while helping the subordinate change his or her negative view of others.

3. *Vision of how he or she would like to operate.* Many bosses in American organizations tend to manage others by pressuring them through intimidation or the use of power to conform to the boss's way of thinking and doing things. Black bosses open themselves up to inappropriate evaluations when they operate this way. To prevent this, find out the subordinate's vision of how he or she prefers to do the job. This knowledge helps set the stage for developing the most productive way for the subordinate to operate in his or her job role.

4. *Organizational goals, objectives, needs, and expectations.* This information from a subordinate allows the boss-subordinate pair to ensure that the subordinate's goals, objectives, and expectations are realistic and in line with those of the organization. It also ensures that a subordinate's specific job needs are met, thereby positioning the individual to produce at a maximum level. These needs could involve technical aspects of the job, interpersonal or management technique, or job execution.

5. *Working conditions.* If a boss knows how a subordinate works best, then the pair can make maximum use of opportunities to complete work quickly and efficiently. Some subordinates, for example, like to be given tasks and resources and left alone. Others like to touch base periodically with the boss to ensure that they are on track. This information allows a boss-subordinate pair to define how they will work together.

6. *Thoughts regarding job positions and task accomplishment.* This knowledge allows a boss to obtain a subordinate's viewpoint about how the work can best be accomplished. Subordinates tend to perform better

if they feel that their ideas have been used to define their job roles and determine how the work will be completed.

7. *A list of work priorities.* Bosses and subordinates usually have a different set of work priorities and may not know the relative position of the tasks on each other's list. Many times, bosses have their own set of work priorities for subordinates but do not inform subordinates of what they think those priorities should be. Inevitably, subordinates do not work on a job task when the boss thinks they should be working on it. A simple solution is to periodically discuss the subordinates' list of priorities to ensure that they are working on the appropriate task at the proper time.

8. *Level of authority.* Subordinates need to be clear about their level of authority for the work tasks they have been charged with completing. A boss needs to know whether there is a conflict between how he or she sees the level of authority versus how the subordinate sees it. A potential conflict can be prevented if the boss is aware of the subordinate's viewpoint regarding the level of authority.

9. *Work profile.* Knowledge about a subordinate provides insight into how to manage him or her to achieve maximum job output and growth. A profile of a subordinate can provide the necessary knowledge. We suggest that you use the form in Figure 8-1, "Profiling the Boss-Subordinate Relationship," to gather information on your subordinates. The following are some of the things you should learn about each of your subordinates:

- The subordinate's job needs, interpersonal style, and mode of operation
- How the subordinate's decision-making processes work
- Whether the subordinate is a reader or a listener
- The subordinate's strengths and areas needing improvement and how these may be used, strengthened, or corrected
- Whether the subordinate is political or nonpolitical in the organization
- Whether the subordinate is a team player or an individual worker
- Whether the subordinate is people- or task-oriented
- What the subordinate does well, how the subordinate learns best, and what motivates him or her
- The subordinate's job interests
- How the subordinate defines rewards and punishments[1]

1. Based on Peter Drucker, *The Effective Executive* (New York: Harper & Row, 1966), pp. 93–99.

Tips for Managerial Success With Subordinates

The following list provides guidelines for achieving a productive and mutually satisfying boss-subordinate relationship:

1. *Tell your subordinates how you work best and how you would like them to work.*

2. *Share your organizational goals, needs, expectations, and criteria for success as they relate to the job.*

3. *Give your subordinates a clear job description for their role or ask them to develop one for your approval.*

4. *Share your list of priorities and your criteria for setting them.*

5. *Create a motivating and supportive atmosphere for subordinates.*

6. *Do not become competitive with subordinates.*

7. *Delegate appropriately by considering your subordinates' interests, willingness, abilities, and experiences.*

8. *Coach and counsel your subordinates.* Coaching is used to provide subordinates with skills and knowledge. Counseling helps provide subordinates with direction and is also used to determine why they are not using the skills and abilities they possess.

9. *Give continual performance feedback to subordinates.*

10. *Use knowledge about different racial boss-subordinate dynamics to develop a productive relationship.* Black subordinates tend to need organizational support and seek to verify for themselves whether the black boss will be supportive. White subordinates tend to initially challenge and test the black boss's intelligence, experience, and ability to handle the job. If white subordinates are properly managed, they will stop this type of behavior.

11. *Encourage subordinates to give input or feedback on job procedures, work problems, morale, and personnel needs.*[2]

12. *Discuss the level of authority subordinates will be allowed to have in carrying out job assignments.* Levels of authority vary in different organizations. Possible levels include: (1) full authority to decide and act; (2) authority to decide, act, and report; and (3) authority to decide and recommend.

2. Judy Simmons, "Managing Organizations: Listen, Learn and Lead," *Black Enterprise* (November 1978), p. 56.

13. *Learn your business.* The more you know about your organization's business, the more valuable you are to your company. In this context, *business* refers to how the product or service you provide reaches the consumer. How is a product first created? How is research and development conducted? How are the prototypes developed? How is the product tested, and what are the results of those tests? How are your products or services sold? How are targets developed for production and for amounts of service delivered per unit of time? The more you are aware of these activities and the part you play in the whole service/product-delivery chain of events, the more opportunities you will have to impact the business in a creative and innovative way. Remember, we are not telling you to be an expert in each phase of the operation; just know what is happening in areas other than your own. If you concentrate primarily on your part of the production chain, your focus will be narrowed, and you will become an expert in only one phase of the operation. Experts tend to be kept in their area of expertise rather than promoted up the corporate ladder. Therefore, bright young managers who are plotting their careers must plan ways to learn about their business's total chain of events.

14. *Create ownership in your subordinates.* One of the key roles of a manager is to create a motivating environment so that people perform at their maximum potential. An important means of achieving this goal is to create in subordinates ownership of the business. If employees have to contend with repetitious or mundane tasks and do not know how they fit into the profit-making or service-delivery business, they will not produce at their maximum. All they will do, essentially, is follow orders. On the other hand, subordinates who understand the importance of their part in the whole chain of events and feel responsible for the successful accomplishment of that part will use creativity and innovative thinking to positively impact the business. This will make it much easier on you as a manager and will also free up your time so you can plan ways to increase production or improve service.

Have a publicly displayed feedback mechanism (e.g., charts and graphs) so subordinates will know how they are performing against the monthly production or service-delivery target. In that way, you are telling them directly that they either did or did not meet their goals. If they did not, then they can bring some of their creativity and innovation to the forefront and work as a team to get the appropriate results.

15. *Make your expectations clear.* Share with your subordinates what is truly important in the organization and what you will be looking for

at performance appraisal time. Our experience has shown us that most people perform at their best when they understand what is expected, how it is to be accomplished, and when it is due. You will be a more productive and efficient manager when you delegate authority and state clear expectations. Then you can move out of the way and allow people to work on their own as adults. This gives you additional time for your own innovative thinking and creative activities.

If you fail to tell your subordinates what you expect of them, you face the possibility of disappointment. They are unable to read your mind; in an attempt to deliver what they think you want, they may guess wrong. You will then be faced with the challenge of correcting or changing their behavior after the fact, which is more difficult to do. It is much easier and more productive to tell subordinates what you expect and what you will grade them on before they start the task or job.

You owe it to your subordinates to give them a clear understanding of what counts in the organization in terms of their delivery of products or services. We have found that often subordinates really do not know what to emphasize in their jobs—what is important and worthwhile and what is not. Take report writing, for instance. It is essential that a manager clearly indicate what needs to be covered in a report, how precisely it needs to be explained, and who will read the report. Without that explanation, a subordinate may miss the key reason for the report, spend valuable time in overwriting, or miss the mark entirely. For subordinates to perform at their peak in terms of transmitting information via a report, they need to learn from the receivers of the report exactly what they expect. In short, when subordinates are given a job, they will work faster and make fewer mistakes if four major areas are covered: (1) the exact prerequisites of the job, (2) the quality desired, (3) the time limit, and (4) how the work will be delivered.

16. *Build healthy competition.* Set up friendly competition within your area of responsibility by sharing key facts from the various organizations. For example, if you operate in a manufacturing organization at the plant-manager level or at the department-head level, you can compare the case cost of a product from other departments with the case cost of a product from your department. You may also compare the time that various departments spend in the delivery of a service. If you have four manufacturing departments operating under you, share case costs between the four departments. You can create an atmosphere in which people develop their own friendly competition by trying to outdo each other in a positive, as opposed to a destructive, way. The end result is

that you drive the case cost down. If you happen to be a department manager of a three-shift operation, run the competition between the shifts. Be sure to use all the aforementioned techniques to develop the appropriate atmosphere. Publicize the results so everyone can keep track of the competition. Develop a reward system. Give gold stars to your best workers to redeem for a prize—a case of beer or steak dinner. Have pizza parties to celebrate milestones. Be creative. People like to know you appreciate their efforts. It builds team spirit and boosts morale.

17. *Stress minority development.* Because blacks, women, and other racial and ethnic groups are not a normal part of the "good old boy network," the information casually shared between white males tends not to be shared with females or nonwhite males. As a result of this gap in the informal information-sharing process, neither females nor nonwhite males experience the same growth rate as white males in the organization. Black/minority development can reduce or close this gap. In black/minority development, blacks and other minorities can learn the vital skills they need to become properly socialized in the organization—and still get organizational data commonly shared on the golf course. They can learn how to get sponsors/mentors and how to network more effectively. They can learn how to become a part of the system that they would normally be left out of and how to handle racist or sexist issues that might arise in that organization. Techniques for developing blacks and other minorities include reading relevant books and attending courses and seminars for minorities.

18. *Teach subordinates to control their careers.* Your organization should be prepared to give you and your subordinates the resources you need to plan and organize your careers, but do not expect the organization to control your careers. It is the responsibility of individuals to request what they need for growth and development. Our assumption here is that your subordinates at least meet the organization's minimum performance requirements. If a subordinate expresses a desire to be more productive and to do more, then be willing to meet the resource and growth needs that will position the subordinate to increase his or her output. Teach your subordinates not to be concerned about using resource help when they need it—either in a technical area or in a task-execution area. Organizations always have people who know exactly how to get things done, and subordinates are expected to use these valuable resources.

Be aggressive and seek outside managerial training for your subordinates. Most organizations have budgets for outside training activities. If the budget is limited, choose seminars or events wisely. Have your organization order audiotapes, videotapes, books, and periodicals that can be helpful to your subordinates in doing their jobs and in career planning and growth. What you do for your subordinates careerwise is up to you as their boss; your company will not do it for them.

19. *Share promotion requirements with your subordinates.* Help them understand the promotion system by explaining how promotions are made and who makes them—an appointed committee or one person at a certain level. If promotions are made by a committee, then it is your responsibility to ensure that your promotable subordinates are given opportunities for exposure to the committee members. As your subordinates are exposed to those individuals who make promotions, be sure your subordinates do not convey only their desire for a promotion. You do not want a white manager saying, "Oh, your people are just working hard for promotions; they don't care about the organization's business." You need to stress the importance of growth and the desire for additional responsibility—not just a better title.

Work with your subordinates on the "what counts" factors that get people promoted. Many organizations have written requirements specifying what is necessary for promotions to certain levels. Basically, you must help each subordinate present a picture of someone who is talented and who can produce the appropriate high-quality business results on time. Determine what is required for promotion: leadership, ability to meet business goals, ability to deliver on hot organizational issues, assertiveness, innovativeness. Be sure to give subordinates regular and timely feedback on their performance. Help them find out how their performance stacks up against the required performance standards. Ensure that they get the appropriate amount of visibility in your organization. They will not be promoted if decision makers do not know them.

20. *Teach subordinates the importance of having mentors.* Subordinates need the support of people other than their bosses. Mentors can teach your subordinates additional ways to accomplish organizational tasks and can share technical information with them. It will be advantageous if at least one mentor is an upper-level, well-respected manager or is a power broker in the organization. There will be many occasions when mentors can speak to others in the organization about the outstanding work completed by one of your subordinates, which will carry more weight than your message about the outstanding work. This will also

provide visibility for you in the organization by displaying your competence and talents as an outstanding manager.

21. *Require your subordinates to manage coworkers' racist and sexist
behavior.* As a boss, it is to your advantage to look after the best interests
of all your subordinates. Since you also have other important roles to
fulfill, you will not always be available to subordinates to help them
work issues and problems that result from the racist and sexist behavior
of others in the organization. When subordinates continually run to you
to describe and complain about the racist and sexist behavior they are
experiencing, you may at some point question whether or not they can
take care of other portions of their job. It is critical for them to be able to
manage and neutralize people in their environment who are behaving
in a racist and/or sexist manner. It may be helpful to purchase some
publications, books, pamphlets, or videotapes that show how to do
this, or perhaps your subordinates may want to attend outside workshops, courses, or seminars. As a boss, you have the right to require
your subordinates—both minorities and majorities—to manage racist
and sexist behavior that interferes with the effective performance of
their job.

Other Organizational Relationships

In addition to building an effective relationship with his or her boss and
subordinates, the minority manager must build effective relationships
with sponsors/mentors, key peers, and subordinates (other than his or
her own). Since the importance of mentors/sponsors has already been
discussed extensively in earlier chapters, we will focus in this subsection
on the latter two types of relationships.

Relationships With Key Peers

It is extremely important to have good relationships with key peers.
A lot of hands-on work in an organization is completed as a result of
interactions between peers. As a reminder, no one person can know
everything. In establishing working relationships with peers, you can
be more informal. However, some of the same guidelines apply as you
would use in establishing relationships with upper-level managers. You
need to identify the powerful and influential peers. What kind of skills,
experiences, and abilities do they possess? From which of these do you
need to draw? It can be to *your* advantage to draw from skills and

experiences different from your own, because this will add to your base of knowledge. Keep in mind, competition among peers exists. Therefore, a position of strength for you is to find out what your peers' needs are and be responsive to them. In this way, you can reduce some of the negative competitiveness.

As we said, with peers, your behavior can be more informal. That is, you may walk unannounced into a peer's office, but never into that of an upper-level manager. The peer-to-peer level is probably the easiest level in which to build an after-working-hours relationship in terms of social comfort and shared interests. Family members tend to relate better to other families on a peer level. But of course, this is also contingent on shared needs and interests—and whether the parties involved can enjoy each others' company.

Effective peer-level relationships take on great importance when you realize that peers can band together to focus the resources of any organization on the various tasks, which can improve bottom-line results. In well-run organizations, you will find that peers work well together. However, in relationships between black and white managers, you are most likely to have to deal with threat factors and power issues. Too often, minorities must deal with white managers who have limited experience, or no experience at all, with diverse people. In using such individuals as resources, you can usually count on a threat factor being present.

Even if you have a peer who is threatened by you, or if you feel threatened but need to use that person as a resource, you still need to build a relationship. In this case, start the relationship in a formal manner. Call or send a note requesting a meeting. Go in with an agenda or a list of questions and start from there. At the second or third meeting, ask the person whether you could talk over lunch. Slowly move the situation from the formal office into the informal lunchroom or coffee-break area. If, over a period of time, this does not work, just stick to the office with a written agenda. The important thing is to build some kind of relationship based on mutual needs. If you can only get your needs met in a formal setting, then do it and feel all right about it.

Relationships With Others' Subordinates

Building good relationships with subordinates other than your own (i.e., individuals who do not report directly to you but are at a lower organizational level than you) is essential because they possess the most up-to-date hands-on data on how to accomplish tasks. Subordinates can supply you and, through you, your boss with detailed information. You may often find that you need to obtain from other areas data associated with your job that you cannot obtain from your direct subordinates. Therefore, you need to have a network of subordinates in other areas from which you can draw data. For instance, you may work in the area of marketing and have a project that requires knowledge of the new tax laws. It would be to your advantage to be able to pick up the phone and get the information from a person you have built a relationship with in another area even though he or she is not your direct subordinate. So you need to nurture relationships with sets of subordinates who are strategically placed and have strategic information that you can tap into very easily.

You should also sponsor/mentor subordinates who show potential. This helps subordinates increase their participation and contribution to the total organization. It will also help sharpen your skills and add to your knowledge base. You may, in addition, find subordinates with whom you enjoy interacting and who enjoy your social interests. This is why older white upper-level managers play golf with younger white subordinates. Younger managers get tips and coaching from the older managers who, in turn, keep tabs on what is going on in the organization. This is an example of a give-and-take situation.

Again, we point out that this is a sticky issue for black managers. Whites need to understand that in many cases, black managers look upon this kind of networking as "kissing up" (playing up to the boss), as opposed to seizing an opportunity. This is a holdover from slavery and still persists even though it is generally understood that a great deal of information about business is passed along in social circumstances among whites. We find that whites also share data with blacks in these circumstances.

To recap, relationships in your organization are the bread and butter of the business. You need to be as serious about them as you are about your other tasks and projects. For most individuals, relationships can make or break their careers. How smoothly your career runs will usually depend on how effectively you build your relationships with key people.

Using Resources

One of the characteristics of a good manager is the ability to recognize and use resources. Organizations prize this ability very highly. Positive job results occur when the correct resources are used. The use of resources can provide a growth experience because it enables you to learn new information thta might have been closed to you if you had not searched it out. The use of resources is not automatic with many people. For blacks, it may have negative racial implications based on past experiences. There are three key issues with blacks relative to the use of resources:

1. How can white peers, supervisors, and others be used as resources if they exhibit racist behavior or are reluctant to share their expertise?
2. How can whites be used without a loss of self-esteem, dignity, and pride?
3. How can whites be used when they are likely to pass a negative evaluation on the black individual?

As we have already seen illustrated in Jack's case, protective hesitation is coping behavior that often prevents blacks from using resources. At some point, a black manager has to say to himself or herself, "I don't care how I am viewed by a resource. That person has what I need, and I will interact with that person to get it, regardless."

We have established that no one can be successful in an organization without seeking and using the expertise of others. A person's career progress is tied directly to the use of resources, which allows new information to be integrated both vertically and laterally. Vertical integration means adding to your present knowledge base; lateral integration means taking new knowledge from many sources regarding topics that you do not already know something about. This concept is shown diagrammatically in Figure 8-3.

Once you have decided to use resources, determine whether you need vertical or lateral resources. When a lateral resource is needed, you should seek input from a minimum of two people; often, more are required. When a vertical resource is needed, obtaining input from one outstanding resource is sufficient because you are building on your existing knowledge base. A good thing to know is that you can get strokes and praise from your boss and organization for using resources because they know you grow in the process and become more productive. Also, ideas are easier to sell if you show evidence of having used resources, especially if they are highly respected or powerful. The process for using resources is outlined below. Additional helpful infor-

Figure 8-3. Vertical and lateral integration of knowledge from resources.

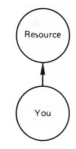

Vertical integration

Building on existing knowledge

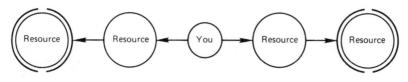

Lateral Integration

Obtaining new knowledge

mation on how to overcome reluctance and hesitancy in asking questions of whites can be found in the solution to Problem I in Chapter 2.

1. *Be clear about why you are using resources and the area in which you want help.* Be as specific as possible about the information you need.
2. *Locate a good resource.* If you do not personally know of someone, ask a trusted friend or acquaintance to suggest a resource.
3. *If you are concerned about the reaction of the resource to your request for information, then find out how the person responds to blacks or women.* If such information is not available, then predict the person's reaction on the basis of whatever information you have and weigh the personal risk for you against how badly you need the information.
4. *Decide on an approach to use, and proceed.* Refuse to quit until you obtain what you want. Preplanning and strategy can take you far. Remember, if the resource becomes nasty with you, you can

always back off and try someone else. Do not become discouraged and give up.

5. *If you are a black boss, try sending a white subordinate to do the resourcing and report back to you.*

6. *Have your boss or the resource's boss ask the resource to work with you, thus making the resource accountable to the boss for the quality of the resourcing.*

Since resourcing is so vital to getting work done, you need to develop strategies for identifying and using all available resources. Here are some approaches you can use:

1. *Be proactive in developing relationships in your organization.* Increased responsibility, financial reward, promotion, etc., result from the effective relationships you build. Through these, you will be perceived as a team player and gain both visibility and credibility.

2. *Sponsors and mentors may be the most important resource base you have.* Make sure you have several. There are many people who need to coach you, but a mentor/sponsor will also be interested in the quality of what you need.

3. *Attend in-house and outside training/learning events when possible.* Make it your business to find out what is available and tell your boss what you need. People, both inside and outside your organization, can share information that provides you with different perspectives, tell you what is new or different in your area of expertise, and help you stay updated.

4. *Resourcing and networking are very closely related, so always be alert for opportunities to build relationships with various people.* Be aggressive; you will need different kinds of information to keep your career moving and your growth opportunities open.

5. *It is helpful to establish a resource list.* Make a list of people and their areas of expertise. Then make personal contact with each of them. Write each person a note; have an informal chat with him or her during a coffee break or for a moment or two before or after work; or join the person for lunch. The best plan, however, is to set up a formal meeting so that you can have some quiet time with the individual. This is a legitimate work-time activity and is permissible in most organizations.

6. *Spend some time in your local library.* We often forget that all we need to do to stay current is get a computer printout of the latest

articles, books, and pamphlets. Many companies have libraries on their premises. It is legitimate to utilize them during working hours. Take advantage of the books and periodicals that your company will purchase fo ryou or your organization. This helps both you and others in your organization keep abreast of new trends, problems, issues, and ideas.

7. *Make resourcing a part of your career development plan.* Make sure it fits in with the goals and objectives of your organization, particularly if you want to do something out of the ordinary. Work the issue of resourcing with your boss such that he or she can clearly see how it will help you do a more effective job.

Reading Cues

We constantly receive messages from our environment. Nature provides us with information about what is going on around us as well as what is likely to happen. People also provide indications of what is happening as well as what is likely to happen. Some of these messages are explicit; we do not have to guess at their meaning. However, many are implicit, leaving us to speculate as to what the messages mean. When we must interpret a variety of information to make sense of a particular message, then we are reading the "cues."

Most of us are accustomed to reading the many cues nature provides. A weather forecaster might say that rain is not forecast for today, but you see dark clouds in the sky, the air feels heavy with moisture, and tiny flying bugs have collected in clumps as if expecting something to happen. The sky did not roar, "No matter what those weather instruments say, I'm going to rain!" Nature implied that an event was about to occur. You take your umbrella with you as a precaution because, even though the explicit statement was that rain was unlikely, the implicit messages were to the contrary. Nature was giving signals, which you interpreted on the basis of some additional messages and through logic, past experience, and emotional reaction to all the information. As a result, you put two and two together to predict what was really likely to happen. Regardless of whether it rained or not, you read the cues and were prepared for the possibility.

This same process applies to reading cues from people. We define *reading cues* as the integration of explicit, implicit, verbal, and nonverbal information about an event or impending event or about things that occur during an event that tell us what may be hidden beneath the more obvious information. This is accomplished by using affective and cognitive modes—that is, using emotions as well as logic. It is what we call "reading between the lines" of verbal and nonverbal information in an exchange. We look for what is not obviously stated and for discrepancies in body movement and gestures.

When it comes to reading messages from people, and particularly organizational messages, our ability to collect implied information and interpret it breaks down. Many of us shroud the reading of organizational cues in mystery. Reading cues, however, is essential to effectively tap into an organization's informal communications network. It is unrealistic to believe that people always have the latitude to openly discuss with us exactly what we want to know in explicit terms. There are secrets in all organizations, and it is inappropriate to discuss them openly. However, organizations do have ways of legitimately sharing data with those who are astute enough to pick up the information. Cues serve this purpose by allowing people to give enough information, without violating any confidences, to let others make a guess at the event. Being able to pick up cues is an additional way outstanding managers distinguish themselves from average managers.

Blacks have survived from slavery to the present by highly developing their ability to read cues. Curiously, however, blacks seem to fail to integrate and apply this cultural ability when placed in the context of the organization. Here, they believe, it is not necessary or appropriate. They believe that organizations will be fair and open to everyone. They throw away their cultural knowledge of reading cues because they do not understand what it is, that it is still necessary to their survival and success, how to apply the skill in an organizational setting, and that whites pass a lot of sensitive information through cues. If black managers fail to integrate and apply what is usually a normal part of their cultural background, it can serve as yet another barrier to achieving success.

There are a number of reasons why the reading of cues is so important. Just as we must be aware of nature's cues because weather forecasters cannot always predict the weather correctly, we must be aware of organizational cues because people in the hierarchy cannot, for many reasons, openly tell of coming events before they have crystallized or become a reality. Good managers will realize and respect this and be open to seeking information that may be suggestive of what they want to know. Often, people will attempt to prepare you for some change or impending decision that may affect you by hinting at it. If you are able to put the many pieces of information together, then you can speculate about the coming event and be prepared to deal with it when and if it happens.

If you cannot read cues, you will miss a large part of the information that moves through the informal communications network. It is this network that often allows you to get early information about what is happening in the organization. The sooner you know what is going on, the sooner you can act in your own behalf or at least be in a position to react appropriately when the information is formally shared with the entire organization. Reading cues helps in your decision-making process. It may at some time be critical to your career advancement to be able to read cues. It can give you an edge on your competition. You will often need to read the cues to recognize both your supporters and your adversaries.

The ease with which you read cues makes you stand out from your peers because it shows you can understand the organization's implied messages. For instance, it is impressive if, in a meeting with high-level people, you are able to read the cues about when it is most appropriate to speak up or be quiet. Upper-level managers like subordinates who can read power figures and their needs and respond to them without being directly asked to do so. Also, being able to read cues makes you appear to be an intuitive manager—that is, one who possesses the ability to make the right decisions based on what others think and say is insufficient data.

As we stated earlier, blacks tend to have a culturally based and highly developed ability to read cues. A remark that is often heard as an explanation of this skill is, "I just felt in my gut that it was the right thing to do." It is important to trust your gut feelings. They reflect the cues you are reading that you've observed below your level of consciousness. This is the emotional, or affective, mode of reading cues. When listening to people, look for the contradictions between what is said and their body positions. This is the logical mode of reading cues. When powerful people seem to be interacting with you in an out-of-the-ordinary manner, they are usually giving you cues. Be sensitive to reading those cues. Outstanding managers are constantly reading such cues and work to develop this skill to a high degree. The following are some tips on reading cues:

1. *In meetings, be especially attentive if you sense something different is occurring.* You must be alert to reading information that seems to be leading to some conclusion. Continue to look and listen until you see a pattern by using your gut emotions and logic. Put all

the cues together until you can draw some conclusion about what is happening.

2. *When you hear indirect information being shared that tells you there is a hidden message, listen to and closely watch what follows so that you can be prepared to draw some conclusions based on both verbal and nonverbal actions.*

3. *When information is not explicit, you cannot interpret its underlying meaning until you have collected* all *the implied information.* This may occur over an extended period of time, as you gather information from several meetings, from comments made at lunch or in the halls, from memos, and so on.

4. *When reading cues from someone, never ask the person for verbal confirmation.* The person will not want to give it. That is why you got the information in the form of a cue in the first place. Asking for confirmation causes the person giving you the cue to become disgusted and to question your capabilities for subtle comprehension. Instead, ask a series of indirect questions using cues to verify the information, but do this only if needed.

5. *Be sensitive to the many ways cues are given; some are given within a single situation, whereas others are given over a period of time.* One secret to reading cues is to integrate seemingly isolated events, comments, and observations over a period of time to gain needed information.

6. *Very important information is usually given by cues over a period of time, not all at once.*

7. *Practice by making yourself aware of incoming data, whether it is direct or indirect.* Discuss what you think you heard or saw with someone you can trust. Put information down on paper and try to making a logical conclusion based on all the data you have received.

8. *Be willing to learn from others, especially from other blacks, about how they read cues.* Your own family—parents, grandparents, uncles, aunts, etc.—may be a wealth of help to you.

9. *Understand that indirect information sharing is an Anglo-Saxon norm and therefore a norm in the American organization.* This approach is not wrong; it is merely a different form of communicating for some ethnic minorities.

Successful Confrontation

Successful confrontation involves facing an issue, usually one about which there is conflict, in a way that enables mutual agreement to be obtained and action steps developed and implemented. Our discussion deals specifically with successful confrontation within the context of multicultural management. We are primarily concerned with confrontation as it applies to blacks facing and resolving conflict with whites. However, we do not mean that this section is only for blacks; white managers· can certainly increase their confrontation skills, especially when in conflict with blacks. Other ethnic minorities will also benefit from confronting whites and blacks in ways that ensure a more successful resolution.

People generally know how to do their jobs, but they may not know how to manage or deal with conflict that arises in the course of fulfilling their various job roles. Using successful confrontation skills allows people to manage the conflict so they can perform their job functions. When conflict arises among white managers in performing tasks, it is not uncommon within the organizational culture for the involved parties to gloss it over and do nothing. In time, the power structure will settle the issue, and most people are content to follow its decision. With the entrance of blacks and other ethnic minorities into the dominant organizational culture, normal organizational reactions to conflict fail to work well because blacks and some other ethnic groups respond differently to conflict, cognitively as well as emotionally.

We have already ascertained that blacks will resist power when their self-esteem is in question. Furthermore, in organizations, blacks tend to operate in a more personal manner, whereas whites tend to operate in a more depersonalized manner. As a result, blacks tend to take disagreements more personally, which may lead to dysfunctional behavior, such as overresponding. Whites, on the other hand, not understanding how blacks operate, often approach blacks in ways that seem cold and insensitive. This triggers anger in blacks because they feel as though they are not being taken seriously or as though the white person is trying to put, or keep, the black person in his or her place. A black individual may feel as though he or she has been manipulated and controlled by the white person and become angry. The white person, seeing or sensing the black person's anger, tends to become more insensitive, confused, and controlling and feels forced to use his or her organizational power. This sets up a situation wherein the black feels placed in a slave-master position, and the conflict escalates. Some blacks withdraw and become passive-aggressive. This means the individual acts out the anger in some dysfunctional way or attempts to "get even."

Blacks cannot afford the luxury of walking away from conflict in an organization. When they do, regardless of who is to blame or who initiated the conflict, whites tend to project all kinds of negative things on the black individual. If blacks do not work to help resolve the conflict, they find that whites consider them a principal cause of the conflict. Another reason blacks need to learn successful confrontation is that whites in an organization tend to punish blacks by confronting them with negative feedback that is often not well thought through and may be inappropriate. This is especially true if the white person is in a power position. Although whites do not tend to be very confrontational with each other, they tend to be so with blacks for the purpose of control and punishment. If the black individual is beyond the Entry Phase, this behavior from whites almost always leads to conflict.

Let us now introduce you to a five-stage confrontation model that can help you deal more successfully with conflict:[3]

Stage I: Approach. In this stage, you approach the individual and raise the subject that is in disagreement. The subject should be brought up in a functional manner so that the other person is willing to listen and discuss the issues. Both parties should avoid a display of emotionalism because it will divert attention from the issues under discussion.

Stage II: Impact. At this point, the black individual should impact the other person with his or her interpretation of the issue. Confront the other person by sharing your feelings, attitudes, and opinions about the issue. Be sure to give the other person an opportunity to respond with his or her feelings, attitudes, and opinions.

Stage III: Probe. In this stage, each person should probe the other's feelings, attitudes, and opinions. This can be accomplished by asking questions and repeating the answers to ensure understanding of the facts. This stage is used primarily to narrow the focus of the conflict so that only the facts involved in this particular incident are being discussed.

Stage IV: Follow through. Follow through in this stage by being as cognitive as possible. Be less emotional, and select the appropriate pieces of the narrowed conflict by making logical sense out of the facts revealed in the probing stage. At this point, allow logic to lead you to the next stage. You should now have a picture of how and why the conflict arose.

3. The five-stage confrontation model was developed by Dr. Duke Ellis while he was serving as Assistant Dean of Student Affairs, School of Professional Psychology, Wright State University, Dayton, Ohio.

Stage V: Closure. In the closure stage, mutuality is sought. Areas of agreement are discussed, and mutually acceptable action plans or thoughts are accepted. If, at this point, you cannot reach mutuality, stop the process and leave each other's presence. Perhaps both parties need more time to think through the situation. Meet again at another time, and repeat the entire five-stage process. At some point, one or both of the parties will compromise.

Here are some additional pointers that are helpful in a conflictual situation:

1. *It is always appropriate to attack a person's process, but never the person, in a meeting where others are present. Process,* as used here, refers to the sequence of events used by a person in an interaction. Look at how something was done. You can search for deficiencies in a process and examine them by pointing out problem areas or stating your negative reaction to how something was done. Examining a person's process of interacting is a key to good management.

2. *You can confront superiors in a one-to-one meeting behind closed doors but not in a meeting in front of others.*

3. *When inappropriate pressure is placed on you and you can ascertain that a person is attempting to intimidate you, place the pressure back on the other person by asking questions.* Then let that person deal with your questions.

4. *When you are in a meeting with others and are verbally attacked, ask for clarification of a point made by others to give yourself time to think about a response to the attack.*

5. *When someone writes or states something that you do not agree with, say, "That is your perspective. However, I have some concerns about it."* Then point out some specifics and give your perspective on the information.

6. *Say that someone has "made an error in judgment" or perhaps has "misunderstood" instead of saying, "You are wrong."*

7. *Sometimes, it is essential to acknowledge that a person's negative feelings and thoughts are valid.* After the acknowledgment is made, say to the person, "Now where does that leave us?" Or, "What's next?" Do not *always* deny others' negative feelings and thoughts.

8. *Approach an issue by asking questions and giving answers that narrow the focus to points of immediate disagreement that can be resolved.*

Eliminate any other issues that do not have a direct bearing on the problem at hand.

9. *When you read criticism directed at you personally, react emotionally by yourself and with trusted friends and peers.* Then go back and look at the written information from an organizational rather than a personal perspective. This allows you to see the strategy of others more clearly. This applies especially to written performance appraisals of you that are completed without your input or knowledge.

10 *When a white person reacts negatively to your attempt to help, try to remain productive in your reply.* "I tried to help you, and you reacted negatively. I don't feel good about it. I've got more data in the area under discussion, but I can't seem to get it across. Can you help me understand what went wrong? Can we work things out so that we can both benefit from this interaction?"

11. *Peers and those below your peer level can be rebuked in private and in meetings.* However, with hierarchal superiors, blacks should sublimate their anger and use that energy to manage the conflict by outthinking or outmaneuvering them.

12. *When appropriate, people can be taken to task with theory, information, and probing questions.*

13. *To help prevent confrontation when presenting a proposal to managers, have alternatives available to allow for the managers' input.* This provides them with some degree of latitude and ownership.

14. *If you find yourself disagreeing with someone in a meeting and you know a fight will ensue that you cannot win, let the other person do all the talking.* Gather data about the issues that concern you. Say, "Thank you," and leave. Then write a report about those concerns. Use the report to say some of the things you would have said in the meeting had you felt free to do so.

15. *When you have to reprimand a person during a verbal confrontation, be sure to stroke the person when you win and offer some assistance.*

16. *When people in your organization are having difficulty with a manager in another organization, do the following:*

   - Meet with that manager and state that the manager's approach is hurting the efficiency of your organization. Then ask, "What can we do to solve this problem?"
   - Focus your efforts on the process and not the content.
   - Negotiate or establish a different process to accomplish the work.

17. *Look for contradictions.* Point them out and discuss them.
18. *When appropriate, use Dr. Carl Rogers' mirror technique by repeating the person's statements to give him or her an opportunity to "see them as a reflection in a mirror."*[4]

Personal Barriers (Person to Person)

Some job barriers are personal and may involve such issues as personality differences that get in the way or personal racism or sexism that prevents a smooth working relationship. In the case of major job barriers, successful confrontation can be a simple step-by-step process:

1. *Meet in private with the person with whom you are experiencing the conflict.* Do not involve others unless or until the situation becomes so critical that it is beyond the ability of you and the other person to work on a resolution.
2. *Probe each other by asking questions about the barriers or what you see as the barriers.*
3. *Make comments and give your reactions.* Avoid personal attacks and character assassinations.
4. *Agree on the barriers that prevent effective cooperation.*
5. *Identify the cause of the barriers.* Deal with cause and effect relative to behaviors, not attitudes.
6. *Agree on the facts—those behaviors seen and experienced that cause conflict.*
7. *State your philosophy on the barriers and how you would prefer to operate.*
8. *Allow the other person to state his or her philosophy and how he or she would prefer to operate.*
9. *Seek agreement on alternatives to eliminate the barriers. Both parties then practice the agreed-upon new behavior.*

Task-Execution Barriers (Work Group to Work Group)

Some barriers are created because different groups of people have their own ways of getting a job done that differ from those of another group

4. For basic information on the mirror technique, see Chapter 28 of *Psychology Today: An Introduction* by Communications Research Machines, Inc. (New York: Random House, 1979).

with which they must work in order to execute some task. Use the following process to deal with such barriers:

1. *As the manager, make a tentative list of major task-execution barriers as you see them.* Make your list specific with regard to behaviors so that the list can be clear to everyone.
2. *Identify the key thought/action leaders/peers from both work groups.* These are the individuals in the two groups who can and do challenge the normal thinking in an organization and the normal way things get done.
3. *Meet with these individuals.* Have a one-to-one meeting with each person.
4. *Refine the list of barriers by exploring with each person how you see the barriers interfering with task completion.* Show each person your tentative list of barriers, explore his or her viewpoint on this subject, and refine the list based on the person's input.
5. *Develop a barrier priority list with each of the individuals.*
6. *Meet together with the thought/action leaders/peers to adjust the priority list of barriers so that everyone agrees on the same priority list.* Then identify and agree on a proposed action plan to eliminate at least the major barriers.
7. *Present and sponsor the plan to the entire group—i.e., both work groups together.* The thought/action leaders/peers will help sell the plan and see to its execution.
8. *Assign formal responsibility and accountability to selected individuals from both work groups to ensure proper implementation of the plan to eliminate the barriers.*

Leadership

Lloyd Ward, a regional vice-president of PepsiCo, Inc., and a highly valued black leader of his organization, shares with us the following thoughts on leadership:

. . . Leadership is a skill that must be mastered to "play above the hoop." It is an essential skill required to gain full recognition and value in today's ever-changing world.

Leading skills are different from managing skills. Managing involves planning, organizing, controlling, and doing. Leading involves visioning, aligning, empowering others, and constancy of purpose. Leaders have passion and are comfortable with being uncomfortable. Great thoughts and effective leaders normally operate outside conventional wisdom. Reverend Jesse Jackson says, "If you can see it in your mind, feel it in your heart and have the will to do it, it can be." Wayne Calloway, CEO of PepsiCo, Inc., says, "A point of view is worth ten I.Q. points."

The challenge of black leadership in a white culture is not so much taking leadership action, but rather getting followership response. In general, the majority culture does not have leadership expectations of minority constituents. We are expected to be managers, followers, doers—not leaders. This is both our biggest challenge and our biggest opportunity.[5]

There are three essential elements to leadership: (1) feeling a healthy dissatisfaction with the status quo, (2) having a view of new possibilities that could improve the current situation (leaders live in possibilities), and (3) empowering oneself to take a stand and make a difference. These leadership requirements are universal; they transcend race, gender, and ethnic background. Beyond this, specific leadership skills can be learned and mastered.

Tom J. Peters, coauthor of *In Search of Excellence*,[6] says there's a leadership crisis in America. America is overmanaged and underled. We agree with this wholeheartedly. The result is that there aren't many effective role models of leadership—white or black.

Taking Leadership

It has been said jokingly that today's leader is someone who looks at where the crowd is going and runs really fast so he or she can get in front of it. It is not very funny when you look at the kind of leadership we seem to have today and realize that there is more than a little truth to that joke.

What are *real* leaders like? In our experience, black managers who function effectively and take leadership are individuals who:

- Bring tasks to conclusion, work jobs to completion
- Act independently when appropriate
- Are creative

5. Lloyd Ward, Cincinnati, Ohio, interview with the authors, May 6, 1989.
6. Tom J. Peters and Robert H. Waterman, Jr., *In Search of Excellence* (New York: Warner Books, 1988).

- Use good interpersonal skills and get along well with different kinds of people
- Use resources effectively
- Free up their bosses by doing part of the bosses' jobs
- Make good decisions
- Are courageous about taking appropriate risks
- Do many jobs and do them all well
- Manage their bosses well
- Manage their area in the most effective manner from a corporate or an institutional standpoint
- Use a good sense of timing in managerial situations
- Provide constructive dissension in the organization to improve results
- Accept setbacks and bounce back without a loss of productivity
- Actively seek opportunities to contribute
- Read the direction of the organization and provide leadership
- Manage racist and sexist behavior
- Resist power appropriately
- Resist black self-hate
- Make quick assessments of people
- Manage organizational conflict well and use it to make the organization more productive and a better place to work
- Motivate others to follow their lead
- Look for ways to expand products, services, and the total business operation
- Behave in a mature, adult way and are not organizationally immature

More than ever before, we are in need of strong leadership from people who understand what it means to be a leader. There are principles of leadership that are important to understand and follow. Leaders *do* lead. As a leader, you will already be in front of the crowd because you will be doing something different than the crowd.

Key Principles of Leadership

1. *Leaders exercise leadership by "going forth in front of and before others."* A leader becomes the spokesperson for people who cannot, or are not in a position to, speak for themselves. Leaders make their leadership obvious to all onlookers and followers. This also means that

leaders should expect their visibility to have both positive and negative consequences. As a leader, you must be prepared for "stones" as well as praise to be thrown your way.

2. *Leaders provide vision and a process for connecting the vision to the functional self-interest of others.* Leaders must provide a vision for others and be able to articulate it in such a way that others can understand and buy into it. Simply put, leaders "see." Others can "buy in" when the leader can make it clear what is to be gained for the individual, the team, the organization. Minorities should never expect people to follow them out of blind faith, but people will follow if they clearly understand why it is in their best self-interest to do so.

3. *Leaders provide people with support to help remove barriers that prevent effective task execution.* People must be free to execute the visions. Therefore, leaders must know and use the kinds of resources that can clear the way for task execution. Leaders take initiative to clear paths in the direction in which people need to go. They will thoughtfully manipulate people and events to eliminate those barriers that would stop their people's progress toward achieving the desired goals.

4. *Leaders provide counseling and coaching when required.* It is very important for a leader to understand the difference between counseling and coaching. A leader provides counseling when a follower or subordinate understands what needs to be done and how it needs to be done, but does not act. A leader provides coaching when a person needs to do something but does not know how to accomplish the task. A coach spells out the game plan and then tells the members of the team how to execute the plan. A good leader has to know the difference because, in one case (counseling), it is necessary to motivate, and in the other (coaching), it is necessary to instruct. Confusing these two types of input can frustrate the other individual or completely shut him or her down.

5. *Leaders gain power and influence through the interpersonal relationships established between themselves and the members of their group.* Leaders gain power by being articulate and respected and by taking responsibility and ownership of events. Leaders develop charisma and have a rapport with people. Minority leaders develop the ability to relate across socioeconomic and cultural lines. They appear to be at ease with laborers, professionals, whites, and others. They speak with authority and are respected by others. Leaders listen to others and talk *with* others—not above or below them. When leaders give and show respect to others, they receive respect, even from adversaries.

6. *Leaders understand business needs and strategically develop methods to accomplish tasks.* Leaders not only understand clearly what the business needs are but also who their supporters are and how to use them. Leaders also understand their adversaries to the degree that they can anticipate what strategies to use and the results of those strategies. They understand what problems are involved in doing the job and strategically and tactically work out the method by which business needs are met.

7. *Leaders influence group members' contributions to the successful accomplishment of tasks.* Leaders engage members of their group in such a way that the contributions of others are critical to the accomplishment of tasks. Leaders are not afraid to delegate responsibility to others. They may be the spokespersons for their groups, but they do not try to do everything themselves. Leaders involve their key people in the decision-making process. It is essential for leaders to make their subordinates feel that they are a valuable part of the plan. True leadership is being able to make people feel that they are working as associates versus being in a less-than or inferior position.

8. *Leaders recognize that building talents and know-how is an important part of the accomplishment of current and future tasks.* Successful leaders utilize and build on the talents and know-how of their people and incorporate them in current as well as future tasks. They provide resources for their people as well as further training opportunities. Leaders let their people know that they have value and expertise that is needed for task accomplishment.

9. *Leaders develop a "can-do" attitude among their people.* Outstanding and exceptional leaders do not say to their people, "We have a problem." They say, "We have an opportunity." They discover the positives in negative situations. Leaders believe that to effectively resolve an issue, you must see it as a challenge and an opportunity. This way, people will not start dealing with an issue from a defeated viewpoint. The only question in people's minds will now be, "How will we meet the challenge to achieve success?" not, "Can we be successful?" Furthermore, with leadership, the use of the word *we* instead of *you* or *I* is very important. *"We* have an opportunity," or, *"We* will meet the challenge," signifies that there is a united group and force that will go forth and conquer.

10. *Leaders exhibit proactive, rather than reactive, behavior.* Leaders develop a clear vision of the future, which permits meaningful preplanning. They plan for action, eventualities, strategies. Proactive strategies,

visioning, taking the initiative, and having the ability to anticipate potential difficulties keep leaders from being surprised and put in a reactive mode.

11. *Leaders recognize and impact environmental boundaries and constraints.* Leaders are well acquainted with the boundaries within which they must operate as well as the constraints of their organization. However, they do not remain confined by these but instead set out to create strategies that will impact both the boundaries and the constraints. They use strategies that will open up the organization to new possibilities without shutting down the task or the people involved in executing it. As a result, leaders must be aware of the possibility of conflict and be prepared to constructively recognize, surface, and contend with it and plan for its resolution.

12. *Leaders address both content and process in task execution.* Leaders concern themselves with what is being done (the content) as well as how the task is accomplished (the process). In this manner, leaders involve others in deciding both the content and the process. They share these responsibilities with others, although the leader is the focal point around which things get done.

Those who have the qualities and the inclination to take leadership need to reflect seriously on the demands of being in a leadership position. They need to be prepared for the hardships, as well as the joys, associated with leadership. It is often scary and lonely to be out in front of others and know "the buck stops" with you. However, for some individuals, there is no alternative to taking the leadership position. It is a calling and a challenge. It is done without thinking because there is an inner need to have a vision and to take charge. For those who feel compelled to lead, there is another joke that applies: "Unless you are the lead dog, the scenery never changes."

The Management Operation Funnel

Through the 1980s and into the 1990s, a significant number of blacks have moved into middle-management positions in American organizations. Just as blacks bunched up as a group at the entry levels in the earlier years, the "glass ceiling" now stops movement into the upper levels. Very few companies can show an equitable distribution of minorities throughout their hierarchy.

Blacks who have "made it" have reached the middle levels by being given an opportunity by their organizations to perform at an acceptable or above-average level. Although these black managers are performing their job functions, their organizations are socializing them into behaving and operating in a certain way that fits with the organization's cultural norms. In accepting this socialization completely and living within those boundaries, blacks help to create the "glass ceiling" that stops further advancement.

In the upper levels of the organization, managers are expected to perform a leadership role for the rest of the organization. However, leadership, for many, remains a set of elusive qualities. When a person is told, "Take leadership," or, "Become a leader," the main task becomes figuring out just what that means. Admittedly, there are many aspects to being a leader. Each aspect has its own set of behaviors. For example, when we envision people who have displayed outstanding leadership, one common quality they exhibit is "charisma." To understand charisma so that this quality could be acquired, the task becomes one of pinpointing behaviors that can be copied.

What all this means is that to push beyond the invisible barrier into the upper levels of management, people—blacks in particular—must fight against the organizational socialization they have undergone. To move ahead, the individual manager must distinguish himself or herself from the other middle-level managers; he or she must become a "leader." When we stand back and look at how all this gets played out, it is rather analogous to watching the operation of a funnel—the kind of funnel used in the kitchen. That is, you pour a lot of liquid in the top and get a small stream out of the bottom. So it is with middle managers flowing into the top levels of management. We call it the "management operation funnel"[7] (see Figure 8-4).

The funnel is made of two parts. The wide part is called the "maintenance mode" of operation, and the narrow part is called the "leadership mode" of operation. The top half of the funnel describes how middle-level managers tend to behave, and the bottom part describes how individuals behave as they take on a leadership role. The sieve in the neck of the funnel is the point at which a sorting-out process occurs.

Maintenance Mode

Individuals who operate in the maintenance mode are very protective of their organizational position. They often feel lucky to have made

7. The management operation funnel was developed in conjunction with Dr. R. Jerome Jenkins, Director of 7 Hills Neighborhood Houses in Cincinnati, Ohio.

Figure 8-4. Management operation funnel.

**An individual who operates
in the maintenance mode:**

- Exercises minimal
  creativity and innovation
- Manages tasks while ignoring people needs
- Manages the status quo
- Exercises minimal initiative
- Develops few products/procedures
- Tends to evaluate conditions/results
  but fails to make suggestions or act
- Tends to placate upper management
- Attempts to blend in with others
- Relies on leadership, usually from above
- Tends to avoid responsibility
- Is overly cautious
- Tends to work alone, fearing evaluation
  from others

**MAINTENANCE
MODE**

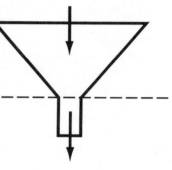

**An individual who operates
in the leadership mode:**

- Leads the business
- Uses leadership that influences and impacts
  the system
- Develops new products/procedures
- Stimulates upper management's/others' thinking
- Adds value to output
- Uses focused and concise thinking to get results
- Does strategic planning
- Uses creativity, innovation, and initiative
- Is appropriately balanced in meeting people
  and task needs
- Accepts responsibility
- Uses insight and anticipates needs
- Freely uses resources and includes others
- Stimulates change and improvement

**LEADERSHIP
MODE**

it as far as they have. Many feel they have worked hard to get where they are and see it as a stamp of approval for their hard work. They do not want to do anything to jeopardize their position. They know there are stiff penalties and harsh punishments for upsetting the organization. This protective stance leads to little exercise of creativity and innovation. What's worse, if the boss is not as smart as the subordinate, the subordinate middle-level manager is going to be extremely cautious about suggesting new ideas or developing innovative proposals. It is less risky to do the job at hand and not push the organizational limits with new ideas.

Managers operating at this level tend to manage tasks while ignoring or neglecting people needs. Socialization, in most organizations, leaves little room for managers to use their people skills because the focus is on the task they are assigned. These middle-level managers are held accountable for the results of projects and tasks. Little emphasis is put on the appropriate functioning of the people within the organization. When needs are met in terms of task accomplishment, nothing may be said or acknowledged. Only when people-management processes break down do managers get reprimanded or punished for their inability to meet people needs. Seldom do these managers receive an obvious reward for working effectively with their people.

It comes as no surprise that middle managers are socialized to manage the status quo. The organization tends to protect itself by building inertia into its operating systems. It does not want its culture upset with new ideas and people "making waves." Therefore, it encourages its managers to exercise minimal initiative. It makes it risky to develop new products and procedures. It provides a hierarchical chain and some degree of bureaucracy to monitor change efforts.

Managers in the maintenance mode evaluate conditions and results. They articulate whether something is good or bad, appropriate or inappropriate. They make judgments. Seldom do they set forth the ideas and suggestions that would change things. They prefer to "play it safe" and not take risks. A great deal of their energy is spent in placating upper-level management. The ever-present question is, "What do you want?" Ironically, what is needed is often not clear to the upper-level bosses. Those at the upper levels may attempt to look downward to identify organizational needs, but usually with little success. The middle levels merely respond by saying whatever they think the upper levels want to hear. Their socialization tells them to do otherwise is too risky. "Don't make waves."

Another issue, especially among black middle managers, is the need to blend in with others. The idea is not to do anything that would make them stand out and be seen as different from the organization's white male middle managers. These blacks want to be invisible, particularly if they are faced with issues pertaining to black-white interrelationships and interfaces.

These middle-level managers rely very heavily on leadership, usually from above. They want to find out what upper-level managers want, move to meet those needs, and do nothing further. The danger in doing this is that leadership from above is normally cut off from the realities of the day-to-day work processes. Upper-level managers are seldom in tune with present-day needs. Always looking upward to see what upper-level management wants merely builds in more organizational inertia. Ideas for meeting the new or changing needs of an organization tend to originate at the bottom—not at the top.

This same group of black middle-level managers tends to avoid responsibility. Most of us see this without even realizing it when we hear comments like, "Well, my boss did not discuss this with me," or, "I was not told that these particular issues were important," or, "I was not given the go-ahead on that task." Sometimes, we see organizations where all of the middle-level managers—both black and white, male and female—tend to avoid responsibility for fixing a problem or situation. They always look to upper-level management to give them directions in terms of what to do. These organizations usually have few or no written, concrete goals and objectives that they share with everyone throughout the organization. Therefore, these organizations are not self-directing.

Black managers in the maintenance mode tend to be overly cautious more often than their white counterparts. Many are aware of institutional racism and its repercussions if they do things differently from their white peers. Some overfantasize about the risk involved in doing something differently. They literally frighten themselves into inaction. As a result, many black managers tend to work alone, fearing evaluation from others. This is an especially critical point because all of the aforementioned behaviors reflect a dread of evaluation, not only from the organization but from the individuals who interface with those in the maintenance mode.

Leadership Mode

Individuals who operate successfully in the leadership mode—that is, persons who have gone through the sieve in the neck of the funnel—have learned to cast off enough of their socialization to behave differently. This group of people has figured out how to live with, yet get around, possible negative repercussions and do something different. They move forward to visibly distinguish themselves from their peers. They accomplish this by working their agendas through others. They get more work done not only by using others but also by getting two, three, or more different sponsors and supporters to help, guide, and advocate for them. They make sure that they are clear about organizational goals or objectives from above and changing needs from below. This allows them to lead the business in which they are involved. If the business consists of providing information to others, then they find out what information is needed; they find out how to get data through with high quality; and they lead their people. They lead in a way that influences and impacts the system.

Leaders try to influence an organization to produce new products or use new procedures. When influence fails, they use an emotional base to impact and push the system. They are usually successful at it. The understanding is that in order to keep the business vital and productive, constant change and forward movement must be built into the organization. Managers operating in the leadership mode tend to develop new products and procedures. These products and procedures are based on identified needs from outside and inside the company or organization. What they know is that whatever procedures or products exist within the company, there is always a better way of doing things. The individual in the leadership mode is constantly looking to improve both products and organizational procedures to get jobs done.

Managers operating in the leadership mode also tend to stimulate upper management and the thinking of others—peers as well as subordinates. This contributes to an organization's vitality. They do this by asking questions and by doing "blue-sky thinking" with others. They attempt to answer the question, "What if?" Leaders rarely shut out others by making the kind of declarative statements that imply they have the problem solved. They tend to operate in a way that leads people to their ideas and allows others to feel included. They add value to the output of an organization. For example, if an organization is producing an informational or consumer product, black individuals can add value to it because of their tendency to look at the human side of the product's use: how they can influence people to use the product in a different way or use more of the product. In other words, they can add value to the output by considering the way human beings use the product from viewpoints other than the white norm.

Managers in the leadership mode use focused and concise thinking to get results. They are capable of looking at broader concepts and then narrowing them down to specifics. This allows people to get outstanding results. They not only think and talk conceptually but are able to visualize the end result and turn it into specific behavioral actions.

They also do strategic planning. Instead of just looking at today's needs, leaders look at how today's needs will fit with tomorrow's needs so that each time external changes occur, it is not necessary to totally change a product, technique, or procedure. Success rarely occurs through happenstance. The person in the leadership mode understands that jobs don't get done by trial and error or by luck, but through clear and thoughtful planning. This individual makes things happen and ensures that the required job does indeed get done in the best possible way with the intended quality.

People operating in the leadership mode also use creativity, innovation, and initiative. Now, what does this mean? If they are aware of an organizational problem or issue—involving either people, a product, or procedures—then they will initiate some action to focus on a creative and innovative way of resolving the difficulty. They will do this by informally involving others. Instead of being locked into what has been the status quo, people in the leadership mode are not as concerned about "rocking the boat" or "making waves" as they are about producing high-quality results. They also look for and define an appropriate balance in meeting people and task needs. Creative precedents and standards have been set that focus on meeting people needs as well as producing high-quality results. When these are placed in motion, the norm for organizations is high morale, high-yield productivity among employees, and efficient operations. Examples of creative programs initiated by individuals in the leadership mode are on-site child-care facilities and profit-sharing programs.

Black middle-level managers who move through the neck of the funnel and operate in the leadership mode also readily accept responsibility. Even if they have initiated something that turned out badly, they stand tall and say, "Yes, I did it for these reasons. Here are the things I learned." Next time, that particular mistake will not be repeated. They also use insight and anticipate the needs of upper-level managers so that they can meet those needs in addition to meeting their own personal leadership needs and the needs of the organization.

They freely use resources, and they include others in situations where they are trying to be creative and innovative because they do not feel threatened by others. Black managers who operate in the leadership mode do not adhere to the principle that a boss is someone who knows all the problems, has all the insight, and knows all the solutions. Instead, they adhere to the principle that a boss is an individual who can lead and direct people to identify the problems and possible solutions as well as help with the process of selecting solutions. In some cases, the boss may have the best solution. Managers in the leadership mode operate under the theory that the smartest manager is the manager who can access the smartest people in the organization. In this way, they stimulate change and improvement in the organization.

In working with and observing black middle-level manager behavior in workshops, in seminars, and on the job, we see managers act out their organizational socialization. They do this by being overly cautious in evaluating situations, by avoiding responsibility, and by not suggesting what should be done. They tend to sit on their creativity because they do not want to push the organization to make the culture more conducive to meeting changing needs.

Now one might ask, "How does this differ from what whites do?" It doesn't differ except in its consequences and in how blacks get evaluated at promotion time when upper-level managers look at the quality of their contributions versus their expectations. Clearly, in today's marketplace, minorities are expected to help their organizations get an edge on their competition. Top management is looking for more minority *leaders*, not just more minority managers.

A difference in consequences is that as people go through the funnel, hit the area of the sieve, and begin to trickle out, the number of whites who emerge does not cause a problem because the majority of the people in the organization are white. Since the number of blacks at the middle-management level is limited, it becomes critical that more blacks move from the maintenance mode to the leadership mode to provide a resource base from which managers can advance. Because fewer blacks reach the entrance of the funnel, as people go through the sorting-out process, nearly all managers coming through the bottom of the funnel will be white. As a result, there will continue to be only a small number of blacks who move through the bottom of the funnel into higher leadership positions. One thing that should be pointed out to organizations is that they need to work on getting more blacks in the middle-management level so they will have a larger number coming out of the funnel.

Organizations need to present blacks with additional information that can counteract, or place in a better perspective, the natural socialization process that takes place in any organization. Organizations need to require and help white managers to be more comfortable in sharing some of the unspoken and unwritten rules and laws of the organizational culture. Blacks must learn to push the limits of the organization to help facilitate appropriate change. Blacks must learn the difference between adapting to the organization's culture and being assimilated. Creative leadership is most often lost in the process of assimilation.

The way to use this management operation funnel model is to

identify where you are and look at the specific things you do that prevent you from meeting your personal goals and objectives. Then take a look at where you need to move. Develop an action plan that consists of behavioral steps you can implement to get you through the neck of the funnel (if you operate more in the maintenance mode). Take a realistic view of the risks involved and check your perceptions against those managers who clearly operate in the leadership mode. If you do this, the organization will take note and help you speed through the funnel.

As you develop your behavioral action plans, you need to use resources to help you refine those plans. Use trusted friends, bosses, and peers and certainly your mentors and supporters to help you refine what you want and need to do differently. Learn how to take the leadership mode concepts and break them down into specific behaviors you can learn to distinguish yourself while at the same time working within and using the culture of the organization. By no means are we suggesting that individuals kill themselves off by running amok. Use strategic planning to distinguish yourself from people in the maintenance mode so that you gain positive visibility and your organization comes to rely on you. Because there are still so few blacks in upper- and top-management positions, those who make it beyond the middle-level ceiling will be expected to perform at what is demonstrably a leadership level. That means they will be expected to make a difference in the organization. Otherwise, there is no need or justification for expending the extra effort and expense to ensure that blacks move into decision-making positions in organizations. At this time in the development of black managers, they have no choice. They must make a difference!

9

Environmental Strategies

Chapter 9 provides guidelines for dealing with the environmental system—the setting in which individuals operate within the corporation. Specific topics include strategic management, the effective use of power, and black development.

Strategic Management

Strategic management is a process that causes change and results through others. It is an organized way of thinking and planning, of using special techniques for achieving some goal.

Research and experience indicate that the use of strategy is an essential skill for black managers in negotiating and attaining success in the white corporate system. Many black managers take great personal pride in the development of in-depth strategy skills. Blacks who are ambitious and who have high levels of skill and ability have to use strategy against institutional as well as personal racism to impact the system. They must plan in order to affect the outcome of any given situation. Everything becomes important—dress, style, and timing. To implement strategy, blacks must have high levels of interpersonal and behavioral skills and political savvy—higher than whites, because whites do not have to overcome racial barriers to attain success. Overall, strategy is a very important component in enabling black managers to use their job skills to achieve success.

There are numerous reasons why strategic management is essential to black managers in successfully negotiating the white organization. It helps to balance power by compensating for racial bias and for a lack of organizational power held by blacks. It helps blacks accomplish work tasks with less expenditure of energy. Strategic management is an essential part of managing the racial attitudes of others. Its use is fundamental to blacks in white institutions in order for them to be heard, responded to, and given available job opportunities and resources, because external forces work on blacks to reduce their impact on the system.

Blacks need to use strategic management whenever their survival in the organization is in jeopardy. It is certainly essential when programming successful career moves. Strategic management is necessary when attempting to change a long-standing work practice or procedure, the direction of an organization, or the organizational culture; when reorganizing a work area; or when anticipating a conflict with someone possessing greater organizational power. When attempting to resolve a critical organizational issue, the use of strategic management is paramount.

The following list presents twelve key principles that you should understand in using strategic management:

1. Identify people with power in your organization.
2. Know what you want (i.e., change or bottom-line results) and when you want it.
3. Predict the reaction of the people involved in a situation.
4. Assess the personal risks involved in reaching your goal.
5. Know how much risk you are willing to take.
6. Deal with conflict; do not avoid it.
7. Have a face-saving contingency plan for withdrawing in case it becomes necessary.
8. Know how to make the power of the people involved work for you and not against you.
9. Use the power of the boss; others will respond to it.
10. Identify the critical issues and problems in your organization.
11. Use an effective interpersonal behavioral style with whites.
12. Stay on the offense by asking more questions than you answer.

The following are some simplified steps for using strategic management:

1. *Identify what you want to happen and when you want it to happen.* This then becomes your goal. Make sure you are pursuing a legitimate organizational goal that will benefit your line of business.

2. *Weigh the probability of obtaining your goal.* If the probability is low, then use strategic management.
3. *Develop a rough tentative plan of action by conceptualizing your ideas.* Look at your ideas in a broad sense, but do not work out the details yet. Test the ideas for logic and see whether they meet both organizational and personal job needs.
4. *Identify your adversaries, supporters, and resources in the situation.* Use strategy to neutralize your adversaries.
5. *Connect your goal to the needs of your supporters.*
6. *Consider the needs of your adversaries and incorporate them in the plans for meeting your goal.* If you do this, they will have less need to fight you.
7. *Bounce major ideas and concepts off your resources.*
8. *Predict how your supporters and adversaries will react to your attempt to reach your goal.* Make the prediction based on your knowledge of these individuals. Consider what they like, how they behave, what they are good at doing, what their strengths and limitations are, whether they are readers or listeners, what they need in order to use their strengths for you, and so on.
9. *Incorporate the above information into your tentative plan of action to meet your goal.*
10. *Informally run your tentative plan past one or two resources, friends, or trusted peers.* This is especially essential if the goal is a high-risk one or very important to your success.
11. *Lay out your tentative plan, either on paper or in your mind's eye.* Test each step of your plan by predicting the reactions of the people involved. If a negative reaction is predicted, then consider asking a supporter to help you neutralize the reaction. If this is not possible, then modify your plan.
12. *Be flexible.* Modify your plan (allow others to help) until it is workable.
13. *Implement your plan and make "in-flight corrections" as appropriate.*

Visibility

Since visibility is vital for advancement in organizations, it is also a vital part of strategic management. Minorities, not being a normal part of the informal communications network or present in any significant numbers in upper management, tend to be overlooked. Blacks also play into this invisibility by trying to "blend in" with their peers.

The criteria for selecting managers for important assignments include "personal knowledge" of the managers by those who make the assignment decisions. If decision makers are not aware of the minority managers who are ready for important assignments, those managers will not get a fair shot at opportunities. Blacks must allow their hierarchy to see what they can do!

Black managers need to ensure that they get the right kind of visibility by taking advantage of opportunities to share information about themselves in a positive light with the decision makers. Be creative in finding ways to show your hierarchy how good you are and the value you bring to your organization. To get you started, here are some of the ways minority managers can get the right kind of visibility:

1. *Ask to attend meetings or briefings with your boss.* Do not wait for your boss to ask you to attend.
2. *Volunteer to attend your boss's meeting with his or her boss.* Make a presentation or give an update on one of your important projects.
3. *Volunteer to share information at your boss's organizational meeting with his or her manager.*
4. *Ask to represent your boss's organization at meetings that your boss cannot attend.*
5. *Volunteer to do some of your boss's work tasks if he or she does not have time to do them.*
6. *Seek mentors who will help provide opportunities for you to be visible in the organization.*
7. *Develop relationships with upper-level managers to allow them to help coach and develop you.* You will receive visibility through them.
8. *Periodically, share with your hierarchy the status of your key work tasks; in other words, "Toot your own horn."*
9. *Allow people to get to know you on a more personal basis by attending organizational social events.*
10. *Always have something to contribute at every meeting you attend.* Never get caught being silent during meetings, even if all you can do is summarize what has already been expressed.

Networking

There is a modern business culture that has grown up around the communications process called networking. The process is often misunderstood and misused, especially by young blacks who see themselves as upwardly mobile. First, let us tell you what networking is not.

It is *not* an opportunity to brag to your peers about how important you are or how much money you make. It is *not* time spent showing off your expensive clothes or buppie car. Talking about how wonderful the Riviera is this year, your trip to the Islands, or your great skiing trip is best left for your leisure social hours.

Networking *is* serious business and *is* an opportunity for you to profit from others' expertise and experience as well as share your expertise. Networking *is* individuals' sharing data relative to the attainment of goals in a controlled and unified environment. It *is* time to exchange information and ideas with others who are seeking the same thing. You do this with anyone who has information that can be of use to you in attaining your goals. It is reciprocal; you are expected to share information with others in their effort to attain their goals. Now let us take a look at what you gain from networking:

1. *It is a chance to get information of all sorts.* Information is potential power. Leaders and organizational "movers and shakers" gather lots of information and put it to use for their benefit.
2. *It is an opportunity to bounce ideas, issues, problems, and concerns off others to get different perspectives.* We are often too close to something to see it clearly, and others give us fresh views. Many people have had similar experiences and can offer possible solutions to problems and concerns. Others can help you develop ideas, sell new concepts, etc.
3. *It is a learning opportunity.* It is difficult to keep up with all the new developments in business and industry. Networking can help you stay updated and in the know. It can also help you rapidly expand your expertise in your areas of interest.
4. *It is an opportunity to influence others and be influenced.* Many people may change their minds about a number of things once they have your information. Or you may be missing some vital data relative to your decisions or your opinions of something or someone.
5. *It is an opportunity to go around the normal organizational hierarchy.* Now before you misunderstand, networking is not an opportunity to tell on your boss or to complain about terrible working conditions. It is a legitimate way for people in organizations to have contact with others to whom they would not normally have access. It is an opportunity to discuss issues, problems, and concerns with people to get and give insight into organizational matters.

6. *Networking can build relationships.* This is extremely important because in this way, you will get necessary visibility in your organization and find people who can support, counsel, and coach you. People get to know you and what you can do. You also learn on whom you can rely. If you are isolated in your job—particularly from your ethnic or gender group—you need to make a special effort to create networking opportunities for yourself.

7. *It helps you keep your fingers on the "pulse" of the organization.* Have you ever noticed how some people always seem to know what's going on before anyone else? This happens through effective networking.

For minorities, networking needs to occur on two fronts: (1) with members of their own ethnic group and (2) with whites in the organization. As you read the following text, substitute your ethnic group whenever we refer to the term *black*. Blacks need to seek out, cultivate relationships with, and network with other blacks to:

1. *Share learnings from a black perspective.* Your added value is a part of who you are as a member of a group of people who have developed unique skills based on their group experience. Stay close to these skills because they are a part of your cultural degree along with your individual differences.

2. *Get information or discuss issues you do not want to discuss with whites.* Every group of people have intracultural issues and information they feel are best kept among group members because they are commonly understood by group members and because these people do not have to deal with racist or sexist components among themselves.

3. *Ventilate.* Again, you need to converse with people who can see things from your experience base and who understand what you are feeling and why without requiring lengthy explanations or becoming judgmental.

4. *Get energized.* Simply, blacks know best how to energize each other.

5. *Work strategically.* Most important blacks are best at helping other blacks with strategy because they automatically take into account the conditions of racism and the impact it has on everything you do. Strategies must always contain ways to neutralize the racist elements.

6. *Receive and give coaching.* This differs from coaching across cultural lines because the data automatically take the racial factor into account.

7. *Share information needed by other blacks.* Blacks need to share experiences and learnings with each other. This enhances personal development and organizational growth.

8. *Receive psychic support and encouragement.* These two factors are needed for good mental health in the organization. Racism can easily make black managers feel they are "losing it." In addition, blacks need someone cheering them on, particularly in the face of all the inherent barriers that remain in American organizations.

9. *Be role models.* Blacks need to see and experience their successes to know that success can be achieved.

10. *Eradicate the isolation that can occur.* For all the reasons stated in this subsection on networking, there is nothing more dangerous for a black manager than to be cut off from needed contact with members of his or her group.

11. *Keep abreast of changes in the marketplace.* Although this information can be found anywhere, it will not have the additional data that might apply to you as a black person. Other blacks can help supply that.

12. *Keep from being oversocialized.* Oversocialization puts blacks in a position of not using their added value for their organization. It creates white people in dark skin and feeds into black self-hate. Other blacks can help you stay in touch with who you are and how you impact the system as a black person.

13. *Mentor other blacks and be mentored.* Blacks must mentor each other just as whites mentor each other. That is how you move upward in an organization. We are *not* saying, "You must not mentor across racial/gender lines." We *are* saying, "Don't let individuals make you feel you are wrong to mentor other blacks." In some respect, you have an obligation to help other blacks become successful.

14. *Learn how to be successful.* Many blacks have outstanding track records and positions in the organization. Learn from them how it was accomplished.

15. *Get black development.* All the upper- and top-level black managers we talked to had black development. That is, they learned those unique and differing skills it takes blacks to use to break

through organizational barriers to achieve and keep top-level positions.

American organizations are built on white male traditions, values, and ways of conducting business. Because of this, blacks must be aware that they may need to learn vast amounts of information about how white male business is normally conducted and about the white organizational culture and expectations. Blacks therefore need to seek out, cultivate relationships with, and network with whites to:

1. *Receive counseling.* Blacks need to receive useful, valid, and honest feedback from whites they trust and respect as blacks learn how to operate effectively in the organization.
2. *Receive coaching.* Blacks need help from whites in learning how to negotiate most effectively in the organization. From whites, they can receive critical information on all the ways organizations respond best to individual needs.
3. *Be mentored/sponsored.* Most organizations make decisions on pay raises, increased responsibility, and promotions behind closed doors. Those who make it are the managers who have upper-level men and women speaking for them and fighting for them behind those closed doors. These men and women also share vital information with the managers as to the best course they should take to meet their personal organizational goals.
4. *Gain visibility in the organization.* Networking allows the white hierarchy to examine you. It gies you the opportunity to let your hierarchy know who you are, what you are doing, and what you are capable of doing if given the chance.
5. *Influence the system through the informal communications network.* To get your goals and objectivs met, you can use the informal system to sell your ideas and programs as do whites.
6. *Get information into the system.* Often, the hierarchy uses the informal system to receive data about what is going on in the organization. Many changes occur because people at the lower levels make their needs and wishes known through the network.
7. *Keep current.* Networking with whites gives you a fairer chance of keeping up with current events in your organization.
8. *Receive training/development.* When you establish networking re-

lationships, whites are more likely and willing to share their training with you and help you meet your development needs.

9. *Learn corporate goals, needs, and norms.* Networking with whites provides you with all kinds of insights and understandings regarding what your organization perceives as its needs and goals. You also obtain a better understanding of the organization's norms, how others perform against these norms, what is sacrosanct, and how the norms relate to the processes of everyday business.

10. *Allow whites to become comfortable with you.* Many of you may say to this, "Who cares?" or, "I thought whites were already comfortable with me." You need to care because goals get met by your ability to interact effectively with all the people with whom you must work. The degree of comfort that whites have with you will depend on a number of things. But remember all whites have been touched by racism and sexism, just as all black have been affected by these factors. For this reason, all groups are adjusting and readjusting the data they have about each other, and networking can help people get more positive data about you.

11. *Learn various corporate skills.* Because blacks and women were not always a normal part of the business world and are still relatively new, there are many corporate skills to be learned. Networking provides an easy way to rapidly acquire these skills.

Network both inside and outside your organization. It is more convenient to network with people to whom you have ready access, but do not forget your outside opportunities. Join professional organizations, especially in your job field. It is important to use outside organizations to stay connected to the community. Serve on community boards and committees. You may find these contacts to be invaluable. Set up networking activities with blacks outside your organization if there are none in your organization. Participate in formal knowledge meetings if they are available to you. Many communities have breakfasts, lunches, or dinner meetings sponsored by community organizations and businesses.

How you network is largely up to you. We will suggest some obvious ways, but be clever and innovative. Develop a positive attitude about networking and make it as much fun as it is informative.

Socially

1. Host an informal get-together or take the time to attend others' get-togethers.
2. When your organization sponsors parties, attend. If you don't like those kinds of parties, think of them as an extension of your workday.
3. Give a party or go when a coworker asks you to attend his or hers. You may decide not to stay long, but put in an appearance.
4. Attend community and/or professional organizational meetings. Also, attend when such groups have informal get-togethers.
5. Have meals with a group or with individuals. Set a date to have breakfast, lunch, or dinner with people with whom you would like to network.
6. If you are a religious person who attends church and church functions, use those occasions as opportunities for networking.

At Work

1. Use premeeting time to network. Arrange to be at your meeting early.
2. Network during meetings. It is acceptable.
3. If you have break periods in your organization, use them more productively and network.
4. Arrange to have lunch at work with people with whom you would like to network, whether you are brown bagging it, going off the premises, or eating in the cafeteria.
5. Set up a formal meeting on company time to network; it is an acceptable and common business practice.
6. Take a moment to stop someone in the hallways for a brief· conversation and share data.
7. Occasionally, stay after work to network.

During Play

1. Ask someone to join you at a sport or game you enjoy viewing.
2. Play a sport or game that gives you an opportunity to network, such as tennis, golf, racquetball, or swimming.
3. If you have a hobby (such as photography, building models, or just flying kites), involve some others you would like to talk to or join someone else in his or her hobby. Use this as a networking opportunity.

In taking a look at the communications networks in an organization, let us briefly review the different systems. First, there is the formal network, which is the official verbal or written means of issuing directives, orders, and so forth throughout the hierarchy. Then, there is the informal network, which we have just finished discussing. This system is made up of people at various organizational levels who pass information and learnings, often in the form of organizational cues, through social activities, at work, and at play. The information will contain various data, including editorial comments, differing perspectives, and personal opinions. However, there is also a third communications networking system, called "the grapevine" (also referred to as "the pipeline").

The Grapevine

The grapevine satisfies the needs of black employees to pass and receive information, especially when they experience exclusion and insufficient support from the regular informal communications system. The grapevine is very much like the regular informal network but with some differences and additional funcitons. When the informal communications network only serves the common needs of the white members of the organization, the grapevine meets the common needs of the black members. They add their own editorial comments, perspectives, and opinions based on their shared experiences, attitudes, feelings, and viewpoints.

The grapevine is also a support system for blacks that goes beyond the type of support system needed by whites. That is to say, the grapevine passes messages of encouragement, warnings, and sometimes chastisement. The grapevine is often the system used by more experienced blacks to instruct and coach other blacks on organizational norms, culture, and politics. In addition to passing information, the grapevine servies the following vital functions for blacks:

1. It helps them learn how to use their anger and other potentially dysfunctional behavior in more beneficial ways.
2. It helps them make contact and establish relationships with other blacks for mutual survival and psychic support.
3. It enables blacks to help each other sort out mixed messages received from the organization.
4. It provides corrective measures when negative feedback has been received.

5. It helps blacks identify the skills they bring to the organization.
6. It acts as a pressure-release valve when organizational stress and strain reach the saturation point.
7. It provides blacks with needed strokes and encouragement, especially when things get rough.

In these cases, the grapevine is the cornerstone of black development. (Black development relates to the growth activity of black managers and is discussed in the last section of this chapter.) The grapevine exists in predominantly white organizations (businesses, service organizations, and educational institutions) as a means of communication for survival and success. Like the regular informal communications network, the grapevine is based on social interactions, work relationships, and play.

Although networking and the grapevine are vital to the survival and success of black managers, too many blacks fail to use them effectively or do not use them at all. In his narrative, Jack conveyed loneliness and a sense of being the only person struggling with a system not fully understood. In reading about the phases Jack went through, we saw that Jack initially did not avail himself of networking opportunities. In fact, Jack did not see the importance of developing a black support system until he was "knee-deep in alligators." He certainly was not ready to become a part of the regular informal system.

The most common reason why some blacks fail to link with at least the grapevine is obvious: black self-hate. "If I am unvalued by the larger society, then how can I value the intellect of other blacks whom I perceive as being just like me?"

Another reason many blacks do not link with the grapevine is the "dumb-nigger syndrome." The individual thinks, "I cannot allow whites to see I do not know or do not understand, nor can I allow other blacks to see this. They will all think I'm dumb. I'll reinforce the stereotypes people have about blacks." Such individuals are primarily concerned about their self-image. In their need to appear superior and supercompetent, they devalue the common experience and information sharing provided by the grapevine. The piece that is missing for these blacks is there is great value in the link with the grapevine. They do not understand the critical importance for their survival and success of such a subsystem within the broader informal communications system. *Nobody* makes it without adequate information, and nobody makes it alone.

The Effective Use of Power

Webster's Ninth New Collegiate Dictionary defines *power* as (1) the "possession of control, authority, or influence over others" and (2) the "ability to act or produce an effect." We define it as (1) the ability to define what is real and to act on it, (2) the ability to get others to respond to meet some prescribed end point, and (3) the ability to act independently. In simplified terms, power is the force people use to get things done. The more things people get done, the more power they accrue.

Power flows from a "freed-up" personal attitude and mind-set. People who exercise power usually have feelings of personal freedom that enables them to act and behave in ways that set them apart from most others. When we look at power from a black manager's vantage point, we still see too many blacks in organizations who stop themselves from progressing because of their negative thoughts and feelings about the use of power. Over the last twenty-five years, we have seen a shift in the way many blacks view power. In the early 1970s, many blacks in corporate America viewed power in a negative light because blacks, as a group, have been victims of the inappropriate use of power. Since a few blacks have had the experience of rising to the top levels in organizations, they now have a different perspective on the use of power: They now see the positive benefits of possessing power.

As we conduct training sessions for blacks across the country, we find we must spend time helping some of them examine their attitudes about possessing and using power. Most black managers have at some point been faced with the need to examine their feelings about using power on others. Although the feelings and reactions vary based on each person's experiences, we have found some common reactions among blacks to using power. Many blacks do not feel good about using power on others or at least feel uncomfortable about it, as though they should not have power. This is a normal response to having been in an inferior position to whites. Many blacks still tend to think of power as a means of victimizing rather than as a tool for making things happen.

A major issue blacks face in using power is black empowerment. Their right to use power in the organization is a confusing issue for blacks, and it is definitely a racial issue. Blacks are placed in the untenable position of being caught between the proverbial "rock and a hard place," and whites tend to reinforce that position. Organizations sometimes promote blacks and give them organizational power or place them in positions of authority and then move to defuse their power in the organization.

Black empowerment becomes operative when an organization authorizes and enables black managers to accomplish various tasks for the good of the organization. That part is easy. The difficulty and confusion arise when black managers attempt to use the empowerment. Whites tend to react and subtly pressure black managers into not using their organizational power charter. This ambiguity causes stress and anxiety in black managers. More specifically, when black managers give directives, whites tend to react negatively, insist on certain behavior and results, make demands, or get visibly angry. Blacks can certainly see for themselves that whites do not react this way to white power figures. In addition, white subordinates are alert to, and frequently test for, indications that the organization will not support a black manager's empowerment.

A person possessing power can give rewards when individuals behave appropriately and punish when they behave inappropriately. However, we believe that a person possessing power has a responsibility to employ that power appropriately and not misuse people in the process. Having power in an organization can mean more money, prestige, job satisfaction, success, and personal leverage with others; an opportunity to run things your way; a nice private office; better assignments; and the opportunity to work for a better boss.

Managers who are assertive, aggressive, and ambitious have a goal of attaining power in organizations. To gain power, these individuals strive to sell themselves in a way that will influence organizational leaders. This behavior tends to be new to most blacks in organizations and may seem alien to them. As a group, blacks tend to be more accustomed to being managed than to manage. Blacks must deal openly with themselves and their concerns about power and learn to feel comfortable using it; power can help them use their creative ideas an unique skills. Blacks need not equate power with victimization or dysfunctional behavior; rather, it is a way to make beneficial things happen for the organization and for themselves.

We try to get blacks to think about the positive uses of power. Of course, people can misuse their power. However, if you behave with integrity, the use of power can open up many new opportunities in organizations. Power can be used to remove barriers that prevent people from producing at their maximum levels. It can be used to change the way people behave, and it can cause organizations to develop new products and services. This, in turn, affects the bottom-line profits and the quality of services produced by organizations.

Although there are different kinds and different uses of power, we will focus primarily on the following four kinds of power because these are the ones used most often by blacks in attaining success:

1. *Organizational, or position, power is power you earn.* It is bestowed upon you by the organization because of the position you hold. Authority to use power is given as a result of your organizational role. The higher your position in the hierarchy, the greater the authority to use power. For instance, vice-presidents in a company are listened to more than others at a lower level and are responded to faster when they issue orders or give directives.
2. *Expert power is gained as a result of technical expertise and an organizational reputation for competence in your field.* This is based on achieved organizational results.
3. *Power of influence, or interpersonal power, is your ability to influence other people.* This is usually done by indirect means, such as with the use of aggressiveness, assertiveness, or tenacity. Your ability to behave in a reasonable manner with others and to reason also plays a role in interpersonal power.
4. *Charismatic power is the power that causes people to stop talking and look up when you enter a room.* It is an attention-getting presence based on personality, likability, and social skills. Charismatic power is greatly influenced by your dress—having a pleasing appearance, neat hair, and shiny shoes. People with such power seem to exude inner strength and tend to dramatize what they do. They are perceived as winners.

Listed below are some key principles for the use of power that are especially important to blacks. Keep in mind that these are a selection of principles, and we would like to refer you to Michael Korda's book *Power! How to Get It, How to Use It* (New York: Ballantine, 1987) for further information. This is a good book to read to increase your understanding of power. If you are black, we do suggest that as you read Korda's material, you keep in mind that you may have to translate some of it to fit the reality of how you most successfully relate to the dominant culture:

1. *If you are a black in a power position, people will automatically challenge you.* When this happens, relax and think about the challenger and why you are being challenged. If you decide to engage the challenger, use the following rules of thumb:

- If the challenger is a subordinate or a peer, you can use "raw power" on him or her by having an open discussion without fear of retribution. You can confront issues, express your opinion, question others, seek common ground for understanding, and seek compromises. This will work because your power is equal to or greater than that of the other individual. This is an example of the use of position, expert, interpersonal, and charismatic power.
- If the challenger is your boss or another higher-up, take your lead from the person in power. Wait for him or her to open the discussion with a question. This sets the tone of the discussion. Ask questions until you understand why you are being challenged. Use expert, interpersonal, and charismatic power to respond in a way that does not strip the other person of his or her dignity. If you do not know the answers to some of the questions or concerns, say you will find the answers and get back to the person later. Stick to logic in the discussion by starting with the other person's understanding of the situation and helping him or her think through the issues involved. If the discussion turns into an impasse, withdraw and say, "Perhaps we could discuss the matter further at a later date." If this is not acceptable, the other person will say so. At that point, continue the discussion as best you can. Manage your emotions in such a way as to permit communications to continue until the higher-up ends the session.
- If the challenger is your boss or another higher-up, use charismatic power and the power of influence. On some occasions, you may be successful in using expert power, but this will work only if the higher-up invites you to use expert power.

2. *If you are in a power position, you can personalize negative information in an interaction with subordinates.* (By *personalizing negative information,* we mean accusing the other person of something negative.) However, as a subordinate, you should not personalize negative information when talking to a higher-up (including your boss). In essence, you can personalize negative information with people below you in the hierarchy, but not with those above you.

3. *Power can be assumed by challenging organizational norms at the*

appropriate time. If you have an idea that violates an organizational norm and if the implementation of your idea will meet organizational goals, then you should push and fight for your idea. Use the power of influence, expert power, and charismatic power.

4. *Power is always involved when you meet with upper-level managers.* You cannot change this. You must respect their power by at least listening to them. There is no way to remove the power factor from the interaction. In this case, you should use charismatic power, the power of influence, and/or expert power.

5. *Timing is important when you talk to a power figure:*

   • Subordinates can interrupt for clarification and amplification.
   • Subordinates should not interrupt for negation or confrontation but should wait until the power figure finishes his or her point.
   • Subordinates should not interrupt to defend themselves.

   If you are the boss or higher-up in the situation, you can interrupt people at any point. If you are a subordinate, you can accrue power from your self-control by following the above rules. Now, if you are angry enough and feel black rage, you may *choose* to interrupt a power figure to confront that person. If you decide on this course of action because you deem it important to you, be sure to follow sound rules of confrontation (see Chapter 8) and stick to factual and logical data. Rely on the power of influence.

6. *Black managers can increase their charismatic power by developing a smooth style of operation and dressing in a stylish corporate manner.*

7. *Use the power of your insight to move to the heart of a problem when you are a member of a problem-solving group.* Influence and charisma are helpful here.

8. *Competing with your subordinates is a misuse of your power as the boss.* You are the boss, and there is no need to continually prove it; you already have position and exert power.

9. *Additional organizational power may be gained by developing a style and a behavioral pattern that are a combination of your own style and behavioral pattern* plus *the successful power style and behavioral pattern of your boss, your mentor, or other power figures.*

10. *One key to the use of power is to be flexible and use the different kinds of power appropriately.*

11. *Blacks can use charismatic power to compensate for a lack of organizational power.* Charisma can be their best source of power until they gain other kinds of power. Pay attention to the people who respond to your use of charismatic power; use it with them often.

Black Development

Throughout this chapter, we have occasionally made reference to *black development* but have not yet provided a detailed definition of the concept. Quite simply, black development is the process and act of learning those skills and techniques that are unique to the survival, adjustment, planned growth, and success of blacks. These things are learned predominantly from other blacks who are successful in white institutions. The end product of black development is another black person who can be successful in white institutions.

Black development provides blacks with:

1. An opportunity to come to grips with their need for different or additional relevant training and development
2. An opportunity to learn to harness the potential energy of rage and convert it into useful behavior
3. An opportunity to learn how to interact effectively with others who possess suppressed racism as well as those who display overt racism
4. Insight into how to recognize corporate norms of behavior and identify the differential consequences that some of these norms have for blacks
5. Insight into how to seek help with technical and managerial matters without feeling a loss of dignity
6. An opportunity to develop skills that allow them to identify and change those aspects of the black-white interface for which they are repsonsible
7. An appreciation for the added value of blacks and teaching how to effectively input these values into the corporate system.

In essence, black development is needed to reach the success phase and beyond. How do you begin your development program as a black manager? Black development starts with:

1. *Learning about and knowing yourself.* This opens the door for you to understand how you relate to others and to your environment:

   - Know how you learn best: reading, listening to others, reflective observation, experience, experimentation.
   - Admit what you do not know. Denial is unproductive and keeps you from learning.
   - Be clear about your strengths and shortcomings. This enhances your ability to quickly gain what you need.
   - Be clear about your personal barriers and key issues. You cannot control what you cannot see.

2. *Trusting your black intellect and that of other blacks.* This includes learning to resist black self-hate, trusting the wisdom and experience of other blacks, and trusting your own experience and gut feelings.
3. *Understanding the effects of being black in white institutions.*
4. *Developing a knowledge and an appreciation of the black experience and culture in America.* This is extremely important for the development of positive self-esteem and a sense of rootedness.

In addition to knowing what is involved in beginning your black development you need to know what is important to learn. The key components of black development are to:

1. *Understand the four phases of black development and use them to guide yourself.*
2. *Understand your blackness and its meaning relative to existing conditions in your organization.*
3. *Understand the double bind of needing information from whites while needing to maintain a sense of competence in a racist atmosphere.*
4. *Understand and learn the effective use of resources to increase your expertise, add to what you know, provide new knowledge, and give psychic support.*
5. *Learn to use an effective style that conveys energy, personal organization, and confidence with the ability to read cues, manage emotions, and use strategy.*
6. *Learn to manage the racist behavior of others.*
7. *Develop a support system.* This means knowing and using your advocates and knowing and managing your adversaries.
8. *Know your boss's expectations.*
9. *Know your job role.*
10. *Understand and use effective ways to obtain appropriate performance feedback from your boss.*

11. *Understand the four basic types of power and how and when to use each.* Also, learn to appropriately resist power when necessary.
12. *Use goal-setting techniques.*

How do you undertake the process of black development? Here are a number of productive approaches:

Techniques for Black Development

1. *Identify and use black and white advocates.* Pick these to fill your learning needs. They can be at your organizational level or above.
2. *Observe white and black power figures in action.* Watch their interaction with others and your interaction with them. Observe how they influence others and use power. Listen to their thought processes and watch how they handle conflict. Discuss these issues with the power figures and duplicate some of their behavior, fitting their successful processes into your own style.
3. *Attend meetings with your boss and other high-level managers; observe their interactions.* Make yourself appropriately visible.
4. *Read cues in interactions to learn how people you work with interact.*
5. *Choose role models for certain behavior and incorporate that behavior into your personal behavioral style.*
6. *Attend relevant outside seminars to extend your information base and compare what you know with what others know.*
7. *Learn to think like racists so you can anticipate their reactions and plan effective responses.*
8. *Attend relevant inside training sessions.* Translate the material for yourself when it does not allow for differential consequences.
9. *Develop and use a personal reading program.* Read diversified materials; allow for differential consequences and the impact of your blackness/gender when applying some of the concepts presented in the material.
10. *Seize opportunities to make significant contributions to your firm.*
11. *Learn to prethink and plan every major move you make.* Anticipate the reactions of others and factor that knowledge into your planning. Freely use cultural paranoia and protective hesitation to be proactive.
12. *Use other blacks and common cultural wisdom to test new behavior and new learnings, to plan strategies in order to minimize risks, and to make sure plans and behavior reflect sound thinking.*
13. *Learn to use white mentors/advocates as an aid in getting your needs met in the organization.*

10

Other Directions for Success

This chapter provides guidelines for a number of strategies that black managers should use as they seek success in the corporate world. The first section discusses how black managers can most effectively sustain their presence in today's marketplace; the second and third sections deal with gathering information and assessing personal needs. The chapter closes with a section on the career-planning process.

Key Actions That Blacks Can Take to Sustain Their Presence in the Marketplace

Before we proceed further down the path toward a career development process, we will look at what we believe blacks need to do to sustain their presence in the marketplace. This is good preliminary information to have as you continue your personal planning efforts. The following are ten courses of action blacks can use to positively enhance their position in the marketplace:

1. *Utilize training materials appropriately.* Take advantage of both in-house and outside training materials. These would include books, videotapes, audiotapes, and periodicals to help you technically and managerially. Use technical workshops and seminars, but please do not dismiss workshops, seminars, and learning experiences that offer growth opportunities for managers and leaders. Blacks tend to forget

that they are held accountable for acquiring and developing their own managerial skills. Even though companies are cutting their training budgets, they still allow employees to take advantage of selected training opportunities. If a particular training opportunity fits your career development plan as well as the company's overall objectives and goals, make it a point to attend. Be sure to consider the training in light of your blackness or ethnicity. Make allowances for "differential consequences."

2. *Recognize the importance of networking.* Participate in networking within your culture and across cultures. Each month *Black Enterprise* magazine advertises networking and business-card exchange activities it sponsors in selected cities. If you are located in or near one of these cities, it would be to your benefit to take advantage of these networking opportunities. Part of networking involves bonding with other blacks to build relationships and to give and receive support and development. Remember to take advantage of your own company's networking opportunities for vital information and growth. A good place to build a stable networking system is right in your own backyard.

3. *Build positive self-esteem.* Throughout our travels across the country and in working with both minority and majority managers, one thing stands our—black managers tend to discount or underestimate the importance of self-esteem. A lack of self-esteem has a distinctively negative effect on attitude and behavior, especially for blacks.

"Self-hate" is also an important issue with blacks. Today blacks, as a group, are still as susceptible as ever to the effects of white racism and the erosion of a positive self-concept. It is important that blacks have some understanding of what they, as blacks, have contributed to history and also what they are capable of contributing. Help yourself by building your own self-esteem. Attend workshops and seminars that are geared toward black development. Be willing to share your experiences and listen to the experiences of other blacks. You will not only learn additional skills but also have an opportunity to get feedback relative to where you see yourself. You will then have further opportunities to help others to build their self-esteem and increase minority participation in the organization.

4. *Maintain a "superstar" mentality.* Despite what you have been told about blacks' advancement in the marketplace, if you look around you or ask a few questions, it becomes clear that it takes more than innate ability and education to be successful. You must adopt a "superstar" mentality. Today, as it was more than twenty years ago, a black person

must still do 150 percent to a white person's 100 percent to be seen as achieving the same results. Indeed, more energy is required to successfully accomplish many of the same tasks as whites. Blacks continue to be scrutinized on the job and evaluated subjectively by bosses. In addition, barriers to job success continue to interfere with work progress. Therefore, you need to plan to give 150 percent, not 100 percent. For example, if you are required to work eight hours a day, work a minimum of ten. If you are supposed to be at work at 8 A.M., be there at 7 A.M. If quitting time is 4 P.M., stay until 5 P.M. Use the additional time to do extra work. Take the same tactic as an army general or highly skilled chess player. Strategize, plan your moves, and think things through carefully before automatically reacting.

5. *Take group responsibility.* Black people must continue to feel responsible for each other. As long as this society, as a whole, is willing to blame the misdeeds of one black person on an entire race, we cannot stand alone, as do whites. If a black entrepreneur defaults on a bank loan, the bank will automatically scrutinize *all* black people who apply for loans—unlike whites, who are judged individually. On the other hand, if that same black entrepreneur is very successful, whites tend to react positively to only that one person. Obviously, it now becomes important that blacks, as individuals, become as publicly successful as possible because it reflects on the race as a whole.

6. *Share your learnings with each other.* If blacks are to prosper as a group in the American marketplace, those who are successful must pass along their learnings to the new black members of the various professions. Young blacks entering the marketplace must be willing to learn from the experiences of seasoned veterans. If they do not, valuable time will be spent rehashing the same learning experiences that "senior" blacks have already undergone. Learn organizational politics from senior blacks. Learn to determine what things are important in a corporation. To be successful, you have to employ business strategies that often are not the kinds taught in textbooks but the kinds learned from experience in the marketplace. Data and information tend to be passed along through the relationships you build. Whites learn from each other how to negotiate their system. Blacks tend to cut each other off by not sharing. If blacks are to gain equality in business with whites, then part of that equality must be achieved by sharing their learnings with each other. By so doing, they can build themselves a psychic support structure. In this way, blacks discover that they are not alone and that there is no need to try to solve all their problems and issues by themselves.

They must build group strategies to remove barriers. For instance, let's use the previous example of the barrier in banking. One black individual alone has very little power in "taking on" a bank or changing the mind of the bank's white loan officer, but a group of black individuals possesses clout. These are the same kinds of principles that blacks used when they boycotted in the 1960s. So sharing learnings with each other becomes a critical strategy for blacks as they take on racist institutions that set up barriers to their progress.

7. *Join professional organizations.* Joining professional organizations is important for two corporate reasons: (1) It enables you to take advantage of new learning opportunities and network with people, and (2) it gives whites an opportunity to interact with blacks on a professional level. There are still some white professionals who do not have an opportunity to interact with black professionals. Be open to providing an opportunity for whites to learn how to interact with black professionals. Some of the people with whom you interact may be managers from your own organization whom you would otherwise not have an opportunity to meet. Suppose you experience a crisis on the job—one not easily solved by the people in your immediate hierarchy. There is a high probability that another company resource may prove to be just what you need. Accessibility to the resource may be limited or difficult if you are not known. Become involved in whatever professional organizations are available. Whether you volunteer for a committee or engage in minimal activities, it is important to attend at least some of the meetings. Whites need to become accustomed to seeing your face. This will begin to make you more visible in your organization.

8. *Exercise individual initiative.* Since we are talking about what is happening in the marketplace, with companies cutting back on personnel and consolidating operations, ensure that you are working on the "hot," or "high-priority," issues in your present organization. *Make sure you're working on the right things in the right area at the right time.* Make yourself invaluable to the organization by positioning yourself in a key area. When you begin to exercise your individual initiative, creativity blossoms.

We encourage blacks to get in touch and/or stay in touch with their cultural background. Solutions to many of the problems that are plaguing the marketplace today can be found within one's own cultural experiences. Blacks have some unique experiences and learnings that can be helpful in the marketplace. Blacks have long been accustomed to making something out of nothing—an important business skill to have at this particular time, given the many business cutbacks that the country is experiencing. For example, unlike whites, who are accustomed to managing large budgets, blacks have always had to be creative about taking a small amount of money and stretching it a long way. This kind of skill can be critical to some businesses in helping to cut costs. This is just one example of what we mean when we say to exercise your individual initiative and keep close to your cultural roots. These are the kinds of learnings that become critical for success in today's business world—in addition to making you a more valuable asset to your company.

In your job position, learn the organization's priorities, goals, and objectives. Do not wait for your boss to assign you specific tasks in order to meet those goals and objectives. Think about some different approaches and sell them to the organization. In other words, go out and make things happen on your own as opposed to waiting for you boss to tell you how to proceed. Remember, small things often become important. A lot of us "miss the boat" by focusing on major portions of a project or interaction when some minor details can be critical to the end result. A small courtesy may spell the difference between a yes and a no.

9. *Develop career strategies based on your needs and what is happening in the marketplace.* A career strategy must have at its core a good, well-defined career plan because it helps identify your needs. Look at your needs in terms of what is happening in your organization. Look at your organization's priorities, goals, and objectives. Also, look outside your organization for trends. Your strategy will mean nothing if it is developed independently of sensitivities and trends as they apply to the marketplace as a whole. For instance, if you are developing your career strategy around the expansion of your staff job, and you put that against the backdrop of what is happening in the marketplace today, you will clearly be able to see that you may wake up one morning and find that your job no longer exists. Your company could conceivably reorganize you out of a job, thereby making your career strategy and plan irrelevant. If you view your needs against the backdrop of the marketplace, that might be an indication for you to do one of two things: You could consider seriously looking into entrepreneurial endeavors, or you could conclude that you need to position your organization to move you into a profit-generating line position.

10. *Make your work system accountable.* If you go back to the early 1960s, you will see that a lot of companies tried to actively recruit black

professionals. In many cases, they were unable to locate the black professionals they sought. Companies, in turn, gave scholarship funds to high-school and college students to try to increase the size of the professional black work force. Gradually, blacks entered the doors of corporate America in the mid-1960s. They stacked up at the entry level, obtained additional relevant training, and moved ahead. Now they find that they have moved in critical masses to the middle-management level of various industries.

At this point, given the current political and economic climate, companies are starting to back away from affirmative action. At the same time, in a very subtle way, they are giving minorities a message that "race" is no longer an issue. Of course, "race" *is still* an issue. An additional issue is the ambiguous message white corporate America has given to blacks concerning black upward mobility. Many blacks clearly see black managers get promoted because they seem to do their jobs and cause no trouble in the organization—i.e., they do not push the system on behalf of black interests. They appear to comply with the establishment. However, blacks have not appeared to notice that these same black managers are experiencing higher stress and gradual loss of value to the company. White managers are now distressed over the loss of black energy, creativity, and innovation and because blacks are not making the right things happen in their organizations. This is a growing complaint, even though these same white managers are the ones who rewarded the blacks for their compliance. In many cases, white managers are saying, "We've got the wrong blacks in key corporate positions." Minorities have "let the system off the hook." Now the system no longer has to meet its affirmative action goals and objectives. Loss of accountability by the system has made the future tentative at best for neoconservative blacks and frustrating for the rest of today's black professionals. Black managers in corporations must insist that the system remain accountable.

In summary, some of the courses of action that we are proposing are interrelated in terms of how they operate. For instance, in making the work system accountable, it now becomes important for you to join professional organizations. If you are in a professional organization, you've got some voice in how the organization operates.

Group responsibility is important. Whereas a protest is risky or ineffective if it is done by a single individual, it can become less risky and more effective if it is done by a group. For instance, if you were against your company's participation in South Africa, one man's or woman's voice is not going to count as much as one or two black organizations together voicing their displeasure. Therefore, band together as a group to make the system accountable. How you plan your strategy is going to be critical to your being able to stand as a group and not just as individuals. Blacks and other minorities must make the system accountable if they are ever to realize true equal opportunity.

Corporate America promised black America over twenty years ago that it would have parity in the marketplace. To date, this has not happened. In fact, the opposite has started to happen. Complaining about what blacks do not have is one thing; banding together as a group, taking responsibility, and exercising initiative to make the system accountable are another.

Blacks, both neoconservatives and others, need to revisit the dream they struggled for during the last twenty-five years. Priorities need to be reexamined and the lessons learned in the 1960s again taught to young blacks. The battle has not been won but has only moved to a different front. And black managers still need each other's strengths as much as they ever did.

Information Gathering

This section addresses what we call "the information-gathering tour." This tour will assist you in understanding what is needed for success in your organization. An information-gathering tour is defined as a number of meetings with individuals in and outside your organization to obtain information needed to plan for success. In the "Building Relationships" section in Chapter 8, we set the stage for you to identify and meet with people who can share information needed to develop your plan.

In many training sessions with minority managers, we suggest using the information-gathering tour as a way to get in-depth and useful data. Sometimes, minorities react by saying, "I don't see others doing this, so I don't think I should do it." We then tell these individuals that they need to plan for success to increase their odds of being successful. Although the information-gathering tour is not an absolute necessity for attaining success in an organization, it will greatly increase the odds for success and greatly reduce the time required to attain it. Of course, merely obtaining the information will not, by itself, ensure success. This information must then be used to develop a career plan.

If properly executed, a data-gathering tour becomes an opportunity to learn from both the technical and nontechnical experiences of others. This approach can reduce by months the time it takes to move through the development phases talked about in Part Two. As an example, if young black managers start their career with an organization by going on a data-gathering tour, they can find out in two weeks what it takes to make a contribution to the organization instead of discovering this through months or even years of on-the-job experience.

It is advantageous for an individual new to a company or an institution to go on an information-gathering tour between three and six months after starting a new job. The specific time should be determined by the individual. He or she should have sufficient opportunity to meet and get to know people in the organization before starting the tour. We suggest the three- to six-month time frame because some people are more friendly and personable than others; for these people, three months is sufficient. For those who tend not to be friendly, a six-month wait may be more appropriate. Three to six months should be enough time for individuals to identify the organization's outstanding and average performers. An individual who is new to an organization because of a transfer within the same company or institution should go on an information-gathering tour after two to three months.

The information-gathering tour should be organized by selecting people with whom to talk to obtain valuable data. Select a minimum of four people who fit the following criteria:

- A black and a white who serve in a position comparable to yours in your organization or another organization in your company or institution.
- People who have been members of your organization for two, five, and ten years.
- A man and a woman (if possible), to obtain different perspectives.
- A person who is seen as a sharp and outstanding performer.
- A person who is seen as an average performer, so that you can clearly identify for yourself the boundaries and indicators of the company's acceptable-performance range.
- People who work in and outside your field of endeavor, so that you can broaden your information base regarding task disciplines in order to position yourself to be a manager.

Prepare an agenda to use in these meetings. You may want to send the agenda to people before you meet with them so they can be better prepared for the discussion. The agenda should be structured as follows:

I. Purpose of the meeting.
II. Discussion of personal background, such as where you grew up, the school you attended, previous jobs, experience, and other ice-breaking information. Be friendly and personable, not distant and businesslike.
III. Discussion of information. The following questions should be asked. You may wish to expand or modify the list to suit your individual needs.
   A. What are the key ingredients for success, both in this organization in general and specific to my field of work?
   B. What advice would you give someone in my position about how to make a maximum contribution to this organization?
   C. What are the characteristics and behaviors of successful people in this organization?
   D. What things, both technical and nontechnical, do you think I should learn in the next year?
   E. What are the most important organizational norms of which I should be aware?
   F. What results are successful people in this organization expected to produce, both in general and in my specific field?
   G. What do you have to do to get additional responsibility in this organization?

Take notes on the data you receive. After meeting with several people, reduce and consolidate your information into a list that answers the question, "What is needed for success in this organization?" Your information should reflect the views of a cross section of the organization's members.

Assessing Personal Needs

As further preparation for your career development plan, complete a form similar to that shown in Figure 10-1 to assess your personal needs. This form will help illuminate your personal needs before you attempt to document a career development plan. The quality of your career plan hinges on the clarity of information you have about yourself before you write the plan. Find a quiet place, give in-depth thought to the ques-

(Text continues on page 380.)

Figure 10-1. Needs assessment form.

Date: _____

Part A: Personal Needs

When I think about my personal growth needs, the top five areas I
would like to work on are:
1.
2.
3.
4.
5.

To help me grow and develop professionally, I will use these
resources:
1.
2.
3.
4.
5.

As I grow and develop my skills, these are the possible barriers and
difficulties I perceive I will face:
1.
2.
3.
4.
5.

To help me remove the barriers and deal with the difficulties, I can use
these resources:
1.
2.
3.
4.
5.

I see these as my areas of strength:
1.
2.
3.
4.
5.

Part B: Organizational Needs

As I think about my present career needs (those things I believe should be in place in order for me to be successful in my job), my top five needs are:

1.
2.
3.
4.
5.

The resources I require to get my present needs met are:

1.
2.
3.
4.
5.

When I think about my career, here is what I want:

1.   In two years:

2.   In five years:

3.   In ten years:

As I look at where I want to go with my career, I see these as potential obstacles:

1.
2.
3.
4.
5.

To help me overcome the perceived obstacles, I can:

1.
2.
3.
4.
5.

(continued)

Figure 10-1. (continued)

The resources I can use to help me overcome the obstacles are:

1.
2.
3.
4.
5.

The strengths I bring to my present job are:

1.
2.
3.
4.
5.

My special talents are:

1.
2.
3.
4.
5.

---

tions, and jot down your answers. Put them aside for a day or two. Then go over your answers again to see whether they represent exactly how you feel and what you believe to be true. Now file this information away for future use. You will need it as input when you work on documenting your career plan.

The Career-Planning Process: What Do You Want?

Blacks and other minorities are leaving corporations in larger numbers than they have in the past twenty years. There are several reasons for this increase: (1) a lack of advancement opportunities, (2) corporate politics that block the attainment of personal gains, (3) economic downturn, and (4) personal needs to pursue entrepreneurial opportunities.

One of the major factors causing corporations to downsize and restructure to cut costs is the need to compete in international markets. Also, stockholders in major companies are demanding bigger returns on their investments; therefore, cutting costs and recapitalizing are a must. Blacks are getting caught in this restructuring process, which follows the "last hired, first fired" pattern. In addition, a disproportionate number of blacks are in staff jobs, and these jobs are usually the first to be cut. Blacks are also experiencing increasing dissatisfaction in terms of personal fulfillment in their jobs. This causes a large number of them to seek second jobs and careers, which may mean "going out on their own."

In the past, American institutions made bold promises to blacks about equality of opportunities. However, no amount of individual corporate/political sophistication learned by blacks has made a lasting impact on equal opportunity in corporate America as a whole. White upper-level managers in charge of profit-making organizations must at some point recognize that a disproportionate number of black managers are leaving the corporate world and do something about it. One way to keep blacks in corporate America is to look beyond the traditional career development model to the personal career development model as it relates to self-fulfillment. The need for personal career development, though, is by no means limited to minorities.

It is vital that blacks learn to think in terms of career planning as early as possible after starting a new job. It is important to begin planning your career early to avoid being trapped in a position that will become just another job. Let us examine the differences between a job and a career. A job has a nine-to-five time orientation. It is more structured and controlled and offers little responsibility. There is little opportunity to impact the business of the organization. A job is task-related and ends at some point. It offers less mobility, is impersonal, and is not highly satisfying. A career is oriented toward discharging a responsibility. It is less structured and offers more flexibility. Its boundaries are not clearly defined. There is room for change and the exercise of initiative in a career. A career is ongoing and has the potential for becoming more satisfying and providing a bigger reward because it can be designed to meet personal as well as job needs.

Another reason it is very important for blacks and other minorities to plan their careers early is because it helps to either eliminate, reduce, or compensate for the effects of a number of important barriers in the work scene. Career planning helps to:

- Compensate for a lack of black role models.
- Reduce the effects of racism and sexism, which prevent blacks and women from being able to take advantage of available opportunities.

- Manage the white fear of blacks.
- Reduce subjectivity in evaluations and increase objectivity.
- Reduce or eliminate low trust among racial groups by removing doubt so trust is no longer an issue.
- Raise blacks' awareness of the effects of their blackness in a corporate setting.
- Eliminate racial stereotypes.
- Eliminate whites' concerns about reverse discrimination because career plans are usually worked up and down the hierarchy, with agreement from key people.

Subordinates in general should always be sure that they have a career plan that is reviewed and updated at least every twelve months. For blacks at the lower levels of management, this is a must. New employees should initiate a career discussion with their boss after being employed six to twelve months. This gives the subordinates sufficient time to survive a probationary period and become acclimated to the work environment.

What is career planning? Before we discuss the details of the career-planning process, let us look at a simplified career development philosophy. Career planning is a process that generates a dynamic plan, which positions and allows a person to use his or her talents, skills, and potential to their maximum levels in a way that brings personal fulfillment and rewards. It is a plan designed to help an individual get what he or she wants. Simply stated, career planning is nothing more than the appropriate matching of an individual's skills and interests with the business needs of an organization.

Each of us has a personal list of needs, desires, likes, dislikes, goals, skills, and interests. The organization has a similar list. Figure 10-2 shows the two as separate entities. If you were working in an organization whose characteristics coincided perfectly with yours, then the two separate lists would coincide. However, people and organizations are rarely, if ever, perfectly matched.

Therefore, it is *not* practical to expect that the two lists will coincide. Realistically, there is an acceptable area of overlap, shown in Figure 10-2. The main objective of career development, then, is to maximize the size of the overlap area. If the overlap area is maximized, employees will produce at their greatest potential and will continue to grow and develop professionally. Employees produce at their maximum when they are interested in their work, their job needs are met, and they are having fun.

Figure 10-2. Career development model.

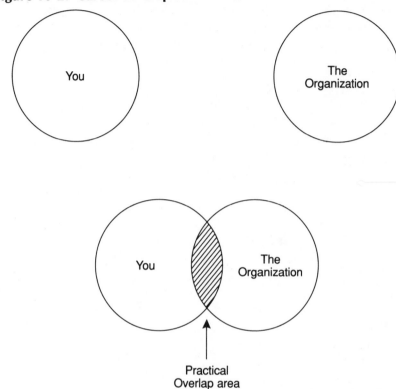

Because blacks are leaving corporations and other organizations for the previously mentioned four reasons, there is a critical need to expand this model to look at what we call personal career development.

Personal Career Development

When you look at Figure 10-3, you can see how an individual relates to his or her organization. The career development process should be viewed as a total concept, which includes personal career development. An individual and an organization are two separate entities, both having identified needs—goals, likes, dislikes, objectives, desires, wishes, and so on—that are compatible. The overlap area is where you maximize your growth and development and where the organization can utilize your talents to produce maximum results. You need to look at yourself

Figure 10-3.   Personal career development.

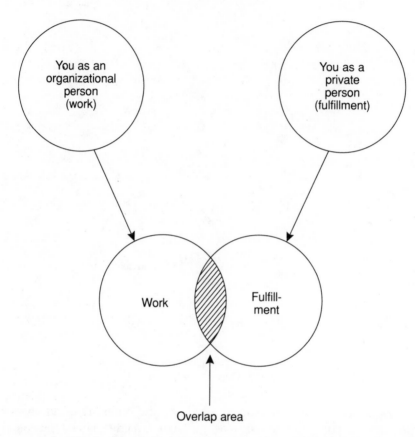

Overlap area

as a productive human being. See *yourself* as two separate entities: as *a person needing work* and as *a person needing fulfullment*. On the basis of how fulfilled you are, the overlap area represents how much satisfaction you receive from your work. When the overlap area is very small, that is an indication that you need to look at yourself as a productive human being.

Ask yourself the following:

1. To feel fulfilled, what do I need and desire?
2. Do these needs and desires fit the tasks I perform?

There has to be a reasonable overlap in these areas. If there is, go on to ask yourself two more questions:

1. Do my job tasks fit my career goals and desires?
2. Do my career goals and desires fit the needs and desires of my organization?

Again, there has to be some compatibility here. If the overlaps are small, you have pinpointed the probable reasons for a stalled career, which can take the form of lack of the following: development, professional growth, appropriate job results, and job satisfaction.

Let us paint a picture of the setting and the manner in which you need to collect these kinds of data. First of all, find a private, quiet place. Think of yourself as a *private person* (see Figure 10-3), not in the organizational sense but as it relates to your "ego self." Imagine your "ideal self." What would it take to meet your fulfillment needs? What are your "ideal" goals? What things need to occur to create the perfect situation; what things need to be in place—objectives; goals; realistic needs, wishes, and desires? Refer to the "Needs Assessment" form (Figure 10-1), which you completed in the preceding section. Make a two-column list showing (1) the things you need and want most and (2) the job tasks you do not like. This will give you a good picture of where you are right now in terms of personal fulfillment.

Now do the same exercise for yourself as an *organizational person* and make another two-column list showing (1) the things you need and want most from your career and (2) the things you do not like about your job and/or organization.

Compare your private and organizational career development lists. If your career needs overlap those required for fulfillment as a private person, the overlap is the area in which you will achieve the greatest growth and development and the most productive job results. The larger the overlap, the greater the probability that growth and development will occur and that you will produce excellent job results.

In comparing your two lists, avoid judging what is right or wrong. As the television detective says, "Just deal with the facts." Decide where your organizational person (work) and private person (fulfillment) overlap. This is your area of greatest potential. This is where your interests lie and where you need to concentrate the bulk of your energy. Now you have a written picture of those areas where the "sameness" works for you.

Analyze your position in the organization. If the area of overlap between you and the organization is small or nonexistent, you have identified a source of job dissatisfaction, inability to grow and develop, a stalled career, and so on. You need to take action steps to increase the overlapping area. By working through this model, you can increase your options inside your company—that is, transferring to another division or department, changing your career field, getting additional education, or asking for special assignments to enhance your position. A number of other options can be developed that will better suit both your needs and those of your organization. These options will be developed later.

In addition, the process you have just used allows you to understand your needs, goals, and desires to the point where you are now able to see and examine options outside your company, such as entrepreneurship or a different kind of job. Corporations will continue to lose highly respected, highly qualified, and talented black individuals unless white managers encourage blacks to take an expanded view of career development. White managers must learn to be more comfortable in helping blacks examine their options. A white manager can help a black manager decide whether his or her current job is meeting self-fulfillment needs.

Job dissatisfaction, dysfunctional behavior, low morale, lost work time, and an inability to join in the work team are examples of what can happen if an individual's personal fulfillment needs are not met within an organization. Personal fulfillment is a critical concept to look at relative to where employees of all colors and cultures are today.

White managers should use this process as a model for discussing career development for black managers (as well as white managers) and be aware that in the 1990s, white managers have to address the self-fulfillment needs of minorities or they will tend to become less productive or even leave the corporation.

Now that you have completed the preliminary steps, you are ready to meet with your manager and use the following ten-step process to complete your career-planning efforts. Share all the information that you have generated up to this point:

1. *The manager should share his or her managerial philosophy on career planning.* This includes fundamental beliefs, concepts, and attitudes about career planning.

2. *The subordinate should share his or her philosophy on career planning.* Make sure you understand each other's positions.

3. *Identify three to five areas in which the subordinate does well and three to five areas in which the subordinate needs improvement.* Remember to use your "Needs Assessment" form (Figure 10-1). Discuss the information on this form in depth so that each of you understands and agrees on what the areas are and why improvement is needed.

4. *The subordinate should fantasize and describe work scenes in which he or she is most motivated and produces at the highest rate.*[1]

    A. At this point, we are asking subordinates to use the same process they employed when they were children and fantasized about being adults. The boss can set the scene by asking the subordinate to fantasize operating in his or her work world while the boss, figuratively speaking, watches through a one-way mirror. The boss can see the subordinate, but the subordinate cannot see the boss. The boss can start by asking the subordinate to paint a verbal picture of the scene. The subordinate should paint the picture by telling the boss what the subordinate is wearing, to whom he or she is talking or listening, the location of the secne (the office, the field, a plant, a laboratory), whether he or she is standing or sitting, who else is there, what action is taking place, and the purpose of the action in the scene. The supervisor should ask additional questions if and when the need for clarification arises. Repeat this for at least two scenes, with subordinates fantasizing where they would like to be in two years, to cross-check data from the first scene. The supervisor should listen, ask questions, and jot down the key aspects of the work scenes. The supervisor should pay particular attention to needs, likes and dislikes, desires, motivating factors, skills used, and tasks or jobs that give happiness and pleasure.

    B. Repeat the process, with the subordinate fantasizing five years into the future.

    C. Consolidate the information from A and B.

5. *The supervisor should discuss his or her perceptions of the subordinate's fantasized work scenes from step 4.* In this discussion, look for factors that motivate and inhibit work output as well as the common threads that run through all the work scenes, such as leadership, control, and use of power.

6. *From the discussion in step 5, the supervisor and subordinate should extract key objectives, needs, desires, interests, and likes to be met in the next assignment.*

7. *Summarize the preceding information in clear and concise terms, using the following format:*

1. Dr. Ronald B. Brown, management consultant with Banks Brown Consultants in San Francisco, shared this concept and process with us.

- Three to five areas in which the subordinate does well
- Three to five areas needing improvement
- Key objectives, needs, desires, interests, likes, and dislikes
- Key motivators
- Description of desired job, without naming a specific role

8. *The supervisor should test the plan by discussing the summary with his or her manager to seek input and agreement and to obtain information on the needs of the organization as they relate to the subordinate's needs.*
9. *The supervisor should arrange a step-level counseling session with his or her boss.* The purposes of this meeting are: (1) to give the subordinate an opportunity to use the experience of the supervisor's boss and (2) to allow the supervisor's boss to formulate his or her own opinions and perceptions about the subordinate's career direction.
10. *The supervisor and his or her boss should search various organizations—including their own—to find a job position that matches the subordinate's desires, interests, and skill level.* The subordinate and supervisor should then review the available career options.

People at various levels of the hierarchy can play a role in the career-planning process. Each level has a responsibility to secure the effectiveness of the process.

Third-Level Boss

- Probe, monitor, and test career plans.
- Provide resource and organizational input to the process.

Second-Level Boss

- Probe, monitor, and test career plans.
- Provide organizational information needed in career plans.
- Work out the career plans with the next level of the hierarchy.

First-Level Boss or Supervisor

- Initiate and develop the career plan along with the subordinate.
- Work out the career plan with his or her boss.

Subordinate

• Work with the supervisor to develop the career plan.

Here are some key points to remember about planning your career:

1. Be proactive and push the direction of your career.
2. The fantasizing process is innovative and novel, and it is an effective way to quickly collect your thoughts, feelings, and ideas into an organized whole.
3. The boss's interpersonal skills must be well developed in order to contribute most effectively to career planning.
4. Barriers that look difficult to overcome should not stop career planning.
5. Career planning is a logical follow-up to a performance-improvement plan.
6. Understand that career planning for minorities is different from that for white males because race and/or gender are involved and must be considered.
7. Keep the overlap area in mind when you do career planning.
8. The boss should communicate the subordinate's needs up the ladder.

Implementing Your Plan

Subordinates should be given time to select their future assignments from the career options made available. A time range or specific month and year should be chosen for a move to the next job assignment.

The subordinate's selection should be reviewed by the supervisor with his or her boss. This will establish a contract or plan for the subordinate's future. (The subordinate should be given a copy of the contract or plan.) In some cases, it will be appropriate for the subordinate to change assignments immediately. If so, this should be done. The subordinate's supervisor should review the contract or career plan for implementation at least two months before the time of the job change (if one is scheduled to occur).

It is the subordinate's responsibility to ensure that proper time and attention continue to be focused on his or her career plan.

Part Five
Facing the Future

As corporate America advances toward the twenty-first century, it will face the challenges and opportunities of managing an increasingly diverse work force. In Part Five, we offer readers and their organizations ways to combine and focus the information in the preceding chapters in a way that will help them respond most effectively to these challenges and maximize their opportunities.

Chapter 11, "The Management of Diversity," introduces the topic of how to manage a diverse work force for optimal productive output. The concept of added value is presented as a way to identify and use the assets that individuals of different cultures bring to the workplace. By the year 2000, most new people entering the work force will be minorities, including women. In fact, *minority* could gradually disappear as a term applied to the peoples of the diverse work force. Hence, it will become increasingly important for managers to learn how to manage *all* employees appropriately.

Chapter 12, "Corporate and Institutional Opportunities for the Future," views black managers against the backdrop of the corporate world. In addition, we suggest some approaches that can help organizations learn how to get the most from their minority employees.

11

The Management of Diversity

Management of diversity refers to the management of a diverse work force so that individuals in that work force perform at their maximum potential by using all their skills, competencies, talents, and added values. *Added value* is a term representing those important additional assets that individuals acquire as a result of belonging to a group and apply to some task or in some environment. These important additional assets are that group's unique experiences, values, behaviors, skills, and talents that have been learned and traditionally handed down from generation to generation.

Today, both the concept and the practice of diversity are hot issues in corporate America. This trend will continue into the twenty-first century because of the projected changing demographics in the workplace. It is expected that white males will hold a minority of the jobs after the year 2000.[1] Over the last twenty-plus years alone, blacks have made major inroads in an effort to reach the boardrooms of American businesses. White managers have been required to learn how to manage and be managed by blacks. By the 1990s, most companies will have become increasingly aware that in the corporate chain, there are both men and women, and there are many cultures—blacks, Hispanics from various cultures, Asians from various cultures, etc. Learning how to effectively manage the multicultural organization or group—the diverse work force—is rapidly becoming a major issue.

Before we proceed, let us clarify what the term *diversity* means to

1. William B. Johnston and Arnold H. Packer, *Workforce 2000* (Indianapolis: Hudson Institute, Inc., 1987), p. 95.

392

us. *Webster's Ninth New Collegiate Dictionary*[2] defines it as, "The condition of being different: variety." Diversity only involves differences, not judgments regarding those differences. Being different does not make one good or bad, right or wrong, superior or inferior. Being different adds another perspective or dimension to a task, an issue, or a situation. Differences among us—our diversity—as a work force affect bottom-line profits and services. The ultimate objective of learning how to effectively manage diversity is to value, identify, and use the added values of ethnic groups and cultures in a positive way to meet organizational needs, goals, and objectives so as to increase profits and deliver high-quality services.

The Age of Diversity

In the early years after the signing of the Civil Rights Act of 1964, this nation accepted that it must take affirmative action to create opportunities for black citizens to become equal in status to white citizens. That meant taking a stand to create preferential opportunities for blacks and, later, for women. Few have been happy with how affirmative action has worked in practice. Whites felt minorities were given an unfair advantage in the marketplace—white backlash. Blacks felts they were being hired not on competency but on color—tokenism. No one has been satisfied with affirmative action because its main goal was to respond to numbers. Diversity focuses on using *all* people as resources and seeking to use differences to create dynamic results.

Affirmative action had its place in opening up the marketplace. Something had to be done to initially open doors that had been closed and create a critical mass of nonwhite males in organizations. Since most of these doors have now been opened, there is a real need to advance beyond focusing on blacks, women, and other minority groups sequentially to focusing on the skills and talents of all American cultures. Figure 11-1 shows the key components of the management of diversity.

In the 1960s influential black Americans took white Americans to task on their discriminatory laws and practices. White Americans responded by taking affirmative action to right what they felt were long-standing inequities. With affirmative action, whites were made to feel a

---

2. *Webster's Ninth New Collegiate Dictionary* (Springfield, Mass.: Merriam-Webster, Inc., 1988), p. 369.

Figure 11-1. Key components of diversity.

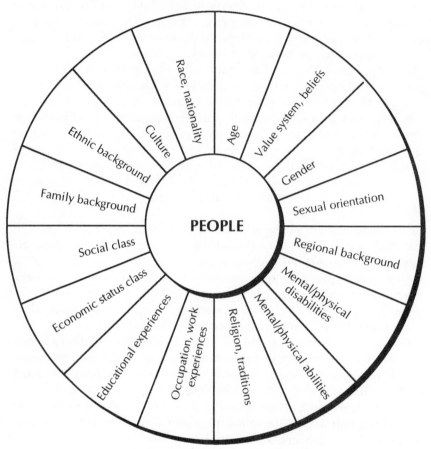

moral and social responsibility for the "poor, downtrodden blacks."
Over the twenty-plus years we have worked with black and white mixed
groups, guilt has been one issue we have had to help whites overcome
so they can move from the past to help deal with current issues. A
current issue is blacks do continue to be relegated to a "less-than"
position and have had little value in the marketplace other than their
mere presence representing an end to discrimination. However, managing diversity demands that every group take responsibility for its
actions and that each individual take responsibility both for his or her
own group and for himself or herself. Using diversity is based on need:
the need of groups to glean expertise from other groups and from

individuals who are different from each other. Valuing diversity involves recognizing that each group has "gifts" and potential. There are no "special" or "less-than" groups of people. Different groups need to be treated in ways that pull the best from them, not the worst. It is as simple as that.

One concept that works against the management of diversity is the melting-pot concept. Immigrants and ethnics are told to assimilate. Affirmative action stresses assimilation—integration. Forced integration does not work well, and certainly, assimilation is all but impossible for some ethnic groups. What are ethnics being told, anyway, concerning becoming a part of the melting pot? Is it that they must become white Anglo-Saxon Protestant males? Must we all attempt to be unrecognizable culturally? In a melting pot, flavors lose their identity; the strongest flavor prevails. The colors of the different ingredients become one. You can end up with an unrecognizable mush, sometimes strong but not very tasty. Some cultures have blended and, as a result, lost much of their past identity and uniqueness. It is difficult to blend some people into a melting pot. Some people do not blend, no matter how many of the outward manifestations of the dominant culture they try to adopt. And sadly, many ethnics who do try hard to assimilate end up having to deal with other weighty issues, such as isolation from their identified group, group ostracism, and cultural self-hate.

The management of diversity teaches cultural pride, high self-esteem, the value and utilization of other cultures, and national unity. How? By embracing the natural order of the American society, which is more like the ingredients on a plate of salad than a melting pot. We are peoples from throughout the world. We bring to this land our own uniqueness, combining the learnings of our ancestors from our original countries with our personal experiences in America. The different ingredients in a salad are mixed together, but they are not blended; each piece keeps its own texture, flavor, and color—i.e., its own integrity. The management of diversity allows cultural and ethnic groups to keep their own integrity. It teaches us to value those differences and use them for the benefit of the whole; neighborhoods, organizations, or the country.

A most obvious example of using a group's "differences" to the best advantage is how the military used one of our American Indian tribes in World War II. Because Germany was constantly breaking the secret codes used to transmit American military data, someone suggested the idea of using Navaho Indians as radio operators. Suddenly, Navahos found themselves thrust into the role of highly valued, much-sought-after radio operators who could pass military and troop data without the Germans ever knowing what was being said. As information was passed from Navaho to Navaho, the Germans were going crazy trying to crack a code for which there was no key. Navaho is a spoken language that was never written. German cryptographers therefore had no sources from which to learn Navaho. The Navahos brought tremendous added value to America's success in World War II.

If we are to respect each of our nation's various cultural and ethnic groups, some of you may well ask, "What, then, is the glue that keeps us together? How do we live, work, and produce in harmony?" Although there are some major differences between us as cultural and ethnic groups, there are also significant commonalities. It is these commonalities that bind us into a nation (see Figure 11-2).

Our most commonly held values are, of course, our love of America and the love of freedom. Most groups of people came to America out of choice and in search of freedom. For the early Africans, captured and forced into servitude, the freedoms of America were hard-won. Every group feels it has earned the right to be American. All of America's diverse groups love and respect the institution of family and of tradition. We share in the making of American traditions and the celebration of American holidays. We all believe in the right of the individual to self-actualization. No matter our color or gender, we all have stories about the least of us becoming the best of us. Regardless of which groups of people in this country openly claim allegiance to the "Protestant work ethic," the fact is that *all* groups survived and prospered in this land through perseverance and the sweat of their brows. You can doubtless add other commonly held values, ideals, and dreams that hold the United States of America together as a nation.

Affirmative action is almost a dead issue. This is the age of diversity. As America sees its number-one economic position slipping in the world marketplace, the time has come to realize that we can no longer waste our human resources. We must become less concerned with the packaging of the resource and more concerned with the contents of the package. We have the world's greatest talent here. We must learn to use it.

Added Value

In the years to come, we will be hearing more and more about added value and its place in the business world. Simply, added value is the cultural background we have to supplement our education, training,

Figure 11-2. Salad dressing.

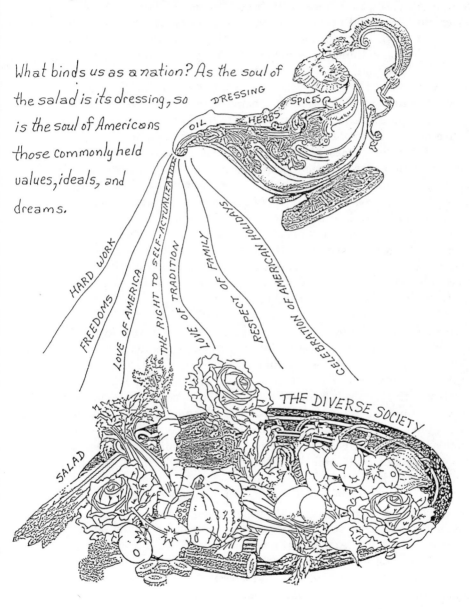

What binds us as a nation? As the soul of the salad is its dressing, so is the soul of Americans those commonly held values, ideals, and dreams.

and work experiences in doing our jobs. Technically and professionally, blacks work in organizations with the same basic skills and abilities as whites, as one would normally expect. Blacks are expected to have the same education, training, and/or experience to do the job. However, blacks bring something more to the job. They bring an added value from the unique life experiences they share as a group. These experiences were gained from the struggle through slavery, their survival as freedmen, and the successes from being a part of the black culture operating against tremendous societal barriers. These learnings add to the basics and worth of their participation in the marketplace.

Added value comes from the traditional life experiences of any group of people over an extended period of time. Cultures have centuries of practice to build the basis for their common wisdom. You are enrolled at birth. When you learn your lessons well, it can be said that you have graduated into the job market with a cultural "degree." The level at which you can perform based on your learnings can be thought of as having earned a bachelor's, master's, or doctoral degree. Your ability to use your added value depends on how well you were assimilated into your particular cultural group and whether or not your group placed a high value on what it had to offer.

Many people are taught to reject their cultural learnings in favor of a larger culture thought to be American. The so-called American business culture is a myth. In reality, business here is conducted based on Western European traditions. Other cultures have impacted and are impacting those traditions, but they remain essentially the same. The problem with assimilating into the Western European culture, particularly for ethnics, is that you relinquish that which is of value. You place yourself in a position of not being able to offer anything different from what is already established. You deny your organization its right to tap into your unique skills, abilities, and perceptions, which would enhace its success and help it to grow.

Every culture in the world has added value. Because of this fact, our heterogeneous society should be able to do more than any homogeneous society ever could. Since we are not in fact doing so, it is because we have not learned to value, access, and use the vast cultural resources we have at our disposal. It is important for all of us to understand that when the cultural added values of various groups are combined, it yields a broader base of operations from which to problem-solve and increase skill development. It enhances both creativity and innovation.

Accessing Added Value

To begin learning how to manage the diverse work force, we must, as usual, begin with ourselves. Racism and the melting-pot concept have been with us a long time. One cannot expect to unlearn long-standing untruths and misconceptions overnight. One does begin by admitting that racism, sexism, isolation from some groups, inappropriate information or lack of information, fear mongering, and indoctrination through various media have impacted how we feel about groups other than our own. Traditional attitudes about some groups of people continue to be handed down, even though many of us are no longer aware of the origins of those attitudes. In general, unless there is a compelling reason, most of us live out our lives without ever examining why we feel the way we do about some people or how we were taught to view some groups in such a negative light. We seldom question the validity of what we have learned. Even fewer of us check it out for ourselves.

Once we can admit our own personal ignorance and inappropriate learnings about other groups of people, we are ready to learn what is real. Even though people of various cultures and ethnic groups live side by side today, we know incredibly little about each other. We call ourselves an integrated society, but we are still segregated in ways that inhibit us from knowing one another. We do not have authentic social interactions. We do not avail ourselves of the many opportunities to build authentic positive relationships across cultural lines.

Across Christian America, Sunday is our most segregated day. Whites and blacks go to their respective churches and network with each other in isolation from other groups. Whatever leisure-time activities we indulge in, we do with members of our own group. We work together each day, and at the end of it, we cannot wait to quit each other's presence. We consciously or unconsciously find ways to avoid each other. Is it any wonder we have learned so little about each other?

Managing diversity demands that we come together in an open learning mode. If you are not aware of another's added value, you cannot use it. You cannot use your own if you do not recognize that you have it. That means we must ditch the notion that we should not see differences. They are real, and they are a part of what makes us who we are. There is a negative message in trying to ignore another's differences: Those differences are valueless and somehow "bad." Our differences, not our commonalities, are what make us "special." We must begin to learn enough about ourselves and other groups to be able to make initial generalizations about each other. Until we learn about our various cultures, we cannot guess what added values a particular group may have that can be accessed and used. Later in this subsection, we will share some general cultural added values of certain groups, which we have gathered over the years from members of those groups. These are just a few of the cultural learnings and skills gathered from the hundeds of workshops we have conducted. The participants shared with us the important values and skills handed down to them from their parents, who got them from their parents, and so on. Whether or not an individual practices these values and skills varies from individual to individual. Nevertheless, they were still a part of their group cultural upbringing and, as such, are a part of their cultural heritage.

To avoid possible misunderstandings of generalized cultural added values, we must first be clear about the differences between generalizing and stereotyping. Relative to people, the concept of stereotyping is easiest to explain. Most of us have stereotypes about somebody. The dictionary defines the verb *stereotype* as "to repeat *without variation*."[3] It means to conform to a *fixed pattern*, lacking individual distinguishing qualities. As a noun, a *stereotype* is a *fixed picture* of a group representing an oversimplified opinion, an affective attitude, or a judgment. Stereotypes are almost always negative pictures of the individuals in the target group.

Those of you who are old-movie buffs and have seen movies from the 1930s may be familiar with a black character actor who often appeared in those early films, Stepin Fetchit. He was always typecast as a black servant—slow, dull-witted, and bumbling. This was the stereotypical picture many whites had of black males. Even the famous Rochester character of the Jack Benny team was easily frightened and had to be looked after by the smarter, protective white male. Then let us not forget Amos and Andy, of both radio and television fame. These programs convinced many whites that all blacks were childlike and helpless in the face of life's ordinary challenges. How were whites to know any different, since intimate and personal contact with blacks was rare? Blacks, on the other hand, protected their privacy from whites, since it was often in their best interest to allow whites to keep their stereotypes. Blacks knew they were seen as less threatening by this image, and they often got things done for themselves by allowing well-meaning whites to "help" them.

When we stereotype people, we do not allow for individual differ-

3. *Webster's Ninth New Collegiate Dictionary*, p. 1156.

ences within a culture, nor do we take into account the possibility of a person in that group totally abandoning the group's cultural values, traditions, habit, or skills. When we stereotype, we take what few notions and what little information we may have about a group and assume that every individual in the group fits what we believe or think or know about that group. We create stereotypes out of generalizations when we do not check out our assumptions about a person who belongs to a group on an individual basis. The individual may have many characteristics and skills of his or her own and may at the same time have learned to operate in a proficient manner from some cultural base different from his or her own. Stereotyping stamps the members of a group the same way a printing press stamps out identical pages for books. Stereotyping keeps us from ever truly knowing how members of cultural groups behave or learning about their values, skills, and traditions. Cultural impact is only one, though important, aspect of a person, so stereotyping inhibits us from knowing the individual.

Generalizations are more difficult to deal with because we struggle to separate our generalizations from stereotypes. Again, we turn to the dictionary. With regard to an overall picture or as applied to a wider class, the verb *generalize* means "to make inductions or general inferences; to be prone to make vague or indefinite statements."[4] With regard to a group of people, the noun *generalization* means a response made to a stimulus similar to but *not* identical with a reference stimulus. We could generalize, for instance, that the average black American *tends* to be more animated in conversing than the average white American. Unlike stereotypes, that does not imply a fixed pattern. There are plenty of exceptions to these generalized styles among both blacks and whites.

Generalizing about things we have information about is a normal brain activity. We do not store or think about everything we know in our world in terms of specifics until we must deal directly with some one thing. We group information under categories for convenience and conservation of space. For instance, we know that generally trees have green foliage and brown trunks. As long as we are in the city, we can be comfortable with that generalization. Once in the forest, we instantly become aware that foliage comes in colors other than green or has various shades of green and that trunks come in many shades of brown, or may not be brown at all. We must now individualize the trees or be more specific relative to the whole forest of trees.

4. *Webster's Third New International Dictionary* (Springfield, Mass.: Merriam-Webster, Inc., 1981), p. 945.

So it is with people. Groups of people have observable behaviors and habits. People belonging to the same group will have similar habits, behaviors, attitudes, and value systems. We can make some generalizations about that group based on what we think we see and know. When we interact with and get to know an individual from the group about which we have generalizations, then we must relinquish our generalizations in favor of the specific data we have about that individual as a specific personality. That person will fit or not fit our generalizations based on how deeply he or she is entrenched (encultured) into the group's culture.

A generalization is *only* a place to start, not an end to the process. When you begin to learn about the collective habits, behaviors, attitudes, and values of a group of people, you have only a reference point from which to interact with an individual from that group. That person must now be gauged against what you know about the group to which he or she belongs. Now the person becomes specific: an individual who happens to belong to this group, displaying more, less, or none of the characteristics of the group. Generalizations tend to be neutral or positive. Yes, all people are individuals, but they are also members of various groups that help to shape and mold who they are, and generalizations can be made about groups.

Generalizations can be made about groups of people when you understand that cultural groups evolve because of long histories of common experiences shared by numbers of people facing the same environmental demands. Culture itself is shaped by both past and present demands made on it from its own society and its members' input and reactions in that society. It is formed and evolved by the environment in which it exists as well as by the events acted within it and upon it. It encompasses all the experiences it has encountered and all the reactions to those experiences. People and their cultures have histories that have given birth to value systems, attitudes, skills, technologies, arts, sciences, etc. However, not *all* members of a cultural group have been raised in their culture, have learned to value and accept their own culture, wish to acknowledge their culture, practice their cultural skills, and so on. Remember, cultures also change and evolve as different demands are made upon them. When we learn that a particular culture holds some value in high esteem or has a long history of dealing successfully with some environmental demand, we can safely make a generalization that this is a cultural added value of this particular group. We cannot, however, assume that each and every member of that group holds the same value or is proficient in that skill. To do so is stereotyping. You must check it out by getting to know the individual member of that group. He or she may or may not exemplify what you believe to be a cultural value or skill.

For instance, blacks seem to love to dance and expose their children quite early to dancing movements. This may seem quite evident to you by the number of blacks you see on the dance floor exhibiting what seems to be a natural sense of rhythm. But if you walk up to Susan, a black woman, and automatically assume that she can dance just because she is obviously black, she will be both insulted and angry. You did not *see her* dance, not did you ask whether she would like to dance with you and collect your own data about her. If you had taken the time to dance with Susan or watch her, you might have learned that she is clumsy on the dance floor and that she has two left feet. For whatever reason, she never learned to dance as well as a lot of blacks do. It was all right to know that, generally, blacks do dance well because it is a part of the black culture and children are usually exposed to dance early. It is fun, and it does not require a membership in the local country club, but *all* blacks were not exposed to dance, nor did they all learn. By insisting that Susan *must* know how to dance and not allowing for individual differences within her culture, you have done more than generalize; you have stereotyped her.

Now that you understand the difference between stereotyping and making generalizations, we can take a look at some cultural generalizations that can be translated into cultural added values. Many of us are quite skilled and accomplished in some areas because we were taught and had to practice these skills as a result of being members of a certain group. These skills and values are most commonly taught in ways that the person learning them is not consciously aware of the process. It is a part of that group's tradition and how that group has learned to get along in the world and conduct its business. We are often unaware that we have these skills. It is just something we normally do. Remember, individuals show their cultural skills more or less depending on how deeply they have assimilated their culture. In learning to manage the diverse work force, we must begin to learn about other people's cultural degrees as well as our own. Many whites struggle to remember their roots because their groups have tried so hard to assimilate into something they believed was an "American." Try to remember the skills and values you were taught as a child. They originated from somewhere. Some of you of mixed ancestry will find you have multicultural skills already. These are the things you automatically know how to do.

The following list of cultural added values includes only a chosen few cultural groups and, of those, only a few of their general cultural added values. There are, of course, many more cultural groups, and they have many more values than those listed here. If you do not find yourself here, try naming your dominant culture and discovering the skills and values from that group. Try guessing how those skills can be applied in the workplace. If your group is listed, try adding other skills you have learned from belonging to your group and listing how you may use them. Many cultures have common skills and values. (See the discussion of the salad-dressing concept earlier in this chapter.) Let us remind you: The added values below are generalizations about these groups based on their cultural historical learnings. Be careful about turning them into stereotypes. Be aware of individual differences within groups, and take the time to learn about an individual before you assume that he or she has a particular cultural skill or value.

Cultural Added Values

1. *Irish.*
   - Generally, the Irish are verbal people who are given to eloquence in speech and to humor. An encultured Irishman or Irishwoman can break the tensest of moments with an appropriate quip or humorous story; this is a good person to have on a team in tight negotiations.
   - The Irish tend to teach neighborhood involvement and a sense of obligation to neighbors. In the work environment, they would tend to want to pull their work force into a community, with people helping people.
   - Irish people learn about justice and what is or is not fair. They tend to be loyal to what they believe in and like. If a company "plays above the rim," it could not have a more loyal employee.
2. *English.*
   - Most of us are familiar with the English culture, on which much of how we do business and run our government is based. English added value tends to be a part of our daily lives: our judicial system, social services, legislature, and of course, punctuality.
   - The English are known for their "stiff upper lip"—their perseverance against the odds. Here are people who will tend to charge ahead for their organization no matter what.
   - We get a lot of our concepts of the rugged individual from the English, no doubt because of their propensity for constantly

exploring and moving about in other parts of the world. You can expect some degree of independence and testing the limits of the organization, which can help keep it vital.

3. *German.*
   - Although Germans do not tend to be a very emotionally affective people—rather stoic, in fact—they are very strong-willed and stubborn. Once a decision is made, you can count on them to see it through—for themselves and the organization.
   - Self-discipline is highly valued among Germans. You need not stand over them to make sure they will finish what has been started. Just point the way and leave.
   - As hardworking people, Germans seek precision. In their creativity, they will tend to be very methodical and thorough. You would certainly want these people to attend to all necessary details.

4. *Black.*
   - Blacks are people-oriented. The institution of slavery made them learn how to quickly size up people and rapidly formulate strategic responses. Having excellent people-assessment skills and being able to think quickly on their feet make blacks valuable in dealing with people issues in the organization.
   - Because of a tradition of having limited resources with which to work, blacks have learned how to be exceptionally good at creating something out of almost nothing. Given today's climate of dwindling resources, these are good people to have around. Blacks will automatically focus on how to stretch a resource or make do without it.
   - Blacks are less classist than Europeans and have had to live in a multiclass and multicultural environment. They have learned how to move easily across socioeconomic lines and how to successfully live and negotiate in multicultural environments. This is a most valuable asset in sales, marketing, and a number of organizational efforts.

5. *Jewish.*
   - Jews have learned to love debate and the knowledge gained from questioning and seeking answers. Jews can push an organization to clarify its visions and goals such that people can understand their organization's mission. Through the process of learning their religion, Jewish people have developed highly refined debating skills.

- The Jewish sense of duty is legendary. One might greatly rely on that value to see that the organization remains true to its values and its charter.
- Because Jews have historically been the victims of oppression and slavery, they have learned tolerance of others and have compassion and empathy for others who are oppressed. Knowing this, it is not surprising to find a large number of Jewish individuals involved in some form of public service and advocacy of human rights.

6. *Mexican*.
   - The Mexican people have a passion for a great many things, and they are not shy about showing it. The energy they bring to a job can be a great motivator for an organization in tackling its toughest jobs.
   - Mexican attitudes are rooted in the "now." Mexicans tend to focus on the most pressing issues at hand. They have little patience with dragging issues out; instead, they will want to very quickly compress long lists to the most essential items. They will deal with less pressing matters at a later date. Mexicans can help the organization to very rapidly focus in on and pare down the critical issues.
   - A valuable skill within the Mexican culture is that of building interpersonal relationships. The ability to be personable—even with strangers—give respect, and behave with honor is looked upon with great favor. Mexicans are naturals in the sales area or any area requiring the art of persuasion.

7. *Chinese*.
   - The Chinese, although furious fighters, will seek harmony and conflict resolution first. Because of their love of harmony and order, they make competent mediators. Organizations can rely on Chinese employees to seek resolutions designed to leave people in win-win situations.
   - Chinese are probably best known for their patience. They are most often willing to work hard and wait for rewards; that is, up to a point. They are even-tempered but stubborn. These are probably the characteristics that have kept China from truly being conquered. They simply wait out the enemy. Chinese have great value in helping the organization see long-range projects through.
   - Organizations would do well with leadership from Chinese employees. They bring a strong sense of relationships, struc-

ture, and organization. They tend to be focused, with a fine eye for detail, and driven to succeed.

8. *Dutch.*
   - The Dutch are known to be a frugal group. They hate waste and value saving and investing their money. The Dutch bring to us the value of taking care of what we have and better using what we gain. Many of Dutch extraction find themselves drawn to areas of finance.
   - Organizations have value in encultured Dutch, for they are persistent in their tasks. Relative to more visually expressive groups of people, the Dutch would seem unemotional. They are slow to anger and offer a calming influence in chaotic situations.

These are but a few of the many rich and varied cultures that make up American society. We will repeat, as a reminder, that cultural generalizations are merely the starting points for understanding what an individual who belongs to a group *may* bring in terms of added value, not what he or she necessarily *will* bring. The list does not, by any means, contain all of what each of these groups have to offer.

How to Make Diversity Work in the Workplace

Over the last twenty-plus years, we have collected some key ways to make diversity work in the workplace. This information applies to both majority and minority managers and subordinates. Some of this information was obtained directly through personal management and leadership of diverse people; some of it was obtained through observation and from training and development sessions we conducted. This information has been shared with others in various training and development seminars and has been found to be invaluable because it yields positive results.

As you review the information, look at it as integrated information that when properly used, yields the desired results. A potential trap for you is to try to separate the information into "good general management practices" and "good management practices for a diverse work force." Sometimes, it is inappropriate and impossible to make such a separation. Individuals who have little or no experience with minorities or women in the workplace may try to categorize this information into neat little packages rather than looking at it as being necessary to properly manage a diverse work force. This is good management information that can be used for any group of people in the work force. Although its use may be optional in a monolithic organization (an organization that contains only or mostly white males or primarily members of one culture), we firmly believe its use is necessary to obtain good performance and good output from a multicultural work force. At this point, no useful purpose is served by attempting to separate the information into categories. It is good information, and it does work when used to manage a diverse work force:

1. *Take responsibility for your own attitudes, behavior, and job performance.* It is safe to say we have all been victimized by the effects of racism and ethnocentricity. If we are to learn to work together, we must *unlearn* what is inappropriate relative to people who are different from ourselves. How you perform for the benefit of your organization will be judged on how well you can use your expertise and added values and those of others with whom you share the workplace.

2. *Feel and take real ownership in your organization.* Minorities have been acting like renters in organizations—i.e., taking little or no responsibility for the direction of their organizations. Owners do what is necessary to make things right. When you rent an apartment and the plumbing breaks down, you call the landlord or building superintendent and complain. When you are a home owner, you call the plumber directly, or if you have the know-how, you fix it yourself. Blacks must stop complaining about all the things that are wrong and take ownership in their business—doing what needs to be done.

3. *Empower yourself to make a difference in your organization's results.* If you wait for others to give you the power to push for excellent results, you will probably have a long wait. Organizations expect their really sharp people to empower themselves and distance themselves from their peers by achieving outstanding results. Assuming power is the surest way to get power. Blacks can hold themselves back by not contributing all they have, waiting for permission, being afraid to "make waves." People who assume power take calculated risks.

4. *Recognize and understand cultural/ethnic/racial differences in the workplace.* Respecting what others have to give and making opportunities for *all* your people to contribute are ways to get the best out of everyone. People will feel they are valued employees and work for excellence.

5. *Learn about the cultures of people who are different from you.* When you learn about the values, skills, and needs of people different from

you, you open the door to learning more about yourself. You are in a better position to use your added value and the added values of others. You then know how to meet peoples' needs and motivate them to give their best.

6. *Learn to use differences to enhance productivity and service.* Productivity is more dynamic when there are infusions of differing perspectives, skills, and talents.

7. *Effectively use your expertise, personal image, and visibility.* Your talent may speak for itself, but that is usually not enough for the minority in the workplace. It is easier for you to be misunderstood, usually because of differences in style. Minorities have to sell themselves as well as what they can do. The right personal image is important. Exposure is also important. Minorities are often overlooked in companies run by white males. Because of limited contact with you, they do not know you or what you can do. Activities such as networking and mentoring are important, since they will allow your hierarchy to know you and see what you are capable of doing.

8. *Adapt rather than accommodate and assimilate.* Never compromise your integrity, your values, your standards, who you are, and your sense and understanding of what is just or fair. Instead, choose to learn what is looked on with favor and respect in your organization and add those things to your repertoire of behaviors.

9. *Learn the unwritten rules of the organization.* All groups and organizations have rules—ways of behaving, dressing, getting things done, etc.—that are in the realm of common wisdom and understanding shared by the individuals who formed and perpetuate the group or organization. These rules are not written but are passed to new members through informal contact and initiation. Minorities as new members, are not in the group and must make opportunities to form the kinds of relationships with group members that facilitate their sharing the unwritten rules. That means networking with whites and acquiring mentors whom you can also observe as they conduct normal business activities.

10. *Effectively network with both majority and minority members of the organization.* We constantly stress networking because it is impossible to do your best in an organization without the help of many others. Those who claim to have risen in an organization on merit alone, with no help from anyone, are both naive and unaware of those who mentored them in the background. In taking all the credit for themselves, they have denied the helping hands behind them.

11. *Value and use mentoring.* The mentoring process is the normal and traditional way organizations identify and help the chosen few up the corporate ladder. As a minority, you cannot wait to be chosen. Your organization may not know how to recognize your talent and potential. Instead, you do the choosing. Choose to grow in your organization and establish relationships with a number of important people who can help you reach your goals.

12. *Understand the mentoring process and teach it to others.* Make sure you learn and understand how your organization reproduces itself. Then you have an obligation to teach others how to do the same. Whites know how to mentor each other, so you will have to help your organization learn how to mentor minotirites. As a minority, be a mentor to both minority and majority members. Set the example and be a role model.

13. *Use alternative solutions to all problems and issues.* One of the great benefits of operating successfully in the multicultural work environment is your access to a vast reservoir of problem-solving techniques. Allow others who are different from you to bring their perspectives and expertise into problem-solving sessions. That old cliché is true: "There really *are* more ways than one to skin a cat."

14. *Explain the organizational ground rules to all employees.* Often, in the joining-up process, blacks do not receive a proper explanation of the organization's official and unofficial rules. Some whites do not want to appear overbearing or will assume that people closer to a black member will fill him or her in appropriately. Do not assume anything. Seek out the new employee and ensure that he or she has all the information needed to make a successful start.

15. *When in doubt, check it out.* It is constantly surprising how blacks and whites hold back during interactions with each other for fear of saying the wrong thing, hurting someone's feelings, or making others angry. Asking is and always has been a simple matter. If there is a question in your mind as to how your statement or behavior may be perceived by another person, share your concerns with him or her. In such situations, other people will appreciate your desire to be sensitive and correct. They will be willing to help you with your concern and, in the process, give you more information about themselves and their cultural group.

16. *Be open and share yourself with others, especially those who are different from you.* Cooperation and good working relationships come

with trust. Trust is earned—by allowing others to get to know you and by getting to know them. Building understanding between yourself and others who are different from you is just good business. People need to know what kind of person you are: what you like and dislike, how you want to work with others, and what you need. You must know those things about others. Take the time to build some famiIarity with the people around you. It will pay off big in the end.

17. *Learn to express your true feelings to others.* We are not suggesting that you do this tactlessly. Others, especially blacks, are very skilled at assessing verbal and nonverbal cues, whether you are aware of giving them or not. Hiding or hedging your feelings usually does not work. Blacks will pick up some data from you and interpret it based on their personal experiences with you or others like you. Being candid earns you respect, regardless of whether the other person likes what you are feeling. Expressing how you really feel will open a door with the other person so that dialogue can take place. If there is a problem, things can be worked out if the other person knows how you feel. If your feelings toward the other person are good, share that information as well. Sharing positive feelings is as important as being honest about negative feelings.

18. *Respect individuals for all they are (added values).* Getting the best out of people is easy. Allow them to fully contribute all they have to give.

19. *Respect the added value of groups.* Through centuries of facing hardships, attaining successes, learning, and growing, cultural/ethnic/racial groups are proud of their abilities to contribute. Never ignore the contributions various groups of people have made to humankind. That is what helps build a sense of pride and good self-esteem in people.

20. *Create an environment such that all have equal opportunities to be successful.* Every time an employee is successful, the whole organization benefits. It is a waste of time, money, and resources to allow the environment to put up barriers to the potential attainment of success by any segment of its population. Develop the kind of environment that is flexible enough to accommodate all members and that will encourage *everyone* to perform at their maximum level.

21. *Encourage and include subordinates.* A boss's success hinges on how well his or her subordinates perform. When you include your subordinates in the work processes, they can be clear about the job and buy into obtaining outstanding results. It is important to tell your people

when they are doing well—especially blacks, who rarely get any information until they have failed.

22. *Develop and use good people skills.* In an effort to produce the product or service, some organizations seem to forget that their people are the ones behind the product or service being offered. People must be maintained as well as the machines they use. Good people achieve results from the effective use of people skills. This becomes increasingly important as the work force diversifies. Good people skills must be broad and flexible because all groups are not maintained in the same way.

23. *Deal with people where they are, not where you wish them to be.* As you learn to become a multicultural manager, you must learn to be careful about imposing your values, dreams, understandings, perceptions, expectations, and needs onto others. That is disrespectful, inappropriate, and dysfunctional. If people move to where you would like them to be, it must be their decision, not yours. You may influence, but not insist.

24. *Do not give up your uniqueness—that is why you were hired.* Organizations need and want your added value. Without it, there would be no need to keep you around when it is easier and more economical to hire another white male. Smart organizations are already seeking to benefit from the diversity in their midst.

25. *Realize it is not always what you say but how you say it and what you do or do not do.* Minorities, in general, are mistrustful of white support because of a long tradition of broken promises and rhetoric. How you state your commitment to multiculturalism in the workplace and how you back up your words with the appropriate behaviors will be closely watched by blacks and other ethnics.

26. *Understand when it is important to be a team player and when it is not.* Blacks have a false reputation for not knowing how to be team players. This gets manifested by black silence at the conference table. Often, blacks feel intimidated by aggressive white males and decide that silence is a safe plan of action. Asians also appear not to be team players. Many Asian cultures teach that it is inappropriate to speak up until, or unless, you have it all together and have something of importance to say. In these cases, it is important for minorities to understand, value, and learn to adapt to how team playing is done in American organizations. It is often vital that you be seen as a functioning member of a team. It is perfectly fine if you prefer to work alone. There are

always plenty of opportunities to do that when you are not expected to interface with others.

27. *Be aware of how people interpret your behavior and words.* It is a mistake to assume that all groups of people see behavior the same or hear and interpret words in the same manner. Knowing about the values and behavioral norms of other groups will help you understand how your words and actions are likely to be perceived. If you say or do something that is likely to be misunderstood or seen as negative, take the time to explain your words or actions and how you want them to be interpreted. Know enough about other ethnic/racial/cultural groups to stay away from their "hot buttons"—those behaviors and words that are offensive and insulting.

28. *Know what counts for success in your organization.* As a black, your organization is unlikely to tell you directly what counts. Few people are told. You are also unlikely to receive that data indirectly, as whites normally do—in the local tavern, on the golf course, or sharing a leisurely beer on the boss's patio. Therefore, you must actively use your network, your mentors, or various creative opportunities to gather the data that will tell you what counts for success in your organization.

29. *If you are a minority, get support for your work before presenting it to management.* It is a good idea to build in support for your work before you approach management. This will minimize any questions about your ability to think through your project or handle the details of the work and ensure that any resistance it meets is not just plain racist or sexist. Running it past someone else will tell you whether it is a good idea. Some blacks' exuberant style will threaten whites and cause them to withdraw from even listening. Put together rough drafts that will allow others to provide input. Run your work by enough respected people so that your presentation can include these people's favorable responses to your work. Name names. Your management will feel you have done all you could to ensure the success of your work and will be more willing to listen.

30. *Understand and support minority clustering activities.* White males seek other white males to network, share lunch, talk about their day, or just be with their own kind. This is clustering, although they do not see it that way. When women and ethnic minorities seek each other out for the same purposes, the organization complains that they are "clustering." Different groups of people *need* to spend *some* time with their own groups on the job for the same reasons white males do: to obtain support, information, and encouragement. Organizations must support

this activity, and minorities need to understand that clustering is no substitute for interacting with members of the total organization. It is in your best interest to do both.

31. *Understand the concepts of "cultural paranoia," "protective hesitation," and "differential consequences."* (These three concepts are defined in the Introduction and Chapter 1.) Recognize that the first two activities are healthy responses to the present-day racial climate. Use them as strategies, not as excuses for not performing. As learnings about management are acquired, both majority and minority managers must look for the racial and gender components of the training to see whether its usage might have negative consequences for minorities.

32. *Recognize that most ideas represent different ways of doing things and do not respond in right/wrong or either/or ways.* There is nothing more debilitating over a period of time than for minorities to constantly hear, "That will not work," or, "That's not the right way," or "Obviously, you do not understand how things are done here." Minorities almost never hear, "That's an interesting approach. How does it work?" or, "Let's explore how this might work." Most whites live comfortably in a European mind-set of "either this *or* that," it's "right *or* wrong," that is "good *or* bad." There is nothing wrong with that except that some other ethnic groups do not share that mind-set. Their expectation is more inclusive: "We'll do this *and* that" or "a little of this *and* a little of that." When their suggestions are not explored, listened to, considered as valid possibilities, or incorporated into the ideas of others, they soon believe their contributions are not valued or wanted. They will stop contributing over and beyond what they are told to do. The organization misses out on their added value, and everyone loses.

33. *Listen and see things from the other's viewpoint whether you agree or disagree.* Many people confuse understanding with agreement, the way children do. They have needless arguments because one party is trying to share a viewpoint and the other party is resisting because he or she believes that to see is to agree with what is seen. Regardless of whether your experience or perception is the same, you can listen and seek understanding of how the other person has perceived or understood something. You will have your turn to share your viewpoint after the other has finished and you understand his or her perspective. Perhaps there will be someplace to merge the two viewpoints. Perhaps you will merely end with two opposing viewpoints. However, show respect by allowing someone different from you to have a legitimate viewpoint, which for him or her is as valid as your own viewpoint. You can always make room for compromise if it's necessary to act on something.

34. *Use your power of observation.* Watching others is an excellent way to learn a lot of things: who has power, how whites interact with others, how ethnics interact with each other, how various people get around organizational obstacles, etc.

35. *Learn how to deal with conflict.* Stay with it and work through difficult confrontations. Shutting down and running away will not solve anything, and the conflict will rise again later to bite you. As a minority, you must involve yourself in resolving conflicts because, if you do not, you will be held responsible for the conflict. The organization will see you as the troublemaker, and being fair has nothing to do with it. When whites walk away from conflictual situations, minorities believe the whites do not care. They feel that since whites are in power, they do not have to care. The minorities become angry, bitter, and resentful. Whites believe the conflict is past and become confused and angry because the minorities will not forget it. It is always best to stay with conflict resolution until all parties are at least satisfied.

36. *Take risks with people who are different from yourself.* As greater numbers of nonwhite people enter the American marketplace, it will be crucial that we quickly become acquainted with each other and find the common grounds on which to work together. If we are to survive as a productive nation, this is necessary; if we are to remain the top-producing nation, it is absolutely essential. This demands that we risk engaging each other in such a way as to build trust and knowledge of each other's worth to access the added value of all. The risks of engaging each other are always less than we perceive, and the risks of not engaging each other are greater than we know,.

37. *Assume people have positive motives unless/until you find out otherwise.* We have found the majority of racist behavior is a result of programming and ignorance. Working to remove personal racist behavior in the workplace is not about dealing with "bad" people; it deals with people learning about other people for themselves through personal contact and investigation. It is about deprogramming a nation of people who have been lied to about a lot of things for centuries and have, for the sake of convenience and/or profit, held on to these notions. When you assume that people's motives are positive, you give them a chance to prove whether they are or not. If their motives are negative, you always have time to deal with them. When you assume the worst about people's motives, you cut off their avenues for proving anything other than what you believed. Just as you want others to give you a chance to be your best, so must you do the same for them. More often than not, you will not be disappointed.

The multiracial, multicultural work force is with us now. It is in our best interest as a nation to begin today to educate our emerging work force as well as our existing work force to manage and produce in this diverse environment. We must establish the means to work in harmony and collaboration. At no other time in all the world's history have so many diverse groups of people chosen to unite under one flag to work and live together. We are, again, a nation of pioneers. We have the challenge and the opportunity to show the rest of the world the way.

12

Corporate and Institutional Opportunities for the Future

This final chapter of *The Black Manager* addresses the issue of how organizations can get the most from their minority employees. The first section of the chapter examines some of the challenges facing corporate American and describes what organizations are doing to promote change. The last section offers a number of suggestions for how corporations and institutions can most effectively manage an increasingly diverse work force.

Real Challenges for the Future

Our experience has shown us that blacks and other minorities are leaving corporate, private, and public organizations to go into business for themselves at a rate that causes concern in organizations. There are no official statistics, but many people are concerned about the long-term effects of this situation on the ability of minorities to reach upper-level positions in *Fortune* 500 companies or governmental and private institutions. Although entrepreneurship is one of the gifts of a free society and should be open to all its members, a critical number of highly skilled minorities must remain in corporate America to ensure that there is a pool from which to select top-level managers for organizations.

As we work with people in organizations across the country, we continue to meet strong, high-energy minorities who have two business cards—one for their official 9 A.M. to 5 P.M. job and one for their after-hours entrepreneurial job. Because we see this often, it indicates to us that minorities are being underutilized. Sometimes, white managers try to find excuses by saying that some minorities just want to make extra money and therefore have two jobs. We know that the phenomenon goes beyond this explanation. When individuals feel they are appreciated and have the latitude to use *all* their skills and abilities in their job roles—and they are having fun—they tend to throw all their energies into that job. Hence, many of the minorities would not have two jobs if their personal fulfillment needs were being met.

Highly skilled people are leaving corporate America because they are frustrated and feel that they cannot contribute at a maximum level in their organizations. They tell us they are prohibited from contributing because their organizations overmanage or ignore them. Diverse creativity is not respected or sought, and too much organizational "bureaucracy and red tape" are involved in delivering optimal results. Although there are some who would contend that these individuals are too independent, the primary cause of the "minority drain" is the inappropriate way they are managed. Minorities, who are now more mobile than in the past, are beginning to realize that they have added value and are looking for places to display it that will allow them to contribute more significantly to the bottom-line results of their organization. Therefore, the biggest challenge facing corporate America in the immediate future is to learn how minority talent can be retained and how the added value of minorities can be accessed and utilized to benefit American businesses and organizations. America continues to face increased competition around the world and cannot afford to lose opportunities to use the talents and skills of its total work force. How that competence and talent are accessed will differ from traditional methods and will not be the same for all groups.

Organizations must create a new mind-set that moves them away from affirmative action activities to embrace the management of diversity. The term *mind-set*, as used here, means a change of viewpoint such that organizations believe that their products and services will have higher quality and value if they employ a diverse work force as opposed to a monolithic one. The objective should be to learn to manage a diverse work force for better business results instead of merely participating in corporate "social responsibility" activities. However, affirmative action has served us well up to this point. It caused organizations to open their doors to groups of people who were prevented—for whatever reasons—from entering before affirmative action programs were instituted. Affirmative action efforts also caused some minorities to be given opportunities to obtain job and career development. This positioned them to be selected to move up in various organizations to positions of decision-making authority. So rather than knock the technology of affirmative action, let us move ahead to embrace the new technology of "the management of diversity." The time has come for the evolution of a technology that is more relevant to meeting the needs for success in the global competitive marketplace.

Affirmative action was basically a way to focus on the status of minorities and force opportunities for them in organizations. It was primarily concerned with numbers of different people in the work force. Managing diversity is a way to focus on *all* employees to create an environment that allows them to contribute to their maximum potential by using their added value. It is primarily concerned with the quality and level of contribution of the total work force.

What Organizations Are Doing to Cause Change

Numerous newspapers, magazines, and trade journals are filled with stories of how companies and organizations are moving to meet the challenges of managing a diverse work force and obtaining the most productive output possible from that work force. They are providing training and, in many cases, requiring their employees to attend training events to help them become aware of the need to manage a diverse work force differently from the way they traditionally manage a work force that tends to be monolithic relative to race, culture, gender, and ethnic background.

Since a few organizations are convinced that change is necessary for the growth of their business, they are going beyond the awareness stage and are striving to teach their managers how to manage people from different cultural backgrounds. These organizations are struggling to understand the long-range implications of employing a diverse work force. A few have learned that they produce and deliver higher-quality products and services when they employ people of many cultures. This is not to say that whites cannot produce excellent products and services. It means that when people from diverse backgrounds are added to the work force and are managed appropriately, the products and services will reflect the application of additional skills, abilities, experiences, and talents. This, in turn, will improve bottom-line results. Specifically, some corporations and other institutions are gearing up for the changing work force by taking the following steps:

1. *Developing appropriate recruiting programs that actively seek, interview, and employ people from diverse cultures and backgrounds.* These organizations are aware that they cannot recruit minorities by using traditional recruiting approaches. They also have the expectation that adding minorities to their work force will make a positive bottom-line difference to their business.

2. *Matching potential-employee day visitors with individuals from the same ethnic background.* Essentially, when people visit organizations or on-site job interviews, day hosts from the organization are selected from the same ethnic group as the visitor. This allows the minority to feel more at ease and ask the questions that are really important to him or her. Some key questions could be: "Where should I look for housing? What behavior should I expect from the community, both inside and outside of the company? Where can I get a haircut or find a beauty shop?"

3. *Matching new employees during the joining-up process with resources from the same ethnic group.* The resources are selected because they can share personal information from a minority perspective about how they successfully joined up to the organization. Of course, white resources should also participate in the joining-up process for the new employees. In this way, minority individuals will learn the best from both worlds and will be positioned to become successful more quickly.

4. *Assembling packets of information for new minority employees.* These packets of information include data such as: local cultural events in the community, names of local minority leaders, local and national events that pertain to specific cultures, local and national organizations for certain cultural groups, and the location of minority business services— e.g., beauty shops; barber shops; and ethnic restaurants, nightclubs, and radio stations. Information about how to contact local minority professional organizations is also included. For those organizations that already give "welcome to the community" information, ensure that you include a section with specific information on the needs of minorities; this information is very useful to them.

5. *Encouraging minorities to establish sanctioned employee groups.* These groups are given a budget that allows them to hold networking sessions on company time, set up leadership groups that invite speakers in to talk about managing and leading techniques, and have training sessions

to meet their specific needs. Some of the groups have a yearly meeting to which they invite white managers and outside speakers. These groups act as a bridge between minorities and majority managers and give minorities psychic support.

6. *Inviting diverse speakers to talk to all employees about issues of diversity.* By doing this, organizations demonstrate that people from different backgrounds should be respected and valued. Many majority employees may not have had an opportunity to interact with minority power figures in the work environment; having a speaker come in helps whites develop an appreciation of other cultures and also offers role models to minorities.

7. *Sponsoring on-site training and development sessions for managers to learn how to manage a diverse work force that includes women.* These training sessions cover: sexual harassment, awareness of other cultures, and basic multicultural management and leadership skills.

8. *Sending managers to outside courses to learn management and leadership techniques that can help them achieve improved business results from a diverse work force.* These courses teach managers how to manage for success across racial, ethnic, and gender lines.

9. *Allowing minorities to attend specialized development sessions.* These sessions teach minorities how to be successful in the workplace. They do this by starting the training where the minorities are, not where they should be. Minorities examine their workplace attitudes, mind-sets, and behaviors and make the appropriate corrections. It helps minorities to take personal ownership in building careers in the organization.

10. *Sending minorities back to school to obtain advanced degrees.* Since some organizations cannot find the talented people they need in certain specialty areas, they encourage and pay for minorities to get additional or advanced degrees. This enhances the opportunities for minorities to contribute better results.

11. *Using outside consultants to teach racial awareness and management skills and to provide hands-on consulting services to both managers and nonmanagers.* This provides people with an in-house support system as the organization undergoes the internal changes necessary to learn how to get the maximum productivity from a diverse work force.

12. *Changing and monitoring in-house personnel practices to ensure fair treatment of all employees.* Organizations are rethinking and changing how job performance is evaluated and how promotions are made. They are training interviewers to reduce the inherent bias that is present in the interviewing and hiring process.

13. *Holding managers accountable and rewarding them for effectively managing across racial and gender lines and developing, sponsoring, and mentoring minorities in their organizations.* This action is effective in convincing majority managers that an organization is serious about changing its management practices. It strongly encourages managers to make development of *all* people an integral part of their job roles.

14. *Purchasing videotapes and audiotapes, books, and formal programs on how to motivate and use the skills of a diverse work force.* Material is being added to the field of multicultural management at an increasing rate, and organizations are beginning to take advantage of what is presently available.

Suggestions for Corporations and Institutions

Figure 12-1 gives an overview of the building blocks for the management of diversity in the work force:

1. *New knowledge.* To learn how to manage a diverse work force, an organization must start by familiarizing itself with the technology of multicultural management. This gives the organization a firm foundation and enables it to define its business needs with respect to the management of diversity.
2. *Development.* By making an active effort to develop its members, an organization will increase and enhance their skills and position them to use their abilities to the fullest.
3. *Recruiting.* An organization must establish a multicultural recruiting program to ensure a diverse work force with regard to racial, ethnic, and cultural differences.

Figure 12-1. Organizational building blocks for the management of diversity.

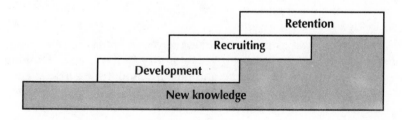

4. *Retention.* After an organization has recruited people from diverse backgrounds, it must then support and develop them to ensure that they stay in the work environment and add value to the organization's goods and services. (Retention is discussed in depth later in the chapter.)

Smart organizations use the leverage of a diverse work force to cause change in the way they conduct business. Many organizations are grappling with change because of both domestic and international competition. There is an urgent need to reduce the cost of producing goods and services which improving quality. Profit margins are shrinking, and investors are demanding a fair return on their investments. Government revenues have been reduced, and the economy is demanding change. Minorities are a powerful force for organizational change because they are moving into the professional ranks of organizations in increasing numbers. Since they must be managed and led differently, they offer organizations an opportunity to simultaneously change the way business is conducted along with the way people are managed.

Minorities are accustomed to change, and they bring a different perspective on how business can be conducted. If given the appropriate amount of managerial freedom in organizations, they challenge the status quo, which, in turn, helps keep organizations vital and productive. Since they possess a different mind-set, they set up a different kind of competitiveness, which looks more collaborative and conceptual than the typical Anglo-Saxon model. Minorities tend to come from an inclusive, rather than an either/or, mind-set. When allowed to use their added value, they work to include people in decisions at the earliest possible time. This creates ownership in the employees who actually do the work and yields better goods and services that meet the organization's cost and quality objectives.

Obtain New Knowledge About Multicultural Management

When appropriately used, the new multicultural management technology can help to improve business results. This technology can be learned by reading literature on the subject, attending training and development sessions, watching videotapes, listening to audiotapes, and using skilled consultants. Unfortunately, most business schools have not recognized the need to offer courses in multicultural management techniques. The courses that *are* offered in a few of the business schools are mostly theoretical—not "hands-on" learning experiences. It is important that courses be designed to teach techniques, not just theories. Organizations should require their leaders, managers, and supervisors to learn multicultural management technology and use it to achieve better business results. Multicultural management technology deal with ways to manage not only minorities but everyone in the organization.

The new knowledge gained through learning multicultural management shows organizations how to use the talents and added values of all people. One of the reasons America is losing its technological edge in the world marketplace is because of international competition from companies that are not constrained by conducting business in the same old way. America must, therefore, learn to use all available talent. Traditional mind-sets dictating that minorities are only good at certain kinds of jobs must be cast aside. If we in America can learn to use the talents from our many different cultures and ethnic groups, we will become an unstoppable economic force. A diverse work force consisting of minority and majority groups of people brings different skills, perspectives, and experiences to the table and can look at situations in ways that can forge creative solutions from chaos.

Develop the Organization

To make maximum use of multicultural management, organizations need to develop themselves. Since organizations are comprised of people, it is the people who need development. Often, when we work with organizations to help them learn how to effectively manage minorities, they focus mostly on output—goods and services. The point they seem to miss is that people create the goods and services through the use of equipment. Goods and services are not produced independently of people resources. To change the quality and quantity of output, organizations have to change both people and the equipment they use.

Organizational leaders usually become stressed and get upset when you talk about changing people. The secret is that people must change themselves. All organizations can do is provide people with information and resources and state their job requirements. If properly motivated, people will change themselves. Many managers tell us that they do not have time to train and develop their people. This then becomes an excuse to do nothing. When upper-level management rewards managers for developing others, then a priority will be placed on training and developing people.

When minorities are hired into previously all-white business situations, they will eventually behave in a way that forces the organization to train and develop them. This occurs because white managers will not get the maximum performance from minorities unless the white managers learn how to manage them effectively.

When organizations train and develop their managers to use multi-cultural management, the managers learn to understand the cultural, gender, and ethnic differences that give added value to all employees. They learn that adhering to a single managerial style will not cause all people to produce goods and services at their maximum capacity. A different type of openness will be seen in communications between bosses and subordinates. This openness will allow people to define issues, problems, and concerns and to problem-solve to remove barriers to performance. This will have bottom-line results in terms of producing better goods and services.

Organizations especially need to train and develop minorities to get the full measure of performance from them. Although white bosses need to learn to equip minorities with the skills it takes to progress in hostile organizations, minorities need to learn how to adapt to hostile environments and still be successful. Minorities are no longer willing to restrain themselves and hold back on using their skills because white managers are threatened. Minorities, especially blacks, need to learn to appreciate their added value and understand how to use it to get better business results.

Black managers in every organization that we have dealt with are very angry because they are positioned in such a way that their skills, talents, and creativity cannot be fully used. White managers usually get upset when they see that blacks are very angry and try to "put a lid" on the anger. Since it requires energy to remain angry, people who are consistently angry cannot give their maximum energy and effort to their job role. It is therefore crucial that organizations do something to *help* free minorities from their anger. Minorities also have a responsibility to *help* free themselves from dysfunctional anger.

Upper-level white managers in charge of large numbers of people that include minorities can be taught to lead and manage those below them in a way that gets better business results across racial, ethnic, and gender lines. Imagine large organizations that spend millions of dollars to produce goods and services to make a profit or meet the needs of others but yet waste millions of dollars due to inappropriate management across racial, cultural, and gender lines. These same managers refuse to admit that they are not getting the most from their minority employees. Stockholders, upper-level managers, and minorities need no longer tolerate this waste of human potential. Organizations must develop themselves and all their people; the dividends are enormous.

Now that we have established the need to develop organizations, the question becomes, "How can it be done?"

1. Upper-level managers should develop business-need statements containing reasons why the organization should implement a program to manage diversity in the work force.
2. The upper-level management group should capture the vision of success in a written description stating how people will interact when they learn to manage diversity.
3. End-point objectives should be written in a "be able to" format describing the behavior that is expected of people when they learn to manage diversity.
4. A written strategy should then be developed to define the approach to be taken to train managers in the organization.
5. With this information as a backdrop, a program can be designed to specifically define the elements and events of the training effort.
6. A timetable should be included to ensure that training events are conducted in a timely manner.
7. An individual reporting to an upper-level manager in the organization should be responsible for managing the program; this can be a full- or part-time position.

A good program must start with upper-level managers' setting the tone by stating, "In the future, all managers will be required to train and develop *all* their people so that the organization can realize the full measure of potential from them." The message that the organization will recruit, train, and develop minorities to use their added value along with the added value of majority individuals must be made public within the organization. The expectation is that the organization will see increased business results. Opportunities will be provided for all managers to learn how to manage across racial, ethnic, cultural, and gender lines. Those who learn and implement the techniques of multicultural management will be rewarded. Open, honest, and constructive feedback on job performance should be given to all employees. People development and the management of diversity will become normal meeting agenda items in the same way as other business issues are routinely discussed.

Managers, especially minorities, should be allowed to attend training and development sessions outside the working environment. Inside training and development sessions should become a normal part of life in the organization. All managers should be expected to sponsor and mentor minorities, just as they do with whites. Both inside and outside consultants should be used to support the program efforts. These consultants can teach courses and consult with managers and work groups as they participate in the program.

Develop a Recruiting Program That Yields Results

An individual should be assigned the responsibility for minority recruiting. It may be helpful to appoint a small committee to assist the minority recruiting manager in his or her efforts to locate and hire minorities. It is very difficult—and in some cases, almost impossible—to recruit minority professionals using normal recruiting techniques. This is true because there may not be many minority individuals in certain professional fields, they may be difficult to find, or they may not wish to leave home or relocate. The cultural background of some minorities causes fear and concern when they are approached with the subject of relocation. Therefore, white managers recruiting them must be aware of these concerns and respond appropriately. In many cases at predominantly white universities, minorities may not use the placement office in the same way as whites do. Even experienced professionals are not easy to locate.

Before organizations institute a program of management of diversity techniques, many of the strong minorities may be seen as threatening or aggressive. This may be construed as negative. However, through the multicultural management program, it becomes apparent that aggressiveness is a desirable characteristic and will cause the employee to take initiative, question decisions and policies, and push to create better bottom-line results. Whites also learn how to spot talent more readily in minorities than they could before. Their expectations for the minorities are higher than they were in the past. A number of things can be done to ensure successful results from recruiting efforts:

1. *Invite professors and administrators—both minority and majority— from target schools to your work site.* Show them the kind of job opportunities you have to offer their graduates.
2. *Appoint an employee—preferably a graduate—to be the organization's campus recruiting contact.* He or she can act as a coordinator for

requests from the university in addition to doing on-campus recruiting.

3. *Participate in job fairs on campus and in large communities across the country.*
4. *Sponsor student and faculty projects on campuses.* This can be done through minority student organizations and through academic departments.
5. *Give spare, surplus, or new equipment to colleges.*
6. *Give scholarships, grants, and research monies to college departments that produce graduates who fit organizational needs.*
7. *Send minorities to informally visit campuses to make contact with minorities and their student organizations.*
8. *Provide colleges with organizational speakers for classes, activities, and especially, minority student organizations.*
9. *Send minority employees to do campus prerecruiting.* This approach allows current employees to make personal contact with potential employees among the minority students. It will help if the employees are graduates of the college.
10. *Train organizational employees to properly interview minority students.*
11. *Hire search firms to locate experienced minority professionals.*
12. *Make contact with the armed-forces discharge center to get the names of professionals who are being discharged and are looking for jobs.*
13. *Develop a summer program to hire high-school graduates to gain experience in industry.* The students should be those who have been accepted into a college degree program.
14. *Conduct a summer-intern program for college students at all levels to interest them in future employment.* Assign someone to stay in touch with the students during their college careers.
15. *Match minority students on an interviewing-day visit with a minority-employee escort.* The employee should be from the same minority group as the student whom he or she is escorting.
16. *Assign a minority-group member to help a new minority employee find housing.*
17. *Interview new minority employees and ask them for ideas on how to improve the minority recruitment program.*
18. *Actively seek assistance from all minority employees in developing the entire minority-recruitment process.*

Institute a Retention Program for Minorities

Institutions and corporations have found that recruiting a minority employee does not guarantee his or her longevity with the organization.

A retention program should be established to ensure that both majority and minority employees remain with the organization on a long-term basis. This program could be operated through the personnel department, another staff function, or a line organization. One person should be assigned responsibility for the program to ensure its success.

Although it may be difficult for some organizations to face reality and realize that there are retention issues, problems, and concerns among minority employees, it is certainly to the organization's advantage to help managers deal with the situation before it causes minorities to leave the organization. It is very costly to recruit, train, and place a new employee on site. It probably costs more to recruit a minority employee than a majority employee because of the additional effort required. Therefore, there is a monetary reason to prevent minorities from leaving the organization.

Typical Retention Issues, Problems, and Concerns

An effective retention program can help white managers and minorities resolve difficulties that present barriers to job effectiveness. All minorities in the organization should be invited to participate in the program; they can be very helpful in making it work well. The following are typical retention issues, problems, and concerns that we have heard expressed many times in various organizations across the country:

- Supervision and management of minorities are poor and inadequate.
- Minorities are positioned as "visitors" to organizations and not as legitimate contributing members. Majority organization members treat them as outsiders; consequently, the minorities behave as outsiders.
- There is a lack of opportunities for development. Majority managers tend to refrain from sponsoring and mentoring minorities. Many minorities do not know the importance of having sponsors or mentors, nor do they know how to get them.
- There is a lack of job opportunities for growth. Minorities are not given the good assignments that lead to greater responsibility and promotions.
- There is lack of appropriate performance feedback. White managers tend to find it very difficult to give constructive and helpful feedback to minorities in a way that can make a positive difference. In many cases, minorities do not ask for feedback.

- Workable career development plans are not created. Minorities are rapidly moving away from seeing employment as merely a job and are looking at it as a career.
- Minorities are prevented from using their creativity, added values, skills, and talents. Many white managers are threatened by their minority subordinates and tend to suppress their creative output. If the managers are biased against minorities, the work output of the minorities then becomes less than optimal.

Pointers for Retaining Minorities

Most American institutions and corporations find it difficult to admit that there are retention issues with regard to minorities. When they do decide that things are not going well, they tend to want to move immediately to resolve the issues. Many times when we consult with organizations, they want us to give them a "laundry list" of action steps before attempting to teach their organizations about multicultural management. We usually refrain from giving a list of solutions because the organizations cannot successfully implement the solutions if they do not first understand what the problems are and why they exist.

We usually start the corrective process by gathering information about the organization. Then we analyze the data and make recommendations that include learning experiences—courses, seminars, and/or workshops—to teach managers and nonmanagers how to define, understand, and resolve the difficulties involved in managing and retaining a multicultural work force. However, since we cannot readily use our normal process in this book, we will share some key pointers for the retention of minorities. Many organizations have found these approaches to be helpful and successful:

- Assign at least one resource person—minority or nonminority—to a new or transferred minority employee. The resource person can share information about the organization.
- Develop a joining-up plan for the new person in the organization.
- Select the appropriate boss/supervisor to ensure a fair joining-up process and increase the odds for success.
- Send the new minority employee on a data-gathering tour (see the section entitled "Information Gathering" in Chapter 10). This will give him or her an opportunity to join up quickly and become a productive member of the organization.

- Have the new person's boss quickly share the following information:
  —His or her goals and objectives and those of the organization
  —Organizational job needs
  —Criteria for job success
  —How he or she works best
  —Job expectations
- Set standards of job excellence and expect everyone to meet them.
- Help the new minority employee develop a job plan for growth and success.
- Provide the necessary resources (people, equipment, books, tapes, etc.) that the employee needs in order to be successful.
- Provide job growth opportunities for minorities. The process used to select people for these opportunities needs to be closely monitored to ensure fairness for all employees.
- Provide opportunities for exposure to members of the hierarchy. This ensures that those who make career decisions will get to know the minorities in the organization.
- When decisions that involve minority employees are being made, involve the minorities in the decision-making process. This is a good way to build loyalty and a sense of belonging to the organization.
- Require minorities to be responsible for documenting a career development plan. This should be done with the assistance of resources in the organization.
- Develop and use an effective performance-feedback system. Insist that supervisors give feedback to minorities on a regular basis; ask for a brief summary of the feedback and the response from the minority individual.
- Ensure that career and promotion boards/committees have minority representation as a normal way of doing business.
- White and minority managers should develop mentorship and sponsorship relations across racial and cultural lines.
- Ensure that white managers include minorities in the informal communications network.
- Make the supervisors/bosses of minorities accountable for their success. This will ensure that minorities are treated fairly and given the appropriate opportunities to contribute to their maximum potential in the organization.

Pointers for Promoting Minorities

Some organizations tell us that they would like to promote minorities but do not have anyone ready for promotion. We then help them understand that minorities have to be developed for promotions in the same way that majority people are developed. The following are some straightforward approaches that can be used to help position minorities to take advantage of promotional opportunities:

- Require a one-page report on the status of minorities every three to six months. This will signal the supervisors of minorities that the organization is serious about learning how to provide minorities with an opportunity to give the best they have to offer. This information should be passed to the upper-level manager who has been charged with ensuring that minorities receive a fair opportunity to contribute to the organization's business.
- Evaluate minority individuals and select the outstanding performers for organizational fast tracking. This means that minorities who rate higher than the organizational norm should be selected for those job positions that lead to faster promotions and increased job responsibility.
- Those minorities selected for fast tracking have a development plan that clearly states the job areas in which they need to succeed. The plan should include a timetable.
- Select the assignments for fast trackers; do not leave the selection to the informal management network.
- Ensure that the criteria for promotion are clear and are public knowledge.
- Provide fast-tracked individuals with an opportunity to participate and interact with middle- and upper-level managers. If this does not happen routinely in the minority's job position, allow the minority to informally join the middle- and upper-level managers as they conduct their normal business activities.
- Develop a plan for promoting fast trackers.
- Give your top-performing minorities an opportunity to attend personal development sessions and advanced professional training outside the corporation or institution.
- Ask top performers to represent the organization on community-service boards and in charity efforts.

Suggested Readings

History

Bennett, Lerone, Jr. *Before the Mayflower*. 5th ed. Chicago: Johnson Publishing Co., 1982.

Blauner, Bob. *Black Lives, White Lives: Three Decades of Race Relations in America*. Berkeley, Calif.: University of California Press, 1989.

_____. *Racial Oppression in America*. New York: Harper & Row, 1972.

Lerner, Gerda, ed. *Black Women in White America*. New York: Vintage Books, 1973.

Weinstein, Allen, and Gatell, Frank Otto. *American Negro Slavery*. 3d ed. New York: Oxford University Press, 1979.

Management

America, Richard F., and Anderson, Bernard E. *Moving Ahead: Black Managers in American Business*. New York: McGraw-Hill, 1978.

Auger, B. Y. *How to Run Better Business Meetings*. St. Paul: Minnesota Mining & Manufacturing Co.; New York: McGraw-Hill, 1987.

Benson, Carl A. "The Question of Mobility in Career Development for Black Professionals." *Personal Journal*. May 1975.

Bradford, Leland P. *Making Meetings Work*. La Jolla, Calif.: University Associates, 1976.

Broadwell, Martin M. *Moving Up to Supervision*. New York: Van Nostrand Reinhold, 1979.

_____. *The New Supervisor*. Reading, Mass.: Addison-Wesley, 1972.

_____. *The Supervisor as an Instructor*. Reading, Mass.: Addison-Wesley, 1968.

Cameron, Randolph W. *The Minority Executive's Handbook*. New York: Warner Books, 1989.

Clark, Chris, and Rush, Sheila. *How to Get Along With Black People*. New York: Third Press, 1971.

Cohen, Peter. *The Gospel According to the Harvard Business School*. Garden City, N.Y.: Doubleday, 1973.

Cooper, Ken. *Nonverbal Communication for Business Success*. New York: AMACOM, 1979.

Davis, George, and Watson, Glegg. *Black Life in Corporate America: Swimming in the Mainstream*. Garden City, N.Y.: Anchor Books Edition, 1985 reprint.

Drucker, Peter F. *The Changing World of the Executive*. New York: New York Times Books, 1982.

_____. *The Effective Executive*. 1st Harper Colophon ed. New York: Harper & Row, 1985.

_____. *The Frontiers of Management: Where Tomorrow's Decisions Are Being Shaped Today*. 1st ed. New York: Truman Talley Books, Dutton, 1986.

_____. *Managing in Turbulent Times*. New York: Harper & Row, 1980.

_____. *Technology, Management and Society*. New York: Harper & Row, 1970.

Fernandez, John P. *Black Managers in White Corporations*. New York: Wiley, 1975.

_____. *Racism and Sexism in Corporate Life: Changing Values in American Business*. Lexington, Mass.: Lexington Books, 1981.

_____. *Survival in the Corporate Fishbowl: Making It Into Upper and Middle Management*. Lexington, Mass.: Lexington Books, 1987.

Fiedler, Fred E., and Chemers, Martin M. *Leadership and Effective Management*. Glenview, Ill.: Scott Foresman, 1974.

Ford, David L., Jr., ed. *Readings in Minority Group Relations*. La Jolla, Calif.: University Associates, 1976.

Fordyce, Jack K., and Weil, Raymond. *Managing With People*. 2d ed. Reading, Mass.: Addison-Wesley, 1979.

Guest, Robert H.; Hersey, Paul; and Blanchard, Kenneth H. *Organizational Change Through Effective Leadership*. Englewood Cliffs, N.J.: Prentice-Hall, 1977.

Hart, Lois Borland. *Moving Up! Women and Leadership*. New York: AMACOM, 1980.

Hersey, Paul. *The Situational Leader*. New York: Warner Books, 1985.

Hersey, Paul, and Blanchard, Kenneth H. *Management of Organizational Behavior Utilizing Human Resources*. 5th ed. Englewood Cliffs, N.J.: Prentice-Hall, 1988.

Johnson, John H. "Failure Is a Word I Don't Accept." *Harvard Business Review*. March–April 1976.

Johnson, John H., with Bennett, Lerone. *Succeeding Against the Odds*. New York: Warner Books, 1989.

Jones, Edward W., Jr. "Black Managers: The Dream Deferred." *Harvard Business Review*. May–June 1986.

_____. "What It's Like to Be a Black Manager." *Harvard Business Review*. July–August 1973.

Kanter, Rosabeth Moss. *Men and Women of the Corporation*. New York: Basic Books, 1977.

Kepner, Charles H., and Tregoe, Benjamin B. *The Rational Manager*. 2d ed. Princeton, N.J.: Kepner-Tregoe, 1976.

Korda, Michael. *Power! How to Get It, How to Use It*. New York: Ballantine, 1987.

Lakein, Alan. *How to Get Control of Your Time and Your Life*. New York: New American Library, 1974.

Likert, Rensis, and Likert, Jane Gibson. *New Ways of Managing Conflict*. New York: McGraw-Hill, 1976.

Lumsden, George J. *Impact Management: Personal Power Strategies for Success.* New York: AMACOM, 1979.

Maccoby, Michael. *The Gamesman: The New Corporate Leaders.* New York: Simon & Schuster, 1976.

_____. *The Leader: A New Face for American Management.* New York: Simon & Schuster, 1981.

McFarland, Dalton E. *Managerial Achievement: Action Strategies.* Englewood Cliffs, N.J.: Prentice-Hall, 1979.

McGregor, Douglas. *The Human Side of Enterprise.* New York: McGraw-Hill, 1960.

MacKenzie, Alec. *The Time Trap: The New Version of the 20-Year Classic on Time Management.* New York: AMACOM, 1990.

MacKenzie, Alec, and Waldo, Kay Cronkite. *About Time: A Woman's Guide to Time Management.* 1st McGraw-Hill paperback ed. New York: McGraw-Hill, 1981.

Mager, R. F. *Preparing Instructional Objectives.* 2d ed. Belmont, Calif.: Fearon Publishers, 1975.

Maier, Norman R. F.; Solem, Allen R.; and Maier, Ayesha A. *The Role-Play Technique.* La Jolla, Calif.: University Associates, 1975.

Mali, Paul. *Improving Total Productivity.* New York: Wiley, 1978.

_____. *MBO Updated: A Handbook of Practices and Techniques for Managing by Objectives.* New York: Wiley, 1986.

Molloy, John T. *John T. Molloy's New Dress for Success.* New York: Warner Books, 1988.

_____. *The Woman's Dress for Success Book.* New York: Warner Books, 1984.

Moskal, Brian S. "Ascent of the Black Manager." *Industry Week.* October 4, 1976.

Nierenberg, Gerard I. *The Complete Negotiator.* 1st ed. New York: Nierenberg and Zeif Publishers, 1986.

Nierenberg, Gerald I., and Calero, Henry H. *How to Read a Person Like a Book.* New York: Cornerstone Library Publications, 1971.

Northrup, Herbert R., et al. *Negro Employment in Basic Industry.* Philadelphia: Industrial Research Unit, Wharton School of Finance and Commerce, University of Pennsylvania, 1970.

Potter, Beverly A. *Turning Around: The Behavioral Approach to Managing People.* New York: AMACOM, 1980.

Roeber, Richard J. C. *The Organization in a Changing Environment.* Reading, Mass.: Addison-Wesley, 1973.

Saracheck, Bernard. "Career Concerns of Black Managers." *Management Review.* October 1974.

Schein, Edgar H. *Career Dynamics: Matching Individual and Organizational Needs.* Reading, Mass.: Addison-Wesley, 1978.

_____. *Organizational Culture and Leadership.* 1st ed. San Francisco: Jossey-Bass, 1985.

_____. *Process Consultation: Its Role in Organization Development.* Reading, Mass.: Addison-Wesley, 1969.

Schleh, Edward C. *Management by Results.* New York: McGraw-Hill, 1961.

_____. *The Management Tactician.* New York: McGraw-Hill, 1974.

Smith, Howard P., and Browner, Paul J. *Performance Appraisal and Human Development.* Reading, Mass.: Addison-Wesley, 1977.

Souerwine, Andrew H. *Career Strategies.* New York: AMACOM, 1980.

Vance, Charles C. *Manager Today, Executive Tomorrow.* New York: McGraw-Hill, 1974.

VanDersal, William R. *The Successful Manager in Government and Business.* New York: Harper & Row, 1974.

————. *The Successful Supervisor in Government and Business.* 4th ed. New York: Harper & Row, 1985.

Walton, Richard E. *Interpersonal Peacemaking: Confrontations and Third-Party Consultation.* Reading, Mass.: Addison-Wesley, 1969.

Walton, Richard, with the assistance of Allen, Christopher, and Gaffney, Michael. *Innovating to Compete: Lessons for Diffusing and Managing Change in the Workplace.* 1st ed. San Francisco: Jossey-Bass, 1987.

Williams, Kenneth A. "The Black Executive as a Subject for Research." *Business Perspectives.* Fall 1972.

Psychology

Aronson, Elliot. *The Social Animal.* 2d ed. San Francisco: Freeman, 1976.

Berne, Eric. *Beyond Games and Scripts.* New York: Grove Press, 1976.

Bhagat, Rabi S. "Black-White Ethnic Differences in Identification With the Work Ethic: Some Implications for Organizational Integration." *Academy of Management Review.* July 1979.

Communications Research Machines, Inc. *Psychology Today: An Introduction.* New York: Random House, 1979.

Fast, Julius. *The Body Language of Sex, Power, and Aggression.* New York: M. Evans, 1977.

Grier, William H. *The Jesus Bag.* New York: McGraw-Hill, 1971.

Grier, William H., and Cobbs, Price M. *Black Rage.* 2d ed. New York: Basic Books, 1980.

Harris, Amy Bjork, and Harris, Thomas A. *Staying OK.* 1st ed. New York: Harper & Row, 1986.

Harris, Thomas Anthony. *I'm OK, You're OK.* New York: Harper & Row, 1969.

Hill, Napoleon. *Think and Grow Rich.* 1966 (new and revised ed.), North Hollywood, Calif.: Melvin Powers, Wilshire Book Co.

————. *The Think and Grow Rich Action Pack.* New York: Dutton, 1988.

Hill, Napoleon, and Stone, W. Clement. *Success Through a Positive Mental Attitude.* New York: Pocket Books, 1985.

Leavitt, Harold J. *Managerial Psychology.* 4th ed. Chicago: University of Chicago Press, 1978.

Schein, Edgar H. *Organizational Psychology.* 3d ed. Englewood Cliffs, N.J.: Prentice-Hall, 1980.

Sheehy, Gail. *Passages: Predictable Crises of Adult Life.* New York: Bantam Books, 1976.

————. *Pathfinders,* 1st ed. New York: Morrow, 1981.

Silverman, Robert E. *Psychology.* New York: Appleton-Century-Crofts, 1972.

Storr, Anthony. *Human Aggression.* New York: Atheneum, 1968.

Sociology

Allport, Gordon W. *The Nature of Prejudice.* 25th-anniversary ed. Reading, Mass.: Addison-Wesley, 1979.

Billingsley, Andrew. *Black Families in White America*. 1st Touchstone ed. New York: Simon & Schuster, 1988.
Pannell, William E. *My Friend, the Enemy*. Waco, Tex.: Word Books, 1968.
Popenoe, David. *Sociology*. New York: Appleton-Century-Crofts, 1974.
U.S. Riot Commission Report. *Report of the National Advisory Commission on Civil Disorders*. New York: Bantam Books, 1968.

Research

Selltiz, Claire; Wrightsman, Lawrence S.; and Cook, Stuart W. *Research Methods in Social Relations*. New York: Holt, Rinehart and Winston, 1959.
Statistical Abstract of the United States: 1990. 110th annual ed. Washington, D.C.: U.S. Department of Commerce, Bureau of the Census.
Turner, Roy, ed. *Ethnomethodology*. Baltimore: Penguin Books, 1974.

Index

[An italicized number indicates a figure; the letter "n" after a number indicates a footnote.]